Nationalism and the Israeli State

Nationalism and the Israeli State

Nationalism and the Israeli State

Bureaucratic Logic in Public Events

Don Handelman

Oxford • New York

First published in 2004 by
Berg
Editorial offices:
1st Floor, Angel Court, 81 St Clements Street, Oxford OX4 1AW, UK
175 Fifth Avenue, New York, NY 10010, USA

Berg is an imprint of Oxford International Publishers Ltd.

Library of Congress Cataloging-in-Publication Data
A catalogue record for this book is available from the Library of Congress.

British Library Cataloguing-in-Publication Data
A catalogue record for this book is available from the British Library.

ISBN 978-1-85973-785-9

Typeset by JS Typesetting Ltd, Wellingborough, Northants.
Printed in the United Kingdom by Biddles Ltd, King's Lynn.

www.bergpublishers.com

Contents

**For Noa and Gaya
Daughters of the present
Sisters to the future**

Acknowledgements

words words
are thrust into
our mouths by
the intentions of others
and flung out
of our mouths
in quest of those others
who by then
are
words words

Even so, my thinking on the subjects discussed in this book has been influenced for the better through discussions over the years with the following friends and colleagues: Myron Aronoff, Amnon Aronson, Daniella Aronson, Hanna Barag, Hugh Beach, Eyal Ben-Ari, Yoram Bilu, Jean Briggs, Yoram Carmeli, Selim Deringil, Shlomo Deshen, Terry Evens, Sidra Ezrahi, Yaron Ezrahi, Michael Feige, Jackie Feldman, Harvey Goldberg, Deborah Golden, Ithamar Gruenwald, Haim Hazan, Bruce Kapferer, Tamar Katriel, Elihu Katz, Carol Kidron, Baruch Kimmerling, Gideon Kressel, Smadar Lavie, Galina Lindquist, Emanuel Marx, Piroska Nagy, Ronit Nikolsky, Robert Paine, Riv-Ellen Prell, Su Schachter, Don Seeman, Moshe Shokeid, David Shulman, Pieter Vanhuysse, Connie Webber, Jonathan Webber, Pnina Werbner, Richard Werbner, Eviatar Zerubavel, Yael Zerubavel. My deepest debt, of intellect, of feeling, is to the late Lea Shamgar-Handelman. Yaron Ezrahi and Hanna Barag helped especially, with thoughtful, valuable comments and discussions on a number of chapters.

The research discussed in Chapters Eight and Nine was supported by the Shaine Foundation of the Hebrew University. Yona Weitz, a research assistant on that project, has helped in manifold ways in collecting and discussing field materials.

Parts of this book were written during a Senior Fellowship at Collegium Budapest, 2001–2002. My warm thanks to the staff of the Collegium, especially the librarians, for providing such comfortable conditions for scholarly endeavor.

words words
skulk deep in the
throat nervously
awaiting the tongue's
catapult to
launch them over
the teeth and
into the world as
words words

List of Figures

Part I
Preamble: Designs and Depositions

–1–

The Collapse of Versailles and the Nation-in-Arms

And I do now what every memory dog does:
I howl quietly
And piss a turf of remembrance around me,
No one may enter it.

Yehuda Amichai (1995: 410)
By permission of HarperCollins Publishers.

One warm evening in the late spring of the year 2001, a private Jewish wedding reception in West Jerusalem turned into an ellipsis that collapsed brutally when the floor of the reception hall, named Versailles, fell away from beneath the feet of the celebrants, plummeting them precipitously into the level below. Twenty-three people were killed; hundreds injured. The disaster was videotaped by the wedding photographer, and the dramatic footage – in which people abruptly vanish into a huge, yawning hole that swallows their screams – was telecast round the world.[1] Rescue personnel – police, firefighters, volunteers – arrived quickly, and thousands gathered outside police cordons to gawk, comment, gossip, pass the time, calling relatives and friends on mobile phones to fill them in. The mood was more one of sadness than anger: was there no surcease from catastrophe? Once more, Israeli Jews were called on to suffer, to bear their already weighty burdens. Much of the rescue work was telecast. The disaster occurred well into the second Intifada, the uprising of the Palestinians in the West Bank and Gaza, against Israeli occupation. Rumors spread rapidly that Palestinians had bombed Versailles. Denied officially, these stories continued to circulate. Army units of the Home Front Command, itself responsible for civil defense, were ordered in to do the bulk of the search-and-rescue. These units have had extensive experience in many parts of the world. The task itself was carried out by young soldiers, most hardly out of their teens, doing their national service. The conditions were hazardous. The threat loomed that the entire building could collapse atop them at any moment. The jagged remains of the building looked bombed out, blown up – a war zone, a site of suffering, a startling and numbing vacancy in the built landscape within which soldiers labored to separate the human and the once-human from the debris. They worked for over forty straight hours almost without respite, in the glare of spotlights, in the heat and dust, until their commanders agreed there were

3

no corpses left to be recovered. The commanding officer of the Home Front Command called off the search.[2] Television announced that this was the worst civilian disaster in Israeli history; and government proclaimed that a 'ceremony' would be held to mark the close of the rescue effort.

This 'ceremony' is in my terms a 'public event,' and the discussion of the Versailles occasion in this chapter will introduce and foreground theoretical issues that engage with my ongoing attempt to develop a theory of 'ritual form,' begun in a previous work (Handelman 1998a). I argued there that as a roof concept the term 'ritual' includes a multitude of occasions that have little or nothing in common with one another, apart from being glossed as belonging together. The term 'ritual' obscures more than it clarifies and should be abandoned. Instead I use the term 'public event' to refer to sites of performance whose designs are intended in relatively coherent ways to convey participants into versions of social order. As the flow of living so often is not, public events are put together to communicate comparatively well-honed messages. The currents of mundane living may be quite uncertain in terms of direction and outcome, yet the converse is true of public events. Public events are indigenous phenomena that exist in the life-worlds of their participants, and are graspable as such by external observers. The mandate of public events is to engage in the ordering of feelings, ideas, and people through certain kinds of practice. The *logics* of design of public events, of how these events are put together, are crucial to how these events work and to what they can accomplish. To enter within such forms is to be captured by and caught up in the logic of their design – and so to be operated on by the event, regardless of why it came into being, or for whatever motives it is enacted. In this book I give center stage to that which I call the 'event of presentation.' I associate this kind of event especially with modern state and state-influenced social orders. The logic of design of the event of presentation I call 'bureaucratic logic.' I stress immediately that bureaucratic logic does not refer to institutions of bureaucracy as such, and I will clarify this shortly.

This chapter addresses the Versailles commemoration as a public event of presentation organized through bureaucratic logic by the State to shape the nation-in-arms, the embodiment of the national. Chapter Two discusses bureaucratic logic in depth, and traces this logic from Eastern Europe to socialist Zionism in Palestine. Chapter Three takes up one example of the State's use of bureaucratic logic in the shaping of Jews as national in their citizenship, and certain of the consequences of this for ethnicity and inequality in Israel. Apart from these three introductory chapters, this book is divided into three further sections. The first of these contains two chapters that take up public events – holiday celebrations and birthday parties – in Israeli Jewish kindergartens. This section addresses the socialization of little children into the encompassing horizons of the Jewish state and into the linearities of bureaucratic logic. Nationalism and bureaucratic logic induce and induct children into living within and through the classifications of the modern state, in the name of greater values of peoplehood, history, heritage, and destiny. The three chapters of the third section address the ways in which the State presents itself to its publics through the opening public events of its three national days – Holocaust Martyrs and Heroes Remembrance Day, Remembrance Day for the war dead, and Independence Day. These events are presentations of social classification emphasizing social categories made to represent fruition and maturity; and so that participate together in the great cosmic drama of national destruction and rebirth. The fourth section, of two chapters, addresses the eternalizing of history, national and personal, through opening and filling holes of absence: one chapter addresses the significance for Israeli Jewish nationalism and memorialism of turning the 'absence' opened by violent death into the 'presence' of sacrifice; while the other discusses the evocation of presence from absence through personal narratives of Holocaust survivors. The Epilogue addresses Israel as a cyborg state, one in which the unlike qualities of the emotional and the machinic are torqued into one another. Each chapter adds to the idea of 'public event,' but each can be read separately as a contribution in its own right to 'ritual' studies and to a perspective on Israeli social order informed by anthropology.

The collapse of Versailles and its commemoration expose two dynamics that intertwine and knot together in events of presentation of the modern state. One dynamic, nationalism, is so prominent and dominant, and is openly contested by numerous constituencies. Nationalism has been likened to a religion, in part because of the intensity of its totalizing impact.[3] Endless reams are written on nationalism, pro and con, popular and scholarly. Nationalism often is showcased in statist events of presentation. In contrast to the other dynamic, I will say relatively little on nationalism. That other dynamic, 'bureaucratic logic,' is pervasive and deeply embedded in the routine grounds of daily life in modernity. If nationalism is thought of as a religion, then this religion is informed by bureaucratic logic, its 'rituals' shaped through this logic. As noted, I distinguish between bureaucratic logic and bureaucratic institutions. In my usage, bureaucratic logic is a way of invoking, shaping, and organizing existence. The logic constitutes the grounds through which bureaucratic institutions are shaped into social existence.[4] As such, the logic is much more pervasive than are bureaucratic institutions; moreover the logic also constitutes the grounds for numerous other social configurations. In this usage, bureaucratic logic has not been named as such. This logic is ignored by scholars of the state and modernity, yet it is practiced incessantly in the everyday living of so many of the societies these scholars study. Ingrained and implicated in daily lives, bureaucratic logic shapes much of the ordering of social life in the modern state, because this logic is central to the shaping and making of order through the invention and application of classifications. The ubiquity of schemes of classification saturates our lives. The practice of inventing and applying classification is so ordinary that it occludes the pervasive power of bureaucratic logic in shaping forms of living, including those of state institutions, nationalism, and remembrance.

Numerous public events in modern states – occasions large and tiny, national and other – are deeply informed by the formative capacities of bureaucratic logic. This perception is overlooked in numerous studies of statist 'rituals' which understand these events first and foremost as straightforward symbolic reflections of social and cultural order.[5] Ignored are the ways in which the logics of *form* in these events shape the messages and feelings that the form of event configures and conveys. The practice of form is the performance of significance. This has not been lost on regimes of the modern era.

Bureaucratic logic is a way of generating lineal forms of classification – a dynamic for the creation and organization of linear form, that in its multitude of applications makes, shapes, and counts social life into existence in so many ways. Bureaucratic logic is a logic of form, yet more so it is *a logic of the forming of form*. Consider that form is omnipresent, in that nothing exists without shaping; and that the dynamics of this shaping, ongoing, never finished, is what I intend by form. All phenomenal worlds are forming, formed, forming. Without social forms, can there be social ordering and its fragmenting? Form is essential to the existence of any and all phenomenal worlds, since without form there is no embodied perception. Yet social form exists only through practice, through the practice of the logic of form that is making form through this practice. The forming of form is that of continuous practice, without which particular social forms would cease to exist. Therefore every act of the forming of form brings form into existence. Form in this regard is more than visual. All the senses are forming.

All peoples must classify their worlds in order to exist together socially. This was the contention of Durkheim and Mauss (1963), elaborated on by Douglas (1966, 1999) and Schwartz (1981) among others (Allen 2000), one never successfully challenged. Bureaucratic logic exists as one possibility of the forming of classification that peoples have imagined in forming their worlds and themselves. Yet the lineal rudiments of bureaucratic logic are part of the stock of possibilities that describe being human. The possibility of bureaucratic logic is always present as an imaginary, though one that itself is not a sufficient cause to bring form into being. The logic offers possibilities for the configuring of moral and social orders, always related to social and historical formations that enable it to be shaped into, and so to shape, existence. This is why bureaucratic logic is related intimately to the routine making of change – through the changing of classification – in the lived world. And this is why this logic of the forming of form has cosmic implications – forming and shaping as originary, implicating over and again some sort of genesis.

Bureaucratic logic has a much wider cachet than the institutional. Bureaucratic institutions are prime loci of this kind of forming, but so too are numerous other sites of perception and organization in our lived worlds. Bureaucratic logic has become a hegemonic dynamic of the forming of consciousness in worlds of modernity. Most modern states and other kinds of complex organizations simply could not exist as they do without the ways in which bureaucratic logic contributes to their ongoing shaping and operating – tautological, yet so. Therefore this pervasive logic must not be treated as an adjunct of other phenomena – for example, of ideology – that 'really' make the world work. Bureaucratic logic is active in all projects of lineal organization in modernity (if not at their outset, then as an emergent property of their development). Bureaucratic logic makes many of the worlds we live in, and enables many of them to work as they do. As such, bureaucratic logic pervades the symbolic representations of modernity in the most commonsensical and unnoticeable of ways.

The state creates, reproduces, legitimates, changes, and sanctifies itself through everyday practice. Nowhere is this done more powerfully than through the lineal classifications generated by bureaucratic logic in institutions that acutely compact and concentrate such classification – the legal and judicial, the bureaucratic, the military, the police, athletics and other contests, and most educational setups.

Versailles Collapses, the State Ascends

The State made order at Versailles. The course of the search-and-rescue mission was to remove the living and the dead from the ruins of the celebration of life, family, kin. The ratification of a new marital bond had turned into the public wreckage of disembowled lives that spilled out into the public domain. The hundreds of celebrants had thousands of ties with others within Israel. Their networks spread, far, wide, deep. The reverberations of ruination traveled with speed and penetrated with force. Versailles smeared the border between private and public with its entrails. There were rumors of a terrorist attack, and the building indeed had fallen in upon itself. The metaphor of Versailles was too close to the greatest of ongoing, pervasive fears among Israeli Jews – the terror that the State could cave in upon itself, either because of threat from without or because of weakness from within, or one leading to the other.[6] A spectacle of flawed construction (social no less than physical), deep within civic society, the ruined remnants of Versailles had to be mended, domesticated, controlled. And this had to be seen to be done, and could be done only by official organs of the State. Versailles was an offence, not to democracy, but to the regnant society of law and order (as Israel is often described by its officials). The State mounted its own spectacle to co-opt and to dominate that of the wreckage. A public event of the making of order – of doing violence to violence to undo violence – was superimposed upon the uncertainty of the unexpected, on behalf of the people.[7] *How* order was seen to be done is crucial to understanding the public events discussed in this book. From the perspective of television the public event began with the televising of the rescue effort, while the closing 'ceremony' summarized this performance, presenting it as a national effort, directed by and on behalf of the State.

The Versailles Public Event

A rough and ready stage – a makeshift platform of wooden planks – is put together in front of the ruined building; and behind the platform, a large, irregular, gaping hole into the dark ruins. In front of this opening are two parallel rows of symbols. Closest to the backdrop of ruins are the following: rubble, piled into a crude pyramid, to one side of which is the emblem of the Home Front Command, and to the other, national and army flags. In the next row are chairs for the dignitaries, and, to the other side, a podium and an unlit memorial flame, balanced on a makeshift tripod. Above the row of chairs is a sign, reading, 'Home Front Command.' Standing, talking, joking, milling about in front of the stage are the young soldiers (some hundred of them) still in their work fatigues (see Figure 1).

The participation of these anonymous grunts is crucial, looking towards the stage and the dignitaries who will show there. Their presence together is the embodiment of the nation-in-arms, as I will discuss shortly. Their exhaustion and dirty uniforms are living evidence of their cooperative efforts; but no less of the intelligence, acumen, and effort of the higher echelons, the commanders of bureaucratic infrastructure who have ordered and organized the rescue effort. The condition of the soldiers is the 'presentational evidence' that the officials responsible are doing their job; while the task of the people is to gaze together towards the elevated dignitaries, to hear their words, and together to demonstrate fortitude and solidarity. Filling space between viewer and stage, the soldiers foreground everything on stage seen by the viewer. The viewers become the nation-in-arms – seeing themselves in the present in the young soldiers, and in the past in themselves, to be led and emotionally fed by the dignitaries. The dignitaries in turn foreground the ruins within which the soldiers have labored. The architectonics of this event are intended to give the officials control over both the ruins and the rank and file, and through the latter, control over the television viewers.[8]

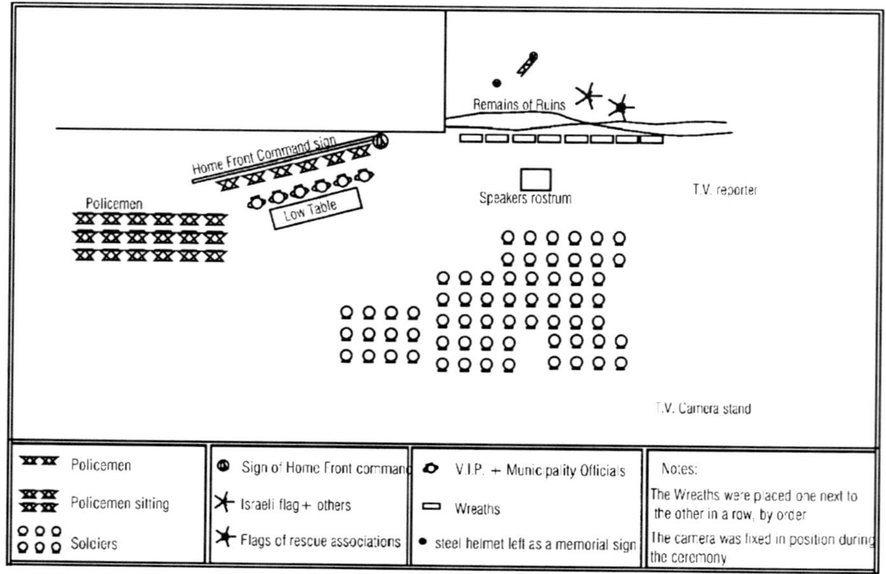

XXX Policemen	**⊕** Sign of Home Front command	**◐** V.I.P. + Municipality Officials	Notes:
XXX Policemen sitting	✶ Israeli flag + others	▭ Wreaths	The Wreaths were placed one next to the other in a row, by order
OOO Soldiers	✶ Flags of rescue associations	● steel helmet left as a memorial sign	The camera was fixed in position during the ceremony

Figure 1 Versailles memorial event, spatial layout.

From the platform a television commentator announces that this is a 'ceremony of remembrance' (Heb. *hazkara*), of 'unification' (*hityakhadut*). Both terms are used during commemorations, the latter term especially to denote the coming together, the joining together of people, of people and memory, of the living and the dead, so that all are closed off together, enwrapped (and at times enrapt) in communion among themselves, to the exclusion of everyone and all else. Together, the performance of remembrance and unification is a powerful practice of the closing of boundaries around a collection of people who, secluded together, then belong together, attending to a common focus shared by all. The 'ceremony,' says the correspondent, is expected to be 'impressive'. She tells us that many members of the Knesset (the Israeli parliament), including a woman minister, are present, as well as numerous volunteers. We see none of them. The nation-in-arms is primarily a military family, the family-in-arms, given birth by crisis, cradling the state with its arms, the bereaved family (*mishpakhat hashkhol*) mourning its dead, uncovering and discovering its unity beneath the shroud.

As the dignitaries file onto the stage, a sergeant-major announces them by name and position, at a staccato tempo. The next four acts – the last three from Jewish ritual – are found in all state or statist occasions of commemoration.[9] The opening act, the lighting of the memorial flame, iconic of remembrance and re-membering, often comes first on these occasions. The assistant commander of the Home Front Command lights the memorial flame without ado. In rapid succession, rabbis associated with the Command read Psalms (*Tehilim*) and recite the Mourner's Prayer (*Kaddish*).[10] A cantor then sings, God Full of Mercy (*El Malei Rakhamim*). The next, lengthier segment consists of four speeches from the podium, the speakers representing the government, the municipality, the police, and the military.

Each speech is delivered by a representative of an official category of state. Together, these categories constitute a lineal taxonomy that delineates the state's organization of responsibility for the welfare of the citizenry, according to categories of national policy (the minister), local government (the mayor), public order (the police commander), and national security (the Home Command general). These speeches are all declarations of official responsibility and achievement. The first act – lighting the flame – is done by an officer of the military, in its role as the physical protector of the citizenry; here the prime intervener in remaking order out of chaos. The next acts are done by functionaries representing the category of religion – Judaism, the official religion of the State, is always present on such occasions. Whatever else it is, the State is Jewish.

The opening speech is given by a retired general and Minister of Tourism. He is the leader of an extremist political party that advocates the 'transfer' of the Palestinians of the West Bank and Gaza.[11] He praises the coordination of all the organizations involved in the search, with special plaudits for the Home Front Command and its rescue work around the world: 'Our little Home Front Command extended its arms [outwards] and carried out rescues at site after site.' He underlines that, 'What distinguishes *Am Yisrael* is our [sense of] responsibility for one another and [our] solidarity . . . All those who celebrated the wedding [in Versailles] are our family.'[12] He closes by saluting the soldiers on their rescue work. They look exhausted.

The Minister stresses that Israeli Jews are the few ['our little Home Front Command'] against the many: enemies are legion; Israel, always the underdog, is beset by them (see Gertz 1984). These few are unusual, for they feel responsible for and solidarity with one another. Together they are one family, kith and kin, who embrace the dead and injured of Versailles. This family is not based on citizenship but is restricted to Jews, the people of Israel. In the Minister's rhetoric, Israel is a Jewish state – the State is the nation, the nation the state. No others have space in this discourse.

The next speaker is the Mayor of Jerusalem, the head of a city officially reunited under Israeli rule following the 1967 War, yet in fact one divided, apart from the bureaucratic infrastructure through which Israel controls the Palestinians of Jerusalem. The mayor invokes the broader, national situation. There are internal disasters (like Versailles) that cannot necessarily be prevented, he says, and there is the external enemy that can be defeated. 'We're in a war,' he continues, referring to the battle against the Palestinians. He points to how the police 'charged' the Versailles wreckage to rescue the injured. (He uses the term, *mista'arim,* one way of referring to soldiers who charge the enemy). In the context of war against the external enemy (who has had nothing to do with Versailles) he offers his condolences and best wishes. The dead, injured, and bereaved of Versailles are co-opted to the war effort. Like the Minister, the Mayor commends the way all the official agencies have worked so well together; and praises their members for working straight through the Sabbath, the day of rest. The implication is one of personal sacrifice for the good of the whole. The troops in the foreground are restless, fidgeting, shifting position, turning their heads and looking around, as the mayor speaks.

The police commander and the general commanding the Home Front continue these themes. The general commends all the administrative units involved, military and civilian, and discloses the codename of this military operation. He uses the metaphor of family, saying that though all waiting, suffering mothers are the same, whether in Kenya, Turkey, or Greece, when the disaster is at home and in one's family, the catastrophe is so much greater. Like the mayor, he connects the disaster to 'Arab terror' – to a nearby Jewish neighborhood of Jerusalem that is fired upon night after night, and to how well the Jewish people of Jerusalem stand up to this. His troops, hardly mentioned, fidget and shift, muttering among themselves, looking in all directions, away from the stage as he declaims. For minister, mayor, and general, the Versailles disaster is positioned as tragedy and trial from a national perspective. It is added to the many tribulations that State and people survive, indeed triumph over.

In the final phase, wreaths are placed next to the pyramidal pile of rubble – first by the speakers and then by representatives of the firefighters, the emergency medical services, the volunteers, and the neighborhood administration in which Versailles is located. It is only here that the volunteers – a popular response of civil society to disaster – appear in their own right, yet silenced, without voice.

The State ascended, taking shape, making order from the ruins of Versailles. The State did so in the name of nationalism, using the logic that I am calling bureaucratic. Bureaucratic logic was essential to the *kind* of order formed into practice at the site of the collapse. This logic has two imperatives. One is to generate categories whose boundaries are, as much as possible, exclusive and inclusive, so as to exclude utterly that which does not belong to a particular category, and to include fully that which does belong to that category. The other imperative is to order these categories as a hierarchy, so that within the same taxonomy of classification, higher levels of category subsume lower ones. This kind of lineal taxonomy was shaped into existence in the Versailles commemoration.

The boundaries of each social category presented during the commemoration divide neatly and rigidly into those at the lower level. This national taxonomy differentiates between categories of officialdom and rank and file (the anonymous soldiers). The category of officialdom subdivides into two sub-categories, secular and religious. The sub-category of secular officialdom sub-divides further into sub-sub-categories of state, municipality, police, army. Every one of these categories, sub-categories, and sub-sub-categories are clearly demarcated from one another, both on the same level of hierarchy and between levels of hierarchy. The most overarching level of the taxonomy expands into the categories of the sub-level, which in turn expands into the categories of the sub-sub-level. In the converse direction, the sub-sub-categories collapse into the categories of the sub-level, that collapse into the overarching level. There is no overlap among categories. Throughout the event the boundaries between these levels and between these categories are unchanged.

Moreover, the spatial geometry of the site does not change. Seats, podium, memorial flame, pile of rubble, all stay in their positions throughout. Time too is segmented neatly. The shift from one segment of time to another is itself categorical. Therefore each action is complete within itself, and the addition of acts, one to the other, is the way the form of this event is practiced into existence. The event can be understood as the addition of acts that have limited relationships to one another, apart from being placed in a certain sequence. The movement from one act to the next is similar to a bureaucratic-like decision to close the practice of one category (or level), to open another, then to close the latter, and so forth. All movement within the event is lineal – in space, to and from the memorial flame, to and from the podium, to and from the wreath-laying; through time, from one commemorative act to the next. Movement in space, movement through time, are taxonomies composed of segments of space, segments of time, the categories of which are formed into existence through sequencing, each segment divided neatly from every other.

The entire event should be imagined as a series of rectangular boxes or modules of different sizes, all clearly labeled, some atop one another, others laid out along a single plane or vector. Each box defines its contents, and wholly contains these. The forming of the event is akin to arranging the boxes in relation to one another. Boxes can be rearranged, added, deleted, without significantly changing the event, and certainly without changing its logic of form.

These segmenting dynamics played their parts in making order at Versailles, from the decision at higher levels to call in the army, to the work at lower levels, picking through the debris. The State took command of the mess, and bureaucracies went into action to restore order; to keep the onlookers outside the site; to separate the living, the injured, the dead, from one another; to shift the injured to hospital; to make the dead disappear from view; and, finally, to celebrate the sorrow of the catastrophe. Vast numbers of detail were dealt with by specialists in more or less orderly fashion, applying various classifications to get the details of the mess categorized and sorted out.

None of this is unusual in the response of a modern state to disaster. We expect this from well-organized bureaucracies. Yet I want to underline the following: The State celebrated itself in sorrow, and its bureaucrats mounted a public event of commemoration at Versailles that was organized according to the logic used to make order within the site itself of the collapse. Central to this celebration of sorrow were the ways in which the State presented itself, and how it congratulated itself through its functionaries on a job well done, a heartbreaking task, like so many others in this embattled country, one that simply had to be done. There are powerful continuities of sameness between the ordering and practice of the rescue operation and the ordering and performance of the state commemoration; and, in doing so, to accord accolades to state-owned and state-sponsored ways of remaking order from chaos. Though these continuities between everyday bureaucratic practices and state 'rituals' are not obvious, they nonetheless are the usual, given that bureaucratic logic informs them both.

The Home Front Command does a 'ritual' to formally close all of its major rescue efforts, though in most cases these missions have been undertaken abroad. This instance differed in that the government declared its own participation, and so its own sense of responsibility. Unusually, the State offered not long after to pay compensation to the families of the dead and injured, thereby implicitly classifying them as victims of an attack on itself.[13]

The Nation-in-Arms, The Family-in-Arms

> Nothing is more whole than a broken Jewish heart.
>
> Menakhem Mendel of Kotsk

The collapse of Versailles was perceived by officials as an attack upon the State itself, especially during the second Intifada, when all efforts were being made to keep the country safe from sudden stabs of terror. Edifices expected to be reliable gave way, as if yet another domain that the State had to stabilize through rules and regulations was out of control. The State was failing to keep structures under its purview upright. Such occurrences did not happen by accident – someone was subversive, someone was to blame, and just as the victims were unearthed from the rubble, so the culprits too would be dug out from the self-protective dens they had dug deep within the moral fiber of the country.[14] The rescue effort and the commemoration presented the people as a nation-in-arms, the joining together of people and army, civilian and military, united with one another as a great family-in-arms (see Smith 1991: 79, on the metaphor of the family in relation to constructions of national identity). The family embodied in its members, the nation embodied in its families, the nation embodied in its members – metaphors that make the nation and the nation-state into organic entities whose borders and their closure become 'natural', in the sense of existing in the natural order of things.

In the early years of the State the idea of the army making over the Jewish people of the nation-state through military service was prominent and popular. The military was of the nation, the nation made into the buttress of the State. Ben-Eliezer (1995: 283–4, see also 1998a: 193–221, 2001: 147) comments that in those early years the diverse population of Jews was turned into a nation-in-arms, perhaps an army-nation (in the nineteenth-century French Republican sense). The distinction between civil and military was blurred, while '. . . the idea that war is not always the less-preferred choice and that peace is not always worth the price,' dominated. 'The population,' Ben-Eliezer continues, 'was constructed as a fighting nation, not for the sake of a liberal democracy but for the purpose of war.' The army was perceived to embody an ethos of voluntarism, comradeship, emotion, and intimacy, all of which aroused feelings of moral order among the people in relation to the state. More than any other force in Israeli society, the army stressed that security and survival demanded the doctrine of 'no choice' (*ain breira*) but to be united, closed, guarding the borders of the collectivity, taking the war to the enemy.

All of this is somewhat less so today. Yet the rhetoric of 'no choice' – shutting down reflection, dissent, the serious consideration of alternatives – appears like clockwork when crisis looms and the State is perceived as threatened, the existential condition today during the second Intifada. Then the state is turned uniquivocally into the Jewish State, the State for its Jewish citizens, and they become its nation-in-arms, its family-in-arms, its bereaved family uniting the living and the dead. Events of presentation are a prime medium through which the nation-in-arms, the family-in-arms, are enabled to embody the premise of 'no choice.' These events often are those of civil militarism (Kimmerling 1985, 2001; Feige 1998) – the pervasiveness of military-like, categorical thinking in Israeli civil life – not only through the ubiquitous presence of the army but also through the semiotics and rhetorics of participants in numerous events like the Versailles commemoration.

The Versailles performance was intended to convey this imaginary of the nation-in-arms, the nation embodying the state in and as an army. The intimacy of metaphors of nation-in-arms, family-in-arms, bereaved family, are crucial to the State's monopoly of physical violence (see Elias 1988). There is no small irony in this. The military is a bureaucratic organization of especial power, shaped particularly to wield disciplined violence as the state, against its enemies. The modern army cannot do without bureaucratic logic, without this logic of decisively incising borders, interiorly, exteriorly. As Marvin and Ingle (1999: 69) comment, 'What keeps killing organized is a clear border. Borders allocate killing authority.' The army in combat acts by deforming, un-forming, and re-forming whatever its power penetrates. The military presence of bureaucratic logic is on display whenever and wherever persons in military uniform appear. Then the display of categories generated by bureaucratic logic is open, visible, and potentially brutal, in contrast to the more shrouded qualities of such categories in civilian life. The nation-in-arms, united in sentiments of solidarity and in the preparedness for violent tasks, takes into itself the shaping force of bureaucratic logic and acts through this militarily as the State. There is no contradiction between deep feelings of solidarity and their shaping through bureaucratic logic.[15] The shaping done through bureaucratic logic has its own aesthetics, and this will be addressed in Chapter Six, on the public event that opens the annual Holocaust Remembrance Day.

The nation-in-arms comes to the fore in public events of national commemoration and celebration. People are mobilized no less for bereavement, memorialism, and celebration than they are for war. All are occasions that re-member crisis by taking it and its overcoming into the heart of the collectivity, as the nation-in-arms arises once more to do its accounting and recounting. These occasions are imbued with the doing of violence to violence, and with sacrificing parts of the collectivity to overcome the chaos of destruction. These qualities they share in common with war. The guarding of national boundaries is given over to Jews, perceived as organic members of the collectivity. Therefore the borders of the collectivity are continuous with that which they enclose. To menace the border is to attack the interior of the collectivity, since there is no principled distinction between border and interior. The border becomes that place (or space of mind) where an Israeli Jew is menaced (as Israeli governments never tire of reiterating).

The nation-in-arms is a radical stance of inclusion and exclusion, one that severs collectivity from networks that traverse national boundaries in mundane lives that have more globalizing referents. Momentarily the borders of nation and state become isomorphic, and fuzziness or overlap are hardly tolerated from within. Non-Jews and foreigners are sharply excluded from the collectivity. Israel, proportional to its population, has a high number of foreign workers. The Versailles commemoration, to my knowledge, made no mention of non-Jews, even though it was likely that they were employed, legally or not, as waiters, busboys, cleaners, kitchen help, dishwashers. The President of the State was reputed to have said a few days after the disaster, that the hall had fallen in because since the 1967 War, Israeli buildings were being constructed by 'foreign' and 'non-Jewish' [Palestinian] labor – Jewish labor is honest and true in the Jewish State, foreign and non-Jewish labor is subversive.

Complementing the exclusion of outsiders and foreigners from the nation-in-arms is the inclusiveness of identity: in the Versailles event no lines of fracture or contestation among Israeli Jews (of religiosity, gender, ethnicity, social class) are shown. The condition of the people is presented as one of classificatory solidarity (Douglas 1987: 96). Whenever this happens, the state is nationalizing the nation. In this sense, Israel continues to be an ongoing, nationalizing state, one that so far has not left its nationalizing phase (Brubaker 1995: 114).[16] This condition enables politicians and bureaucrats to plan public events that nationalize the nation, often by using the theme of cosmic renewal (discussed in Chapters Six through Nine). Warfare as the doing of violence to violence is formative of cosmic renewal. Here as elsewhere, war has been crucial to the formation of the modern state (Dandekar 1990; Mann 1988). The state nationalizing the nation is one of the most pervasive of Zionist narrative enactments.[17] Yet the nation also nationalizes the state, especially through the resurgence of religious fundamentalism, insisting that the State modify its policies and institutions in line with 'authentic' Judaism.

The imaginary of the homogeneous nation-in-arms, taking shape in crisis, is also that of the sacrificing nation. In this self-enclosing nation, wrapped into and enrapt within itself, every member shares essential qualities of being a Jew with all others. This is more than a matter of persons identifying themselves with one another, for they are made the equivalents of one another. In this imaginary each person is in the virtual position of 'soldier', synecdochal with the nation-in-arms. The part, the 'soldier,' embodies the whole, the nation-in-arms. Through the violent death of the part, the whole lives. The part dies so that the whole may live. Hence the epigraph to this section. The Israeli-Jewish heart must be broken so that its missing part makes it whole. In this the commemoration of death is no less the celebration of the whole. The death of the part is a sacrifice on behalf of the whole, but also a sacrifice of the whole on behalf of the whole, given the relationship of synecdoche between the part, in the structural position of 'soldier', and the nation-state as the nation-in-arms. Every member of the nation-in-arms is a prospective sacrifice, and every violent death of a member, a retrospective sacrifice. The nation-in-arms lives anew through the sacrifice of its members, and may well require sacrifice to continue to exist as this imaginary of the nation-state. (On the relationship between sacrifice and state, see Marvin and Ingle 1999; Kapferer 1988).

The commemoration of every violent, sacrificial death is a celebration of the living. If the nation-in-arms is imagined in a broad range of national and statist events in Israel, as I believe it is, then every event of this kind will have an element of sacrifice. Chapter Eight addresses how absence, the holes torn in the social fabric by sacrificial death, is turned into presence through acts of remembrance; and Chapter Nine, how Holocaust absence returns liked a shaped explosive charge through narration. In the Versailles commemoration it is the young soldiers, sent into the perilous, tumbling ruins of the building, who are positioned as the potential sacrifice; just as, in doing their national service, they are the most likely to die violent, sacrificial deaths in battle.

In times of crisis, in times of commemoration (the repetition of crisis), in times of celebration (of repeated escape from crisis), the nation is recast as the nation-in-arms, the military-like body, ever present yet more subdued in the everyday. This homogeneity of inclusion justifies the application of military classification to the nation, but as a taxonomy already integral to the nation, one that emerges in crisis as the nation homogenizes itself. Military classification is not imposed on the nation, for it is the armor of the nationalizing nation, the armor that appears 'naturally' when the nation unifies, encloses, separates off. This shield embedded in blood, used by the state, is apprehended as integral to the existential condition of the nation, organized by the state.

Military classification is bureaucratic: it specifies superior and subordinate levels of hierarchy and the inclusive and exclusive categories (and associated duties and tasks) that constitute each level. The modern army is not democratic; neither is the nation-in-arms. In a twisting, torquing movement, nationalism is joined to that bureaucratic organization primed for massive and mass violence. This empowerment is through bureaucratic logic whose métier is to generate forms that reflect hierarchy and exclusion/inclusion, as I will discuss in detail in Chapter Two. As forms of life organized to do certain kinds of classification, nationalism and bureaucracy continually resonate with one another, as they do, too, with public events of commemoration and celebration that themselves are the products of these kinds of classification.

In times of crisis, and in every imagining of the nation-in-arms, Israeli Jews are spoken of as one great family. The kin metaphor highlights the affinities of mutuality that Israeli Jews are thought to feel for one another beneath all the conflict among them, because they have descent in common in the homeland they descended from a very long time ago and ascended to once more so recently. The Versailles hall was celebrating a core kin occasion – the beginning of a new family of procreation – when it collapsed, becoming the bereaved family. One can say that kinship collapsed. In the commemoration of Versailles, these small families of everyday life were swallowed within the metaphor of the great national family. This ramified family restored moral order to the small ones to whom violence was done by the collapse, by mourning their losses, by promising to unearth the culprits, by making present the absence opened by death.

The Event of Presentation

But how can a wall protect if it is not a continuous structure?

Franz Kafka, 'The Great Wall of China' (1999: 67)

As noted, public events are social forms that mediate people into collective abstractions through different logics of the forming of form. Through their performance, these events induce action, feeling, experience, knowledge. These events are designed to cohere cultural imaginaries that usually are more dissipated and obscured in everyday life. The event of presentation is such a form, one shaped by bureaucratic logic. The Versailles commemoration is an event of presentation.

The event of presentation is often designed as a display – a spectacle, a pageant, a tableau, a procession, and so forth. All of these are comparatively open to the gaze of the spectator (and of the participant). Only rarely are there intimations of concealment, the mysterious, the mystical, in such events. In the Versailles commemoration little or nothing is hidden from view (apart from the deep interior of the site of the catastrophe itself, akin to a battlefield). The presentation shows itself as a mirroring of social and cultural order, as a declarative of how things are or as an imperative of what they should become. The event insists that it is what it shows, says, enacts.[18] The Versailles event shows the unified nation-in-arms, ordered and stratified by rank, holding catastrophe at bay (the devastated ruins are hidden from view, now emptied of threat, domesticated, harmless).

Presentation shows its own ordering, demonstratively, allusively, while opening no space for interrogatives. The event of presentation does not question – not the social order it derives from, not the space it maps and traverses, not the (perhaps utopian or millenarian) future it strives for, not the mythistorical past (McNeil 1986: 3–22) that it stands upon. The Versailles commemoration is above all an affirmation of ordering; the speeches are declaratives and imperatives; mourning is a national heritage; only unity, firmness, steadfastness before the enemy, all around, always threatening, will enable survival. The people, the nation, must bear their national burden. The great national project – making citizenship national – continues. The design of this kind of event prefers not to open space for doubt, nor even for plays upon itself – not through irony, nor through parody, but perhaps through kitsch that mirrors and knows itself as beautiful even as it exaggerates (and lies to itself, movingly), beautifully, to paraphrase Milan Kundera (1990). The mirror of presentation that is the event does not reflect social order with any sense of literal truth. The reflecting surface is constructed to mirror that which the designers of such events want to show, yet preferably without hinting at the constructedness of these intentions, this sleight of hand.

In intending to show itself exactly as it is, the event of presentation emphasizes order throughout itself. This ordering may be closer to stasis, with little motion, as is the case of the Versailles commemoration, or it may be in movement, it may be allegorical, or composed of modules coupled together in different combinations. In any case the ordering is expository. Generally these events are organized through discrete categories whose boundaries are shown as clear-cut, often precise, without overlap or interpenetration (thus, in the Versailles commemoration, the categorical exclusiveness of secular and religious, military and civilian, officers and rank and file, officials and officers, those known by name and the anonymous). A major dynamic of presentation is the addition or subtraction of categories, of mass, of signs and symbols, and not infrequently of might. The event of presentation is often a taxonomy of social categories that emphasizes both the neat dividing of complex phenomena and their containment. Loose ends and ironic knots are not welcome.

Events of presentation are the dominant form of public occasion in the modern bureaucratic state, showing, enunciating, and indexing lineaments of statehood, nationhood, collectivity, collective memory, solidarity – so that whether these exist or not, they are shaped as if they do (Willke 1999: 149). Events of presentation are imbued and resonate with bureaucratic logic. Whatever else they are, these events are celebrations of bureaucratic logic on display, though to call them this would destroy their affect. Such events are sites in which the symbolism of the state, of nationalism, of classification intersect most evidentially and powerfully, disclosing their intimacy, representing the national and the nationalizing through classification, through inclusion and exclusion, through the hardening of social boundaries. At issue are the overt symbolic and ideological designs of state and nation and their presentation, but no less the implicit yet powerful forming of these by the logic that gives existential shape and coherence to these presentations.

Though bureaucratic logic is thought to have nothing to do with the making and shaping of national collectivity – which are matters of feeling and the primordial, distant from dusty offices, officious functionaries, rigid rules and rule-bending – this only speaks to the effectiveness with which the modern state masks its reliance on bureaucratic logic in order to function nationally in the day-to-day, but especially in special occasions that celebrate through sorrow and joy the disasters and pleasures of both using and surviving history. Bourdieu (1998: 58) argues, I think accurately, that, 'To understand the symbolic dimension of the effect of the state . . . it is necessary to understand the specific functioning of the bureaucratic microcosm . . . [the agents of which have instituted the state] by producing the performative discourse on the state which, under the guise of saying what the state is, caused the state to come into being by stating what it should be.' My stress is not on the practices of bureaucratic institutions (Handelman 1976, 1978), as is Bourdieu's, but on the practice of the logic which enables these (and other) institutions to take the forms they do, shaping social orders as they do. This I think is what the Israeli materials in this book tell us about in evidentiary though complex ways.[19]

–2–

Bureaucratic Logic

> The line . . . is present in the *induction* and the *deduction* of science and logic. It is present in the philosopher's phrasing of means and ends as lineally connected. Our statistical facts are presented lineally as a *graph* or reduced to a normal *curve*. And all of us, I think, would be lost without our *diagrams*. We *trace* a historical development; we *follow the course* of history and evolution *down* to the present and *up from* the ape; and it is interesting to note, in passing, that whereas both evolution and history are lineal, the first goes up the blackboard, the second goes down.
>
> Dorothy Lee, 'Codifications of Reality: Lineal and Nonlineal' (1959: 105)

The attributes of bureaucratic logic, as a logic of the forming of form are discussed in depth in this chapter. The chapter proposes one trace through which this logic may have developed in Europe during the past few hundred years, and follows one route through which the logic reached pre-state Palestine via socialists from Russia, where it was put to work in the building of the Zionist state-in-the-making.

Before continuing, let me remind about the kind of classification that bureaucratic logic generates. This classification is linear, with two intersecting axes, vertical and horizontal. The vertical axis is composed of levels of classification in a hierarchy of levels in which each higher level subsumes the lower, and is itself subsumed by the level above. The horizontal axis – a given level of classification – is composed of n number of categories, each of which contrasts with and excludes all others on the same level. All the categories on a given level of abstraction are the equivalents of one another. This logic does not produce dichotomous distinctions. A scheme of classification can have n number of levels of abstraction, and n number of categories on any given level. The classification does insist, however, that a given item be placed in one and only one of the existing categories on a given level of classification, and therefore that it be excluded from all the rest on that level. This is a highly prevalent mode of ordering, of sorting contents into categories, and of relating these categories and their levels to one another. This is a way of organizing a classification of individuals, groups, or things, grasped for purposes of classification as nuclear entities. The taxonomies produced may interface, interlock, and compete with one another, yet they discourage overlap and permeability among themselves. Bureaucratic logic is not a democratic dynamic, nor an egalitarian one.[1]

The development of bureaucratic logic comes fully into being when two conditions are satisfied. One condition is historical, and refers to the emergence of the conscious,

19

systematic, classification of information that is made autonomous from the natural, God-given order of things. The dynamic of classifying gains conscious control over the means of classifying. A pragmatic science of classification comes fully into existence. The other condition is that the doing of classification is organized as a system, in the self-correcting sense.

The Monothetic Forming of Form

Bowker and Star (1999: 10) define classification as, 'a spatial, temporal, or spatio-temporal segmentation of the world.' They add that a classification system is 'a set of boxes (metaphorical or literal) into which things can be put to then do some kind of work – bureaucratic or knowledge production.' This kind of lineal classification scheme is called monothetic, and has been traced to Aristotle's *Organon* and to his *Metaphysics* (Ellen 1979). Sokal (1974: 1116), writing of classification in science, emphasizes 'the ordering or arrangement of objects into groups or sets on the basis of their relationships.' If, in science, classification is intended to bring forth relationships that do exist in the natural world, but that may not be easy to grasp and delineate, in social life we are referring to invented schemas of categorization (though their invention may be ancient, their arbitrariness hidden in mythistory). Reified, these schemes are put to work to classify and act on phenomena. In monothetic or Aristotelian classification, precision always is preferred to no precision (Bowker and Star 1999: 103), regardless of the validity of the precise distinctions among categories at a given level of abstraction, or between levels of abstraction. This suggests that often it is more important to classify with preciseness for the sake of creating a world of precision, than it is to worry about how accurately this classification reflects the world it is made to act upon.

Invented schemes of lineal classification are intended to create facts; and C. Wright Mills (1959) commented long ago that to the bureaucrat the world is a (self-obvious) world of facts, to be treated according to firm rules. Undoubtedly there are frequent clashes of classifications invented at different times by different agencies for different purposes. Yet ideally these problems are intended to be resolved through monothetic distinctions. Bureaucratic logic is a procrustean practice – it cuts, shapes, and changes phenomena more with regard to its own hermeneutic of closure than in terms of how these phenomena otherwise exist in their worlds.[2] Though conflicts over particular classifications are continually generated, there is little argumentation over whether this kind of classifying is indeed the way to organize many aspects of public life, including the interface between public and private. Instead this kind of classifying is a self-obvious practicality in a world of facts (e.g. Haines 1990).

Monothetic classification builds closure into its own scheme, because it is designed to enclose totally the world it describes, thereby exhausting the possibilities of that world in terms of the scheme. The scheme of classification folds into itself its own contingencies (cultural, social, legal) that are unfolded under various conditions. Both the folding and unfolding are symmetrical. Bureaucratic logic values symmetry in classification, in both its vertical and horizontal dimensions. Symmetry signifies boundedness, formality, order (Weyl 1952: 16). Exhausting a world of its contents through monothetic classification is the exercising of symmetrical order. Symmetry invokes the locating of every thing in its proper place, thereby enabling a monothetic taxonomy to be a simultaneity of all its categories.

Yet the practice of classification is necessarily a sequence of action, and therefore temporal. A form or scheme of classification is then also 'the simultaneity of sequentiality' (Luhmann 1999: 19). By totalizing itself in these ways, a scheme of classification may be accorded relative autonomy from its social environment. This is especially so for law courts deciding on how to classify in matters of falsehood and truth, guilt and innocence; but it is also so for the multitudes of administrative decisions about classification, for examinations in education, and for a host of athletic contests and games, all of which are concerned with the classifying and re-classifying of candidates and competitors (Handelman 1998a: xxxvii–xli; Hoskin 1996; Hoskin and Macve 1995).[3]

Monothetic classification is associated closely with counting in its simplest sense of adding and subtracting so that one number is not another, with making these kinds of count in which an item goes into one category and not another nor in both. Stone (1988: 128) points to the act of this counting as categorizing, as a decision about what to include and exclude. Moreover, to categorize requires boundaries that inform whether something belongs or not. Such numbers, she argues, are like metaphors – they are 'about how to count as . . . [so that] to categorize in counting or to analogize in metaphors is to select one feature of something, assert a likeness on the basis of that feature, and ignore all other features. To count is to form a category . . .' by emphasizing a feature of inclusion and excluding all else (1988: 129). Therefore monothetic classification has analogical qualities that can be rendered as inclusion, exclusion, the making of hierarchies. These qualities are symbolized with every act of counting of this kind. Every monothetic taxonomy not only totalizes itself, but practices and symbolizes that very totalization in every act of its classifying. These properties are deeply embedded in bureaucratic logic.

Something of the same is so for the performance of an event of presentation. The performance comes into existence through the taxonomies that are integral to that event. The taxonomies contribute to shaping the performance. The logic of form that shaped the taxonomies shapes the performance. The Versailles event fit so fully, symmetrically, and perfectly within itself because the categories of its taxonomy were shaped to expand out of one another and to close hermetically within one another. Experiencing this symmetrical expansion and contraction is the crucial significance of the performance of categories of this kind. The commemoration is militaristic not only because of the pervasive presence of military personnel, but also because the kind of symmetrical taxonomy that inlays the structuring and performance of the event is common to the ordering of much military (and civilian) life. This is a taxonomy that is made to regiment itself, to guard its own borders. This self-sealing taxonomy is one powerful way of forming the nation-in-arms in official commemoration. These are values that are given shape through this form.[4]

Tracing Bureaucratic Logic through Classification

Think/classify
What does the fraction line signify?
What am I being asked precisely? Whether I think before I classify? Whether I classify before I think? How I classify what I think? How I think when I seek to classify?

Georges Perec (1999: 189)

Logics of the forming of form that are more linear and relatively autonomous from natural cosmos are ancient (e.g. Handelman 1995a, Luhmann 1999: 22), and I will not try to account for their histories. However in Europe there is one historical vector of the forming of linear classification that contributes to this discussion in two ways. It gives a sense of a bureaucratic logic coming to the fore and shows the broad spectrum of its influence. Through its European peregrination from the German principalities to Russia, this vector later left its traces in the early history of Zionist presence in pre-state Palestine, and the beginnings there of a highly centralized, bureaucratic proto-state, the precursor of the present State. This vector gathers strength and momentum during the period, roughly of the sixteenth through the eighteenth century, when the formation and practice of lineal taxonomic classification was understood to be under the conscious control and implementation of human agency, and was used deliberately to shape, discipline, and change social order. I break these developments into two overlapping segments: the first discusses changes in the cosmology of classification from which the monothetic emerged dominant; while the second takes up how the monothetic contributed to a sense of proto-bureaucratic community in central Europe. Towards the close of this discussion I bring out the resonances between bureaucratic logic and that which Deleuze and Guattari call the state-form. In my reading, the state-form is a logic of the forming of form, one that converges in modernity with bureaucratic logic, in a torsion of these logics that enseams together the dynamic of monothetic classification with those that Deleuze and Guattari call capture, containment, striation, smoothing.

The first segment of the historical vector traces the consequences of classifying knowledge of the world totally and quite monothetically. In *The Order of Things* (1973) Foucault provides an insightful, historicized perspective on the crystallization of monothetic classification in Europe.[5] He tells us that the sciences of the seventeenth century were informed by ways of seeing the world that can be glossed as 'rationalism.' Through these perceptions, '. . . comparison became a function of order . . .

progressing naturally from the simple to the complex . . . The activity of the mind . . . will therefore no longer consist in drawing things together [through similarities] . . . but, on the contrary, in discriminating' (1973: 54). Rationalism used the idea of taxonomy to make monothetic order: to distinguish, to divide, to locate, to name, and to connect things living and dead according to their natural characteristics, in order to make these things clearly visible. The phenomenal world surrendered and made explicit what was thought to be its essences. Foucault (1973: 131–2, my emphasis) comments that: 'What came surreptitiously into being between the age of the theatre [the Renaissance] and that of the catalogue [the seventeenth century] was not the desire for knowledge, but *a new way of connecting things* both to the eye and to discourse . . . The ever more complete preservation of what was written, the establishment of archives, then of filing systems for them, the reorganization of libraries, the drawing up of catalogues, indexes, and inventories, all these things represent . . . an order of the same type as that which was being established between living creatures.'

Linnaeus began his new way of connecting things taxonomically by modifying but hardly rejecting the Great Chain of Being, the cosmos of God the Creator (Tillyard n.d.), which he enhanced through the precision of monothetic classification. Yet scientific taxonomies helped to shift classification further from the God-given towards the humanly constructed (Weinstock 1985; Frangsmyr 1994; Gould 1987). As an idea of science, the forming of monothetic taxonomy shaped perceptions of the physical world by opening time/space to the capture and containment of all things, living and inert, through their naming, itemization, placement. All things were classified exclusively and inclusively on vertical axes and horizontal planes in concordance with explicit rules that enabled the classified to enter the discourse of the classifier.

To construct a taxonomic scheme there had to be explicit rules for the delineation of categories, and for the inclusion of items within them; for the aggregation of categories at higher and lower planes, and for the resolution of anomalies when an item fit more than one category on the same plane of abstraction. Therefore there had to be rules also for the creation of new categories, through division and addition. The decision-rules of scientific, monothetic taxonomies were understood as conscious and secular constructions, without divine inspiration, yet mirroring its precision. This conception of classification resembled that of a static, monothetic form, rule-governed yet empty of content. More accurately, this dynamic of the forming of form moved relatively slowly, though with definitiveness and the need to assimilate new items uncovered in far away places in this age of discovery. This slow dynamic was closer to movement in the divinely created and regulated natural cosmos. Yet to the extent that the decision-rules of a taxonomic scheme did their work of comparison, contrast, attribution, and distribution, one could also speak of the 'rationality' and 'efficiency' of the taxonomy, or perhaps one could refer to the capacity of the taxonomy to create and store information, though its processing moved slowly.

This idea of taxonomy as a totality of information hardly was restricted to science. Mapping and placing, naming and classifying, became pervasive to the practices of the period. Yet because the taxonomy was a slow-moving dynamic, to render social life visibly taxonomic required the application of considerable force. Force often took the form of power through presentation. In one of Foucault's striking examples, instructions to control an outbreak of plague in seventeenth-century France, the taxonomic map is the territory.

In response to the tendrils of infection, of disorder, death, chaos, the town is sealed. Within, it is divided into sections and streets, each under the authority of an official. Dwellers are locked within their homes, bread and wine reach their doorsteps via small wooden canals that branch out from more central ones. The only people to move between houses are the higher officials and the non-persons who carry the corpses and the sick from place to place, from category to category. The boundaries of this 'frozen space' (Foucault 1979: 195) are controlled by officials, themselves fixed in place. Surveillance within the town is pervasive. Every day each of the inhabitants of a house appears before his allocated window, to answer the roll call of officials: name, age, sex, death, illness, irregularity, all are inscribed and recorded. In this way the totalization of information is emended. 'The relation of each individual to his disease and to his death passes through representatives of power, the registration they make of it, the decisions they take on it' (Foucault 1979: 197).

The application of such social taxonomies is proto-bureaucratic. The minute, visible, forceful application of classification is living presentational evidence of its validity: the town has become, 'This enclosed, segmented space, observed at every point, in which individuals are inserted in a fixed place, in which the slightest movements are supervised, in which events are recorded . . . ' (Foucault 1979: 197). The vision is that of the perfectly governed polity in which: '. . . power is mobilized; it makes itself everywhere present and visible . . . it separates, it immobilizes, it partitions; it constructs for a time what is both a counter-city and the perfect society . . . ' (Foucault 1979: 205; Eliav-Feldon: 1982: 45). The perfectly governed society is one in which every person is classified and catalogued, and therefore in principle, regulated.

The age of the theater and that of the catalogue collided and intersected in numerous public venues, as the following example from Bologna indicates. There, for one hundred and fifty years during the seventeenth and eighteenth centuries, taxo-nomizing science was linked intimately to events of presentation. During this period a public anatomy course – the dissection of an entire human body with accompanying scholarly exegesis and learned debate – was held annually for ten to fifteen days during the carnival period (Ferrari 1987). The dissection was an exercise in monothetic precision and rigor in the naming and classifying of body parts, their functioning and function – a disciplined exercise of taking apart an individual whole, but under the total control of science. The public dissection was a spectacle infused with the scientific (and proto-bureaucratic) de-forming of form.

Of especial fascination here is how this monothetic de-formation emerges from the discourse of science and takes the form of spectacle, of a presentation of parts held up for inspection, one by one. And, that the anatomy course was held during carnival, and was attended also by anonymous masked revelers. Carnival de-formed the monothetic by raucously playing with the body, exposing hidden social innards, upending and jumbling social order, blurring boundaries among distinct categories and torquing them into one another. As this occurred, the dissection and presentation of body parts simultaneously began to make monothetic order in this world of carnival, an order that formed scientific classification out of the de-formation of a human whole that concealed most of its body parts within itself. Here science took the aesthetic form of a proto-bureaucratic spectacle that laid out for didactic inspection that which was usually hidden within the body.

During the eighteenth century, Western perceptions turned the interior integration of the scientific taxonomy – the archive, the table, the catalogue – into one of organic relationships. Foucault (1973: 218) puts this shift in the following way: '. . . the general area of knowledge is no longer that of identities and differences . . . of a general taxonomia . . . but an area made up of organic structures, that is, of internal relations between elements whose totality performs a function . . . the link between one organic structure and another . . . can no longer be the identity [in and of itself] of one or several elements, but must be the identity of the relation between the elements and of the function they perform . . . ' Rendered as components in organic relationships, classified items practiced functions for entire classifications. This more complex division of labor within and among monothetic taxonomies began to shift into that which we recognize as a functional system: a hierarchic assemblage of levels and categories, that are thought to belong more together than apart; each of which contributes specialized functions to the existence of the whole assemblage. The entire assemblage is dependent on the functions of each of its parts, as they are on one another.

Relationships of interdependence informed the taxonomy with a quicker dynamic of purpose and direction, and so provided social life with more proficient fulcrums of power: the ratio of force to social control changed, so that less force could achieve more powerful effects. The premises of monothetic classification were not disposed of; instead its forming was in-formed by more 'systemic' organization. Systemic taxonomizing enabled one to influence in monothetic, totalistic ways whatever was reorganized. Should a part (and its specialized function) be altered, the repercussions would be felt throughout the entire system. As a depiction of organization, the table-of-contents was to be replaced by the flow-chart, while the theorizing of Spencer and Maine, Tonnies and Durkheim, waited at the threshold.

The forming logic that shaped scientific and other taxonomies valued the visual above all other senses. The scientific gaze can be called 'attestive,' following Ezrahi (1990: 72–87), the gaze of knowledge that dispassionately uncovers, dissects, classifies, and displays the facts of phenomena. The attestive eye is no less integral to the bureaucratic ethos. Science and bureaucracy produce, preserve, and use texts without number. Classification commonly depends on the eye. Therefore bureaucratic work is also hermeneutical – its practices and explanations follow from its own premises. Bureaucratic logic moves towards the self-exegetical and the contemplative. Yet this hermeneutic continually implicates the gaze (Jay 1992a), and this is so also of events of presentation like that of Versailles.

The synthesis of the visual, the taxonomic, and the systemic was exemplified by innovative topological designs like that of Jeremy Bentham's late eighteenth-century Panopticon, intended as a site for punishment and work. The Panopticon was a design of taxonomy as spectacle, made systemic. The name reflects Greek roots, meaning 'all seeing.' The panopticon: a circular, tiered building composed of individual cells whose inmates cannot see one another, but all of whom are visible to supervisors in a central tower who, in turn, are hidden from the inmates. The supervisors themselves are visible to the director, who is hidden from everyone. Exterminated from the panoptic sort is sociality, the interconnectedness and interchange of human beings, their seeing and feeling one another as subjects. Present are the 'clients' of the organization, each individual reduced to a body controlled by abstraction, by the geometric: separated, numbered, supervised, put to productive tasks, each within the isolation of his cell – and on continuous display. Who exercises power and why is of no immediate relevance: whoever occupies the tower, the center, the office, the apex of hierarchy, operates the classifying gaze of perfect taxonomy and its systemic control. Indeed, the Panopticon has been called a 'materialized classification' (Jacques-Alain Miller, cited in Bozovic 1995: 24). The Panopticon is the dynamic of the bureaucratic forming of form gazing at the forming of its product, the client, who is enacting the ways in which he has come to be taxonomized. Here this forming logic gives shape and life to a living taxonomy that is in the ongoing performance of presentation.[6]

In the Panopticon, Bentham intended to create a perfectly symmetric cosmology of scopic supervision, its hierarchy analogous to that of God, angels, and humans; yet a secular microcosmos, one consciously invented, synthesizing surveillance, control, and the changing of individuals. In the entry of the prisoner into the Panopticon, Bentham joined bureaucratic logic to an event of presentation, to a show decidedly didactic in content, one to be staged by the 'manager of a theatre' (Bentham 1995: 101). In this entry (Bentham called it a 'masquerade') the prisoner performed and attested to his own guilt and sentencing in order to persuade others not to transgress (Bozovic 1995: 5). The prisoner performed himself as a confession through which his hidden feelings were exteriorized, so that both his interior and exterior fit perfectly within the taxonomizing form he was in the process of becoming. This was similar to the anatomy dissection, except that in the Panopticon the corpse came alive. In performing himself, the prisoner embodied his guilt.[7] As the prisoner performed his entry, he formed himself into a spectacle pervaded by bureaucratic logic; then to be moved deeper into the prison, into his isolated cubicle, to live entirely by this logic of the forming of form, as an ongoing spectacle controlled by bureaucratic logic.[8]

The Panopticon entry contrasts decisively with the behavior of the prisoner in earlier times before his public execution. In Royal France the prisoner performed his own guilt at a great public spectacle of self-fragmentation that reflected and celebrated the holistic power of the king, embodied in the identity of his person and his kingdom (Foucault 1979; Ezrahi 1990: 72–4); while, within the panoptic forming of form, the prisoner performed in seclusion, before a committee of his sorters (including a theater manager), those who executed his shaping. Rather than his own dismemberment through execution, the panoptic prisoner was individuated, torn from his social integument of relationship and exchange, and put to work in a world itself detached, anonymous, autonomous. The panoptic vision brings together the taxonomic and a more modern sense of the systemic, so that the exercise of power could become 'lighter, more rapid, more effective, a design of subtle coercion for a society to come' (Foucault 1979: 209). Such a design would require little fiscal expenditure; would be labor intensive; would be politically discreet; would be relatively invisible; would arouse little resistance; and would raise the effects of social power to maximum intensity and specificity.[9]

In the twentieth century, Weber's conception of rational-legal authority became the cornerstone of much modern thinking on bureaucracy. My concern here is not with the concept's current status, but with how this concept further developed the dynamics of the bureaucratic forming of form. Weber's understanding of bureaucracy implicitly depended on the premise of classification. The rational-legal bureaucratic type (Weber 1964: 329–40) has the following characteristics. It requires a classification of 'offices'. Offices are defined by 'rules' ('a consistent system of abstract rules, intentionally established'). All offices are regulated by a 'continuous organization' of rules that inform the overall scheme of classification. Thus the organization of offices can be understood as a taxonomy of categories of office, regulated by general principles of classification. The contents of a category of office are defined by the boundary rules of the taxonomy in relation to the particular category in question. (Such contents concern spheres of authority, competence, technical knowledge, procedures for making decisions, and so forth.) Offices as categories are situated within a hierarchy of levels of superordination and subordination. The entire schema is understood as a secular construction, one whose practice is intended to exhaust the phenomenal domain to which it is applied. 'Monothetic rationality' is embedded in this idea of bureaucracy; in its abstract, intentional principles of hierarchical organization and integration, and in its clean-cut definitions of categories (i.e. offices) that are exclusive and inclusive. Weber's conception of modern bureaucracy, which he termed 'a power instrument of the first order – for the one who controls the bureaucratic apparatus' (Gerth and Mills 1958: 228), depends on premises both of taxonomy and of the systemic.[10]

The Weberian paradigm of bureaucracy bears strong semblance to the organization of taxonomies, social and scientific, of the seventeenth century, yet now informed by systemic premises. The *raison d'être* of the bureaucratic form is systemic taxonomic practice. In the modern age the shaping of form is purposive, directed, directional. The organization is shaped to intentionally accomplish some goal; and to accomplish this the relationship between means and ends is made explicit and rationalist. The functions of offices are specialized and specific in their complex interdependence. The entire system is infused with a social power whose focused intensity is evident on any of its levels, in any of its parts.

As a generalized system of processing information, this schema is in principle *devoid* of content, just as it is devoid of ethics. The bureaucratic schema can be filled with any content, to be processed in accordance with instructions. This is why it frightened Weber, though he was a German nationalist. This is why Bauman (1989: 106) argues that bureaucracy '. . . is intrinsically capable of genocidal action,' since its operators can target, select out, and seal off a social category from a multitude of others. Wyschogrod (1985: 39) contends that this may be done through a 'sorting myth', a cosmogonic method of dividing off, excluding, and even destroying certain social categories, so as to remake others as organic, as essence, as foundational, as a purified people, as a united family. The monothetic bureaucratic logic that organizes this exclusion and seclusion of the selected category may become the only frame of reference for its victims, the members of the category (Bauman 1989: 123), and therefore their hope and death of hope.[11]

Underscored here over and again are the qualities of modern social organization and of the modern state that use bureaucratic logic to invent and modify taxonomies in the most commonsensical and routine of ways. These classifications, often systemic, proliferate and flourish in the present as never before, dividing any and all social units – group, community, family, relationship – and fragmenting, classifying, and reshaping the humanity of human beings . . . but also destroying this. The inner vision of bureaucratic logic is that of a hermeneutical gaze of 'viewpoints unaffected by standpoints' (Illich 1995: 52). The bureaucratic forming of form is capable of consciously and deliberately creating virtually any reality and of processing its contents.[12]

The development of the Science of Police had profound consequences for moral and social order in the emerging societies of Central and Eastern Europe, and eventually on the proto-bureaucratic state-in-the-making of the socialist Zionists in Palestine. The Science of Police depended on bureaucratic logic, but moved this shaping more explicitly and firmly towards the political, towards the dynamics of organizing and administering community. I turn to discussing bureaucratic logic in the Science of Police.[13]

Bureaucratic Logic in the Science of Police

> . . . to socialize like with like, and to separate that which is disimilar.
>
> Johann Ernst Habenstreit, 'Museum Richterianum, continens
> Fosila Animalia Vegetabilia . . .,' (1743)
> (quoted in Bredekamp 1995: 90)

In the German-speaking lands of seventeenth-century Europe, there emerged the forming of form that was called 'Police,' 'the well-ordered police state,' or 'the science of police' (Raeff 1983; see also Oestreich 1982: 155–65). This form of organization was neither the police nor police state in today's sense of these terms. The science of police deliberately planned and administered the shape and substance of community, such that people would behave as they should for the common good (*res publica*), the good that included them all and that in this case specifically included the desirability of their living happy, fruitful lives. To practice the good of all required standardization and exactness in specifying similarity and difference in order to introduce uniform classifications, thereby to compare and to control persons as specifically as possible (Kharkhordin 2001: 227). So statistical information was collected, bearing on the capacities and resources of populations and their territories. (Rates of birth and death appeared; covert denunciation of neighbors was commended.) New taxonomies based on age, sex, occupation, and health were invented, intended to increase wealth and population, but also to enable intervention in and to alleviate a wide variety of social problems. People would be enabled to live happier lives, as individuals and as groups, within the nexus of concerned regulation. Through correct practices, people were naturalized into perceiving these ways of living as best for the well-being of one and all. These practices of togetherness effected the group-centered character of social order, the sense that good ways of living were integral to social relationships. Though the beginnings of the science of police may have had strong qualities of imposition, with time these ways of living came to be felt as right.

Through what I call bureaucratic logic, the science of police was practiced by promulgating and applying standardized administrative ordinances and rules for behavior within very broad domains of intervention, yet in highly specific detail. So, in various places the science of police set rules for the use of the personal pronoun between parents and children, the dimensions of saddles, the enumeration of what should be drunk and consumed during wedding feasts, the number of people permitted to attend a christening, and so forth. A science of endless, detailed listings of classification in the interests of the 'good order of public matters' (Pasquino 1991: 111). Police regulations tried to organize everything that went unregulated, that lacked clear form in a society of the three estates – this was 'a great effort of formation of the social body,' one that demanded degrees of order that reached beyond law and encroached on domains new to becoming occupied by public ordering (Pasquino 1991: 111). In terms of its institutions, the science of police in the German principalities was more proto-bureaucratic than bureaucratic, yet it established a 'gridwork of order' (Gordon 1991: 20) that paid close, regulating attention to the itemization, movement, and flow of persons and goods.

Above all, the patterning of this gridwork of order and its taxonomies was symmetrical in its control of variance, variation, idiosyncracy. Simmel (1968 [1896]: 72–3) argues that the 'tendency to organize all of society symmetrically . . . according to general principles is shared by all despotic forms of social organization . . . Symmetrical organizations facilitate the ruling of many from a single point. Norms can be imposed from above with less resistance and greater effectiveness in a symmetrical organization than in a system whose inner structure is irregular and fluctuating.' This was so for the Science of Police, and more generally is so for all social forms shaped through bureaucratic logic. Bureaucratic logic generates the symmetries of monothetic taxonomizing.

The science of police operated on both the individual and the group. The ordinances of Police compartmentalized people, their practices and resources, in new ways. Raeff (1983) points out that through compartmentalization (like the number of people permitted at a christening) the family was made more private, separated more from extended kin and social networks. The person was both individualized (and expected to become a more productive worker) and individuated (and accentuated as a unit of counting and governance). Together with this, the group became solidary through its self-managing and self-policing of itself and of its individual members, all for the common good; and persons felt the significance of the organizing community in their lives, as individuals and as group members. Thus the public sphere penetrated deeply within the private, so that the emergence of the private sphere (the family, the individual) incorporated powerful visions of the public good as a collective endeavor, one that contributed to making the private domain reliant on that of the public and its governance. The private sphere was imbued with values of the public, and governance had opened points of entry into the private sphere.[14]

This accords with Foucault's view that individual agency is a modern, bureaucratic conception of that which I am calling both the individualization and the individuation of the person, in terms of which the individual participates in his or her own self-formation (Foucault 1980; Rose 1998).[15] Individuation in my usage refers to the categorical separation of person from person, making each into an individuate through administrative forces external to the person. Bureaucratic logic individuates when it generates taxonomies within which the person is made a member of an aggregate in a particular social category, and is isolated in this way for administrative purposes. Individualization refers to the person perceived as a unique being in terms of psychological qualities. As Lemke (2001: 191) puts it, 'Foucault endeavors to show how the modern sovereign state and the modern autonomous individual co-determine each other's emergence.' The modern state shaped individual agency to fit the spread of pastoral power through bureaucratic institutions (Foucault 1982: 783–5). These institutions individuated the person and tended to the person so individuated. The individual exercised agency within the range of possibilities extended by individuating bureaucracies.

The powerful sense of symmetrical, organic groupness and community that came into existence in the German principalities emerged together with the power of this groupness to shape and to discipline the person as an individuate, yet as the exercise of power that was integral to the happiness of both community and individual. The science of police forged the linkage between the welfare of the group and the well-being of the individual who was managed from outside himself, leading him to value his membership in and feelings of groupness and community. The welfare of community and individual were related to the capacity to divide the group into individual units, and to combine or to recombine these units into community. The capacity of division and unification grew out of the sense of deep, symmetrical, organic groupness. Therefore this capacity did not alienate levels of social order from one another, for culturally they grew out of and into one another.[16]

The Tsars of Russia, beginning with Peter I, brought ideas of the well-ordered police state into the very different grounds of eighteenth-century Russia. Unlike the more interior forming of community in the German principalities, Peter imposed the science of police top-down on Russian social and moral order. His project was to wrench into existence an abstract conception of the state, one that conceived of its policy in terms of rational efficiency in ordering and changing society through didactics, regulation, and prescription (Raeff 1983: 205). Instead of an incompact empire governed loosely from its center but with high degrees of local autonomy, he introduced centralized and centralizing administration, and built a new capital, Saint Petersburg, as the exemplar of rectilinear hierarchy and functional planning (Scott 1998: 194). The bureaucratic forming of form took shape through top-down coercion and compulsion, discipline and regimentation (Raeff 1983: 237; Stites 1989: 19–24). Peter introduced bureaucratic institutions that formally separated government from other domains of life, that required written records, and that paid attention to the minutiae of office (inkwells, furniture, office hours) (Raeff 1983: 203). The terminology of the state, as an apparatus of government independent of ruler and ruled, appeared in Russian in the eighteenth century. The state – the bureaucracy and legal apparatus – was brought into existence in between ruler and ruled in the name of the common good, but imposed from above as coercive form (Kharkhordin 2001). Catherine the Great made the administrative system introduced by Peter more efficient, in trying to shape a society that would reflect the practices of the well-ordered police state, and that would help rather than hinder the modernizing efforts of the state. Her reforms rationalized administration on lower levels of state organization, and effected ways of life on local levels. Nonetheless, Russian statutes continued to stress the repressive and punitive dimensions of police law (Raeff 1983: 224–54).

The science of police worked well in the closely-knit German principalities because the logic of its forming of form had resonated deeply and harmonically among groups, individuals, and moral order. By contrast, the Russian version of Police continued to be imposed from above to hold together the vastness, heterogeneity, and locality of Russia as empire and as frontier state. One could argue that the top-down imposition of order in Russia continued to be a major force for societal control until the fall of the Soviet empire in 1989. Unlike the German case, the Russian has continuously generated profound discontinuities and the lack of organic integration between different levels of social order.

The socialist Zionist leaders who rose to prominence in Palestine came there from Russia after 1905 and then again after the October Revolution. They were well inculcated in social and moral order organized from the top down, but they were deeply concerned that this also turn into a powerful sense of organic community, one that would be felt to grow from the bottom up. They brought with them the shaping force and power of Russian (and then Soviet) bureaucratic organization; but also the more distant resonance of German organic groupness with its interior force of shaping moral and social order categorically, yet nonetheless felt to grow from within itself.[17]

The science of police is close to what Foucault (1991: 103) calls governmentality. The sensibilities of governmentality are important here because they relate directly to forms that constitute the state, and to public events that reflect what is felt to be significant in this State of being (thus, the nation-in-arms and its presentation through the Versailles commemoration). Governmentality should be read as 'govern-mentality', or simply as government – the perceptions that the State should intervene systemically, however loosely articulated the systems, in the lives, relationships, networks, and enterprises of its own citizens, for its own good and for their well-being. Therefore governmentality can be understood as forms of activity that shape, guide, and affect the conduct of persons (Gordon 1991: 2). Paralleling my claim that bureaucratic logic is a logic of practice, the practice of forming in certain ways and not in others, Foucault (1991: 97) argues that governmentality is the practice of forming acts of governing – the reality of governmentality is its doing. Thus the shift into the nation-in-arms through public events like Versailles is a practice of governmentality through which distinctions between state and nation are erased, the heads of state become the heads of the nation, and the symmetrics of inclusion and exclusion are practiced to a high degree.[18]

Governmentality in Foucault's usage is much more than the formal apparatus of state administration – it is closer to a composite reality put together by institutions, procedures, myths, analyses, reflections, strategies and tactics that enable the shaping, effecting and affecting of populations (Foucault 1991: 102–3). The practices of governmentality may be totalistic, top-down, and all-embracing, or (as Rose [1996b: 57, 61] argues for advanced liberal democracies), these practices may exist at the 'molecular level' of social orders, in relation to 'micro-moral domains.' Trouillet (2001: 130), echoing Foucault, points out that, '. . . statelike processes and practices also obtain increasingly in nongovernmental sites such as NGOs or trans-state institutions such as the World Bank. These practices, in turn, produce effects as powerful as those of national governments.'[19] Their effects are state-like. Public events of presentation in the modern state are no less the products of this govern-mental ensemble of the state and the state-like.

Yet much of the complexity in coordinating the mentalities of a governing ensemble depends on the use of the flexibility of bureaucratic logic in inventing and altering linear classification. Bureaucratic logic enables the tailoring of classification to the sorting and organizing of micro- and macro-levels, and to a wide variety of social units of heterogeneous composition. Bureaucratic logic gives to strategies of governmentality a tremendous range of adaptation in the face of complex, rapidly shifting social, political, and economic conditions.[20]

Bureaucratic Logic and the State-Form

On the idea of emergence: 'We don't need something else in order to get something else.'

Murray Gell-Mann (cited in Horgan 1998: 214)

Eichmann deserves to be recognized as the Winslow Taylor of the concentration camp.

Shiv Visvanathan (1990: 269)

Logics of the forming of form address the imagining and formation of phenomenal worlds. The forming of phenomenal worlds is ongoing, never ending. In the case of bureaucratic logic, the métier of the forms of organization that this logic in-forms is that of change, acting on and altering phenomenal worlds continuously, by adding, subtracting, dividing and redividing levels and categories of classification through which these worlds are put together and taken apart. Yet bureaucratic logic is hardly the sole logic of the forming of form we can identify. Most likely there is a vast field of logics of the forming of form – not universals for the shaping of particular social forms, but a fuzzy reservoir of human imaginaries, of potentials of logics of forming.

My reading of Deleuze and Guattari (1988) suggests that their concept of the state-form is a logic of forming. The logic of the state-form complements bureaucratic logic, and this relationship is discussed here. Deleuze and Guattari ask us to imagine how logics of form inevitably emerge from one another, changing themselves as they do. This is especially significant here because the forming logic of the state-form opens towards the state. Bureaucratic logic and the state-form share dynamics which enable them to interact synergistically, to provide together certain crucial attributes of the state in modernity.

The forming logic of the state-form is arboreal and spatial: the shaping is tree-like, deeply rooted, in-place, a fundament of origins and ancestry reaching unbroken from the distant past into the far future, centered stably around an axis mundi that opens in all directions and planes, unmoving, vertical, tall, hierarchical, protective under the cover of its shading; branching and reproducing clearly, exactly. This logic of forming expands by capture, by taking space, by reproducing its form in additional spaces, by making over these spaces into places. The state-form extends itself lineally, a design for quantitative growth of space and population (Patton 2000). The state-form gives especial attention to shaping and controlling its own interiority, as distinct from exteriority. Deleuze and Guattari (1986: 15) write that: 'The law of the State is . . . that of interior and exterior. The State is sovereignty. But sovereignty only reigns over what it is capable of internalizing, of appropriating locally.' Space is striated smooth. The state-form striates the space it contains (Deleuze and Guattari 1988: 385). Striated space 'closes a surface, divides it up at determinate intervals, establishes breaks . . .' (Deleuze and Guattari 1988: 481). This is the lineal forming of measurable spaces, and of standardized measures to determine all similarities and differences within these spaces.

Deleuze and Guattari relate the state-form to (in my terms) the logic of forming that they call the rhizome. Each of these logics is interior to the other, such that in particular social, historical conditions, each generates the other, each emerging from the other; just as, under other conditions, each meets the other through the interface of exteriors that clash. The rhizome grows open-ended networks of indeterminate nexuses that are shifting, incompact, without centers, without hierarchy, so that any point of a rhizome can connect to any other without going through another. The rhizome is a multiplicity of dimensions, not of bounded linear categories. The lines of the rhizome are flat (not vertical) because these lines continually fill all of their dimensionality. Rhizomes that are broken, shattered, scattered, activate one or another line of movement and growth. The rhizomic has no deep structure, no foundational axis, nor the capacity to grow anything except itself, yet without knowing precisely what it is. So the rhizomic cannot trace itself: it has no capacity for self-organization through memory; no capacity to account, to locate, to specify, to count; and therefore no capacity to capture (even itself) (Deleuze and Guattari 1988: 7–20). The rhizome is smooth space, the space of a patchwork of continuous variation without unity of direction (1988: 481). Yet where the rhizome shows nodes of massification, the logic of the state-form is emerging.

The Israeli state, Israeli Jewish nationalism, the project of shaping Jews as national in their citizenship, have always been at war with the rhizomic logic of forming. From the perspective of governmentality, any felt fragmentation (ideological, ethnic, religious) among Israeli Jews is the subversive appearance of the rhizomic. In these terms, Palestinian citizens of Israel, perceived as the enemy from the founding of the state, should be excluded from the arboreal unity that characterizes the community of Israeli Jews. Jews should relate organically towards one another within their community-state; while Palestinians are perceived by Jews as the wild, subversive, threatening (female, irrational, oriental, nomadic, unstable, violent) growth of the rhizomic.

Deleuze and Guattari take for granted that the state-form generates its own apparatus of self-regulation. Yet I am arguing that bureaucratic logic exists in its own right, and that it shapes without necessary reference to whatever forms of organization emerge from shaping by the state-form. Like the state-form, bureaucratic logic shapes and controls the social surfaces of its expanding space through the capture of new territory for the deployment of power. A classification creates space that simultaneously is captured, bounded, contained. Yet whatever lies beyond the boundary of this captured space becomes the basis for further extension. New classifications create their own *raison d'être* for expansion and self-totalization.[21]

The classifications invented through bureaucratic logic also open space within their containment by making new divisions within existing ones. Complementing the arboreal logic of the state-form, bureaucratic logic enables bureaucratic form to expand through a kind of cellular division of difference yet sameness – the adding of more units of organization to itself (a new title, a new office, a new subcommittee). Bureaucratic logic enables bureaucratic form to attend to finer and ever-increasing details (Lefort 1986: 95). Thus, Lefort (1986: 108) comments that, '. . . it is essential to grasp the movement by which bureaucracy creates its order. The more that activities are fragmented, departments are diversified, specialized, and compartmentalized . . . the more instances of coordination and supervision proliferate, by virtue of this very dispersion, and the more bureaucracy flourishes . . . Bureaucracy loves bureaucrats, just as much as bureaucrats love bureaucracy.'

Given the powerful affinity between bureaucratic logic and monothetic classification, the former is continually implicated in the kind of counting that, as noted, is symbolic of inclusion, exclusion, hierarchy. Stone (1988: 128) points out that this language of counting sounds highly political. Inclusion and exclusion are terms that suggest community, boundaries, allies, enemies; selection implicates privilege and discrimination (and social triage and genocide); while the characteristics that define a class of categories or the category itself connote value judgement and hierarchy. Both bureaucratic logic and the state-form symbolize acts of counting and the arbitrary fragmentation or augmentation of numbers into yet other numbers. Every act of counting practices and regenerates this logic.

The dynamic of capture, containment, and taxonomic division within classification has the formidable impetus and coercion of law in modern society. King (1993: 223) argues that, 'in the legal system social events derive their meaning through the law's unique binary code of lawful/unlawful, legal/illegal. An event in the social environment cannot be interpreted simultaneously as lawful and unlawful or as falling both within and outside the scope of the law. These categories are mutually exclusive . . . Any act or utterance that codes social acts according to this binary code of lawful unlawful may be regarded as part of the legal system, no matter where it was made and no matter who made it.' King is saying that in modern social orders the implementation of division and contrast in terms of absolute categories of inclusion and exclusion has something of the feel, force, and aesthetic qualities of legal mandate (see also Gray 1978: 141). In my terms, the phenomenal forms generated by bureaucratic logic have imbedded in them the feeling of the force, impact, and aesthetics of the symmetries of law. These distinctions need not be binary, in the sense of a choice between two and only two possibilities. The crucial point is the maintenance of the logic of form, the symmetrical distinction between inclusion and exclusion. In monothetic terms, truth is necessarily a singularity, not a multiplicity.

Deleuze and Guattari emphasize that the relationship between the state-form and the rhizome is not dialectical, given that each of these imaginaries exists within the other. Their relationship to one another is that of the continual emergence of each within the other, while this process exteriorizes them into near-absolute distinctiveness only under extraordinary conditions. Bureaucratic logic, however, drives towards a perfect fit between the borders of categories, smoothing the interface between a subject to be counted and a category of classification, so that the category wholly contains the subject. This meeting is procrustean, territorializing the subject as a space of subjection, yet also smoothing, shaping the subject to the category, while smoothing each category to others of the taxonomy. As it striates form, bureaucratic logic simultaneously smoothes form.

Bureaucratic logic de-territorializes, in the terms of Deleuze and Guattari, since its formings have the capacity to amputate any and all social relationships (whether of family, kin, community, friendship), thereby severing and separating persons from one another, from their locations in space (thus, imprisonment, transfer, ethnic cleansing, exile), from their usual trajectories of living, and even from their pasts (thus, social erasure and lobotomy) (Bogard 2000: 270). The social surface of the individual can be separated from any organic conception of the 'person,' amputating the social from the personal, making the social surfaces of individuals placed within the same category homogeneous with one another.

In Israel, this smoothing of social surfaces operates in the bringing together of nationality, ethnicity, and minority, as I will argue in Chapter Three. The classification of nationality contributes to the taxonomy of Jewish ethnicity and Palestinian minority, a taxonomy organized so that minority is made inferior to ethnicity. In terms of this taxonomy, superior Jewish ethnicity should show the value of national feeling on its social surface, while this is forbidden to the Palestinian minority.

Through bureaucratic logic, taxonomized space is the smooth depending from the striated, the striated depending from the smooth. The space within taxonomy is made smooth, standardized, homogeneous, every category symmetrically comparable to and relating neatly to every other on the same level of abstraction, and between levels. Simultaneously, the very creation of the entire scheme of social classification depends on its internal borders between exclusive categories. Bureaucratic classification is striating; it is simultaneously smoothing. Bureaucratic classification is smoothing; it is simultaneously striating. The interface between categories in a classification schema is smoothed, so that their 'edges' fit together; while the fitting together of categories is striating.

Bureaucratic logic re-territorializes, in that it generates taxonomies of containment, so that within a taxonomy each category is put into its proper place. Bureaucratic logic joins smoothing to classifying, enabling and enhancing the fit among surfaces. Yet in its capacity to generate form as de-territorialized, as striated and lineal, bureaucratic logic is itself highly mobile without the need for deep roots of the arboreal state-form. Thus, bureaucratic logic can be practiced as its own metaphysics. Unlike the state-form, bureaucratic logic easily shifts its coordinates to shape containment in any terrain. No less, this logic is infinitely expandable, unless ordered to stop. Bureaucratic logic is a near-perfect 'machine' of capture, forming interiority that is always exterior to itself, preparing always to capture exteriorly and to interiorize whatever it grasps and contains. Given its lack of essentialism in forming classification, bureaucratic logic opens time-space for new phenomena like the hybrid, combining or transgressing categories. The hybrid is simply another phenomenon, one that in accordance with this logic requires classification, as hybrid, or as appendage to a taxonomy.[22]

Two examples from the early years of the state will give a sense of the arbitrary power of the directed use of bureaucratic logic, and of the flexibility of this apparatus of capture and containment. (The reasoning is continuing, has not changed to this day, and is perhaps the most potent weapon in the ongoing confiscation of Palestinian lands in the occupied territories.) The Absentee Property Law placed property abandoned by Palestinians during the 1948 War under the control of the Custodian of Absentee Property. Yet some 30,000 Palestinians had fled from one place to another within Israel, and so had not left and were not refugees. Government bureaucracy applied the Absentee Property Law. To wit, any person who may have traveled to Beirut, Bethlehem, or elsewhere, even for a one-day visit, but outside borders that had not existed during the British Mandate, was classified as a 'present absentee.' Such a person, one who was absent in his presence, a non-person in terms of his property rights, indeed had his property confiscated (Peretz 1991). Through this and other legislation, the State gained a goodly portion of agricultural land that had belonged to Palestinians who became Israeli citizens.

Under emergency regulations promulgated by the British Mandate, the military governor could declare any area closed for national security reasons. After the 1948 war the populations of twelve Arab villages were not permitted to return to areas that had been closed, though they had not left the country. Under an ordinance of the Ministry of Agriculture, the land was classified as uncultivated. The owners were notified that if they did not immediately cultivate these lands, the areas would be confiscated. However, the villagers could not enter these lands because the area was closed by military order. So the lands were expropriated and leased to Jewish farmers; and the villagers left homeless (Rouhana 1997: 61; see also, Drury and Winn 1992; Benvenisti 1990).[23]

In *A Thousand Plateaus* (1988), Deleuze and Guattari are steadfast in their ahistoricism, resolute in their commitment to imagining and exploring dynamics of space, the skins of the imaginary. Yet, no less, the shaping of time – its smoothing and striating – is most relevant for the forms of the modern state, and for its public events of nationhood and nationalism. Many scholars have commented on the importance for governmentality of controlling a people's sense of time, of shaping or of adopting shapes of time within which people know themselves and others as historical beings (or as people without history, in Eric Wolf's phrasing) through national imaginings of duration and periodization (Gross 1985; Verdery 1996: 39–57).

In my terms, the smoothing of time refers to metaphysics of the temporal, within which time is made to flow continuously, such that any markers of time embedded in the flow do not impede its movement, but are integral to its continuity.[24] Smoothing does not mean that time is necessarily lineal, in the sense of having a flat temporal trajectory. Jewish time imparts its significance through rhythmic pulsation, as I argue in the concluding section to Chapter Eight, on the opening public events of Israeli

Remembrance Day and Independence Day. The smoothing and planing of time, indeed the very capture of time, enables the modern state to have a national history – either an unbroken past through time or a past that strives through national activity in the present to mend hiatus and to reshape gaps of discontinuity. The senses of national pastness, upon which so-called 'collective memory' often depends, themselves depend from some shaping of national history or mythistory. A paramount device for the smoothing of time in the modern state is the event of presentation, since such events show themselves as fact, without questions, without conundra. These qualities of presentation show the joining and smoothing of present to past as unbroken duration (without showing the joints of their joining).

Yet events of presentation, even as they smooth, also striate time. Most simply the striation of time is its division, especially its classification into intervals in a taxonomy of time, so that any phenomenon within this containment is locatable exactly in its time. Conversely, any group or individual is divisible into its own history as a sequence of time-parts, synchronized temporally yet detachable from one another, like the slices of a salami. State and person are composed of time-parts, whereby any of their durations – often reckoned in years – can be sliced off the salami for purposes of classification. In Chapter Five, birthday parties in Jewish kindergartens are analyzed as events that embody little children as temporal beings composed of separate intervals, separate slices of duration. Clock time striates, however it is counted, as do schedules, timetables and the like. So, too, their synchronizations with one another are themselves classifications whose function is to enable surfaces of categories to juxtapose smoothly with one another through time. Just as mythistorical time is smoothed, so, too, this time must be striated – divided, dated, made lineal and sequential – since our understanding of history requires its mapping, its capture and containment, made interior as national history (see Gell 1992). Generally, the smoothing of national time, national history, also generates its striation, its markings of prominent times; for these, like body markings and incisions of initiation, make a difference in the perception of national and biographical selves.

The Bureaucratization of Politics in Jewish Palestine

> He who holds the hammer sees every problem as a nail.

The dominant ideological narratives in Palestine and later in Israel have given primacy to one or another idealistic vision of a Jewish collectivity, equating individualism with the breakdown of their dreams (Ezrahi 1997: 81–9). All have diminished the individual as a person with agency. Zionist socialism, the dominant organizing force in Jewish Palestine, held a utopian vision of Jewish autonomy and Jewish statehood, to be attained through social engineering. As noted, virtually all of the founders of socialist Zionism in Palestine came from Russia between 1905 and 1926, the last group experiencing the first years of Soviet rule. They perceived themselves as socialists and nationalists, and where they came from influenced how they built Zionist presence in Palestine (Shapiro 1993: 66). Unlike Western European concerns with liberal democracy and civil rights, the founders of Zionist socialism stressed the relationship between nation and nationalism, placing issues of rights squarely within the purview of the collectivity (Shapiro 1993: 79; Yanai 1996).

The vision of the Russian state as an administrative utopia lasted well into the nineteenth century. The few who held power arranged the lives of the others, to organize them for production, combat, or detention, through hierarchy, discipline, regimentation, rational planning, welfare planning, and a geometrical environment (Stites 1989: 19). Yet even as ideas of utopia declined, '. . . the dream of state power refashioning the land and the people was too alluring to die, and it appealed even to the most radical social dreamers who hated the tsarist state and whose ultimate vision was a stateless society' (Stites 1989: 23). The October Revolution augmented obsessions with top-down reform and control, with increasing efficiency and machine-like systemic visions of social and economic production, with Taylorism and Fordism (Stites 1989: 146–9) – in other words, with the forming of form through capture, containment, striation. It is from this milieu of planned, administrative, systemic collectivism, with its Russian echoes of Police and the totalistic encompassment of the individual by the social order, that the founders of socialist Zionism arrived in Palestine.

So much attention has been given to the ideological dreams of these leaders, and yet so much less to the elementary fact that first and foremost they attended to the building of bureaucratic infrastructure as the bedrock for their political and economic vision of a future state. Erecting bureaucracy was basic to their efforts, and this shaping had immense impact on their political and economic organization during the period of the *Yishuv*, the Zionist settler 'community' of pre-state Palestine (Yuval-Davis 1987: 77), and then on forms of organization after statehood. These people were imbued with Russian political culture – with tsarist absolutism, and with government intervention in all spheres of living, dominated by a collectivist orientation (Shapiro 1976: 2). The General Federation of Labor (*Histadrut*), the roof trade-union organization, was established in 1920, and by 1925, David Ben-Gurion, the leader of the major political party of the Yishuv, Akhdut Ha'avodah (and later the first prime minister of the State), claimed that, 'The Histadrut has been built like a quasi-state with self-rule for the working class . . . ' (Shapiro 1993: 70; see also Yanai 1996: 139; Shalev 1992). This quasi-state included trade unions, labor exchanges, workers' kitchens, schools, public works bureaus, settlement departments, and so forth.

The nascent bureaucracy was taken over by the dominant political party, using methods reflecting how the Communist Party in the Soviet Union had gained control of the state by establishing party cells in all important centers of power, leading to control by a powerful, centralized party machine. In Palestine the socialist Zionist leadership built a strong party machine with cells in all Histadrut organizations; and by 1927 their party received an absolute majority in Histadrut elections. The founders of the party became the heads of the Histadrut, while the members of the inner council of the party were mostly bureaucrats in the Histadrut. In the Soviet Union the political leadership that created the bureaucracy became the product of 'an apotheosis of bureaucratic institutions, an ultra-bureaucracy' (Pintner and Rowney 1980: 11). Bruno Rizzi (1985) called this 'bureaucratic collectivism,' 'the ascent of a new, bureaucratic ruling class and the conversion of the means of production into a new form of property, owned through the state in a nationalized . . . form' (Westoby 1985: 2). Something similar occurred in Palestine.

Ben-Gurion's desire to shape his political forces as a disciplined, obedient 'army of labor' (a version of the nation-in-arms, modeled perhaps on Trotsky's idea of labor armies) was rejected by his party. Yet there was no disagreement that the issue was how to build a total organization, materially and spiritually, one that included party and Histadrut (Shapiro 1976: 60). One major Zionist figure called the Histadrut an 'administrative democracy' (Shapiro 1976: 67) – a bureaucracy manned by politicians who used political practices to run organizations, and bureaucratic practices to organize politics. Huntington and Brzezinski (cited in Shapiro 1976) called these leaders in Soviet Russia bureaucratic-politicians, in that only those who were prepared to head the bureaucracy could hold onto political leadership. The Soviet bureaucrat first had to demonstrate his mastery over the operation of systems of bureaucratic classification, thereby passing 'tests' of his expertise, before he moved into the role of politician. These features of the bureaucratic-politician seem to have been the case also in Palestine (and later in the State). Bureaucratic-political practices in Palestine, argues Shapiro, were closer to the bureaucratic politics of Soviet Russia than they were to the electoral politics of democratic states.

The dominant party, becoming Mapai in 1930 (and then the Labor Party in 1969), set out to persuade the other Zionist parties of the Yishuv to reorganize themselves as copies of itself. Mapai supplied these parties with resources – financial, material, land – in exchange for coalition support; and also encouraged them to develop their own bureaucratic infrastructures, which led to close ties between these apparatuses across party lines (Shapiro 1993: 74). Major private enterprises accommodated their practices to Zionist socialist and nationalist rhetoric, arguing that industry too was integral to the armature of Jewish nation-building (Frenkel et al. 1997). The success of the Jewish national in Palestine depended to a high degree on the development of bureaucratic infrastructures. Though limited and embryonic in their resources, these infrastructures did their utmost to organize, control, plan, and totalize numerous spheres of living (including that of public events, largely planned and organized by committee). Though the scale of these activities (like the population) was relatively small, the solution to problems demanded greater centralization of activists, officials, and offices. As activities expanded and the structuring of living became more complex, new taxonomies and standards of classification had to be invented continually.[25]

There also were the distant resonances of Police, with its powerful stress on the embrace of collectivity by the community, in that whatever was demanded by its regulations should resonate deeply with the desires of its members. Ben-Eliezer contends that even as their elders in the Yishuv were intent on shaping a societal infrastructure through bureaucratization, among the younger native-born generation of socialist Zionists the distinction between coercion and consent often blurred, and the will of the collectivity (of its leaders) was intended to be identical with the desire of individual members. He (1998b: 378) quotes a youth-movement speaker: 'We have no state, we are a Yishuv and a movement that counts on volunteering, and we have no regime . . . [but] the movement can declare a regime of volunteering, with anyone who does not volunteer being removed from the group. Today this council should declare that we are a movement of collective volunteering.' Ben-Eliezer maintains that these people were creating a system of domination through the practice of certain kinds of organization over a broad range of interpersonal relations. The erasure of distinctions between rulers and ruled, between rulings and individual desires, was that which Police had accomplished in the German principalities long before. Perhaps in the Yishuv, too, individualism flourished best within organic groups.

On the other hand, the Jewish proto-state was thoroughly pervaded by bureaucratic logic, which organized numerous domains of living, connecting officials and clients through rules, regulations, their bending and breaking. Every act that applied a regulation, that categorized a person, population, or thing, and that argued over proper classification, necessarily practiced and regenerated the bureaucratic logic of the forming of form.

Nonetheless, in the Yishuv, persons had degrees of choice as to national affiliation, as to whether to join a political party, as to what sources of aid to turn to, as to which friends to associate with (especially across the Jewish/ Palestinian interface). This proto-state still was closer to a 'civil society,' in the sense of a 'free association, not under the tutelage of state power' (Taylor 1990: 98). During much of that period it was easier for individual Jews and Arabs to develop social relationships with one another.[26] After statehood, choices were narrowed, even pinched off. Bureaucratic logic was related indelibly to the laws of the land and to regulating its infrastructure.[27] This was a country in which ideas of liberal democracy, espousing the rights of the individual and of 'minorities' against encroachment by the state, did not have and have not had much success.

These first two chapters imply that conceptions of nationality and citizenship in Israel compete in shaping the ethos of the State. Chapter Three addresses the relationship between these categories, and how this has influenced conceptions of ethnicity and minority. Nationality, citizenship, ethnicity and minority constitute a taxonomy of elementary affiliations in this nation-state. The shaping of these categories has powerful effects on that which is presented and excluded in the public events discussed in this book. References to ethnicities and to Palestinians (apart from the latter epitomizing the enemy) are rare in the imaginary of the state-confirming and state-nationalizing events discussed here. Citizenship too is a seldom presence. Strongly present is the use of the Holocaust as a foundational catastrophe that empowers nationalism and the nation-in-arms.[28] The ways in which these presences are formed through public events depend to a high degree on bureaucratic logic.

–3–

Making Jews National in their Citizenship

Here everybody is both Jewish and universal: the soil . . . the
trees . . . the roads . . . the houses . . . the factories . . . the ships . . .
the air . . . the schools . . .the army . . . the planes . . . the language . . .
the landscape . . . the vegetation . . . all of it is Jewish.

David Ben-Gurion (quoted in Peretz 1991: 86)

Israel's Declaration of Independence (14 May 1948) enunciates a Zionist origin myth
of the State, elaborating on the unbroken unity of the Jewish people during three
millennia. The myth begins with the birth of the Jewish people in the ancient Land of
Israel; progresses through their coming into independence, national identity, and
culture; highlights their exile into the Diaspora during subsequent millennia; confronts
their near annihilation in the Holocaust; and celebrates their return to the Land and
their triumphal, national rebirth through the founding of the state. The Declaration
declares Israel a Jewish state, yet one that 'will uphold the full social and political
equality of all its citizens, without distinction of race, creed or sex . . .,' and calls on
the 'Arab inhabitants' of the state to become full and equal citizens.

Two ideas are given primacy though not parity in the Declaration – Jewish national
identity and citizenship. I stated in Chapter One that the great identity project of this
State is shaping Jews as national in their citizenship, and that public events of
presentation are central to this endeavor. This chapter relates how the State used
bureaucratic logic to form a monothetic taxonomy to make Jews national. Policies and
decisions skewed social order away from the potential equalities of citizenship,
towards the dominance of Jewish nationality, with profound consequences for
inequality between Jewish and Palestinian citizens.

Citizenship, nationality, ethnicity, and minority are four categories in a taxonomy
of the Israeli national, though their uneasy fit with one another continues to be worked
out. The State shaped the categories of citizenship (*ezrakhout*) and nationality (*le'om*,
cognate with Hebrew *uma*, or 'nation'). Over the years, nationality has been developed
as the taxonomic strategy to differentiate between Jewish and Palestinian citizens. By
contrast, the categories of 'minority' (*mi'out*), and 'community' or 'ethnicity' (*eda*, pl.
edot) are more the products of Israeli popular culture. Minority almost always refers
only to non-Jewish citizens. Community almost always refers only to Jews. In effect,
the (mainly Palestinian) non-Jewish 'nationalities' of the state level became 'minorities'

on the level of popular culture. Communities are Jewish 'ethnicities' or Jewish subcultures. On the level of Jewish popular culture, these Jewish ethnicities are sub-categories of Jewish nationality. There is a fifth category whose members are permanent residents by fiat, but who are excluded from the other categories – these are the Palestinians living under Israeli military rule in the occupied territories.

Citizenship is legal membership in the State. Citizenship in the modern democratic state is an egalitarian idea – in principle each individual citizen is the equal of every other (Roche 1987: 367, 373; Segal 1988). In Israel, the State divides its citizens among categories of nationality. This has the taxonomic effect of capture and containment, of dividing citizens into those who belong to a Jewish 'nation' or 'people' within the state and those who belong to other 'peoples.' As noted, Jewish nationality or nation divides into ethnicities, into lower-level Jewish communities that ideologically are egalitarian in relation to one another. Minorities, however, are not entitled to be called ethnic, but are perceived by the Jewish majority as a lower, subordinate category. Egalitarianism among Jewish ethnicities parallels hierarchy and inequality between the Jewish majority and the non-Jewish minorities.[1]

Citizenship

As a monothetic legal category, citizenship accords perfectly with the forming qualities of bureaucratic logic. With limited exceptions, one either is or is not a member of the state. Though citizenship may be elaborated in ways beyond the legal (Shafir 1998; Yuval-Davis 2000; Ong 1996; Connell 1990), it bolts the individual to the state, to its legal apparatus, to its rules and regulations. Citizenship is the attribute of the individual, and the unity of the democratic state arises from the moral equality that each citizen acknowledges towards others so defined and classified by the state. Nonetheless as Dumont (1986) among others points out, the democratic state does not require its citizens to share in any essential sameness of being. In principle the identity of each citizen may be distinct from that of any other citizen.

The Declaration of Independence is ambiguous on this point. Israel is called the 'birthplace of the Jewish people,' their natural and historic homeland, and the Declaration proclaims 'the establishment of the Jewish State in Palestine, to be called Israel.' The Declaration declaims liberty, justice, and peace (as these were taught by the Hebrew biblical prophets) in a state that 'will uphold the full social and political equality of all its citizens, without distinction . . .' Is it essentialist Jewish peoplehood or egalitarian citizenship that is the more embracing conception here? As noted, the state is called Jewish and democratic and this sequencing is deliberate, following on the Declaration of Independence. So, Israel is a Jewish state that somehow is democratic – a state no less for its Palestinian citizens.[2] To date this synthesis is impossible.[3]

In principle the law favors Jews over non-Jews in obtaining citizenship for persons born or residing outside of Israel. The Law of Return is the most prominent instance.

The law was passed in 1950 on the anniversary of the death of Theodor Herzl, the visionary of the Zionist state (Azaryahu 1995: 34). This Law entitles every Jew in the world to Israeli citizenship provided they take up permanent residence in Israel (Bin-Nun 1992: 15). Ben-Gurion called the Law of Return 'the foundation stone of the State of Israel' (Hacohen 1998: 61). Citizenship is granted also to those non-Jews who are born into and who reside within the state.[4]

Shaping Nationality

The category of nationality has been a powerful force in shaping a sense of Jewish peoplehood in Israel. In its governmental usage, the national opens a discourse of difference within the egalitarian premise that citizens are moral no less than political equivalents. This discourse of official national distinctions encourages the reification of collective difference. Citizens are classified and separated from one another in terms of their collective, ascribed characteristics, elevating premises of national essence and difference (see Seligman 1992). The state becomes the new framework for the existence of Jewish community, charged with the survival of the Jewish nation (Swirsky 1976: 132). Thus the boundaries of state and nation are blurred in Israel. As noted, in Hebrew there is no popular term for nation-state – the invocation of each term implies the other embedded within it. The shaping of nationality has added powerfully to the strengthening of essentialism through categorical difference. Each Israeli citizen must belong to one and only one legal nationality, exclusive of all others. Though the official usage of nationality was divisive from the outset, initially it did not carry quite the heavily ethnicized, ideological weight that it acquired through time.

After 1948, the invention and shaping of the category of nationality demanded the capture and containment of essential difference, and officially this set the exclusivist contrast between Jewish nationality and others at the highest level of taxonomic generality. As a category, nationality made its initial appearance in the first Israeli census in 1949. Anderson (1991: 166) comments that: 'The fiction of the census is that everyone has one – and only one – extremely clear place [in it]. No fractions.' The Provisional State Assembly (the forerunner of the Knesset) then made the census into the population registry – called the Order for the Registration of Residents (*Pekudat Mirsham Hatoshavim*) – for the purpose of registering and enumerating all persons within the state. Initially the ORR included the categories of citizenship, nationality, and religion.[5] The ORR itself was treated as more of a technical matter.[6] Citizenship was described as an objective, legal status. Religion was left to self-designation – if one defined oneself as Jewish, this was sufficient. Nationality was not defined.[7] But since 1948 the shaping of nationality has been crucial to the official formation of Jewish essentialism, and to its impact on citizenship. The category of nationality has been endowed with increasing authority to define and to classify Israel's population in exclusivist, essentialist terms.

In its original formulation the Law of Return did not define the identity of the bearer of the right of return. Any Jew (understood as one who felt bound to Jewry as a people or as a group sharing a common fate) could exercise this right. In the wake of the racist Nuremberg Laws and the Holocaust, Jewish nationality (like Jewish religion) was understood as a matter of self-definition (though never by the religious political parties). Nonetheless, through the administration of the Law of Return, Jewish nationality was made into a near prerequisite for Israeli citizenship, virtually guaranteeing the latter. Classifying persons as non-Jews negated the likelihood of their applications for citizenship being granted. These developments in classification severely restricted the possibility that Israel could become a democratic, multinational state based on egalitarian citizenship. The power to classify nationality is held by the Ministry of the Interior, which controls the population registry. Usually in the hands of religious parties, the Ministry has done its utmost to make Jewish nationality identical with the religious definition of a Jew.[8] This shaping of nationality almost equates citizenship with the religious definition of the individual.

Who is a Jew?

Much of the honing of the classification of nationality has been done through court decisions dealing with the question of 'Who is a Jew?' (Hacohen 1998). Adjudication has turned on qualities of personhood used to define one as a Jew (see Abramov 1976: 270–320, for the early years of adjudication). Here I discuss briefly three of the most significant cases, two of which are decisions of the Supreme Court.

In 1970, in a 5 to 4 decision in favor of the plaintiff, the Supreme Court ruled in the case of Binyamin Shalit.[9] Shalit, a Jew, had married a gentile. He had asked the court to order the Ministry of Interior to register his children as Jews under the category of nationality. The Ministry had refused. Prior to hearing the case, the Chief Justice had urged the government to erase the taxonomy of nationality from the population registry, but government refused (Lahav 1993: 139). The majority opinion understood nationality as an administrative category for the classification of statistical information. This opinion urged that nationality, understood as the national identity of the person (*zehut le'umit*), be treated partly as a matter of personal choice and self-definition.

By contrast, the minority opinion attributed an essentialist quality to the Jewish person, giving a religious basis to nationality. This opinion argued that nationality exists as a category that separates citizens into groups that are essentially distinct from one another. Membership in a nationality is wholly ascribed, without personal choice. Nationality exists as a totalizing taxonomy within which Jews are separated from all others in exclusive and inclusive terms. Within this taxonomy of nationality a citizen necessarily belongs to a divisive category infused with primordial essence of the national. Following the Shalit case, the Knesset amended the ORR, in order to strengthen the taxonomy of nationality, making it more similar to the religious definition.[10] The primordial foundation of nationality was legitimated further in relation to state and religion.

The case of George Tamarin narrowed the definition of the national by denying that a new nationality had been created in or by the State. Tamarin was registered according to nationality as a Jew and according to religion as 'non-religious.' He understood nationality as a matter of self-definition, while religion signified belief in a transcendent being. Following the Knesset amendment of 1970, Tamarin concluded that nationality had been reshaped as a classification to which he had no feeling of belonging. He asked the Supreme Court to declare his nationality to be 'Israeli,' thereby equating nationality and citizenship, and obviating the 'national' difference between Jews and others (see also Tamarin 1973: 190).

In rejecting Tamarin's application, the court decision of 1972 stated that 'ethnic identity' is derived from 'ethnic-cultural' characteristics.[11] Ethnic identity in this instance is equivalent to the essentialist quality of the Jewish person. The Court added that in Israel there is no basis on which to claim that a unique Israeli nation (or nationality) has been created. A Jew in Israel belongs to the 'natural' and moral unity of the Jewish people. However, the Court did enunciate conditions under which a national collectivity comes into existence, and in this gave to political action a major role. The decision argued that an 'ethnic collectivity' (*kibbutz etni*) can turn into a 'national collectivity' (*kibbutz le'umi*) if its members organize in order to influence society to accept their national values. By giving to nationality a formative political dimension, the Court indirectly touched on the issue of Palestinian citizens, and why their efforts at political self-definition as a national collectivity have been curtailed systematically since 1948.

The third case was heard before a lower court. In 1976, Yokhana Shelakh requested that the Tel-Aviv District Court change her nationality from Jewish to Hebrew (*ivri*). In rejecting her application on the grounds of its redundancy, the judge argued that Hebrew, Israeli, and Jew were all interchangeable names, synonyms (*shaymot nirdafim*), for the same nationality.[12] The Shelakh case makes clear why the State categorically separates citizenship and nationality, since Jewish nationality is perceived to encompass Hebrew nationality and Israeli nationality. An Israeli nationality that included Palestinians and other non-Jews because they have Israeli citizenship would produce transgressions of essence, of monothetic classification, of the order of Arab Jews or Jewish Arabs. The message is that Jews must be national in their citizenship – and this is made so in the Jewish state. Israeli Jews increasingly substitute the term, 'People of Israel,' meaning the 'Jewish People,' for the term, 'citizens of Israel.' Similarly, the term 'Israeli,' as it is used today usually refers only to Israeli Jews. Holding to the paradigm of Israel as a Jewish and democratic state is erasing the distinction between Jewish nationality and Israeli citizenship, driving Israeli Palestinians to the margins of the state and beyond.

Jewish nationality and nationalism are increasingly shaped in terms of religious affiliation. The only officially sanctioned nationality open to non-Jews with Israeli citizenship is religious. The religions in question – Judaism, Islam, Christianity – are monotheisms. The monotheisms forbid overlapping religious membership. The religious forming of nationality fits perfectly with the State's intention that nationality divide populations, exclusively and inclusively, and capture and contain them totally. This strengthens the claim that only Jews are entitled to decide on the topographical shaping of the State, while citizenship is pushed to the margins of ideological discourse.

The invention and forming of nationality as a monothetic taxonomy enables this to function as an administrative instrument for capture, containment, smoothing. The classification of nationality has been turned into an issue of the moral essence of the Jewish person, moving inexorably towards the total metaphysical separation of Jew and Palestinian. The monothetic taxonomy of nationality is pivotal in shaping nationality as hierarchy.

Majority and Minority

The national boundary between Jew and non-Jew often is phrased as that between Jewish 'majority' and various 'minorities' (*bnei mi'outim*), in particular the Palestinian 'minority' (sing. *mi'out*). Majority and minority are another version of essentialist difference between nationalities. The majority nationality is the State and therefore superior and dominant. In the early 1950s the advisor on Arab affairs to the prime minister declared that, 'I opposed the integration of Arabs into Israeli society. I preferred separate development. True, this prevented the Arabs from integrating into the Israeli democracy . . . The separation made it possible to maintain a democratic regime within the Jewish population alone' (quoted in Peretz 1991: 100).[13]

The great success of the national in Israel is that nationality is perceived to be infused with primordial qualities that cannot be changed. By contrast, citizenship is a legal construct, perceived as shapeable through conscious agency. In the taxonomy of the national, every category of nationality is essentially different. Primordial difference between categories is complemented by primordial sameness within each category. Nationality in Israel is constituted as a taxonomic hierarchy that ranks and values the degrees to which the presence of shared essential qualities among persons is encouraged. The Israeli governmental demands of Israeli Jews that they identify as a collectivity characterized by sameness, as a national group, a political nation; but Palestinian citizens are virtually forbidden from defining themselves publicly as a politicized national minority. Nationality for Israeli Jews indexes the governmental project of building people who are national in their citizenship – in the lyrics of an earlier Zionist song: 'We've come to the Land to build and to be built' – to become the battle-ready nation-in-arms as required, gliding familiarly into the grieving family-in-arms as necessary. Nationality for Israeli Palestinians indexes the governmental project that denies them collectivity as nationals, and demands of them to become collected together as individuals and collectively as members of kin groups. The monothetic qualities of nationality in Israel are reshaping citizenship, and are conditioning the latter on the former.

On each side of the essentialist divide between Jews and Palestinians there are secondary distinctions. On the Jewish side, I call the secondary distinctions within essential sameness the discourse of *edot yisrael*. As noted, the Hebrew term *eda* connotes a cohesive community, a *gemeinschaft* or subculture, based on common origin. Within the Jewish sector of Israel the use of *eda*, of community, resonates to a degree with how 'ethnic group' is used elsewhere. There are, however, crucial distinctions that need discussion in order to see how equality among Jewish 'ethnicities' depends upon inequality between the Jewish majority and the Palestinian minority.

Jewish Ethnicities, Jewish Majority, Palestinian Minority

In terms of 'ethnicities,' the history of the State can be divided roughly into two ideological periods. The first two decades were characterized by an ideology of the melting pot (*mizug galuyot*), whose mold was intentionally Western. The bureaucratic implementation of this ideology was intended politically to banish many of the 'ethnic' distinctions among Jews in order to produce the new Israeli person. By contrast the last three decades have been characterized by the emergence of an ideology of ethnic pluralism among Jews whose impact is felt in all sectors of Israeli life.

The formation of Jewish ethnicities in Israel is shaped by bureaucratic logic, nationalism, and commonsensical versions of Jewish history. The narrative of ethnicities complements that of the Declaration of Independence. Thus, in the distant past the forebears of the Jewish people, the Israelites, shared in common the same culture, society, religion, political structure, and territory. Figuratively this is akin to an unbroken, hermetic circle of peoplehood sharply divided from others, containing its own primordial essentialism, like an entire pie fresh from the ideological oven. With the destruction of the Israelite state and society and the spread of exiles throughout the Diaspora, this pie split into neatly divided slices. In this way, Jewish subcultures came into existence, named according to the countries in which the exiles settled – thus, Polish Jews, Moroccan Jews, German Jews, Yemenite Jews, and so forth.

After 1948 the State gathered in the exiles (*kibbutz galuyot*), and these slices returned to their territorial source and to their places within the unbroken, hermetic circle of essential peoplehood. Yet now the circle had boundaries between its slices, according to the countries from which the exiles returned. Figuratively, the ideological pie is divided into slices, though still joined at their base, one to the other, still sharing the same essentialist, foundational culture. These partly divided slices – all now within the unbroken circle of peoplehood and statehood – are the ethnicities of Jewish Israel.[14] The categorization of Jewish ethnicities as distinct entities within a single classification of 'ethnic groups' has been one of the great efforts of smoothing on the part of Israeli governmentality.[15]

In terms of Zionist ideology, this smoothing renders these ethnicities as the equals of one another within the Israeli national. In the analogy of the ideological pie, all its ethnic slices are equal to one another, existing on the same level of abstraction, each slice made of somewhat different combinations of the same essential substance. This egalitarian precept of the Zionist state can be obscured in Israeli realities of class, power, and discrimination (Smooha 1978; Swirsky 1981; Dominguez 1989). Deconstructions of statist Zionist ideology suggest the following.

The Western founders of the state had intended it to be populated first and foremost by Westerners (Patai: 1970: 67), thereby continuing the demographic pattern of the pre-state period, when over four-fifths of the Jewish population of Palestine were Westerners. Given the obliteration of European Jewry during the Holocaust, the bulk of immigrants during the first decade of statehood were Easterners. Easterners supplied the cheap labor for Westerner-dominated agriculture and industry. The more submerged premise in the Zionist melting pot was that Easterners were exotic primitives, similar to Arabs. Yet all Jews came from the same elemental substance, so that they (unlike the Palestinians) could be modernized under State tutelage. If the immediate reality was one of Westerners subordinating Easterners, the intention of the former over the longer duration was to level hierarchy among Jewish ethnicities. Simultaneously, the intention was to finalize hierarchical relationships between the majority category of Jew and the minority category of Arab.

The premise of egalitarianism has been embedded in the ethnic national paradigm of Israeli Jews at least during the past three decades. Eventually, Easterners will attain economic and political parity with Westerners, while cultural pluralism will shape Jewish ethnicities.[16] The ethnic paradigm emphasizes shared, essential qualities as the national template that encompasses all Jews, while subsuming and respecting their sub-cultural differences. Jewish ethnicities are folded within Jewish nationality, within the shaping of Jews who are national in their citizenship.

According to the discourse of national ethnicity, the Jewish people divide into equivalent categories of Jews, characterized by sub-cultural diversities. Because of their essential sameness, Jewish ethnicities are posited as equal to one another, while enabling them to be different from one another within a well-defined, clearly bounded national Jewish collectivity, from which Palestinians as a subordinate minority are excluded. As the governmental constructs Jewish unity as national, so, too, it monothetically divides minorities to weaken their mass.[17] The powerful sense of the national Jewish collectivity, separated and bounded, slides without effort into the vision of the mobilized nation-in-arms, and into its cognate, the family-in-arms, from which minorities are excluded and often are made the enemy. This is the vision of the State presented through the Versailles commemoration.

The most telling, consequential, and ironic point that emerges from this discussion is that the egalitarian premise of ethnicity among Israeli Jews is itself dependent upon the premise of inequality between Jews and Palestinians. The forming of inequality between majority and minority supports, reproduces, and fixes in place the forming of equality among the Jewish ethnicities. Each forming defines the logic of the other – the essentialism of sameness posits the essentialism of difference, and the latter posits inequality.

The horizons of Zionist ideology have merged with those of Jewish popular culture. The legal arguments over nationality continue to drive towards a monothetic taxonomy of national difference. Within this official taxonomy of difference between Jew and Palestinian, Jewish popular culture has produced the egalitarian (yet no less monothetic) discourse of Jewish ethnicities and their hierarchical relationship to non-Jews. Making Jews national in their citizenship continues unabated, refining Jewish nationality at the State level and the discourse of ethnicities at the popular level. All of this points once more to the credo of the 'Jewish and democratic state' as a hierarchic, taxonomic construction in which the 'Jewish' captures, contains, and smoothes the 'democratic' in accordance with bureaucratic logic.

In the studies of public events that follow, Jewish nationality and citizenship often are made isomorphic, and the governmental project of making Jews national in their citizenship comes to the fore. It is citizenship as nationality that foregrounds the mobilized nation-in-arms, the grieving family-in-arms. On the whole, in these public events Jewish ethnicities are hidden away within Jewish nationality. Any hint of minority as a national collectivity in its own right is suppressed. Where minorities appear, they do so as 'honorary Jews.'

Part II
The National and Bureaucratic Logic in Early Schooling

Prologue

Taxonomy can make your head spin. It does mine whenever my eyes light on an index
of the Universal Decimal Classification (UDC). By what succession of miracles has
agreement been reached, practically throughout the world, that 668.184.2.099 shall
denote the finishing of toilet soap, and 629.1.018-465 horns on refuse vehicles . . .

Georges Perec (1999)

The pervasive presence of the national and bureaucratic logic in Israel is to no small
degree the outcome of the participation from an early age of children in public events
practiced in educational settings. This participation begins in kindergarten and
continues through to the end of high school (Shamgar-Handelman 1990). This
Prologue foregrounds the significance accorded to kindergarten and celebration in pre-
state Jewish Palestine and then in Israel. Chapters Four and Five then demonstrate
how kindergarten celebrations begin to enculturate in little children values crucial to
the existence of the state.

Among others, Durkheim (1956: 71) contended that the purpose of education, 'is
to arouse and to develop in a child a certain number of physical, intellectual, and moral
states which are demanded of him by . . . the political society as a whole.' In this way,
'society perpetually recreates the conditions of its very existence' (1956: 123).
Durkheim's comments make two themes salient here: in the nation-state the political
economy of education induces and articulates the ideology and authority of the
national, and the reproduction of social order depends on education.

In the Yishuv the fusion of political ideology and formal organization in order to
shape the maturation of youngsters began in the kindergarten. A veteran kindergarten
teacher reflected as follows on the intimate ties between this collectivity and the
kindergarten system.[1] These were bonds, she wrote, between early-age education and
'the ideas and aspirations that lifted the spirits of those parts of the nation that rebuilt
the ruins of its homeland and rejuvenated this.' The Zionist dream of returning to work
the land of Israel, she added, 'brought the garden into the kindergarten' (Fayence-
Glick 1957: 141). The practices of the kindergarten were linked tightly to the national
in constructing a collectivity with powerful senses of boundedness, inclusion, and
exclusion.[2] Education enclosed youngsters in forms of organization whose application
of pedagogy was capable of shaping ideologically and socially disciplining persons.

Such pedagogical milieus during the Yishuv and then in the State extended beyond
the formal educational system as such. Jewish educators and officials have strongly
advocated the importance of keeping children and youth within what in Hebrew are

called 'frameworks' (pl. *misgerot*), intended to protect, guide, and control youngsters. Israeli Jewish youngsters are positioned from the ages of 2 to 21 within frameworks – kindergarten, school, youth movements (Kahane 1997), and others – that track and evaluate their performance and maturation. These frameworks culminate with compulsory military service (see Ben-Ari 1998; Lieblich 1989), when the 18-year-old is given over by his parents to the authority and service of the State. When an army recruit completes basic training he is given a Hebrew Bible and a rifle and he swears his allegiance to the State. During his national service he is fathered by the IDF and mothered, to a degree, by his family (see, for example, Katriel 1991b: 71–91).

Though frameworks of formal education have softened and loosened during recent years, producing a host of variant setups with much choice for youngsters and their families, the permutations of ideology nonetheless continue to shape expectations regarding enculturation into the Zionist state. To leave a youngster to his own devices, intentions, explorations, desires, continues to be perceived as dangerous by varieties of officialdom. The efficacy of the governmental is perceived to depend upon containment within frameworks, and progression from framework to framework.

Building educational frameworks was central to Zionist endeavors. The first Hebrew-speaking Zionist kindergarten in Palestine was opened in 1911. Its successors, together with local seminaries for teachers, separated Hebrew early-age education from foreign antecedents.[3] The Jewish kindergartens in Palestine cultivated the Zionist spirit of working the land and building the nation, both of which were linked closely to the practice of the national (Doleve-Gandelman 1987). With statehood, kindergarten education was centralized under the authority of the Ministry of Education, and was made mandatory for children at age 5. But numerous kindergarten classes were opened for children from the age of 2. From the 1920s through the present the demand for places in kindergartens almost always has exceeded supply, and nowadays parents place their children in kindergartens well before the compulsory age of 5. In the late 1980s some three-quarters of Jewish 2-year-olds, and close to 100 percent of Jewish 3- and 4-year-olds were enrolled in kindergartens.

From its inception, Zionist kindergarten education was intended to reach through children to also shape their parents, many of whom were recent immigrants. The intention was to turn the child into an agent of the collectivity, bringing its public values into the privacy of the home. As well, through parent-teacher meetings and instructional sessions in preparation for holiday celebrations, mothers were given instructions on how to behave towards their children, on proper attitudes towards the development of the child, on how leisure time with children should be spent, and on the kind of cooking that children would enjoy eating at home. Pedagogy for early ages intensified after statehood. Numerous books of instruction and advice for kindergarten teachers were published, stressing the need to educate parents as well as children, and the importance of enlisting the youngsters as allies in this national endeavor (Rabinowitz 1958; Zanbank-Wilf 1958: 57; Naftali and Nir-Yaniv 1974; Shemer 1966; Ministry of Education and Culture 1967).

The chapters of Part II begin at the beginning of the little child's discovery of the national and bureaucratic logic, by discussing two kinds of public event held in secular kindergartens. Both kinds of event practice an ethos of the governmental, into which the pre-school child is introduced and positioned. One kind of event, discussed in Chapter Four, is the celebration of national holidays. The other, addressed in Chapter Five, is the ubiquitous birthday party. The celebration of holidays speaks quite directly to affiliation with state and nation; and the chapter discusses how the allegiance of little children is shifted from their families to the State through these celebrations. However the relationship of the birthday party to the governmental is more complex. The birthday party celebrates the child as an individual, as he or she is moved from one age category to the next. On the surface of its practice there is no broader significance to the event. Yet the analyses put forward in Chapter Five use this individuation of the individual to argue that the event is no less a celebration of bureaucratic logic, through which the pre-school child begins his or her inculcation into the lineal logic of monothetic classification.

The celebration of holidays in the kindergarten was and is perceived as a prime medium of enculturation (Rabinowitz 1958). Writing primarily of the Yishuv, one educator commented: 'Special stress was given to holidays as a way of teaching tradition, concepts of history, and Israeli folklore to babies through the pipelines of pleasure and joy saturated with experience.' Many weeks were spent in preparations that 'filled, and are filling today, most of the teaching year . . . it is as if the kindergarten life is one long holiday with intermissions for pieces of secularity and intervals of reality' (Fayence-Glick 1957: 141; see also Katerbursky 1962: 153).

In more recent instruction books the teacher is featured as a touchstone of tradition and modernity, keeping alive holidays lost to parents through the trauma of their dislocation and immigration, and innovating new patterns of celebration by borrowing from different Jewish traditions. Such attitudes reflect the unreflective power of governmentality in trying to classify and remake the person. Immigrant parents are said to have little of their own to contribute to ceremony in the state, and so along with their young offspring they must be taught how to celebrate holidays. Golden (2001) argues that new immigrants are classified implicitly as children who must go through symbolic maturation, their personal histories made to synchronize with that of the Jewish state as they join its temporal dimensions.

Hidden in the writings of educators is the premise that control of the child is crucial to the reproduction of the nation-state through the magnification, elaboration, and itemization of its nationalism. The child is the future member and culture-bearer, while as parent-to-be he or she is essential to the formation of the family-to-come. Therefore serious thought is given to designing holiday events in the kindergarten, as Chapter Four explicates. No less, the forming of the little child as that kind of individual who is classified easily is central to the projects of bureaucratic logic. In this respect, the monothetic classification of the individual is done often according to his/her exact age. The most pervasive motif of the kindergarten birthday party is that of exact age, indeed the classification of the child as one who exists and matures through self-recognition of his/her exact age. Ostensibly the party celebrates age for the sake of the personal growth of the child. The child's passage from one numerical age to the next is constructed to mark his/her deepening enculturation into the norms of collectivity (Weil 1986).[4] Less obviously, yet no less powerfully, the birthday party designs experiences of age and ageing that induce the child into the willing practice of monothetic classification.

Chapter Five discusses prominent practices of age and ageing in the birthday party. One of these is the individuation of the birthday child in terms of a cultural classification of time that momentarily fragments his/her self-continuity into discrete temporal categories. Another is the child's reclassification from one age category to another, in accordance with this taxonomy of time. A third emphasizes the experiencing of time as continuity, for categories of age are shown also to be one's personal past, present, future. The birthday party induces the youngster into a taxonomy of time, and into his/her own place within this. In the modern world exact age is 'good to think,' as Lévi-Strauss might put it, for it is inherent to numerous classifications used to shape social order (Musgrove and Middleton 1981: 53). The individual frequently is keyed by numerical age to systems of social classification invented through bureaucratic logic.

Taxonomy indexes practice. Taxonomies should be good to use. Thus Bourdieu (1977: 97) comments that all practice necessarily implicates taxonomies that structure practice as it is being done, producing its taken-for-granted character. In this regard, exact numerical age is a prime classifier in commonsensical classification. Numerical age is used by numerous bureaucracies to place the individual into anonymous social categories. Age-related taxonomies are pervasive; hardly anyone escapes being captured by them, contained and smoothed.

Age is an index of time. For social purposes, temporality must be standardized and regularized. The age of the individual is his/her personal, autobiographical time, standardized biographically in terms of cultural duration. Western cultural time usually is conceived of as lineal and irreversible. Time is divided mathematically into uniform durations that recur with fixed periodicity. These qualities enable the organization and experiencing of time as quantitative, and of its durations as exactly divisible, measurable, countable, and therefore comparable. A length of time is composed of a number of durations of equal length added together (Zerubavel 1981: 2–11, 59–60).[5]

Piaget (1969: 202–29) contended that the little child has a sense of age that is quite discontinuous. For the small child, age is independent of the order of birth, while the arithmetical difference in age that separates persons exactly is felt by little children to be impermanent and mutable with the passage of time. Yet the child must become self-responsive to the taxonomic break between absolute age differences based on the unit of the year. In this regard each year is not mutable, and is exclusive of all the others. During the period of a particular year of his/her age, the child learns that he/she is a member only of that category of age, to the exclusion of all other age-categories based on the year.

This taxonomic break is the abrupt, jerky movement from one numbered unit of time to another, from one year to the next, from one age to the next. A child learns that each of these ages indexes different moral and normative practices. When he/she can turn these temporal rudiments of biography into autobiography, an important stage of personal maturity is evinced. In the not so distant past the precision of personal age was not especially significant; birth date might be remembered in relation to the closest historical event or calendrical holiday (for example, Myerhoff 1984: 159). Today, knowing one's own numerical age – one's exact location in time, synchronized precisely to all other individuals – is considered an elementary index of individual competence.

The precision of personal age combines exact duration and date of birth. In reckoning age, the year begins and ends for each person according to birth date. The birth date enables the individual to construct his/her private year, from one birthday to the next. These years are the cumulative, chronological durations of his/her autobiography, and perhaps the temporal divisions of the self, of self-knowledge as a historical being (Kunz and Summers 1979–1980). Moreover, the birth date articulates the personal year with the calendar year, since both are constituted from the same durations.

Chronological age is an efficient monothetic divider in separating persons from one another. This is imminent, for example, in discussions of age stratification. Age grades and ranks all individuals, forming age strata that cut across the whole of society in relatively enduring ways, since age-graded roles outlast numerous cohorts of role incumbents (Foner 1975: 147, 157–8; Johnstone 1970). Just as each individual can be isolated according to birth date, so all individuals of a particular age category can be counted together as an aggregate. The classification of aggregates expresses a numerical or statistical conception of the individual, one that is efficient for the governmental operating of taxonomies formed through bureaucratic logic.

Numerical age can abruptly crystallize and synchronize social expectations about the biological, emotional, social, and intellectual qualities of individuals. In Israel, for example, children aged 6 are expected to have an attention span of some 45 minutes, and are placed in the first grade. Yet they are enrolled not because they actually have this attention span, but because they turn 6. Similarly, at age 18, Israelis are expected to understand their political system and so are enfranchised. Yet they are not given the right to vote because they demonstrate comprehension of the political system, but because they turn 18. Monothetic criteria of obligations and rights often are determined by age. Israeli Jews are recruited for military service only after age 17. From that age one must carry an identity card, that also entitles the holder to open a bank account in one's own name. A woman may marry without her parents' consent only on reaching age 18, and not whenever she becomes physically and emotionally prepared for this undertaking. These taxonomies depend on exact age as a universal classifier of the individual, one that is constructed, yet naturalized and embedded in cultural order. Knowledge and experience of the temporal order, of its divisions and durations, of its synchronization of individual rhythms with those of social order, are critical to the development of the child.[6]

The kindergarten years in Israel may be the most powerful in positioning the small child within experiences of the taxonomic structuring of age categories. This role of kindergarten and its public events have hardly been examined anywhere. When such studies are reported, they unequivocally point to the place of kindergarten in impressing the ethos of wider social orders on the young child (cf. Hendry 1986; Ben-Ari 1987; Norman 1991: 104–42; Furman 1999; Gracey 1972: 271–2; Lewis 1979; Henry 1965). In Israel the national and bureaucratic logic are integral to this impress.

The analysis of the Versailles commemoration in Chapter One depended upon the discussion of ethnographic detail to demonstrate the logic of organization of the event and how it signified what it did. The progression of analysis proceeds from the detailing of the phenomenon to its exegesis and significance. In this kind of case-study there is no simple reduction and summation of the phenomenon under discussion. This is so also of the analyses of events in the coming chapters.One should keep in mind that a public event is always practiced through its details. So, too, the analysis of the public event is practiced through its details.

−4−

Celebrations of the National: Holiday Occasions in Kindergartens

[This chapter was coauthored by the late Lea Shamgar-Handelman.]

What walks on four legs in the morning, two legs at noon, and three in the evening?

Riddle of the Sphinx

Little children experience themselves and others through the family arrangements into which they are born. Kinship and familism come to be the natural ordering of things, and fill the metaphor of family with so much feeling. Only later is the child made to realize that parental authority is itself subordinate to a broader social order; and that on numerous occasions loyalty to the collectivity transcends that of familial ties. This transition is crucial to the reproduction of social orders of the state and the governmental. All children must learn that their parents are not the natural apex of hierarchy and authority; that the rights of the collectivity will supersede those of familism; and that in times of crisis the metaphor of familism will appear to encompass the individual within the national. The state appropriates the family as the basis of the nation-in-arms and the family-in-arms.

Many of the holidays celebrated in kindergartens index what Firer (1985), basing her research on school history texts, calls the Law of Zionist Redemption. This refers to the metaphysical premise that the establishment of the Jewish State in the land of Israel was the culmination of the cosmic design that moved all of Jewish history in this direction, a secular, messianic redemption based on deeply embedded religious premises (Evron 1995: 223–41). Celebration scenarios highlight the consensus on cooperation between kindergarten and parent. More implicitly, hidden agendas of these scenarios unearth the more problematic relationship between state and family.[1] Numerous celebrations should be understood as versions of the relationship between representations of national collectivity and family, through which youngsters are encouraged to experience that the superiority of the former supplants that of the latter. The kindergarten is the first location where children learn of hierarchy and egality outside the home.[2]

This chapter discusses three cases of kindergarten holiday celebrations in relation to the symbolic formations they configure and convey. The scenarios of these celebrations project the irreversible maturation that the child will practice into existence

61

within himself, in no small measure through the governmentality of the pedagogical.[3] We focus on aspects of these events that are related to our argument on the interplay of national collectivity and family.[4] We give particular attention to the sequencing of enactments. Sequencing is of signal importance in events whose logic of design emphasizes the lineal (see Lee 1959 on lineal codifications of reality). Thus acts that are placed 'before' and 'after' in relation to one another implicate the logic of organization of the whole sequence of enactment. Whether it is put together consciously in this way or not, an occasion takes on much of its significance through the lineality of its sequencing; through the additive accretion of symbolic practices, and through the emergence of a story line. We attend no less to the prominence of social formations in these enactments. These formations will be related to the three kinds of person – teacher, child, parent – whose positioning in relation to one another indexes the interaction between national collectivity and family that is enacted in the kindergarten.

Serious thought is given to the planning of holidays in the kindergarten. Emphasis is placed on the arousal of emotion through symbolic forms that evoke collective sentiments. In general there is the profusion of 'presentational' symbolism: media that engage the senses more than the critical faculties (Langer 1953). Participants experience these enactments by embodying their symbolic forms. Instruction books note that the kindergarten child needs the emotional experience of a holiday, of togtherness and solidarity, rather than logical explanation or historical exposition.

In the views of kindergarten educators, such sentiments are aroused if scenarios are well-designed. The architectonics of celebration should have internal unity, with well-defined segments of opening, elaboration, and closing. Attention should be given to one or more major ideas or motifs, to scheduling in relation to calendrical cycles, to the sequencing of the program, and to clarity of symbolism. These symbols often are both 'living' and 'lived through', such that the physical positioning of the participants, in itself, shapes symbolic formations. The symbol comes alive as participants live through its shape, as collectivity and as individuals. These formations powerfully invoke a metonymy between motifs of celebration and their experiencing, and a synecdoche in which each part of the collective entity replicates and signifies the coherence and unity of the whole. Educators are well aware of this more explicit level of symbolic manipulation, though there is much variation in enactment among kindergartens.

Kindergarten educators often deny that, more implicitly, such symbolic formations actively manipulate relationships between teacher and parent, collectivity and family. Yet the following must be underlined: the very act of isolating together certain categories of people, and of placing them within embodied symbolic formations, will act on and manipulate the relationships between these categories, regardless of the intent of the designers of the celebration. Moreover each category of participant – teacher, child, parent – has significance beyond the immediate persons who participate in celebrations. The teacher is a governmental figure, a 'gardener' whose task it is to grow, to shape, to cultivate, and so to enculturate her young charges. In Israel these tasks so often are made to circle the national. Licensed by the Ministry of Education, and subject in part to its curricula and supervision, the teacher is the first official-like figure with whom the little child comes into continuous contact outside the home. The teacher is in charge of a collection of Jewish children, a small collectivity in which each child in theory is equal in worth and status to every other, and where she should have no vested interest in particular children rather than in others. Her sentiments should be more universalistic in relating to a child's capabilities, capacities, and behavior.

The child's experience and knowledge, sentiment and loyalty, derive almost wholly from the encompassing primary group of the family. In terms of the governmental the child's years of attendance in educational institutions will reconstitute him in the image of citizen, yet one who is national in his citizenship, one whose ultimate loyalties will be to the Jewish State. Though his attachments to family are not attenuated, there occurs a shift in the hierarchy of family and collectivity, of private and public. These processes are begun in the kindergarten and perhaps are most concentrated in its celebrations.

The occasions to be discussed are representative of the range of traditional and modern holidays celebrated in Israel. The first, Hanukkah, is a traditional holiday, but not a holy Day of Rest. Hanukkah commemorates the victory of the Maccabees and the rededication of the Temple in Jerusalem. The holiday is celebrated in home and synagogue. Our analysis of a Hanukkah celebration demonstrates the implicit manipulation of hierarchy, such that the family is shown to be encompassed by the national collectivity. The second case, Mother's Day, is borrowed from modern Western popular culture, and is a wholly secular occasion of no official standing. In this case it is the collectivity that mandates the legitimacy of the family. The third case, Jerusalem Day, is a secular state commemoration of the unification of Jerusalem under Israeli rule following the 1967 War. Our analysis of this case points to the signifying of links between the collectivity and the child, without the mediation of the family. All of these cases insist on the hierarchical elevation of collectivity over family. In their first few years of education, youngsters experience dozens of such celebrations. Explicit themes, contents, and organization vary within and among kinds of celebrations. Yet the types of implicit relationships between collectivity and family that emerge from our cases likely are relevant to numerous other kindergarten celebrations. For the child, it is the cumulative accretion of such experiences that has enculturating impact.

The kindergarten is defined as the child's world, and the only adult who has a legitimate place within it is the teacher — the representative of the national collectivity. Parents (and other adults) are only guests. Nothing better symbolizes this attitude than the chairs in the kindergarten. In all kindergartens visited, no more than one or two full-size chairs were found. The teacher sits in a full-size chair and at her feet, the children on small chairs. A parent in the kindergarten always occupies a child's place.

Hanukkah: Hierarchy, Family, Collectivity

Hanukkah, the Festival of Lights, commemorates the victory of the Maccabees over the Seleucids, and their rededication of the Temple in 165 B.C.E. According to the Talmud, there was only enough undefiled oil in the Temple for one day of lamp-lighting. Miraculously the oil multiplied into a supply sufficient for eight days. Hanukkah is celebrated for eight days in the home, primarily by the lighting of an additional candle each day, in an eight-branched candelabrum, the *hanukkiah* (pl. *hanukkiot*). An extra candle, the *shamash*, is used to kindle the others. Hanukkah celebrates liberation from foreign domination: in Zionist narrative it is a triumph of faith, of the weak over the strong, the few over the many (Gertz 2000: 5–26). The martial spirit of this holiday is thought to reflect on the struggle of the Jewish people to establish a unified national homeland in the present day.

Books of instruction suggest that the major motif be heroism (see also Furman 1999; and Don-Yehiye 1992, on the role of this holiday in the early years of the State). The enactment should evoke the emotional experience of the occasion. The central symbols of the celebration should be the hanukkiah, candles, tops,[5] and the national flag. The locale of the party should be filled with light, and the shirts or blouses of the children white, to give an atmosphere of joyous luminosity. The best time is late afternoon or early evening, for these darkening hours evoke the uplifting illumination of the holiday from the depths of despair. Scenarios suggest that a central hanukkiah be lit by an adult; that the parents light the small hanukkiot made by their children; and that the children form 'living hanukkiot'.

Description   The party began at 4:30 p.m. Thirty-two children, aged 4 to 5, and their mothers sat at tables placed along three walls of the room. Only a few fathers attended. A name-card marked the place of each child. The tables were covered by white tablecloths. At the center of each table were a vase of flowers, bags of candies, and candles equal to the number of youngsters at that table. Before each child stood a little hanukkiah made by that youngster. On the walls and windows were hung painted paper hanukkiot, oil pitchers, candles, and tops, all of which had been prepared in the kindergarten. Against the fourth wall was a large hanukkiah, constructed of toy blocks covered with colored paper, which supported eight colored candles and the shamash.

An accordionist played melodies of the holiday, and the mothers joined in singing and clapping. The teacher welcomed all those present and at a prearranged signal her helper extinguished the lights. Each mother lit a candle and aided her child to kindle his own little hanukkiah. The room lights were turned on. A father lit the large hanukkiah of toy blocks, and recited the requisite prayers. As he did so, the teacher told the children: 'Remember, when father says a blessing, you must sit quietly and listen to the blessing.' More holiday songs followed.

The teacher announced: 'Now we want to make a living hanukkiah. A living hanukkiah that walks and sings, a hanukkiah of parents and children.' She arranged the mothers and children in a straight line, each child standing in front of his mother. An additional mother-child pair, the shamash, stood some feet to the side. Each mother held a candle, and each youngster a blue or white ribbon. Each child gave one end of his ribbon to the child-shamash. In this formation all children were attached to the shamash by their ribbons, and each mother to her own child. The mother of the shamash lit the candles held by the others. The lights were extinguished, the room lit by the living hanukkiah in the gathering darkness of late afternoon. The accordionist played a melody of the holiday, 'We came to chase away the darkness,' as each mother circled her child. The lights were turned on. The mothers returned to their seats as a group, followed by their children.

The children and mothers from one table returned to the center of the room and were told by the teacher: 'The children will be the spinning tops. Get down, children.' They fell to their knees, bent their heads, and curled their bodies forward. Each mother stood behind her child. The teacher declared: 'The whole year the spinning tops were asleep in their box. From last year until this year, until now. And the children said to them, "Wake up, spinning tops. Hanukkah has come. We want to play with you."' To a background of holiday melodies the teacher moved from child to child, touching the hand of each. With each contact a child awakened, stood up, raised his arms, and began to spin. Each mother spun her child, first clockwise, then counterclockwise. Next the mothers became the tops, spun by their children in one direction and then the other. The teacher told the second table: 'You'll also be spinning tops. Each mother will spin her own child and when I give the signal, change roles. Alright? Let's start . . . The children are the spinning tops . . . the parents are the spinning tops.' Those at the third table followed.

Mothers and children held hands, forming an unbroken circle, and danced round and round the teacher. More singing and food followed. As 6 p.m. approached, the teacher gave the participants permission to leave and the party broke up.

Discussion   This event is composed of three major segments whose overt symbolism is explicit. The first focuses on the traditionalism of the holiday, primarily through the hanukkiah. This segment presents the connectivity between past and present. The second works through the make-believe of the spinning top, and evokes the relationship between present and future. The third alters the relationship between family and collectivity.

The first segment presents a series of candle-lightings: mother helps her child to kindle the small hanukkiah, father lights the large hanukkiah, and the candles are lit on the living hanukkiah. These actions are embedded in the songs of the holiday, telling of heroism, victory, and illumination. These themes interlace emotion and experience to join past to present. The blue and white ribbons of the living hanukkiah are the official colors of the State. In the living hanukkiah ancient triumph is fused with modern renaissance. Collectivity is dedicated to temple, temple to collectivity.

Here the idea of family is central. The enactment practices symbolic acts – the kindling of candles and prayers – that should take place within the home and that delineate a familial division of labor. So it is apt for mother to help her small child, in this instance to light the hanukkiah; and for father, the male head of household, to recite the prayers on behalf of the assembly. Yet then the symbolism of this enactment transcends the family. The 'living hanukkiah' encompasses all the mothers and children, while respecting the singularity of individual families, represented here by the dyads of mother and child. Each mother stands behind her child and then walks around and encompasses the latter, delineating the family unit. This living hanukkiah is a symbol of national collectivity, while this collectivity is itself constituted of smaller family units. The living hanukkiah practices the significance of past heroism and dedication into the present. This is done through the mothers and children, whose living bodies compose the shape of this central symbol. The national collectivity is embodied and presented as living through family units, just as the latter live within and through the former. Each is shown as integral to the other. However the connotation is that of the collectivity as a higher order than the family, since here it encompasses the latter.

In contrast to the seriousness of the first segment, the second is playful. Its motif is the top, a holiday toy inscribed with Hebrew letters that denote the miraculous – the multiplication of oil, the victory itself. Through the motif slumber is shattered, the make-believe evoked, and the participants act joyously in the holiday mood. Again the focus is that of the family unit, represented by dyads of mother and child. The hierarchy at the close of the first segment is kept. The teacher activates each child, and the latter performs under the direction of mother.

Then mother and child reverse roles: mother becomes the sleeping top, awakened and directed by her child. Unlike the inscription of tradition in the first segment, the playful is full of potential, as is the youngster who will mature into the adult, becoming a parent, controlling children of his own. This segment projects the child as parent-to-be towards a future in which he/she will replace his/her parents. Through the two segments, past and future are joined together in the movement of generations. Whereas the first segment recreates family and collectivity in the images of tradition and the enduring past, the second demonstrates that parents are not timeless monoliths, and shows the direction of intergenerational succession.

The third segment begins with an unbroken circle dance of mothers and children who revolve around the teacher.[6] This formation reconfigures the relationship between family and collectivity. Yet the circle dance blurs the distinctiveness of particular families, their parents and children, their adults and youngsters. Distinct family units disappear. Instead, the dancers are closer to being discrete and egalitarian individuals, themselves part of (and made over by) a greater and embracing national collectivity, one of axial centricity.

In this and other kindergarten celebrations the teacher is the sole arbiter and ultimate authority. Before their very eyes, children see and hear her control parents. In these celebrations the teacher is not an alternative source of authority to that of parents, as she may be perceived by children in the daily life of the kindergarten.

Instead she is the pinnacle of hierarchy that subsumes the family. Thus the whole enactment is framed by the architectonics of hierarchy, external to but acting upon the family unit. All actions of such celebrations regardless of their explicit content are imbued from a more governmental perspective with this quality of hierarchy. The first segment constructs a version of hierarchy within the family, and then embeds the latter within a hierarchic version of collectivity. The second takes apart and reverses hierarchical relationships among family members. The third emphasizes equality among Jews, all of whom are orientated towards the governmental figure of the teacher.

In the first segment the child is dependent upon and subordinate to his mother in lighting the little hanukkiah. In turn, both are dependent upon the father who lights the large hanukkiah and recites prayers on behalf of the whole family. This series is an accurate presentation of elementary roles within the family. Family units then are made to constitute a symbol of the collectivity, the living hanukkiah. The national collectivity becomes embodied as an assemblage of families (as in the Mimuna discussed in Chapter Three, note 16, the collectivity embodied there as an assemblage of ethnic categories). Here separate families are dependent upon and are subordinate to the collectivity in order to relate to one another, in order to create an alive, enduring vision of tradition and belief. The first segment builds up the symbol of the hanukkiah in increasing degrees of hierarchy. The apex of experience is through the living of this collective emblem. Integral to this are the ribbons in the national colors held by the children. Thus the Jewish motif of the hanukkiah is imbued with the symbolism of statehood; while embedded in this traditional motif of collectivity is a more modern version.

The second segment begins with the presentation of hierarchical family roles. The dyad of mother and child shows the coherence of the family unit. The mother directs the movements of the spinning top, her child, practicing an accurate depiction of status and authority in relation to her offspring. But their reversal of roles shows the independence and equality of the child. The autonomy of children, their founding of families, will be the outcome of their maturation, in which their family of procreation will no longer play a major role. The third segment, the circle dance, entirely omits any presentation of the family unit: the unbroken circle evokes egalitarianism and common effort as the dancers orientate themselves towards their common center of the governmental. The teacher orchestrates their actions, as does the national in relation to its members.

Like the hanukkiah alive, the circle dance is a living collective symbol. But each is in opposition to the other. The hanukkiah depends on the family and on its internal hierarchy for its existence. The circle dance eliminates the family unit and simultaneously relates each participant equally to all others and to a statist apex of hierarchy that is greater than the family. In the sequencing of this celebration the unbroken circle with its apical center supplants the cellular hanukkiah; just as for children the national eventually will supersede their parents as the pinnacle of authority.

Mother's Day: The Creation of Family and Intimacy

This party was celebrated together by some forty children aged 3, 4, and 5, belonging to three separate classes of the same kindergarten. The explicit aim of the teacher was to have the youngsters demonstrate their love and respect for their mothers. This included the giving of gifts by the child to his mother. However the sequencing of enactment conveys a more implicit pattern of practice: the collectivity brings into existence and shapes the bonds of feeling of the mother-child relationship.

Description   Each child prepared a present for his mother: a piece of shaped dough, decorated, baked, lacquered. A small hole enabled this to be strung as a pendant. Each gift was wrapped together with a greeting card. On the morning of the celebration, vases of flowers were placed on tables, as well as an additional flower intended for each mother. The children arrived at the usual early hour; their mothers were invited for midmorning. The small kindergarten chairs were arranged in a large unbroken circle. An accordionist provided music.

Each mother was seated, with her child before her on a cushion. The teacher stood in the center of the circle. From the outset she instructed the children on how to greet and to behave toward their mothers. 'Come children,' she cried, 'let's say a big "hello" to mother! Let's give mother a big hug! Let's sing together, "What a Happy Day is Mother's Day".' After the singing each child was handed a flower. They sang together, 'A Fine Bouquet of Flowers for Mother.' 'Give the flower to mother,' instructed the teacher, 'and give kisses to mother.' Each child turned, gave his mother the flower, and kissed her.

The mothers were arranged in pairs. Each member faced the other and together they held their flowers. The children formed a large circle and holding hands walked around all the pairs of mothers and sang. Mothers and children sat and sang together. The teacher said a few words to the youngsters on the importance of being nice to mother. The children stood, faced their mothers, and sang: 'Let's bless mother, blessings for Mother's Day. Be happy in your life, for the coming year. Arise and reach 120 years [of age].'[7] The teacher instructed: 'Give mother a big hug and sing, "My dear mother loves only me, yes only me, yes only me".' After they had done so, she added: 'Now smile at mother.'

The mothers closed their eyes and each child gave his mother the present made especially for her; and according to instruction gave her 'a very warm kiss.' The children sang together as the mothers hung the pendants around their necks. Each mother and child formed pairs and danced and sang together. The lyrics concerned physical coordination of the 'look up, look down' variety. The teacher enunciated the lyrics, so that they became instructions for movement that were followed with accuracy. All returned to their places. Since the day was Friday, said the teacher, she and the children were going to teach the mothers a song with which to welcome the Sabbath. Then the teacher pronounced the event completed.

One mother stood and declared: 'We want to say that it's true that we're the children's mothers. But we want to thank and to give a present to the real mother of the children while they're in the kindergarten. We want to give her this bouquet of flowers.' A youngster was given the bouquet and presented it to the teacher while the mothers applauded. The teacher offered snacks, and the party closed.

Discussion   The explicit scenario is clear. The children show their affection for their mothers in order to honor them. Feelings of intimacy are expressed through song, dance, gifts, and numerous gestures. The use of these media was intended to present emphatically the strength and the vitality of the mother-child bond. The sequencing of these acts was not intended to convey any hidden agenda. Their purpose was to lengthen the celebration, thereby to giving the children many opportunities to demonstrate their appreciation. Yet there is a more implicit patterning in this sequence: this practices the formation of the familial bond out of collective formations, under the supervision of the teacher. The major formation consists of an outer circle of mothers, an inner circle of children, and the teacher in the center. The child is situated between mother and teacher. Although each child is placed close to his mother, the presentation of affect in this dyad is orchestrated wholly by the teacher.

The enactment initially delineates the social category of motherhood. Mother is welcomed as something of a stranger, and the youngsters are told exactly how to show affection towards her ('Let's say a big "hello" to mother! Let's give mother a big hug!'). Such instruction may be necessary to coordinate the actions of participants, yet these directives also impress that an acquaintanceship is being shaped, as the category of children is being introduced to that of mother. It is as if here the abstract category of mother is being made real for the child. The intimacy of the mother-child bond is made over here as the creation of the teacher.

The first gift follows: a flower given to the child by the teacher that he in turn presents to his mother. This gift is standardized for all the mothers. Like gifts generally, its symbolic value establishes a relationship. Of equal value, this gift forges the same kind of relationship between each child and each mother. Through this impersonal gift the category of mother is articulated to that of the child. This gift accords motherhood to each woman, through the proof of her status – her child who is the giver of the gift. In contrast to the developmental cycle of the family, here it is the alliance of teacher and child that forms and activates the category of motherhood. But the source of the gift is the governmental figure of the teacher, and so the linkage of the category of mother to that of the child is shaped at her behest.

Subsequent actions support this line of interpretation. The seamless circle of seated mothers is fragmented after the first gift. The mothers form pairs: each couple holds jointly their gifts of flowers and is connected through these. Through the medium of the gift each mother is transposed: from being a member within the category of mother to becoming individuated, a person and a mother in her own right. As such she stands for the motherhood and nurturance of a family unit. Moreover, as mothers jointly clasp their gifts, connections are delineated between families as discrete entities. Yet these families still are denied children of their own. The youngsters are kept in their categorical formation that encircles these mothers. From this collectivist perspective, personhood develops within categorical boundaries: first and foremost people are members of social categories, and only then are they accorded the status of persons with their own unique attributes.

The participants resume their original formation. The children stand as a category, face the mothers, and sing their blessings, followed by, 'My dear mother loves only me, yes, only me, yes, only me.' Through this act each child is told to recognize the especially intimate and affective bond between himself and his own mother. This is actualized through the personalized gift each child prepared especially for his mother. This second gift creates the unique relationship between a particular youngster and his mother. Just as mother was accorded personhood in her own right, so now is her child. The category of child is fragmented; mother and child are united; the family unit is delineated.

This intimate bond is presented further as the concentric formation breaks up, and each mother and child form pairs, dancing and singing together. Each pair like each family is a separate and distinct entity. Still, its unity depends upon the teacher who tells each pair exactly how to move in unison. The special bond, crucial to the existence and reproduction of the family, is under her control. This is underlined further as teacher and children teach the mothers a song with which to welcome the Sabbath. Welcoming the Sabbath within the home is exclusively the domain of the wife and mother. Her expertise, should she do this rite, likely is garnered from sacred texts and from having watched her own mother. No external intervention is required. Here she is made ignorant of basic liturgy integral to the traditional home. Instead a representative of the collectivity in alliance with its wards, the children, imparts this knowledge to mother and home.

There follows an addendum to the party, decided on by some of the mothers, and complementing the preceding sequence. One mother on behalf of the others thanks the teacher, calls her 'the real mother of the children while they are in the kindergarten,' and through a youngster presents her with a gift of flowers. Motherhood, the special bond between mother and child, is returned through a child to its source in the enactment, the teacher. She is described as a mother and her kindergarten becomes akin to the home, a locus of socialization that prepares the child for adulthood.[8] But on this occasion it is through the kindergarten that the home is shown to come into existence. And through this final gift this right is returned to the kindergarten embodied in the figure of the teacher. The teacher is a representation of collectivity, and it is to this representation that authority is arrogated to mold these youngsters.

In other words, motherhood is delegated to the collectivity by a representative of the mothers attending the party. In Hebrew, the words 'state' (*medinah*) and 'motherland' (*moledet*, literally, land of birth) take the feminine form. Phrases like, 'I gave my child to the state' or 'I sacrifice my child for the good of the motherland' are common in describing the relationship of family and national collectivity. In these terms the delegation of motherhood to a representative of the collectivity gains significance.

From the perspective of family and home the implicit patterning of the whole event upends and recasts the normal progression of the domestic cycle: through the celebration the collectivity creates the family. The usual view that the little child experiences first is that in the beginning there is the family; that into this nexus the child is born and within it matures; and that with time he leaves and establishes his own home. But on this occasion the progression practiced is as follows: first the collectivity exists and is composed (in keeping with bureaucratic logic) of discrete social categories. Links are forged between categories, and from these there emerge discrete social units, or families. These are accorded the right to bear and to raise children; and from this there emerges the special bond between mother and child. In this process the rights of and obligations to the collectivity are shown to be paramount.

Jerusalem Day: Statehood and the National

Jerusalem Day was promulgated as a civil, state holiday to commemorate the unification under Israeli rule of the capital of Israel following the 1967 War. It is celebrated primarily through official functions, which include a festive march around the perimeters of the city. The major thoroughfares are decorated with the national flag and with the banner of Jerusalem, a golden lion (the emblem of the ancient kingdom of Judah) rampant on a white background with blue borders. Jerusalem was divided between 1948 and 1967 into western and eastern sectors, the former within Israel and the latter controlled by Jordan. Within the eastern sector is Mount Moriah, the Temple Mount, in Jewish cosmology the traditional site of the first temple built by Solomon, and of the second, destroyed by the Romans in 70 C.E. This defeat is customarily reckoned as the onset of the Diaspora, the widespread dispersion of the Jews into exile from ancient Israel. The only parts of this temple complex to survive are remnants of its outermost ramparts.[9]

A stretch of the western rampart is called the Wailing Wall, known in Israel as the Western Wall. Long a site of popular worship, since 1967 the Wall has been made into the most dominant symbol of the Jewish state and its official religion. The Wall is made to evoke a nation whose florescence into a state awaited the return of its people, absent for 2,000 years. As does no other physical presence in present-day Israel, the Wall is perceived to condense the glory and then the desuetude of the past and the national redemption of the present. We raise these points because much of the symbolism of this kindergarten celebration focuses on this motif, discussed further in Chapter Seven on the opening events of Remembrance Day and Independence Day.

Description   Three classes of 3-, 4-, and 5-year-olds, totalling sixty youngsters from the same kindergarten, participated. The celebration took place in the courtyard of the kindergarten on the morning of Jerusalem Day. Parents were not invited. The courtyard was decorated with national flags and cut-outs of the lion of Jerusalem. As requested, most children were dressed in blue and white. Each child was given a small lapel pin depicting the lion. Each class was seated along one side of the courtyard, with the teacher in the center and an accordionist nearby.

The occasion opened with songs referring to the ancient kingdom of Israel, rejoicing in Jerusalem, and the rebuilding of the temple. In a brief peroration the teacher declared that Jerusalem was and always would be the capital of Israel; that this day marked the liberation of East Jerusalem and the reunification of the city by the Israel Defence Forces; and that this day was celebrated by everyone throughout the country.

Four 5-year-olds recited a poem about two doves who dreamt that the people of Israel would arise. The doves flew to Jerusalem and alighted on the Wall. The closing lines stated: 'The children of Israel are singing a song; next year the city will be rebuilt.' The assembly sang of the ancient longing of the Jewish people to return to Jerusalem. As this melody continued, six of the 4-year-olds danced, each holding blue and white ribbons. During the dance each child gave the ends of his ribbons to two others. As their performance ended the children were joined by the ribbons in the form of a six-pointed Shield of David (the *magen david*, commonly translated as the Star of David), the central motif of the national flag.

The teacher told a story of a lonely wall, dark with age, laden with the memories of the great temple, and of the free nation that dwelled here. Enemies burned the temple and drove out the Jews. They tried to destroy the wall, but their implements broke. The gentiles used the wall as a rubbish heap in order to obviate its presence. For centuries in their hatred of the Jews they dumped their garbage about the wall until it disappeared. One day a Diaspora Jew came to see the wall, but all denied its existence. He came to a great mound of rubbish and there learned of the custom of obliterating the Jewish wall. He swore to save it. A rumor spread that precious metals were buried there. The populace swarmed to sift through the garbage, found some coins of value, and uncovered the top stones. Happy, the Jew kissed the wall. The next morning another rumor spread that treasure was buried at its base. People excavated the rubbish and gradually the whole of the wall was revealed. No treasure was found except for that of the Jew – the Wall itself. The Wall still was filthy; but clouds gathered and rain poured, cleansing the Wall.

Dancing, and carrying toy blocks, the 3-year-olds built a wall of roughly their own height. The other youngsters formed a circle, held hands, and revolved singing and dancing around this edifice.

Discussion   Unlike the previous two celebrations, no reference is made in this one to the family. The relationship between the State and its Jewish members is direct, immediate, and hierarchical. The nation redeems the state; the state protects the nation. Both depend on the faith and loyalty of the citizenry, but citizenship is entirely national. The courtyard is decorated in emblems of statehood, and the blue and white dress of the youngsters shapes them into living emblems of the state, embodied with belonging to the Jewish collectivity. Each child is presented as a small part that embodies the greater whole, itself composed of many such parts. As noted previously the ideal relationship between the collectivity and its members is one of synecdoche.

The event is divided into a preamble of songs and speech, followed by the formal enactments. The preamble enunciates themes and sentiments then developed through the enactments. The opening songs connect past, present, future. The words of each refer to verities held as eternal. The first song is about King David, who made Jerusalem the capital of ancient Israel. The second rejoices in Jerusalem eternal. The third tells that the temple, a metaphor of the nation in its reborn homeland, will be rebuilt. The words of the teacher situate these sentiments within constructions of reality in the present-day. The assembly celebrates the reunification of the eternal capital of the Jewish State, the deed accomplished by Jewish soldiers in the people's army, in which these youngsters will serve on completing high school. Jewish collectivity, Jewish nationality, and citizenship made national are virtually isomorphic through the nation-in-arms, through the heroic, through war (see Furman 1999: 157–62).[10] This is how unification – of a city, of a people, of past, present, future – is done.

The enactments begin with a poem of prophecy. The doves dream that the renewed people of Israel will rebuild the city around the central focus of the eternal Wall. The dove is an emblem of peace, harking back to the biblical story of Noah's Ark and the dove returning with an olive branch, signifying an end to God's wrath. The following song expresses the longing of the people to return and carry out this endeavor – prophecy joined to feelings of deepest desire.

Prophecy and desire are realized as six youngsters form the living Shield of David, a multivocalic symbol used by the Zionist movement to signify rejuvenation and attachment to the national (see Scholem 1971). Thus children who sat in a loose assemblage shape the precise, coordinated pattern of the emblem. As in other embodied symbolic formations, just as the participants bring the emblem into being through their collective efforts, so its shape ties them to one another and incorporates them within a greater, encompassing design. Aesthetic and emotion blend part and whole, the blue and white clothing and the connecting ribbons. The implication is that the national citizens of the future will continue together to carry out the design of this emblem, connoting the actualization of the national collectivity.

The primary message of the allegorical narrative of rediscovering the Wall is that if the Jews do not defend their patrimony they will lose it. The world of Israel, of the Wall, must be demarcated clearly from that of non-Jews who threaten its integrity and viability. This is the bureaucratic, national logic of the precisely demarcated state and its Jewish nationality. In terms of religious membership in the nation, either one is a Jew or one is not. In terms of statehood, either one is a citizen or one is not. The outer boundary of permissible membership is set by the national, the desires of the member are subordinate.

The tale posits a series of contrasts between Jew and gentile that derive from a simple postulate: that the Wall, and by analogy the Jewish State, is indestructible and enduring despite all the depredations of enemies throughout the centuries. This is its internal and eternal truth. By comparison all else is transitory. The Jew who returns to his source across the gap of generations is motivated by value, by ideology. His is the wisdom of the spiritual. The gentiles who try to destroy his national roots are driven by materialism. He uses their cupidity to reveal the glory of the Wall. In the context of the celebration the qualities of Wall and Jew are those of the walled, shielded State protected by the nation-in-arms. The attributes of the gentiles are associated with all those who would deny to the Jews their homeland. The tale is at once a metaphor of renewal and a parable on boundaries of national salvation that in the modern world the state views itself as best able to uphold.

The closing presentation actualizes the message of the story through the cooperative practice of the children, just as the embodied, living Shield realized the prophecy of the poetic doves. The youngsters build the Wall from the ground up, just as modern Israel was redeemed through the joint efforts of its Jewish pioneers. The embodied labors of the children signify that which will be expected of them when they attain adulthood and full membership. The children dance in an unbroken circle around the completed Wall, evoking egalitarianism, synchronization, and perhaps the outer boundary of statehood, of inclusion and exclusion. Once more the center of the circle is filled, here by the Wall – an emblem that is hierarchical and authoritative and that above all has been made into a symbol of the Jewish State.

Celebrating the National

In the world of the little child the kindergarten celebration is among the very few occasions when the order of things in wider social worlds directly intersects with and dominates that of the home. This is evident through explicit symbolism. Yet more profound in their impact are the architectonics of enactment. Their significance derives from the very ways in which people in unison are mobilized and synchronized in social formations in order to practice the more explicit scenarios of celebration. The lineal progressions of such formations constitute their own sets of messages, and it is these that we have addressed in this chapter.

These celebrations and numerous others like them make intensive use of embodied, living formations. Some of these take the shape of explicit symbols, like the hanukkiah and the Shield of David. Others, like the unbroken circle and the dyad, remain more implicit. In either instance these are powerful media. Through them the meaning of things is turned into the shape of things. The shape of things is graspable by the senses, as is the case of icon and emblem. Yet in these latter instances the shapes still are external to the human body, to the source of feeling. But in living formations one grasps the shape of things by feeling them from within, by becoming an integral part of their 'body,' and so living through them. The body of being and the body of imagining become one. This is a more sensual experience, one that engages the senses much more fully to create a holistic experiential environment that joins self and symbol. Architects write of haptic space, of coming to know the shape of space and the feeling this engenders through the sense of touch. Through embodied, living formations the visual, the auditory, the tactile, and the olfactory are all 'touched' by the shape of things – indeed, they become this. The significance of form and the form of significance become inextricable – and the nexus of formed significance stresses inclusiveness, exclusiveness, hierarchy.

The sequencing of formations, in keeping with premises of lineality, is at the experiential core of the enactments discussed. These enactments are intended to arouse the heart of the little child, and so to impress upon his being lessons that otherwise may remain more exterior to his sense of self. In particular we have stressed themes that will be adumbrated in numerous ways in the years to come: for example, the relationship between hierarchy and egality. The interior hierarchy of the family is supplanted by and is subsumed within the national collectivity. The national is superior to each of its members, yet they compose it, and it exists only through their coordinated practices. In relation to one another, members of the national collectivity largely are equals. So too, as children grow they will succeed and replace parents, both as heads of family and as Jewish citizens. These processes depend on the proper outcome of maturation: apart from the efforts of parents, bureaucratic institutions are continuously at work, shaping social boundaries of categories and of the entities that these capture and contain, demarcate and define. In kindergarten celebrations the boundaries between people, between family and collectivity, and between the Jewish State and whoever lies outside it are taken apart, constructed anew, and in essence shown to exist as integral to selfness by becoming embodied in participants.

These messages are central to the production and reproduction of Israeli Jewish social order. In kindergarten celebrations these messages are embodied in ways that make them easy to grasp for the little child. Youngsters are full of feeling, but they have yet to develop the critical attitudes that buffer personal choice against the penetration of classification, the demands of group pressure, and the inducements of collective sentiments. Enculturation through celebration, as instruction books for kindergartens accentuate, is first and foremost an appeal to the emotions of little children. Moods and feelings about collectivity, centricity, control, and cooperation are embodied early on by Israeli Jewish youngsters.

Israeli Jewish pedagogy continues to evince ongoing concern that the child be located within frameworks, within institutional setups and settings that guide and shape his development. Even the teenager left to his own devices and strategies to discover and experience life without the organized guidance of ideology and norm is thought likely to grow crookedly, in a wilder way, away from becoming part of the controlled memory of historical continuity, growing apart from the needs that mobilize the nation-in-arms, to mourn as the family-in-arms. Therefore the child must be captured, contained, and classified through bureaucratic logic, and so brought into the proper governmental frameworks that primarily are pedagogical. The bureaucratic logic of the forming of form shapes these little celebrations as instruments that embody inclusion, exclusion, hierarchy – valuing the Jewish State and citizenship made national. Though there are scholarly arguments that changes in the contents of school ceremonies are an index of deeper changes in value, in ideology, so long as there are no transformations in the bureaucratic logic of forming form – of capture and containment – we doubt that this is the case.

–5–

Celebrations of Bureaucratic Logic: Birthday Parties in Israeli Kindergartens

[This chapter was coauthored by the late Lea Shamgar-Handelman.]

> Time, if we can intuitively grasp such an identity, is a delusion: the difference and inseparability of one moment belonging to its apparent past from another belonging to its apparent present is sufficient to disintegrate it.
>
> Jorge Luis Borges (1970: 252)

The enculturation of little children into bureaucratic systems is crucial to the practices of governmentality. Bureaucratic organization depends from bureaucratic logic, and making Jews national in their citizenship depends upon the individual becoming self-permeated with the categorical imperatives of this logic. One should expect little children to be induced into the rudiments of this logic. In Israel one medium of such enculturation among secular Jewish children is the kindergarten birthday party. This event keys the child to exact numerical age, and to the place of age in a monothetic taxonomy of time through which every person within the state is made accessible to bureaucratic classification. Through the birthday party the small child is individuated, reclassified, and synthesized anew as a temporal being. This monothetic reclassification is immediately related to consonant changes in the obligations and rights of the birthday child. Celebrating exact age is a prime example of practicing categorical imperatives into the daily lives of little children. In the conclusion to this chapter we discuss further just how relevant age is to the practice of bureaucratic logic.

Like the holiday celebrations of the previous chapter, there are neither set formats nor fixed sequences for the practice of the birthday party. Nonetheless there are architectonic and performative elements that are widespread. The architectonics include a special chair for the birthday child, a garland of freshly cut flowers, candles, an album of drawings made by the children of the class as well as other gifts, and a cake baked by the birthday child's mother. Customary activities include garlanding the birthday child, birthday songs, lighting the candles, biographical narratives about the birthday child, blessings for the birthday child, lifting the child in the special chair, gift giving, and eating.[1]

Garlanding tends to appear near the beginning of parties, and lifting the child and gift-giving towards their close. These activities do frame some sense of sequencing, but one much less definite than has otherwise been noted. Our interest is more in the adumbration of practices of individuation, reclassification, and the fragmentation of temporal experience that index the smoothing of the little child's interface with the social world as he is moved from one category to the next, and his capture and containment within the latter. These practices cluster in the birthday party, but are not tied to any particular sequence of activities. Therefore our discussion is organized in relation to these practices, rather than to any overall sequence of party activities.

Nonetheless, you should have some sense of how a birthday party is enacted, in order to appreciate that the practice of birthday celebrations is saturated with premises of the forming of monothetic taxonomy. Therefore we begin with an abbreviation of one party. This description is segmented, using roman numerals to indicate different customary activities. Further on we discuss these activities in terms of the practices referred to above, with additional examples from other birthday celebrations.[2]

A Kindergarten Birthday Celebration

The class consisted of thirty youngsters, aged between 4 and 5. The party was in honor of Amir (his name means the crown of a tree), who was turning 5. From his arrival on that warm spring morning, dressed with care, his hair neatly brushed, he was singled out for special attention by the staff and given the first choice of playthings.

I. *Architectonics*   When Amir's mother and grandmother arrived in midmorning they were escorted inside by the teacher and her two aides. Along the back wall of the room were the children's small tables, each with a vase of fresh flowers on its white, plastic tablecloth. The children sat in their small chairs, parallel to three walls of the room. Next to the fourth wall stood an ornate, bright red chair. Its back was decorated with green sprigs and golden ribbons. The chair, used for all birthdays in this kindergarten, stood on a low podium of large, toy building blocks covered with a small carpet. Amir took his place on the red chair, raised above the other children. To his left sat the teacher, in an adult-sized chair; and to his right his mother and grandmother, in children's chairs.

In the middle of the room stood a round table covered with a white, embroidered tablecloth. On it were a vase of fresh flowers, a plate with six unlit candles (five for the birthday boy's past years, and one for his year to come), a garland of fresh flowers, an album of children's drawings, a coloring book, and a small box of marker pens. On the album cover the teacher had drawn a child holding five balloons. Each balloon contained an inscription, forming the following text: 'Amir is five years old! Congratulations!'; 'An abundance of blessings!'; 'Until one hundred and twenty!'; 'Best wishes from the kindergarten children!'; and 'Heartfelt blessings'! – signed by the teacher and her aides.

II. *Opening Songs*   The teacher opened the party by leading the children in two songs. The first was of a kind used at the outset of group activities to focus children's attention and to coordinate their movements under the teacher's control. The youngsters had to coordinate words with movement – 'With the hands, hakh, hakh, hakh [i.e. clap your hands]; with the legs, trakh, trakh, trakh [i.e. stamp your feet]; with the tongue, tak, tak, tak [i.e. click your tongue]', and so forth.[3] The words of the second song were as follows: 'Birthday, lovely party, how pleasant and how lovely that every boy and every girl weren't born in a single day, but only Amir by himself [was born on this day].'

III. *The Garland*   The teacher asked the children: 'Why is Amir sitting on a decorated chair, all dressed up so beautifully? What's he missing?' Children called out, excitedly: 'The garland, the garland!' The teacher asked Amir whom he wanted to garland him. The four boys he called out paraded the garland around the room, while the others sang: 'Today is Amiri's [his nickname] birthday. He has a happy birthday and a garland of flowers.' The boys placed the garland on Amir's head.

IV. *Biography*   The teacher asked the children: 'What do you think, was Amir born so big? Amir's mother, perhaps you'll tell us how he was born?'

Mother: 'He was born in the north, in Rambam Hospital. We traveled through the night, and he was born there in the morning. He had very big eyes, and he looked at me. Father was very happy, and ran to tell grandfather and grandmother and all the uncles. And he said he'll be called Amir.'
Teacher: 'And how did you accept this, grandmother?'
Grandmother: 'With great happiness.'
Teacher, to mother: 'Tell us how he grew up.'
Mother: 'He ate and slept.'
Teacher: What did he eat? Fish? Chicken?'
Mother: 'No, he drank milk.'
A kindergarten girl interjects: 'Also porridge and tea and water.'
Mother: 'And when he grew up a little bit, he began to eat more solid food. And when he grew up a little more, he started to crawl.'
Teacher [to Amir]: 'Maybe you'll show us how a baby crawls. [She gave mother a musical triangle] When mother strikes the triangle, you'll crawl. And when I beat the drum you'll walk like a big boy.'

This sequence of activity was repeated twice more.[4] The teacher told ten children to make five arches, facing each other in couples and raising their arms towards one another. Amir proudly marched through the row of arches, as the children sang: 'What's happened? What's occurred? Our Amir is five years old.'

Teacher: 'Amir, invite your mother and we'll teach her to dance.' The teacher put the children into pairs, and they, Amir and his mother, danced and sang under the direction of the teacher.

V. *Blessings*   The teacher sang: 'Amir has his birthday . . . Let's bless him on his birthday.' The teacher called forward, one by one, those who wanted to bless Amir. The following is a representative listing of the children's 'blessings.'

Boy: 'Don't touch the electricity.'
Teacher: 'It's very important to be careful.'
Girl: 'May he help mother and father.'
Teacher: 'What a wonderful blessing. Its so important to help mother and father.'
Girl: 'May he travel by plane.'
Girl: 'May he be healthy.'
Teacher: 'This is a wonderful blessing.'
Girl: 'May he be a diligent student in school.'
Boy: 'Both at home and kindergarten, may he be diligent.'
Teacher: 'Lovely! Mother, how are you blessing him?'
Mother: 'May he be a good boy.'

VI. *Candle-lighting*   All sang: 'What is, what is the party? In our kindergarten again there is a birthday. This is the most important festival. Candles are lit on the cake. And around them, games. And it's written in chocolate, "Congratulations and all the best!"'

Teacher: 'How many candles are you going to light, Amiri?'
Amir: 'Six.'
The teacher turned to Amir: 'Invite grandmother to light the first candle.'
Grandmother did so, and kissed Amir.
Teacher: 'Amir, don't forget to give grandmother a kiss.'
Amir: 'Now, mother.'
Mother lit the second candle and kissed him.
Amir lit the remaining candles.

VII. *Games*   The teacher turned to mother: 'Now let's see if you know your child.' She covered mother's eyes with a kerchief, and placed a girl before her. Mother touched her and said: 'This is a girl. This isn't Amiri.' She touched another child: 'This is a boy, but he's not Amir.' Then Amir was brought before her, and she called out as she touched his face: 'I think its Amir. Sure, its Amir.' The games continued with charades, as Amir and the other children acted out imaginary gifts and guessed their identity.

VIII. *Lifting the child*   The teacher placed Amir and the birthday chair in the center of the room. Together, teacher, mother, and a number of children lifted Amir in the chair five times, and then one more for next year, calling out the number and lifting Amir higher each time.

IX. *Gifts*   The teacher announced the first of the gifts, the album of drawings done by children of the class, their present to the birthday child, with empty pages at the end for Amir to add his own drawings. The teacher chose the children to present him with the album. Amir burst into tears. His mother tried to calm him and discovered (she said) that he wanted to choose the children himself, which he did. As children sang, 'Here everybody, everybody comes, a large group marching to the birthday party,' Amir received the album, together with coloring book and marker pens, the gift of the kindergarten. In turn, Amir's mother (on his behalf) presented the gift of a large toy to the kindergarten. The teacher then asked Amir to blow out the candles, which he did after strenuous effort.

X. *Snacks*   The aides rearranged the tables. At each child's place they set a slice of the birthday cake (baked by Amir's mother), half an orange, a candy, and a small bag containing sweets and a small toy, the customary gift of the birthday child to each of the other children. The birthday chair was put at Amir's usual seat, while places were set for the adults at the round table. Amir sat in the birthday chair and cried, mumbling that he wanted to sit next to his mother. The teacher moved the birthday chair to the round table. When the children finished eating, they went outside to play, while mother and grandmother said goodbye to Amir and left.

The event has a festive atmosphere whose logic of forming form is that it is a good thing to grow older and grow up. This logic of shaping is not open to negotiation by any of the participants. Growing older is done by individuating the child and reclassifying him according to exact age, yet without neglecting his own continuity through time.

Individuation

The birthday child is singled out from the outset as a unique person. His individuation is prominent in the architectonics of the room, in songs, in his garlanding, and in gift exchange. The chairs (I) are placed in the format of an assembly (*atzeret*), within which the birthday child is the focus of everyone's gaze. In his throne-like chair, on the podium, he is separated from and elevated above the other youngsters. The birthday child is classified and treated as more of an autonomous being, a unique constellation of individual attributes that also constitute a moral being in Western perceptions.[5] As such, he is categorized in terms of numerical age. Here exact (and exacting) age is the only category that separates him from the other children in a taxonomy of time. On this day he is constituted wholly by his age, entirely made of time, a temporal being. The exact age that is his only is present everywhere, in the number of rising balloons and in the inscription on the album cover, in the number of candles, in the act of lifting the child, and in the words of many of the songs.

The process of individuation is also that of fragmentation, readying Amir to be shaped, smoothed, recast as a new member of the category of age 5. This is evident in the words of the second song (II), opening the party with individuation – 'how lovely that every boy and every girl weren't born in a single day, but only Amir by himself.' In terms of categorical time, of birth date, Amir is forced to stand by himself. This is emphasized in his garlanding (III), in which the practice of individuation also intimates reclassification. The garland motif entered the secular kindergarten during the pre-state period, likely in the celebration of *Shavu'ot*, a first fruits festival. Then children's heads were wreathed with flowers. Just as this spring festival signifies a new round of fresh growth, so the flowering youngsters were presented as the first fruits of Zionist practices in the homeland. Comparably, the garland decorates the birthday child as the first fruit of his last round of maturation, the period of one year he has passed through.

In other kindergartens the garland is marked even more acutely in relation to birth date and reclassification by age. The following description is from a party for a girl turning 5. Five children entered the room, each holding a hoop, its rim decorated with flowers. They danced to the song, 'Today is a birthday . . . today is Orit's birthday.' They placed the hoops over their heads, then down around their shoulders. As they sang, 'And she has a garland of flowers,' a sixth child garlanded the birthday child. Hoops decorated like garlands are used here as openings through which children pass head first. Since this passage is on a birthday, it likely is related to age. These hoops reflect the round birthday garland, and, so, the individuation of the birthday child, her reclassification by age, her movement through the threshold of an age category. In instances like this, short sequences are shaped to evoke development and progression, recapitulating and resonating with the experiential thrust of the entire celebration.

The pattern of gift exchange in Amir's party is common to birthday celebrations in numerous kindergartens. Gift exchange (IX, X) joins individuation to classification, indexing the relationship between the individual and membership in a social category. Just as the birthday child is singled out temporarily from the category of kindergarten children, the other children remain generic members of this category. An aggregate, they are treated during the party as interchangeable with one another. The individual and the aggregate engage in gift-giving here.

The gifts are of two kinds, unique and generic. Amir is given a coloring book, marker pens, and the album of drawings. The book and markers are a generic gift from the kindergarten. The album contains drawings, each the gift of an individual child. Here each gift is the same (a drawing), but also unique (the particular composition of a named individual). The drawings are bound together in the album as an aggregate of individual compositions. Each is like and unlike every other, as are the children of the category when one perceives them as distinct individuals who are classified together. This gift demonstrates both the viability of the generic category of children and of variation within it. Indeed the gift of the album constitutes the generic category, through the aggregation of unique individuals. So, too, the birthday child is expected to draw on the empty pages of the album, thereby inscribing himself within the aggregate of the category. In turn Amir gives one gift to the entire kindergarten. Later on each child receives from him a bag of gifts (X). The contents of each are the same apart from the little toys that vary from bag to bag. The little toy grants to each child a measure of uniqueness, yet this individuation is standardized since the match between child and toy is by chance.

The birthday child gives one gift (the large toy) to the kindergarten as an institution, and the same gift, the bag, to each child. Similarly, he receives one gift from the kindergarten (the coloring book and markers), and the same gift (a drawing) from each child. However the drawings differ from one another as do the bags. Though children are shown to vary within the category of childhood, the same forming through classification is shown to embed itself in each child. Gift exchange constitutes the birthday child as both unique and generic in relation to other members of the category of young children within the kindergarten. Here the forming of form – the shaping of the children – combines the generic and the unique within the individual, smoothing his reclassification.

Reclassification by Age

In many kindergartens, as in Amir's, monothetic reclassification is used immediately to relate individuation to obligations and rights that accompany the taxonomic lurch in numerical age. Choices of importance are set before Amir. He must publicly declare his relationships with his peers by choosing whom he wants to garland him. Yet that he is given the right to make this choice on this day is a clear reflection of his individuation. In these parties the impact of monothetic reclassification by age is most weighty in what are called blessings (*brakha* pl. *brakhot*) (V). In ordinary language usage a blessing refers to a benediction, to a request or hope for well-being. But in the birthday party the blessing often becomes a statement of social expectation laid upon the new member of the age category. Some of the blessings directed at Amir are akin to benedictions (e.g. May he be healthy). Others are virtual imperatives, loaded with warning (e.g. Don't touch the electricity; May he not irritate his mother) or with normative injunctions (e.g. May he help mother and father; Both at home and in kindergarten, may he be diligent).

The repetition by children of blessings heard at previous parties constitutes the normative adumbration directed at the social being of the child. The children themselves bluntly tell their peers of the connection between reclassification by exact numerical age and acquiring new obligations. These blessings like the party itself are highly reflexive, in that children take turns being the subjects and objects of participation. In parties of 2- and 3-year-olds a child hears over and again the injunction, 'May you not wet your pants.' And then on his third birthday suddenly it is his turn, because it is he, now, abruptly, who has reached the age of three.

The practice of individuation sometimes leads directly to that of reclassification. After Gil was garlanded on his fourth birthday in another kindergarten, messages of reclassification surfaced immediately. The teacher commented: 'Now, Gil, you're happy . . . but [she turned to the other children] I'm terribly mixed up today. Perhaps Gil is only a year old . . . or perhaps two years old . . . or perhaps three . . . let's hear how old Gil is.' Gil called out: 'I'm four years old and one day.' The teacher responded: 'Yes Gil? So you're already big and not small.' Gil's mother added: 'It's true. Yesterday was his exact birthday.' Gil then recited the verse he had rehearsed, closing with the phrasing: 'Today I'm four years old; I'm not little any more.' The teacher kissed him warmly, exclaiming: 'You really recited it as if you were six!'

The garlanding of Gil leads immediately to the recounting of his age as an additive sequence of years (1 . . . 2 . . . 3), culminating in his self-recognition of membership in his new age category, indeed of his exact age as a sequence that inexorably progresses, as he exclaims, 'I'm four years and one day.' This leads to other byplays on his continuity through time. Gil has become 'big' in contrast to being 'small' in his own past ages. He is no longer 'little,' because he is now 4. And in doing the recitation as if he were 6, he is orientated further toward his own future of additional age categories that continue the same monothetic taxonomy of numbers.

The practice of numerical age-classification abruptly introduces discontinuity, perhaps even fragmentation, into a birthday child's sense of being. The child is taught to perceive himself as a person of temporal parts – of blocks (indeed, building blocks) of time measured by the year. The transition from one exact age category to another requires disjunction and recombination. Yet the child also learns that age constitutes continuity of being. The transition between age categories leaves those blocks of time that indexed his previous ages embedded in the birthday child's personal history. Gil is not only 4 years of age – he is also 1 and 2 and 3 and . . . 4 years of age.

In these celebrations, adults stipulate the becoming of the child as constituted continuously through numerical age. Children like Amir and Gil are made to become individuals who taxonomize themselves, who count themselves into being through the exact addition of years. They learn to be referred by these building blocks of age. This is a segmentary, arithmetic continuity through time. Not only is the exact number of the child's age important but also the consecutive counting of age. These celebrations adumbrate age categories as numerical classifiers that index time. Through counting these age categories, increases in time that are unidirectional are practiced into existence; one only grows older, one only becomes bigger.

That age categories are treated as temporal classifiers is evident in the candle-lighting (VI) and chair-lifting (VIII) at Amir's party. The birthday child is identified with the number of candles, with his reclassification. The order of candle-lighting chosen by the teacher demonstrates the co-presence of three age categories within the same family, activated in order of descending age. Grandmother, the most historical, lights the first candle, mother the second, and Amir, the least historical, the third. The sixth candle points Amir toward the age category to come, the next block of time in the taxonomy. The individual constituted through numerical age can always be captured and contained, divided and fragmented, along the fracture lines of age categories. So, too, the chair-lifting recapitulates the child's life through the enumeration of age categories. Each lift is higher, the number of the year called out in louder voice. Each elevation practices the joyful growth of the child, year added to year, through the present, toward the future, in a taxonomy of being composed of building blocks of time.[6]

Temporal Continuity

The continuousness of time is the necessary complement to taxonomic fragmentation by age. The continuity of the time-self, as Piaget noted, and of self in relation to other, is crucial to self-recognition and to autobiography. This continuity is crucial too for practices of the governmental, in that the individual must hold him- or herself together in order to function as a viable member of social order. In the previous section we noted one kind of temporal continuity that occurs when categories of numerical age are recounted as a sequence of successive ages. This continuity is arithmetic and segmentary. Yet birthday celebrations also practice temporal continuity as the unbroken, flowing synthesis of time. This kind of continuity was encountered in Gil's celebration ('So you're already big and not small'). Here size is a metaphor for age. Such references to changes in size – then small, now big – are more ambiguous than the exacting lurch from one age category to the next. Small turns into big through the continuous weaving and blending of strands of experience. This synthesis of the child's life course is more holistic, its entirety suffused with the continuousness of experience.

This kind of temporal continuity is most pronounced through brief biographical narratives, usually told by parents about the birthday child. Commonly these begin in the past, bringing the child into the present. These narratives inform the child with a past growing and flowing into the present and beyond. Time becomes profoundly integrative because it becomes *the* context within which the entirety of the child takes shape. These narratives tell the child from an adult perspective how he has grown into his own present. The adult, unlike the child, can summarize the child's life-course from a past that is inchoate to a future yet unimaginable. This continuity, no matter how self-evident, is one grounding through which the child eventually becomes national in his citizenship, as one who meshes with his own continuousness of being, as a certain kind of person of value, of ideology.

At Amir's party (IV) his mother begins even before his birth, and then quickly iterates the mother-child bond ('He had very big eyes, and he looked at me').[7] The narrative moves on to growing up, to sleeping, eating, and 'when he grew up a little bit,' the shift to more solid food. Then, with additional growth, Amir acquired mobility – he began to crawl.

The teacher makes this simple story into a performance, one that recapitulates the developmental sequence narrated by the mother. At his mother's behest, Amir demonstrates how a baby crawls, and at his teacher's, how a 'big boy' walks. Then he is freed to march independently through the living arches of children, as they sing, 'What's happened. . . our Amir is five years old.' What has happened is the passing of an age threshold, leading to even more complex behavior on the part of the child. So this sequence ends with Amir and the teacher teaching mother how to dance. The performance of dance when compared to crawling and walking is the most complex of these motor activities. The entire sequence is fraught with implications for his development. The baby, of little competence and accomplishment, is tied here to mother and home; but greater accomplishments are articulated to teacher and kindergarten, as the present selfness of the child thrusts into the future, towards individualism and individuation in the bureaucratic state. In the first game (VII), later on, the teacher further dramatizes Amir's development. Blindfolded, his mother must recognize Amir by her touch. This puts the question of whether Amir is so changed that even his own mother will not recognize him. She does, and so the biography she has given him is indeed his past.

The temporal continuity practiced through biographical narrative is quite different from the temporality of a chronological taxonomy of age categories. Narrative alters the qualities of the child through time, weaving them into an unbroken but ever-changing sequence of development. Amir is described as looking, that becomes eating, and then turns into movement of different degrees of complexity (crawling, walking, dancing). These are accompanied by developments in social capabilities (first taught by his mother, then teaching her; first dependent on his parents, then the first among equals in his class on this day). In kindergarten biographical narratives the qualities mentioned do not depend on exact age, but rather on self-transformation. Selfness is made through time, yet it does not depend for its existence on any categorical blocks of time. Instead narratives emphasize the unity and continuity of the time-self in the creation of the individual as a unit of becoming and being.

By contrast the counting of numerical age (in candle-lighting, in chair-lifting) establishes a continuum composed of equal but absolutely distinct intervals. This produces a synthesis of time that is segmentary – categories of age are additive, divisible, and so forth. This continuum of the enumeration of age imposes an external taxonomic scheme on the child. This no less is biography that produces autobiography. But this kind of synthesis enables the fragmentation of the individual along borders of absolute fracture. In this version of the individual, he can be taken apart in terms of exact age by himself and by others, arithmetically, statistically. Here qualities of the child are understood to derive from categories of age, rather than from one's inner development. Age becomes crucial to comprehending capability. Qualities become an index of age – a child of a particular age is assumed to have the qualities that adults think correspond to that age.

Though these parties are joyous occasions for children and families alike, they are tense for the birthday child. Towards the close of his celebration, Amir bursts into tears

(IX, X). Crying by the birthday child is fairly frequent at these events. The usual explanations are those of over-excitement, over-tiredness, and so forth. Nonetheless one should not overlook the abrupt shift from one absolutist, irreversible age category to the next. Still, the child is wrapped by those surrounding him into a mood of consensus about the positive value of exchanging one age for the next. He is continuously congratulated on this, as if it were his own personal achievement. Yet the celebration shows the child that he is trapped by this consensus into the new obligations expected of him. In the life of a little child the demonstrative addition of a whole year's block of time may well feel weighty and intimidating. A tearful child commonly will declare, 'I don't want a birthday party any more,' and look for refuge in his mother, teacher, or an empty room. In these instances he is returned to perform as the star of the celebration, together with admonitions that, no longer a baby, he should behave in accordance with his new age.[8]

More than a few scholars of childhood socialization argue that it is 'a collective process that occurs in a social or public, rather than in a private, realm,' and that through this process children discover worlds of significance (Corsaro 1988: 2). In Israel, age likely is the very first attribute of the little person to be turned into a monothetic classifier. Later children will come to know other of their attributes (gender, education) as classifiers. In Israel the kindergarten birthday party is a realm of meanings of classification far more complex and polyphonic than common sense dictates. The experiencing of classification – to selfness, to otherness – is crucial to the development of child into adult, imbued with monothetic realities of the state and the governmental.

Age and Bureaucratic Logic

The early experiencing by the little child of the reclassification of exact age is a prime example of a recurring commonsensical event fraught with the celebration of monothetic taxonomizing. Age classification constitutes a taxonomy of time that keys and articulates the individual's temporal order to that of the governmental. This is the kind of early age enculturating we should expect to find in modern states. These experiences of a monothetic taxonomy of time are paradigmatic of the kind of enculturating that shapes bureaucratic logic within the child in social orders where this logic will be essential to his everyday existence. For the individual the logic and practice of bureaucratic classification constitutes ongoing experiences of the categorization of self. In Israel the practice of these experiences begins in the kindergarten and in birthday parties there. Bureaucratic logic is passionately committed to the conception and practice of exact classification. The power of the State, but no less of the governmental, depends to a high degree on their control over the means of classification. Time, as formed by bureaucratic logic, is monothetic: taxonomies of the exact division of temporality into equal intervals, amenable to numerical manipulation. The control of time in the modern state is a prime modality in controlling the behavior and life-course of the individual (see, for example, Verdery 1996). This discussion suggests that governmentality actively forms persons into beings whose senses of selfness resonate with their ongoing classification and re-classification, and who are hounded by the inexorable passage of exact time intervals.

So, what kind of person is most amenable to the classifications of bureaucratic logic? The premises of bureaucratic logic – resonating with those of the state-form – enable its use to fragment any social entity into its smallest, most singular units for purposes of social classification. The most minimal human unit is the individuated person – the individual. Bureaucratic classification frequently recasts individuals as members of aggregates or cohorts who have in common only the taxonomic criterion that brings them together. In this bureaucratic mode of production there are no enduring social relationships that necessarily need be taken into account. Not kin ties, not friendships, not social networks, not community – none of these social forms of connectivity has any principled, cultural mandate to reject the arbitrary (in the sense that consciously it could be otherwise) selections of bureaucratic classification (Handelman 1998a: 76–81). For that matter, the irrelevance of these relationships for premises of bureaucratic logic is thought a criterion of their universalistic objectivity.

In the modern state, bureaucratic logic is used regularly and easily to individuate persons and to aggregate them in categorical terms as individuals. Bureaucracies work most efficiently and cost-effectively with a cosmos of individuates, one in which its members, individuals, deliberately are sorted and resorted into different social categories. From the forming perspective of bureaucratic logic the individual is the sum of all the taxonomic indices applied to him. In this arithmetic, statistical forming of the person, the more the information available on each individual, the more adequate his categorization as a total unit is thought to be. The technological adequacies of information-processing systems are the only real limitations on the complexity of the shaping of the bureaucratized individual.

The effectiveness of numerical age as a taxonomizer is attested to by its widespread prominence in bureaucratic classification. As noted, this idea of exact age depends on a conception of time that is segmentary. The value and validity of exact, numerical age derives from this conception of time, one composed of exclusive and inclusive segments or categories. This conception of time enables bureaucratic logic to shape the temporality of the modern individual, smoothing the individual into the bureau-cratic order, harmonizing him with this, and opening him to the taxonomic manipula-tions of the governmental. We learn to be the kinds of people who resonate with bureaucratic logic, usually without reflecting critically on its premises. This chapter argues that this learning begins early, though there is little information on how this is done. One study of American kindergartens concludes that their experiences prepare children to work in bureaucracies (Gracey 1972: 279). Another argues that the American nursery school shapes a little world resembling large-scale formal organ-izations, thereby providing little children with bureaucratic-like experiences (Kanter 1972: 203). Still another emphasizes that American nursery schools shape structures that objectify time, mirroring the temporal constraints of 'planned time' in wider social orders (Suransky 1982:185).[9]

In Israel, the ubiquitous kindergarten birthday party practices experiences of taxonomic time and monothetic age that are exemplars of the individuation and classification of the individual. This conjunction of individuation and bureaucratic logic is central both to nationalism (the individual as national, the individual as citizen) and to governmentality (the multiple locations of multiple practices of organizing and directing aggregates and their individual members). Governmentality that depends from the bureaucratic likely depends on individuals comprehending themselves as certain kinds of temporal beings; yet no less, on the individual perceiving himself as a self-governing and self-managing entity (Foucault 1982; Rose 1996a, 1989; Lemke 2001). In this regard the Israeli Jewish child, temporally segmented, temporally synthesized, resonates well with this dual thrust of modern governmentality.

Part III considers how Israeli official public-events present themselves through bureaucratic logic and the national. The following chapters are the fruition of the kinds of enculturation discussed in Chapters Four and Five. The chapters of Part III take up major events of commemoration and celebration that open the three national days promulgated by the State after independence. These chapters address theoretical concerns of time, space, and the aesthetics of events of presentation, as well as the still dominant narrative of the Israeli national that emerges from the sequencing of these three Days. The Prologue to Part III shows how premises of the time and space of the national are embedded in the sites of these three opening events and in their relationship to one another. Chapter Six argues that the practice of bureaucratic logic continuously implicates aesthetics, and that this logic and these aesthetics are embedded in, and structure, the opening event of the Day that commemorates the dead of the Holocaust. These aesthetics are dominant in shaping the self-presentations of the State; and in this regard it becomes extremely difficult to comprehend the public events of the state (and their relationship to the national) without factoring in the aesthetics of bureaucratic logic. Chapter Seven compares the opening events of Remembrance Day for the fallen in Israel's wars and Independence Day, showing that when experienced as a sequence these Days encode the national as narrative. Furthermore, that this narrative is itself deeply embedded – structurally, historically – in Jewish culture, understood broadly. When Holocaust Remembrance Day is added to this sequence the full narrative comes forth without equivocation.

When during the 1980s, Elihu Katz and I began to tell of these three Days as the encoding of a Jewish national narrative, it was as if this had not occurred to many of our readers and listeners, though once the arguments were absorbed there was little rebuttal. Today this national narrative of the three Days is perceived as self-obvious. This in itself is a good, if rough-and-ready index of the degrees to which Israeli Jewish nationalism has burgeoned during these years of settling the occupied territories, of the increasing turn to traditional religion, itself becoming more and more nationalist, and of the two Intifadas.

I should note that the conceptual division of labor of the coming chapters could be reversed without difficulty: Chapter Six on the opening event of Holocaust Remembrance Day can be analyzed just as easily in terms of nationalism and narrative; while the openings of Remembrance Day and Independence Day of Chapter Seven can be analyzed in terms of bureaucratic logic and aesthetics. The present division of labor among the chapters reflects the issues that dominated thinking when each of these chapters was written.

Part III
The Fruition of the National and Bureaucratic Logic

Prologue

Daughter: Why did Herzl write *The Jewish State*?

Mother: Because he thought the Jews should have a state of their own.

Daughter: Why is it [Mount Herzl] next to the soldiers' cemetery?

Mother: Because many people were killed in order to get our state, and here [*she points to the cemetery*] is where the ceremony for Remembrance Day takes place.

Daughter: So why, Holocaust Day?

Mother: That is there [*she gestures towards Yad Vashem, over the rise*], and the remembrance of Holocaust Day takes place there.

Mount Herzl, Saturday, 21 March 1987

Like many states of the modern era, Israel designated a particular date to remember those who sacrificed their lives for the existence of the state, and another to commemorate its founding. Unlike most other states, Israel put in place a third date to commemorate the nation's deepest tragedy. The first is named Remembrance Day (*Yom Hazikaron*), the second, Independence Day (*Yom Ha'atzma'ut*), and the third, Holocaust Martyrs and Heroes Remembrance Day (*Yom HaShoah v'HaGvura*). Each is opened by a central state occasion, televised in its entirety. Each event is one in which the State intentionally selects aspects of its self-understood purposes and their foundations, aspirations, apprehensions. Taken in their annual sequence – Holocaust Remembrance Day, Remembrance Day for fallen soldiers, Independence Day – these versions become segments in a dramatic master narrative of the national that encodes time, and therefore history. In turn, this version of history infuses the over all story with deeper significance.

Instead of attempting to address the roles of both the national and bureaucratic logic in each of the events, a different strategy is used. In Chapter Six the opening event of the first of the three days, Holocaust Remembrance Day, is addressed through its relation to bureaucratic logic; and in Chapter Seven, the opening events of Remembrance Day and Independence Day are taken up in relation to the national, and to citizenship as national. This Prologue sets the scene, temporally, topologically, for discussions of these three Days.[1]

Holocaust Remembrance Day precedes Remembrance Day for the fallen by seven days. Remembrance Day is scheduled for the 24-hour period immediately preceding Independence Day. The official event that opens Independence Day includes as its initial segment the closing of Remembrance Day. Holocaust Remembrance Day begins in silence, opening with a solemn assembly (*atzeret*) at the national Holocaust memorial in Jerusalem, attended by numerous survivors and dignitaries. In contrast, Remembrance Day for the fallen begins with a shocking sound, penetrating and synchronizing the different worlds of everyone in the country. On the appointed minute, and for one minute's duration, sirens shriek in every village, town, and city in the land.[2] Human life stills: people stop in their tracks, vehicles stop in mid-intersection; all is silent, yet pervaded by the fullness of the same wail. These same sirens cry crisis. The difference is one of modulation: to cry crisis the wails rise and fall; to intone bereavement their note is uniform. The next morning the same practice is repeated, but for two minutes. On the morning of Holocaust Remembrance Day the sirens wail for one minute. In Israel this wail is the most dominant sound of the presence of absence.

The opening event of Remembrance Day for the fallen has the singular, monotonic qualities of the siren's keen and the stillness of the land. The next morning, the siren's wail signals the beginning of memorial services at military cemeteries and memorial sites throughout the country, in memory of the fallen of different corps, regiments, and other units of the armed forces, and of geographical localities, sometimes down to the neighborhood level. By contrast, Independence Day expands out of its opening event into a variegated and colorful multitude of activities, planned and informal. On the eve of Independence Day there are open-air stages where popular entertainers perform, dancing in the streets, games of chance (otherwise illegal) in city centers, and bonfires and singing. On the morrow there are special services in synagogues, the opening of selected military bases to the public, official receptions, and a host of family outings and picnics. Each opening event is a key to the tenor of activities that constitute the bulk of each Day. Together, these three opening events are a semiotic set: they make meaning together. This set is monothetic, the clarity of the separation of the Days reflecting the bureaucratic logic that forms them as distinct units of time.

Zionist Cosmologic: The Dating of Days, The Shaping of Space

That these three events make meaning together tells us that their scheduling and sequencing are neither natural nor inevitable, but likely are related to the formation of the national, since the sharing of the temporal ordering of existence is crucial to unifying people and to separating them from others. Temporal arrangements are crucial to narrative (Ricoeur 1984: 206–25), and synchronization among people through time is essential to social order (Sharron 1982). Moreover, the chronological coding of temporality as 'before' and 'after' is the production of history (Lévi-Strauss 1966: 257–60; Gell 1992). Time and temporal vision are essential to Zionist cosmology, as they are to those of Judaism (Yerushalmi 1982). So too is temporal rhythm and the pulsation implicit in this, as well as the rhetoric and sentiments of a unique people, beleaguered in the world (cf. Gertz 1984), echoed in the performance of the Versailles commemoration.

Israeli Jews accept the separation, contiguity and continuity of these Days as morally correct, even though the immediacy of transition from the mourning of Remembrance Day to the celebration of Independence Day is felt as especially heartrending. Perhaps this suddenness of transition is felt as moral because it is so difficult. The transition should be hard, for its abruptness encodes temporally the small differences in chronological time between the founding of the State and its War of Independence. This war was well under way before independence was declared, but intensified greatly afterwards. For Israeli Jews the two were identified indelibly and encoded as such.[3] Today, no less, the three Days are felt to be in a natural, fitting sequence.[4]

Nonetheless this sequence exists only because decisions were taken to make it so. Modern states choose their significant dates according to different semiotic and temporal codes, and they may experiment with different calendrical arrangements (Zerubavel 1985). Thus the French promulgated Bastille Day as their 'founding day' only in 1880, following the formation of the Third Republic; while French governments shifted the public focus given to prominent calendrical markers in accordance with prevailing political conditions. So in 1920 the government combined the fiftieth anniversary of the Third Republic together with the solemnities for the fallen of the Great War – and chose a date other than Bastille Day for this (Rearick 1977: 456). In the instance of Australia, its memorial day, Anzac Day (dated to the landing of the Anzacs in Turkey at Gallipoli in 1915), has developed as the major marker of Australian nationhood, rather than the national day, Australia Day. The different valences given to these two dates are intimately related to the formation of Australian national cosmology (Kapferer 1988).

The first Day in the Israeli sequence (though the last promulgated) was set into the period between the end of Passover and Independence Day. Choosing the date was influenced by the Hebrew calendar and other factors.[5] The eve of Holocaust Remembrance Day falls on the 26th of the Hebrew month of Nissan, five days after the last day of Passover. Holocaust Remembrance Day commemorates the murder of millions of Jews by the Nazis and their collaborators and the heroism of those Jews who rose in armed struggle. This Day is identified explicitly with the anniversary of the Warsaw Ghetto Uprising in 1943, which became the exemplar of Jewish armed resistance against impossible odds during World War II. On 19 April the Germans came to strip the Ghetto of its remaining Jews in order to ship them to the death camps, and armed resistance began in earnest. This corresponded to Passover eve in 1943. Judaism interdicts mourning during Passover. Therefore 19 April could not be used to commemorate the Uprising. In Israel the commemoration date was made to coincide with the extinction of the Uprising on 2 May, 27 Nissan in that year. The German command dated the end of armed resistance to 16 May (Krakowski 1984: 211). Accepting 16 May as the date of commemoration, one that enhanced the duration of Jewish armed struggle, would have scheduled Holocaust Remembrance Day almost a week after Independence Day according to the Hebrew calendar. Ending the sequence of the three national Days with Holocaust Remembrance Day would have upended the Zionist master narrative that the legislators were shaping into existence.

The eve of Holocaust Remembrance Day falls seven days before the eve of Remembrance Day, 3 Iyar. This period of seven days corresponds to the traditional period of Jewish mourning following death, the *shiva* (literally, 'seven').[6] On the one hand, Holocaust Remembrance Day, the catastrophe of Diaspora Jewry, is distanced from Remembrance Day and Independence Day, occasions of the arisal of the Jewish State. On the other, Holocaust Remembrance Day is scheduled before these occasions, as their forerunner.

The date chosen for Independence Day was 15 May.[7] In 1948 independence was declared on 14 May, which then became the eve of the holiday. The date in the Hebrew calendar became 5 Iyar, corresponding to 15 May in 1948. The Hebrew and Gregorian calendars are independent of one another, and so the date of Independence Day varies by a matter of weeks from year to year in the Gregorian calendar.[8] Embedding Independence Day in the Hebrew calendrical cycle was no small matter since the holiday then recurs annually only thirteen days after the end of Passover. Passover is the quintessential 'festival of freedom' in Judaism, celebrating the exodus of the Israelites from Egypt. Held on the eve of the holiday the festive family meal, the *seder*, 'is a symbolic enactment of an historical scenario whose three great acts structure the *Haggadah* that is read aloud: slavery – deliverance – ultimate redemption' (Yerushalmi 1982: 4; Fredman 1981).[9] The metaphysics of the Seder text, the *Haggadah*, demand the annual 'fusion of past and present' (Yerushalmi 1982: 4), and the identification of each and every Jew with that ancient attainment of freedom. 'In each and every generation let each person regard himself as though he had emerged from Egypt', reads the *Haggadah*. Passover is a holiday beloved of Israeli Jews, secular and religious alike; and the great majority celebrates the occasion. Independence Day was referred to as the onset of a new period in the history of the nation, continuous with Passover, and compared to the exodus from Egypt (Don-Yehiye 1984: 10–11).[10]

The scheduling of Remembrance Day also required an arbitrary decision, since there was no traditional date to commemorate the fallen in war. The need to memorialize the war dead was felt early on, stressing that arisal and independence were bestowed by their blood. At the outset, memorial ceremonies were part of Independence Day celebrations (Levinsky 1957: 495ff.). By 1951 the Ministry of Defense began to experiment with a separate Remembrance Day, the day prior to Independence Day (Azaryahu 1999: 96; Ben-Amos and Bet-El 1999: 267). By 1954 the Minister of Defense commented that he viewed as 'organic' this attachment of Remembrance Day to Independence Day.[11] Unlike Independence Day, Remembrance Day was not opened by a central event until 1967.

The temporal meta-design of these three Days is as follows. The destruction of European Jewry was followed by the War of Independence, during which the State was founded and through which it kept its freedom as it has ever since through the mortal sacrifices of its people. Given the tragedy of the Holocaust, its Day is followed fittingly by a period of separation (or 'mourning') from the subsequent Days. However, the sacrifice memorialized on Remembrance Day led directly to the revival of the Jewish state and its redemption of the Jewish people. Therefore the celebration of Independence Day is the immediate and fitting continuation of the commemoration of Remembrance Day.

This sequence of semiosis also conveys the following. The degradation and despair of the Holocaust was the harvest of anti-semitism sown in the lands of the gentiles. The Diaspora was the dead end of Jewish existence. Even so, the Holocaust kindled sparks of resistance. The snuffing out of these heroic sparks (the Jewish partisans, the ghetto and camp uprisings) are mourned, but also are celebrated on Holocaust Remembrance Day. For in Palestine, among independent and proud Jews returned to their own land and once more battling against seemingly insurmountable odds, these sparks flamed into ramified armed struggle. The outcome was the Jewish State. In Zionist nationalist visions these developments became the only creative response to the Holocaust. The sequence of the three Days practices a theme of death and the regeneration of life on a cosmic scale (Bloch and Parry 1982).[12]

The scheduling of these three Days is a construct of the State, and their sequencing is accepted as natural by Israeli Jews. The sequence is the national meta-narrative of modern Jewish history, but one with cosmic, temporal harmonics embedded in Zionist ideology. These relationships were enunciated by Prime Minister Levi Eshkol, in his address on Holocaust Remembrance Day, 1964: 'The Martyrs and Heroes Memorial Day falls between the ancient Festival of Freedom [Passover] and the modern Day of Independence. The annals of our people are enfolded between these two events. With our exodus from the Egyptian bondage, we won our ancient freedom; now, with our ascent from the depths of the Holocaust, we live once again as an independent nation.'[13] The Passover narrative of slavery and freedom itself corresponds to the 'basic conflict formula' of the present-day celebration of many Jewish holidays (Y. Zerubavel 1995: 218). This facilitates the identification of the sequence of Days with the struggle against oppression embedded in other Jewish holidays.

Yet in one respect the scheduling of the three Days is more in keeping with the romantic reckonings of modern European nationalism. In the traditional ceremonial cycle of Judaism there is a limited correspondence between the order of occurrence of holidays and their location in a chronology of historical reckoning (Y. Zerubavel 1986). By contrast, these three Days of national reckoning are sequenced in the chronological order of temporal occurrence. The sequence of Days is one of modern history, harmonized with the rhythms of time in traditional cosmology. This synthesis of metaphysical rhythms of time, the traditional narratives these enable, and their encoding of modern chronological history makes the sequence of Days experientially commonsensical and valuable to Israeli Jews. These themes are addressed more substantially in the concluding section of Chapter Seven.

The temporal articulations among the three Days also are produced topologically. In 1949 the remains of Theodor Herzl, the visionary of modern Zionism and the founder of the World Zionist Organization, were brought from Vienna and reinterred in Jerusalem, on the summit of the mountain named in his memory. Mount Herzl affords a vista of three hundred and sixty degrees of Jerusalem and its environs. Herzl's black basalt tombstone bore only the simple inscription, HERZL, eternalized. Herzl's tomb stands alone at the apex, not unlike an axis mundi, separated by broad open spaces from the graves of others. Mount Herzl is a cemetery wherein nationalist history is encoded topologically, through the spatial locations of ancestors and their descendants.

The layout of these gravesites is as close as secular Zionism has come to inscribing itself topographically as a pantheon (see also Yarden 1998). Radiating outwards from Herzl's tomb, at different levels and in different quadrants of the down slope gradient are clusters of graves. At a distance from and lower than Herzl's tomb is that of another Zionist visionary, Vladimir Jabotinsky, the founder of the revisionist movement. At the same level, in another quadrant, is the cluster of graves of the presidents, the inheritors, of the World Zionist Organization, and their wives. The presence on the heights of these chief officials, indeed bureaucrats, of organized world Zionism is thoroughly in keeping with the bureaucratic logic of governmentality that pervades Israeli life. Thus on the highest reaches of the mountain are the graves of modern prophets of Zionism who created the movement to return all Jews to the land of Israel, and the graves of the upper tier of international bureaucrats of Zionism who helped to organize this vision. At their center lies Herzl.

Somewhat further down slope is a cluster of gravesites reserved for the 'Greats of the Nation' (*Gedolei Ha'uma*) and their spouses. These are the presidents, prime ministers, and speakers of the Knesset, the first citizens and political leaders of the Jewish state.[14] These graves are virtually continuous with those of the military cemetery, begun during the War of Independence, that slopes down the northeastern gradient towards dense urban neighborhoods (Benvenisti 1990). The upper slopes of the mountain are carpeted with lawns, shrubs, and flower beds, and resemble most a park dotted here and there by groves and graves. The military cemetery is more forested. The over all composition derives from nineteenth-century European romanticism (see Mosse 1979; and on the forest as a national symbol, Y. Zerubavel 1996).

In 1953 a lower spur of Mount Herzl, jutting from the western slope of the massif, turning its face from the city towards the sea in the direction of Europe (Friedlander and Seligman 1994), was named the Mount of Remembrance (*Har Hazikaron*). On this more distant ridge Yad Vashem, the national Holocaust memorial center, was built; and there the opening event of Holocaust Remembrance Day takes place. Unlike the topological continuity between the highest reaches of Mount Herzl, the 'Greats of the Nation,' and the military cemetery, one must leave this Mount to enter Yad Vashem by a circuitous route. Further discussion of the topology of the military cemetery and Yad Vashem is in Chapter Eight.

The articulation between Yad Vashem, the military cemetery, and the summit of Mount Herzl is one of 'historical space' (Straus 1966: 34), whose momentum is that of a teleology of the national. The temporal sequence is mapped onto, moves through, and infuses space with significance and feeling. Holocaust Remembrance Day is marked on a lower and more distant spur of the Zionist mountain, just as this Day is distanced temporally from those that commemorate and celebrate the Jewish State. On the morning of Remembrance Day a commemoration for the heroism and sacrifice of the soldiery is held in the military cemetery, on the lower reaches of the main massif itself. That evening, as it has since 1950, the venue climbs to the summit to open Independence Day, with Herzl's tomb as the axis of the celebration. The heights are scaled spatially in the temporal order of Days, from destruction, through the struggle for renewal, to the pinnacle of triumph, which also is the source of the vision and the annual enactment of its viability.[15] This integration of time and space is evident in Eshkol's speech, quoted above: 'The very struggle against the adversary [the Shoah] and the victory that followed [the War of Independence] laid the foundations for the revival of our national independence [the founding of the State]. Seen in this light, the Jewish fight against the Nazis and the War of Independence were, in fact, a single protracted battle. The geographical proximity between Yad Vashem and Mount Herzl thus expresses far more than mere physical closeness.'[16] These fruits of the Zionist vision, sculpted topologically, shaped temporally, are seeded in kindergarten, later to be harvested in sorrow and celebration – the bereaved family, the nation-in-arms, the State triumphant.

– 6 –

Opening Holocaust Remembrance Day: The Bureaucratic Logic and Aesthetics of National Mourning

But how can a wall protect if it is not a continuous structure? Not only cannot such a wall protect, but what there is of it is in perpetual danger.

Franz Kafka (1999: 67)

The analysis of the opening event of Holocaust Remembrance Day continues the argument of Chapter One that in the modern state much of what is called 'ritual' is shaped by the forming of form that I call bureaucratic logic. My discussion engages public events of presentation, and how these demonstratively exhibit aspects of Israeli social and moral order. More specifically, I maintain that logics of forming public events, and the aesthetics of these logics, are intimately related to practice. Practice works best when given its senses by aesthetics. Logics of forming form tell how practices of fitting together people, things, worlds, are done. Aesthetics *enable* this fitting together to be done through practice. Forming form and its aesthetics of practice are a set – if a logic of forming form is present, then so are its aesthetics of practice. Nonetheless there is no clean-cut conceptual distinction between logics of forming form and aesthetics. The two are meshed together in practice.

The aesthetic is crucial to all practice in mundane living. Moreover, the aesthetics of practice in public events may not be radically distinct from those of everyday practice. This is so in the opening event of Holocaust Remembrance Day, where forming form is done through bureaucratic logic and bureaucratic aesthetics. This event of presentation is a direct extension of the logic and aesthetics of mundane bureaucratic order. The practice of this event resonates with the hidden presence and practice of the Army, the violent arm of the mundane State. The military logic of forming form is continuous with the logic that shapes the practice of the Holocaust Memorial Gathering.

The Aesthetic Feel of Practice

I use the aesthetic in the way it was first used in the eighteenth century, as sensuous knowledge (Goldman 2001: 181), though here this knowledge is tacit and taken for granted. My use of the aesthetic refers to something like the 'feel' that one has for what one is doing; the feel for the 'rightness' of how one is doing what one is doing, or how this is done in concert – the feel of the senses forming form through practice. The aesthetic in mundane living is related to Bergson's idea of 'habit memory', of attending kinesthetically to one's own body, monitoring what one is doing. This is 'memory etched in movement,' providing ways of behaving unself-consciously that 'engender a *felt sense of rightness* in doing what one does . . . we feel at home in our bodies . . . because we resonate with a familiar dynamics, a tactile-kinesthetic dynamics that we have come to establish as our own way of doing something, whether brushing our teeth, throwing a ball, playing the violin, or walking' (Sheets-Johnstone 2000: 360–1, my emphasis). This sense of rightness or 'fitness' (Hardin 1993: 12) – kinesthetic, sensuous, interpersonal – indexes the aesthetics of living unself-consciously. Unself-consciously, one monitors affectively. This is a sense of 'rightness' not in moral terms, but of *how* one does that which one is doing.[1] Moreover, one self-monitors with sensuous immediacy, feeling presentness through experiencing that is in solution rather than a precipitate (Williams 1977: 133–4).

The aesthetics of mundane living generate and conserve awareness through feeling the 'rightness' of practice, the rightness-in-doing, felt inside oneself, outside oneself, and between oneself and others (see also Inglis and Hughson 2000: 289). Mundane aesthetics are an in-dwelling of tacit knowing that always includes *more than we can tell*, were we able to relate this knowingly (Polanyi 1966: 17–23, 1962: 314). Paraphrasing Polanyi, Katz (1999: 314) argues that 'effective action requires that we disattend our body as we act, focusing away from the point at which our body intersects with the world.' Tacit knowing is the feeling of disattending that moves us beyond ourselves, enabling the exterior world of practice and the interior world of experience to be unified as the exterior world of experience and the interior world of practice (see also Dufrenne 1973: 446). To feel is to transcend (Dufrenne 1973: 377). The aesthetics of practice transcend practice by enabling practice to communicate 'more than we can tell,' while feeling the rightness of not needing to, or not being able to relate this. The aesthetics of practice integrate us with what we do, self-generating and self-organizing this integration as more than we can tell, while feeling the 'rightness' of this. This leads to 'an appreciation of the essential place of aesthetics in all behaviors, however mundane or esoteric' (Katz 1999: 314). In mundane living the aesthetics of practice enable people and social orders to naturalize their own arbitrariness, to know their worlds tacitly as natural, as taken for granted (see Bourdieu 1977: 164; Garfinkel 1967). Without the aesthetic experiencing of practice as it is done, there is no feel of rightness, no feel that this is how doing is doing, how doing is done, how done continues as doing.

Aesthetics are axial to the natural feel of mundane practice as more than we can tell, as more than we can know. Practice fits together person and world, person and person, person and action, action and action – fitting them into and through one another – their mutual forming. Aesthetics – the synesthesic, sensuous feel of things fitting together (and not fitting together) – enables us to proceed formatively, coherently, perspectively, and prospectively in *the nowness of here*. The aesthetics of practice are its persuasive grounds, persuading us that practice is in the process of being done as the kind of practice it is (and is becoming).[2] Aesthetics may be more like an ongoing gestalt, a 'coherent entity' (Polanyi 1966), or an entity whose coherence is continously coming into being, fitting itself together self-persuasively, even as that which it fits together erodes, ruptures, breaks.

Since we must know ourselves indirectly through interaction with others, there is usually a break in any aesthetic of mundane practice. The very feel of rightness constitutes a temporal lag, however small; a lack of synchronization with oneself and with others. As Katz (1999: 315) puts it, 'I see, hear, feel, and express myself through actions that in part always remain behind myself, always just beyond the reach of my self-awareness.' So we are always trying to catch up with more than we can tell.[3] Yet this is also the break between mundane social order and its special occasions, whereby we posit 'more than we can tell' as visions graspable and knowable, enabling us to catch up with ourselves and with others through these visions of making order. This break may open towards radical shifts in aesthetics of practice within public events, or it may continue the honing of the self-same aesthetics, only in different venues.

Bureaucratic Aesthetics in the Event of Presentation

Bureaucratic logic makes monothetic 'difference', forming symmetrical, mutually exclusive, even infinitesimal distinctions, and insisting on their significance. The analysis of the Versailles commemoration in Chapter One showed how within a monothetic taxonomy, levels nest neatly within one another. Yet the higher level does not encompass the lower holistically, since the lower level cannot signify the entirety of which it is a part. There is no synechdoche in a monothetic taxonomy. Bureaucratic logic is enabled by its own aesthetics of practice. Given the significance of ocular centrism in the modern epoch (Foucault 1979; Jay 1992a), bureaucratic aesthetics are those of anatomization – the defining, classifying, specifying, inspecting, and enumerating of all the parts from which some totality is constituted. These aesthetics are practiced in public most explicitly in events of presentation, and these aesthetics of presentation are strongly continuous with those that organize practice in so many domains of mundane life. There is no radical shift in aesthetic from the mundane to the event of presentation.[4]

The event of presentation shapes and shows often symmetrical taxonomies. Taxonomies are put on view, their categories filled, the members of these categories practicing a repertoire of signs and actions. These are living taxonomies, spectacles of bureaucratic logic whose aesthetic feel of rightness enables their enactment. Events of presentation are icons of social order open to public inspection. These events assert the determinacy of the significance that they enclose within themselves. Ocular-centric, their signs and symbols are arranged often as a tableau. The actions of performers (like the categories they embody) rarely overlap, and are carefully allocated, measured, synchronized. Order is continually seen to be formed and practiced during the event.

It is especially ironic to discuss the opening event of Holocaust Remembrance Day in terms of bureaucratic logic and bureaucratic aesthetics. The Holocaust arouses sensitivity and passion – increasingly so – in Israeli Jewish everyday life (see Chapter Nine, and Friedlander and Seligman 1994; Young 1990; Feldman 2000; Kidron 2000). In Israeli popular and academic discourse alike, the ritualization of the Holocaust is attended to primarily in terms of moral, philosophical, theological, historical, and political valences and their consequences, as if the logic and aesthetics of commemoration are irrelevant to how these valences are conveyed. Yet it is through the bureaucratic logic of forming public occasions that the significance of Holocaust in Israel is shaped to an important degree, while it is the aesthetics of this logic that enable these events to take the presentational, taxonomic form that they do, and to be appreciated as such.

To reiterate, the aesthetics of the event of presentation are a direct continuation of their prominence in the everyday life of a social order shaped through the state-form and bureaucratic logic. The practice of these events is the dramatization of bureaucratic logic, and its enablement through bureaucratic aesthetics. This is even more striking, given that the opening event of Holocaust Remembrance Day is tacitly framed and embedded within the ordering taxonomies of military bureaucracy. Military logic is a potent distillation of bureaucratic logic, but one always on the cusp of physical violence. The Memorial Gathering is in its own way a shaped and practiced projection of the submerged military presence the State uses to protect this event. The logic and aesthetics of the event itself continue the protection afforded by the military, so that each is the lineal extension of the other. Before turning to the event itself, I discuss the military formation that practices its protection.

The Military Envelopment of the Memorial Gathering

Like all Israeli state events, the Memorial Gathering is enclosed by a cocoon shaped by military classification. The IDF has a major presence in this opening event, described in the next section. Yet the explicit participation of the IDF is but the tip of the military presence – the Gathering exists as it does by being enveloped by the military. The presence of the military envelope is practical and functional – to ensure monothetic order in keeping with the forming capacities of bureaucratic logic and the state-form. The differences between military and bureaucratic logic are more matters of content and direction than of premises of classification. Therefore my discussion is of the military as the exercise of bureaucratic logic. Both the Gathering and the IDF are metonymic with bureaucratic logic. In terms of a logic and aesthetics of classification and its practice, the military instructions to protect the occasion cannot be separated from the performance itself of that occasion. I turn now to these instructions and their monothetic logic.

The overall responsibility for planning and enacting the event lies with Yad Vashem. Nonetheless the Army instructions to secure and to protect the site of the Gathering envelop and ultimately control Yad Vashem's roles. Though Yad Vashem appears in official control of the Gathering, there are points at which this institution is dependent upon or subordinate to the IDF. At times there is struggle between the overt and hidden enactments – one example will suffice here. The Army's concern is to secure the Gathering against terrorist attacks. The President and Prime Minister of the State attend, as do official representatives of foreign states. Yad Vashem wants the event enacted according to its script. Both Yad Vashem and the IDF are deeply committed to the vision of the State and nation-in-arms as the protective bastions against any future Holocaust. The final rehearsal takes place in the late afternoon, before the Gathering begins. Some hours before, the IDF seals off Yad Vashem as a closed military area, under the Emergency Defense Regulations (see Chapter One). The Army controls all access and movement within this area.

In 1988 the Gathering took place some months after the outbreak of the first Intifada, and the local IDF Commander decided to seal off the site (itself distant from any actual clashes) earlier than usual, in what Yad Vashem personnel described as a fit of 'security hysteria.' Consequently the announcers and members of the choir and orchestra either were either unable to enter the site or were unable to rehearse properly there. This could have affected the performance adversely, and led to discussions between Yad Vashem administrators and Army officers. A compromise was hammered out, but the Army's ultimate control of the site was uncontested.

Both sides in this dispute are organized through bureaucratic logic. At issue is not only a division of labor and spheres of authority, but the very forming and application of taxonomic categories – the relentless creation and invocation of arbitrary, categorical difference. Yad Vashem orders the presentation of the Holocaust in monothetic terms, and the Army does the same to Yad Vashem. Yad Vashem, open to the public six days a week, and receiving in the neighborhood of a million visitors a year, is redefined categorically by the IDF, and on this basis is turned into a fortress, into another order of ordering.

The significance of the IDF's act of closure may be lost on the parties concerned, yet it must be stressed. The official Holocaust memorial is itself remade – ghettoized – within the national landscape intended ideologically to be open. (Landscapes of death and memorialism are discussed in Chapter Eight.) The fortress is besieged within itself, given the status of a protected species, and placed apart. As the participants commemorate the Holocaust, they themselves are set apart as the potential victims of another Holocaust (thereby encouraging their self-classification as such). This irony is foreign to the bureaucratic logic used. At issue is whose taxonomic ordering of reality will prevail. The Army has the advantage, since it envelops Yad Vashem in its timescape. The military vision of order puts in place and territorializes a taxonomy of control and discipline hidden in the main from the Gathering participants, yet intended to embed them all within its surveillance. The classified territory becomes the mirror image peering within itself in a panopticon-like way. The Army creates an event within which order is made yet is not to be seen, complementing the order made to be seen in the Gathering itself.[5] The Army relentlessly and symmetrically divides and classifies time, space, people, and function. There is no ambiguity in classification. Everyone and everything connected with the Gathering is placed in one or another category. The focus here is on Army planning for a Gathering in the 1990s. After this I discuss relevant aspects of the Gathering enacted at that time.

Time was sliced cleanly into two consecutive phases. The first phase spanned four days, from 7 to 10 April, during which preparations and rehearsals were done. The second stage began at 15:00 hours on the 10 April, when military forces secured the area, and lasted until the end of the Gathering at approximately 21:00 hours. The list of Army goals was lengthy and exhaustive: to control all approaches to the ceremonial plaza where the Gathering would be held; to secure the entire area of Yad Vashem and its roads and byways, using foot patrols on the near and distant peripheries, motorized patrols on the roads, as well as positioning bomb-disposal personnel; to establish observation points at controlling locations; to use military police to secure the parking lots; to use civil defense reservists and soldiers of the Women's Corps to search the bags (and where necessary, the person) of all entering the ceremonial area; to use bomb-disposal personnel to check all vehicles entering the area; to have in readiness Medical Corps personnel to treat and evacuate, according to need; and to coordinate with bodyguards of the Security Services (*Sherutei Bitakhon*) who safeguard the seating of Israeli dignitaries. Safeguarding the ceremonial plaza itself was also the responsibility of the Security Services from the moment the dignitaries entered.

To implement these goals the IDF used several hundred military personnel belonging to the regular army, the military police, the border police, the sappers, the medical corps, the women's corps, and the civil defense guard. Military personnel were divided into eleven units: these included a regional command center with communication specialists; forces to secure and to safeguard the approaches to Yad Vashem; a preventive force on a rooftop overlooking the plaza; an assault force for more incisive intervention; and patrols on axes triangulating the entire area of the memorial complex.

This relentless classifying shapes discrete, modular, monothetic categories. Taken together, these categories are organized vertically (those ranked higher control those ranked lower) and horizontally (categories on the same level do not overlap in their contents and functions). The dimensions of each category are measured: the kind and number of personnel, the kind and number of weapons and other artifacts. Together, these categories totalize space and time – they suck in, subsume, and make order among all the phenomena towards which their taxonomy is aimed. Nothing, no one, is left outside the monothetic classifying of space, time, people. The taxonomy includes itself, and so is self-sealing. All are under control and discipline, whether they know this or not. Since the categories are modular, they can be altered, shifted, redesigned, added to or subtracted from the taxonomy without changing the operational efficiency of the classifications. The resemblance to the principles of taxonomizing in the Versailles commemoration is striking.

The effect of having all the categories of the military taxonomy in position on the ground, enveloping and surveilling everyone and everything within the Holocaust memorial, is something like a public event in its own right. An event of presentation, but organized as a concealed scopic system controlling itself, and aimed at the Memorial Gathering. This systemic apparatus is hidden from outsiders without the code to the military taxonomy. Nonetheless the hidden military classification is present and piercingly scopic, in place in space, reshaping the landscape into vectors of force, moving according to preset instructions, holding everything within its gaze. An event that itself is the gaze of control, a symmetric, systemic, covert tableau, the embodiment of bureaucratic logic and aesthetics in systemic motion – a lookout precisely here, a roadblock directly there, a patrol moving through a specified axis, an assault force held in instant readiness.

The military event is an analogue of the state-form, capturing and containing through the forming enabled by bureaucratic logic and aesthetics. The covert military event surveils the entire site of the Memorial complex, enveloping this and the Gathering performed there. The military apparatus cocoons the memorial site in its taxonomic closure, gazing at the displayed tableau of the past, at the practice of Holocaust memorialism. The hidden present (the military) disciplines and orders the visible past (the Holocaust event) that is made to appear as if it controls the visible present. The tableau of the Memorial Gathering is immobile and static, in contrast to that of the military, mobile, flexible, systemic.[6]

The Memorial Gathering

The Memorial Gathering is performed as a panoply of taxonomic categories, one that embodies practices of bureaucratic logic and aesthetics. The setting is the Warsaw Ghetto Plaza (dedicated to the revolt), dominated on one side by a high brick wall (called the Wall of Remembrance, hereafter, the Wall) within which are embedded reproductions of Nathan Rapaport's original bas-relief and sculpture that stand on the site of the razed Warsaw Ghetto (Young 1989a). The bas-relief and sculpture divide the Wall into two sections, two categories; and during the Gathering the focus shifts from one to the other (from right to left, the direction in which Hebrew and Yiddish are written).

The Taxonomy of the Wall of Remembrance

The large bronze bas-relief of the Last March is embedded in the right side of the Wall (see Figure 2). The bas-relief depends through a horizontal axis, depicting Jews – older men, women, and children, all of whom have a ghetto look – clustered together,

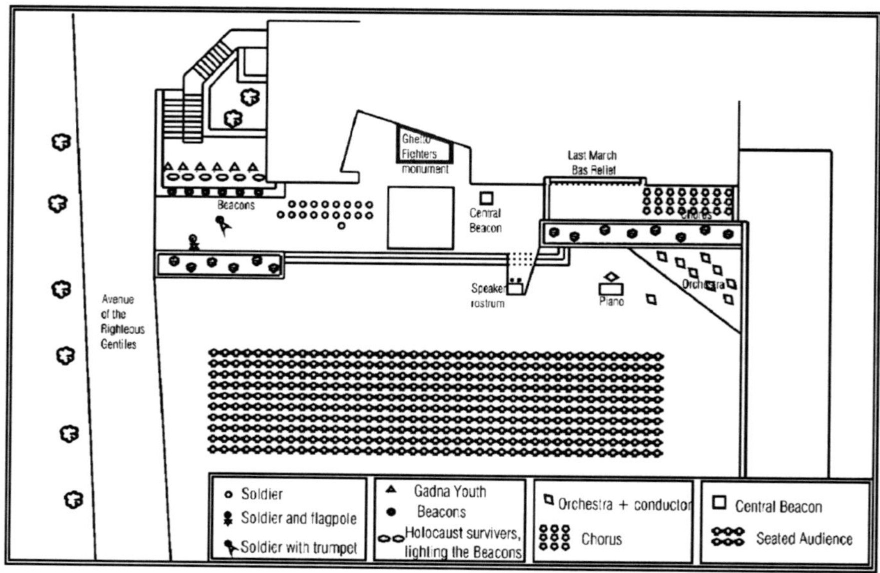

Figure 2 The opening event of Holocaust Remembrance Day, spatial layout.

eyes averted from the viewer's gaze, bent beneath their burdens, walking into a strong wind, sorrowfully treading towards an unknown destination. Whatever the destination, it annihilates them. To the left of the bas-relief is a sculpture of the fighters of the Warsaw Ghetto uprising, vertical and the height of the Wall. Nestled within a rectangular niche in the Wall, these fighters, mostly young, stand tall and strong at the ready, grasping rifles and grenades, facing the viewer and looking straight ahead at a distant horizon. The bas-relief is 'pasted' onto the surface, but the sculpted fighters emerge from within the depths of the Wall, embodying its unyielding strength. In the Warsaw original the bas-relief is placed on the reverse side of the Ghetto Uprising sculpture, so that the two are not seen together.[7] At Yad Vashem, bas-relief and sculpture are positioned in a lineal relationship.

These two scenes constitute a taxonomy of narrative history, one that symmetrically divides Jewish perceptions of history into a before and an after, into categories of destruction and arisal, shifting one into the other.[8] From right to left the scene shifts from the driven despair of generations of Jews at the shattering edge, to the fierce determination of the Ghetto fighters, the maturing of embattled, centered, powerful strength. The narrative moves from the horizontal stretch of the bas-relief, an even plane of suffering that extends indefinitely without surcease, to the unbending verticality of the sculpture, stopping movement through posture, gesture, positioning, signing to the viewer that these Jews will not be driven any further. This is the dominant narrative of the Holocaust in Israel today. The narrative in-forming the taxonomic shift from catastrophe to regeneration is also enacted within the Gathering, so that this meta-narrative is doubled, again symmetrically. I first discuss the visual placement of social categories along the Wall, and then their sequencing during the occasion.

The Wall is made to frame the performance. The social categories of the enactment are laid out lineally along the breadth of the Wall. The vertical sculpture of the Ghetto fighters is used to divide this tableau into segments of destruction and arisal. A central memorial beacon is placed between the bas-relief and the sculpture – but more to the right side, identified with the Holocaust catastrophe. In the early 1990s the flame emerged from a cone, rising high through a spiral of barbed wire, searing and transcending the barbs that tore the flesh, heart, life of the Jewish people, reaching to the very top of the Wall. To the right of this central beacon is a rostrum, used by the announcers of the ceremony and by those who deliver speeches and prayers. Still further to the right are the choir and orchestra. The right side is identified more with civil order. The Jews who suffered and died during the Holocaust were the victimized members of European states.

The categories of the left side are identified primarily with military order. Immediately to the left of the central beacon stands the Honor Guard of the IDF, naked bayonets fixed to automatic weapons. Further left, atop a lower extension of the Wall, are six memorial beacons in memory of the six million Jewish dead. During the event the beacons are lit ceremoniously by persons chosen by the Yad Vashem administration. The beacon-lighters are assisted by paramilitary youth in uniform who hand them lit torches to kindle the beacons. Framing the entire tableau at its extreme left is the State flag. The martial response to the Holocaust – Honor Guard, beacon-lighters, paramilitary youth – is itself framed, enclosed on its right by the Ghetto fighters sculpture and on its left by the state flag. The sequencing of the event shifts, again symmetrically, from stateless Jewish Holocaust victims, betrayed by foreign states, driven fatedly to their deaths, to fighting Jews standing their ground, focused for battle, intergenerational, national – the nation-in-arms as the only viable response to persecution.

Through the performance the visual sequence of bas-relief and sculpture is extended further, from World War II into the present. This sequencing shifts Jews from uprising and rebirth (signified by the sculpture) to the State of Israel (signified by the national flag) where the martial response extends into the future. During the event the entire Zionist version of recent history is taxonomized as a classification of historical events laid bare before the gaze of the audience.[9] The audience sits facing the Wall, dignitaries and speakers in the first row.

Initially the performance clusters around the bas-relief, the unredeemable side of the Holocaust tableau. With the lighting of the six beacons the focus shifts to the martial response. The beacon-lighters are heroes and heroines of the Holocaust – living embodiments of the Warsaw Ghetto sculpture – elevated above the audience on the low wall of beacons, to the very left of the tableau. The Jews depicted in the bas-relief no longer exist in this version of history – either they became survivors (who 'ascended' to Israel) or they are dead 'martyrs,' in the language of Holocaust memorialism in Israel.[10] In any case, there is no mimetic embodiment of the category of 'martyr' within the enactment – only the ghostly outlines of figures long past, frozen in bronze on the bas-relief. When all the taxonomic categories are added together, one to another, they constitute a history that relates Holocaust annihilation to the fighting response, and then relates this martial response to the armed protection offered to Jews by the fortress state and its nation-in-arms (embodied by Honor Guard and paramilitary youth protecting the beacon-lighter survivors, all cocooned within the protective envelope of the Army).

Taxonomy and Rhythms of Time

Adding together all the taxonomic categories is impelled by a Judaic temporal rhythm to be discussed in detail in the conclusion to Chapter Seven. This rhythm is unrelated to bureaucratic logic and its aesthetic enablements (unlike the sliced, modular temporality discussed in Chapter Five). This rhythm is more a moral aesthetic of duration, making living through time a moral pulsation. In the Israeli case this rhythm, to a degree, shapes how bureaucratic logic organizes an event like the Gathering. Through this rhythm the moral value of time pulsates from low to high valence, through the encoding of different durations – through the 24-hour day, the week, holidays, the sabbatical year, and so forth. These pulsations are practiced and lived experientially rather than theorized – consciously or not, they are integral to Israeli Jewish life. This temporal rhythm encodes the downward and upward pulsations of moral presence in the world, including the high valence of holism and completeness, previously of the nation, now of State and nation, that upward pulsation endows. These pulsations encode the perception of native history. When taxonomic categories are ordered as 'before' and 'after', they are impelled into connectedness by these rhythms. More accurately, the aesthetics of these rhythms of time impel taxonomic categories into an ordering that is perceived as 'before' and 'after.' Thus the aesthetics of duration – the rhythms of time – enable the forming of native history.

As conditions of existence descend, entering a period of low moral valence, this inexorably is driven to move from descent towards ascent, towards a period of high moral valence. In living this temporal rhythm there is powerful metaphysical resistance to permitting Jewish (and now, Israeli) history to end as the pulsation into moral descent, fragmenting holism. The rhythm demands moral, existential ascent. The logic and aesthetics of this rhythm shape perceiving the Holocaust as a phase on the way to redemption. In nationalist terms this is redemption through the founding of the State as the haven for the nation. This upward pulsation encodes the relationship between Holocaust Remembrance Day, Israeli Remembrance Day for the war dead, and Independence Day, discussed in the next chapter. This upward pulsation encodes and shapes the taxonomic relationship between categories within the Memorial

Gathering: between descent and ascent; and too, between the martial enveloping of Yad Vashem and the performance of the Gathering within this envelope. The aesthetics of descent and ascent shape time in ways that give significance and meaning to native history.

Taxonomy and the Three Generations

The martial side of the tableau accords fully with upward pulsation. This side is embodied in three symmetrical categories whose temporal linkage is no less metaphysical than historical. These categories are of three generations of fighters, the grandparental, the parental, and their offspring. The beacon-lighters are analogous to the grandparental generation. Born in Europe, they survived the Holocaust and ascended to Israel, aligning themselves with the founders and pioneers. Lighting the beacons of remembrance that are also flames of destruction and sacrifice, they transcend their own pasts through memory of the past in the present. The Honor Guard is composed of young soldiers doing their compulsory military service. They are analogous to the generation of children of the survivors, who have grown to maturity within Israel. They are the state in its martial modality, honoring and protecting the generation of Holocaust survivors. The beacon-lighters are handed their torches by the uniformed paramilitary youth, analogous to the generation of Israeli Jewish grandchildren who belong to the more distant future. Handing over the torches, the paramilitary youth (the unformed future) enable the beacon-lighters (overcoming the disastrous past) to commemorate their remembrance, protected by the Honor Guard (the fighting present). The narrative structuring the length of the Wall and the three-generational paradigm of remembrance are at the heart of the Gathering's significance; and they are formed through the aesthetics of temporal rhythm, pulsing from low to high. Neither the rhythm of Jewish time nor the paradigm of the three generations is explicitly recognized in the Gathering. Though in practice the rightness of these temporal rhythms is recognized, they are also 'more than we can know,' and so they encompass us in their fullness that is beyond our ken.

Planning and Bureaucratic Aesthetics

The presence of bureaucratic logic is plainly evident in the comments of a planner and organizer of early opening events of memorialism, in which the Wall of Remembrance was first used. He stated that the ordering of taxonomic categories, in my terms, along the length of the Wall was primarily a practical matter that matched positioning with available space. Once the decision was taken to use the Wall and the taxonomic categories discussed here, the only space sufficient for the six beacons was on the left side. Since the Honor Guard defended the beacon lighters, it too went to the left side. The national flag, then, also went to the left side and, too, the paramilitary youth.

Since all space on the left side was taken, the choir and orchestra had to go to the right side. This disposition along the Wall, said the organizer, 'has no meaning.'

The distribution of categories along the Wall depended upon, first, deciding which elements to include; and, second, arranging them in relation to one another so that all fit the available space/time. There is in this the arbitrariness of bureaucratic logic, yet also the tacit aesthetic perception (according with this logic) that like goes together with like. Beacons, beacon-lighters, Honor Guard, paramilitary youth, and flag, all fit together, belonged together. Brought into conjunction, the interaction of these signs immediately began to produce their own semiosis, to make emergent, perhaps unintended meaning. This interaction generated the doubled visual narrative and the paradigm of the three generations. Relatively unrelated signs brought serendipitously near to one another relate semiotically to one another – they are felt, aesthetically, to fit together even if this remains tacit (Handelman and Shamgar-Handelman 1993).

The organizers of the first Holocaust memorials at Yad Vashem decided that a proper commemoration should include at least three discrete categories, without specifying their relationship to one another. These were, first, the acts mandatory for a religious memorial (the mourner's prayer and 'God full of mercy'); second, an 'artistic' category consisting of appropriate music and song; and third, a category of speeches and readings. Music and songs, readings and speeches, were synchronized through alternation, so that a song followed a speech or reading, and so forth; while the religious practices were clustered towards the end of the occasion. These categories were defined quite arbitrarily, yet their conjunction produced an aesthetically clean-cut alternation between rhetoric and song that felt right – perhaps in that the discreteness of speech and music was maintained. Furthermore, these secular practices were kept together, separated from the category of religious practices.

Bureaucratic aesthetics shape the exactness of categories, borders cleanly demarcated in relation to one another, demonstrating difference, everything harmoniously in its place. In keeping with this, the sequence of action is divided into temporal segments producing as perfect a synchronization as possible between categories within ceremonial space. This aesthetic of machined parts fitting together is what, above all, enables the performers to be in the right place at the right time. Precise, symmetrical synchronization is the primary integrating force in this event, holding together pieces that otherwise may have little connectivity with one another. There is no space/time for irregularity, fluctuation, uncertainty (see Simmel 1968 [1896]: 73). Crucial to this integration is the announcer, who reports on ongoing synchronization in the event by telling the audience which segment will perform next, thereby articulating segments with one another. This is an expression of bureaucratic logic and aesthetics, since the announcement of each segment is no less the enunciation of its demarcated modularity. In this event the extreme, symmetrical modularity of its segments enables its construction and integration. This modularity allows the organizers to add and subtract modules at will. This is so too for the military envelope, and beyond this for the practice of everyday life in social orders shaped through bureaucratic logic and aesthetics. There are powerful continuities and similarities between the organization of the Gathering and that of the mundane, accentuated here by the positioning of the military envelope between the event and the everyday.

A Memorial Gathering of the 1990s: Sequencing

In this Gathering there were twenty discrete segments. I list them here to demonstrate just how modular they are, depending entirely on symmetrical synchronization decided on before the event begins. I use the segments to discuss aspects of their sequencing relevant to the meta-narrative of the three Days. The sequencing of the segments (and the time allotted each in minutes) was as follows:

(1) The entry of the Honor Guard five minutes before the start of the ritual;
(2) entry of the President of the State (2:00);
(3) lowering the State flag to half-mast (2:30);
(4) lighting the central memorial beacon by the President (3:00);
(5) song by choir (2:00);
(6) speech of the Chairman of the Yad Vashem Directorate (2:00);
(7) song by choir (2:00);
(8) speech of the Director of Yad Vashem (2:00);
(9) cantor sings 'God, God, why did you forsake us?' accompanied by the choir (3:00);
(10) speech of the representative of the partisans' organizations (3:00);
(11) speech by the prime minister (5:00);
(12) reading of poem by an announcer (2:30);
(13) song by choir (2:00);
(14) lighting the six beacons (8:00);
(15) reading by an announcer of a text of 'live witnessing' of the Holocaust (3:00);
(16) readings of psalms by the Sephardic Chief Rabbi of the State (2:00);
(17) saying the mourner's prayer for the dead (2:00);
(18) singing Yizkor, the prayer of remembrance (6:00);
(19) songs by choir (2:00);
(20) singing of the national anthem (2:00).

The total time allocated to the occasion was 60:30.

Like the tableau laid out in space along the Wall, the sequence of acts is categorical, segmentary, modular. Most segments are rehearsed, but participants have no mandate for inpromptu improvisation should anything go wrong with the synchronization. Segments are externally administered by a director or organizer; indeed by 'bureaucrats' who ensure that the performers be in the right place at the right time for the correct duration. The anatomy of this event of presentation is analogous to a bureaucratic exoskeleton that is fleshed out, in place, through time, by performance. The logic of the exoskeleton is like that of the military envelope within which it is embedded, except that the envelope has systemic qualities that enable it to function and to self-corrrect, as do other bureaucratic infrastructures. By contrast the Gathering, set into motion by bureaucratic edict, must play itself out without any capacity for self-correction during performance.[11]

Especially striking is just how restricted is kinesthetic movement, and altogether just how little there is. Some categories of person are fixed in place throughout the event (Honor Guard, choir, orchestra). The members of others move very short distances from the front row of the audience to take fixed positions temporarily on the podium and behind the beacons. At all times the entire tableau is visible to the gaze of the audience.[12] The performer is the (near) perfect embodiment of his category in the performance – he does not expand, restrict, or play with this. Instead he contributes to the vision of perfected monothetic ordering. All of this speaks to a regimen in aesthetic presentation that is beyond the nationalist and the statist, and closest to the bureaucratic logic of forming form, of this kind of ordering of people and things.

Framing

Despite the modularity of the Gathering, there is some framing of sequence at its beginning and end, though this framing itself is lineal and categorical.[13] The IDF Honor Guard – the overt sign of the protective State – takes up position first, awaiting the entry of President and Prime Minister. The military anticipates the arrival of the civil state, just as the military envelope awaits the arrival of the event. The State flag is lowered to half-mast, signifying the entry of state and people into mourning. The central beacon is lit, signifying the entry of the people into remembrance. This sequencing demonstrates the State's protective envelopment of the enactment.

The people do not enter into remembrance before the State enters into mourning. The State disciplines and synchronizes the remembrance of the Holocaust. State control is practiced through the presentation in sequence of a taxonomy of categories of power (the Honor Guard), of authority (the President and Prime Minister), and of peoplehood (the central beacon). The end of the event is performed through collective singing of the national anthem – the occasion is not complete until the State grants it closure. Though this framing signifies the State's control, the logic of classification in presentation is that of the bureaucratic. Put otherwise, how the bureaucratic mind-set organizes the event enables this occasion to signify the State's control as it does.

In this aesthetics of presentation the taxonomic categories are displayed as segments and activated, one by one. Just as each category is added to the next, so, too, the event can be deconstructed into these segments without doing much violence to the occasion as a whole. Despite the variety of physical postures – standing on guard, sitting and holding musical instruments, standing and lighting a beacon, standing and orating, standing and singing – the very immobility and functionality of their embodiments suggest that like proper functionaries most of the participants could be seated behind a desk or wicket. This montage points to the resonance between the bureaucratic logic of the event and its military cocoon, and between these and the ordering of society.

Lighting the Memorial Beacons

Bureaucratic logic and aesthetics shape the lengthiest segment of the occasion, its dramatic highlight, the lighting of the six memorial beacons. Each year a Yad Vashem committee chooses a theme to commemorate in the Gathering, the categories of persons who will represent this theme, and the persons who will embody these categories by igniting the beacons dedicated to the theme. For the enactment discussed here the theme chosen was the fiftieth anniversary of the destruction of the Jewries of Russia, Yugoslavia, and Bukovina. The six beacons were lit by eleven persons. They had been military heroes, partisans, survivors of ghettos and escapees from concentration camps. Some were children during the Holocaust, one was a woman whose own mother and own child were both slaughtered at Babi Yar, and another, a Righteous Gentile who made his home in Israel.[14]

Despite the heroism and suffering of the beacon-lighters, despite the death and pain they commemorated, all was inscribed in the announcers' texts as the enumeration of a precise anatomy of anguish, as a trait list of its attributes and locations.[15] Thus the first beacon-lighter was introduced by the following text (given in part): 'A full fifty years after the extermination of the Jews in the Soviet territories conquered by the Nazis, in memory of the Jews of Lithuania, Latvia, Estonia, and Byelorussia who were murdered . . . the murder of Ponar – near Vilna, the nine in Kovno, Rombli – near Riga, Malitrostiniech – near Minsk, and many other places, ascending first to light the beacon is a new immigrant . . . who was in a prisoner camp in the Minsk Ghetto, escaped and joined the partisans in the forests . . . one of the survivors of the concentration camp, Sergiosko.'[16]

This trait list, together with those of other texts, practice the tacit premise that the enumeration of details in the micro-domain of Nazi actions will produce a comprehensive vision of the multitude of catastrophes that today are called Holocaust.[17] This listing by categories that, as it were, are cross-indexed with other categories is precisely one of the attitudes shaped by bureaucratic logic, enabled by bureaucratic aesthetics, one that equates the symmetric addition and enumeration of mass with a holistic totality.[18] This logic, and its aesthetic of every detail in its proper place, are quite similar to those of the military 'takeover' of Yad Vashem.

Performing Practices of Bureaucratic Logic

That events like the Memorial Gathering are organized through bureaucratic logic and aesthetics makes a difference to the kinds of information these occasions communicate. From the perspective of organizers and audience the Gathering is a moral project of the Jewish State, carried out in the name of the Jewish people. The moral duty is remembering the evils of the past that fragmented and annihilated Jews, and protecting these fragments within the holism of State and people. In the Gathering the practice of remembering is cast as an itemization, an accounting of the past, occurrence by occurrence, point by point – a double-entry book-keeping of remembrance. The practice of bureaucratic logic is enabled by the bureaucratic aesthetics of lineality – classifying monothetically, modularizing arithmetically, itemizing with exactitude. In the Gathering the power of these aesthetics is brought home by the ways in which the military envelops the site within its own taxonomies. Yet as I noted, the premises of taxonomy used by the military are the same as those used to organize the Gathering, and both are the same as premises camouflaged to a degree in daily life. This suggests that the relationships among practices of the event, the military envelope, and daily life are fractal.

The Gathering is a fractal composition, reflecting the logic and aesthetics of military taxonomizing, and both are fractals of bureaucratic logic and aesthetics. Fractals are profoundly symmetrical in relation to their own interiorities. To plumb the logic and aesthetics of the Gathering is to enter into those of the military; to plumb those of the military is to enter into those of the bureaucratics of everyday living. To plumb those of everyday bureaucratics is to discover where bureaucratic logic and the state-form shape one another, and to plumb this is to enter into the Memorial Gathering. The bureaucratic message in the invisible military tableau is made explicit in the visible tableau of the Gathering. This message indexes the practice of exclusivist classification, of fragmentation and itemization, at the expense of the holistic vision of remembrance. The moral project of the State is shaped, modified, and cracked as it passes through the forming force of bureaucratic logic and aesthetics. The vision and feeling of Holocaust stand rigidly to attention, open to minute inspection, petrified in place. The vision shifts towards the totalitarian in its presentation, supporting Simmel's arguments on the semiotic consequences of symmetry.

Bureaucratic logic and aesthetics ironically contribute to separating the Jewish Holocaust from all other atrocities, to classifying it as the unique, historical occurrence of the planned extermination of an entire people – a category with a single member (indeed, a category that paradoxically is a member of itself, and is therefore self-sealing, rejecting comparison with any other heart-rending atrocity). This exclusivist patterning with all its inherent dangers resonates with the monothetic treatment of profound tragedy that characterizes the Memorial Gathering. In this instance, bureaucratic logic and aesthetics support nationalism and remembrance that recursively gather themselves into themselves, an in-gathering that separates Holocaust from too many other instances of man-made mass-death (Wyschogrod 1985).

For numerous Jews in Israel the difference between the Holocaust dead and living Israeli Jews is that the Israelis have 'a state, a flag, and an army,' as the Minister of Education put it on Holocaust Remembrance Day 2001. This formula is signed by the Gathering – the State saves the Israeli Jews from the fate of the Holocaust dead. Zygmunt Bauman (1998) comments that what the Nazi designers of death failed to accomplish in life, turning the world against the Jews, they may accomplish posthumously, turning the Jews against the world. Michael Bernstein (1998: 7) argues that, 'we are hypnotized by what could be called a monotheistic ideology of catastrophe,' in which, 'there must be one exemplary cataclysm, one form of savagery unmatched by any others because only through a single, all-persuasive and all-sufficient instantiation of evil can one truth about human nature emerge.' Hence the insistence that the Holocaust is simultaneously the universal instance of man's inhumanity to man but that this cruelty is particularistic, for it could only be done so utterly and totally to Jews, and is therefore their cultural heritage, their legacy, indeed their property. Their embrace of universal particularism enables quite a few Israeli Jews to feel that a return to the borders of the pre-1967 War would make these the 'borders of Auschwitz' (Zertal 2000: 120). Moreover, Israeli Jews resonate with occasions like the Gathering, given that they are both the practitioners and the practiced of bureaucratic logic and aesthetics in the everyday. The logic of lineal classification and the practice of its enabling are commonsensical to them in how they live much of their lives, especially outside the home. They are not reflexive about their practice of this logic, nor about its aesthetic enabling.

In the use of bureaucratic logic and aesthetics there are intimations of lawfulness, to return to King's (1993) point, raised in Chapter One. King argues that in Western legal systems, law depends for its ontology on a binary code of lawful/unlawful, legal/illegal, and the like. To carry this a step further, law is a prime way of symmetrically classifying everyday acts within monothetic taxonomies with great authority and with powerful consequences. Legal systems generate decisions that clarify and banish conditions of uncertainty, irregularity, fluctuation, vagueness, overlapping, and the questionable. Legal systems underwrite these decisions by sanctifying lineality. King suggests that this logic of the legal is far more embracing and totalizing than the formal system of law as such. Of especial interest here is that binarism meets the criteria of monothetic classification. Therefore monothetic taxonomizing, with a much broader range than binarism, may be substituted for the latter. Moreover forming form through monothetic logic indexes the presence of bureaucratic logic. And so the operation of bureaucratic logic implicates the presence of lawfulness. Bureaucratic logic is authorized to a degree by a feeling of lawfulness in practicing monothetic classification. There is then an aesthetic, itself imbued with a sense of lawfulness, indeed, of rightness, that enables the practice of bureaucratic logic in everyday life. This version of aesthetics helps explain why the bureaucratic logic used in the Memorial Gathering, in the military, and in the everyday, works aesthetically on so many. But, too, why we may be so ambivalent to the practice of this logic, yet without knowing exactly and precisely why.

–7–

Sequencing the National: Opening Remembrance Day and Independence Day

[This chapter was coauthored by Elihu Katz.]

Though rarely enunciated, the most powerful message of the event opening Holocaust Remembrance Day is that only citizenship made national is trustworthy. Citizenship after the Holocaust is that of the Jewish State. This citizenship is integral to the rhythm of ascent from the Holocaust. The opening events of Remembrance Day and Independence Day continue this narrative, presenting why citizenship must be made national, the just struggle to make it so, and the fruits of this ascent, the national shaped by bureaucratic logic and aesthetics.

Opening Remembrance Day, Enclosing the National

> "Where was he wounded?" You don't know
> If they mean a place in his body
> or a place in the land.
>
> Yehuda Amichai (1995: 238)
> With permission of HarperCollins Publishers

The setting is the great earthen plaza that abuts the Western Wall in the Old City of Jerusalem. The contrasts with Mount Herzl are striking. In place of vast, open vistas of West Jerusalem and its hills, of expanses of softly contoured greenery, the plaza and its surroundings are severe, rectilinear enclosures, bordered by looming buildings evoking a host of conflicting associations. To the west, the ever-increasing heights of the rebuilt Jewish Quarter (see El-Haj 1998). To the east, the Wall itself, abutting the bulk of Mount Moriah (the ancient site of the Israelite Temples) on which stand the silver-domed mosque of al-Aqsa and the golden Dome of the Rock. Further east, archeological excavations expose buildings dated to the Second Temple period. To the north, the edge of the Muslim Quarter. Immediately before the Wall, the fenced-in prayer area.[1]

Numerous occasions of state are held in the Wall plaza.[2] The Wall is the perfect setting for making citizenship national (cf. Aronoff 1986; Schwartz et al. 1986; Bruner

119

and Gorfain 1984). In Zionist Israel the Wall evokes the last period of Jewish statehood, and so its modern revival. However the Temple can be linked to the giving of the Torah on Mount Sinai following the exodus from Egypt, to the very beginnings of Jewish peoplehood. The Wall often is referred to as a 'witness' to the endurance of Jewish nationhood, awaiting the return of the people from exile (see the kindergarten celebration of Jerusalem Day in Chapter Four). Signs of Israeli statehood can hardly be disentangled from those of Jewish peoplehood, and those of peoplehood from those of religion (Paine 1983).[3]

The hour is night. At the siren's moan the occasion begins. The plaza is in semi-darkness, the Wall lit. All stand at attention, gazing towards this illumination.[4] The spatial focus is the Heroism Memorial Beacon, in a small enclosure just outside the prayer area (see Figure 3). The beacon itself is encased in a squared conus of dressed stones, evoking those of the Wall. Within the enclosure stands an Honor Guard of four young soldiers. The flagpole, the national flag at half-mast, is aligned with the beacon, between the enclosure and the prayer area. Facing the enclosure, standing at a marker on the ground, is the President, flanked by two officers, one of whom is the IDF Chief-of-Staff. Well behind these three stand invited members of the bereaved families, and behind them to the borders of the plaza, other spectators. On the northern side of the plaza are two small rostra, one for invited speakers and one for the announcer. On the southern side, a large honor guard closes off the space of the event.

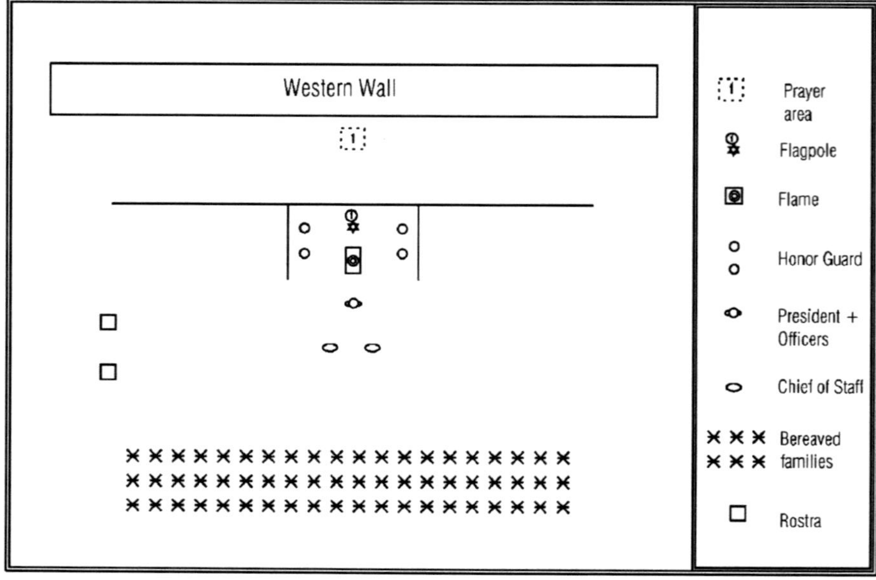

Figure 3 The opening event of Remembrance Day, spatial layout.

Apart from these solitary markers of presence, the large plaza is space filled with emptiness and still shadows. Only the flag moves, fluttering fitfully in the quiet breeze. The moan of the siren dies, the event proceeds in silence. The three figures walk forward at a measured pace. Two female figures appear, one a bereaved mother (alternatively, a war widow), the other a young female soldier bearing a lit torch. The two officers stop, the President continues alone. At the enclosure's entrance he meets the two women. The soldier gives the torch to the bereaved mother, who hands it to the President. He advances into the enclosure, lighting the memorial flame. A bugle sounds. The President communes before the flame, as the two women reenter the shadows. The President speaks briefly before the enclosure, facing the flame, telling of the unification of the people in memory of the fallen; of the bereaved family and its sons, the fallen; and of the necessity of sacrifice and its commemoration. His rhetoric may refer to the Wall as this holy place, as the witness to ancient destruction, and now to revival.[5] The President takes his seat next to his wife, in the first row of bereaved families.

The focus shifts to the speaker's rostrum, to speech, reading, prayer. During this period the middle of the plaza remains empty, a lengthy expanse separating the bereaved families and speakers from the memorial flame, where flickering fire and fluttering flag are the only motion, against the serene, still, backdrop of the Wall. The Chief-of-Staff speaks, addressing his remarks to the bereaved families. This is followed by the sole secular reading, for example, from the work of a noted Israeli Jewish author on the theme of dead soldiers gazing down at those left behind, apologizing for the sadness of the latter; yet they, the dead, were obliged to do battle. And God receives them as His sons. The chief rabbi of the IDF reads from the Book of Psalms. A bereaved father recites Kaddish, the mourner's prayer. And the IDF cantor sings 'God, full of mercy . . .' The assembled rise, remaining in place until the President exits, conversing with members of the bereaved families on his way. The opening event has lasted some fifteen minutes.

Much of the power in numerous events of presentation focuses on the evocation of mood through formations of signs, space, rhetoric. This is so here. The spareness and simplicity of the occasion are striking. So too are the stillness and darkness, the vacant spaces, the restricted movement, the absence of the dead made present. These aspects, echoed in rhetoric, evoke a focused cast of mind, mood, feeling. The unity of signs is not to be broached. The occasion is characterized by the synthesis of person, position, performance, and place, from which variation and individualism are effaced; though signs of Israeli Jewish collectivity and collective endeavor are prominent.[6] Though brief in time, the occasion evokes the eternality of a moral and social order pervaded by the problematic of the nation-in-arms, heroism, death, the family-in-arms, and the mourning family – one without solution save continuing sacrifice, and the profound meaning given to death made powerful in its service to people and State.

This understanding of sacrifice is that of presence turned to absence in exchange for a strengthened, national collectivity. The agency of exchange is heroic death.

Through heroic death the people generate the state and its citizenship as national. To a great extent, heroic death in battle is a function of nationality. In heroic death the people willingly surrender their lives so that others and the collectivity itself may live. Thus in the President's 1969 speech, he stated: 'In the name of the whole House of Israel we elevate the memorial candle to the souls of all our dear ones who gave their life for our freedom and [the] release of our souls . . . and their pure sacrifice will be accepted, forever and ever.'[7] (Heroic sacrifice is discussed further in Chapter Eight.) This occasion evokes presence from absence. Just as in Holocaust memorialism the dead are named 'martyrs' and given 'remembrance citizenship' in the Jewish State, so the opening of Remembrance Day re-members the fallen in the greater, eternal collectivity of the living and dead.

The living momentarily reach out to touch the dead, signing their presence out of absence, but then drawing back to address them from afar. This is done at the very outset in two ways: the kindling of the flame by the apical figure of the state hierarchy, and by the semiotic alignment of signs during those moments. The memorial flame is brought into being by the living in memory of the dead.[8] The rising flame signs the presence of the dead, their re-membering among the living. Through this conjuncture the living rearticulate the memory of the dead. The kind of collectivity in which the membership of the dead is reasserted is crucial to interpreting this occasion. Here the alignment of signs, during and immediately after the flame's kindling, is pivotal. Four signs are aligned lineally and continuously, in increasing magnitudes of rank and encompassment: President, memorial flame, flag, Wall. This requires further discussion.

The President is formally head of state, though with limited powers, mainly ceremonial. Elected by the Knesset, encumbents are expected to be aloof from the political hurly-burly. The presidency is de-politicized by design, and presidents should be figures of moral stature, upholding principles and values important to state and people. Popular presidents have had qualities of the father-figure about them. Absent from active participation in this event is the partisan, political leadership of the country – its prime minister and cabinet. The head of the Jewish State on behalf of its people remembers heroic sacrifice by lighting the flame, re-membering the dead in the greater encompassing collectivity of the living and dead, greater because the dead are beyond the living, recast closer to eternal ideals.[9] Together these living and dead constitute the State as national, actually, historically. Yet the State, signed by the national flag, is again a greater encompassment. The State is not merely the sum of its citizenry or of its people. The State exists independently of its members. It is to the Jewish State that all the Jewish dead and living give their allegiance, and from which they accept their obligations.

This lineal alignment of symbols of increasing magnitude and encompassment is itself encompassed by the Wall. This 'holy place,' this unyielding 'witness' to history, is embedded in the land throughout the ebb and flow of ancient destruction, exile, return, and sovereignty once more. As the Wall endures all tribulations, so too in Zionist mythos do the Jewish people, and so do they endure the loss of their heroic offspring. Here the Wall signs the people, from whose enduring memory of themselves, in the Zionist imaginary, Jewish sovereignty has been reformed in the present. That which the Wall signifies receives fresh vigor and strength through the trials and victories of State and people. In increasing orders of encompassment, the sign of flame nests within that of flag, as both then nest within the sign of the Wall. The concept of 'encompassment,' building on Louis Dumont's (1970, 1979) discussions of hierarchy, describes this nesting. Encompassment suggests that values embedded in higher-order levels contain those of lower-order levels; so that higher-order values have the capacity to generate lower-order ones. We return shortly to these relationships.

Yet there are two qualities of ambivalence here. The Wall, signifying the Jewish people, may be understood as the people encompassing the State; and this complexifies the Zionist imaginary. As discussed in Chapter Two, the Zionist vision was one in which all Jews would move to the Jewish state, state and nation eventually becoming coterminous, though with the authority of the Zionist state encompassing its people. The State would be the prophetic culmination and salvific fulfillment of the teleological national endeavor. These ideals are consistent with Remembrance Day memorials on Mount Herzl, and with the transition there from Remembrance Day to Independence Day. But the Wall projects more ambiguous versions of the state/people relationship, ones more in keeping with religious and nationalist trends that have greatly accelerated their momentum since the 1967 War.[10]

The second note of ambivalence relates to the incipient dualism of a military/civilian division – of those in uniform and those not, with the implication that each sector is ordered by antithetical principles (see Ben-Eliezer 1998a). In the event this incipient opposition is stabilized by two factors: the sequencing of discursive action, and the spatial hierarchy characterizing the major signs. Following the lighting of the memorial flame, there are six discursive acts, in the following order: the President's speech, the Chief-of-Staff's speech, the reading by a civilian, the reading of psalms by the IDF rabbi, the recitation of kaddish by a bereaved father, and the recitation of 'God, full of mercy,' by the IDF cantor. The action of this sequence alternates between civilian and military. Less obviously, this sequence falls into three parts, each composed of a civilian and military figure and each given over (roughly speaking) to a different discursive genre. The President and Chief-of-Staff do speeches, the civilian and IDF rabbi do readings, the bereaved father and IDF cantor do recitations. Through this alternation and pairing there is a vivid expression of partnership and synchronization between the civilian and military sectors, in their joint commemorating of heroic death. The occasion and its versions of moral and social order depend on the full cooperation of these sectors. Yet the civilian sector is dominant: the President begins this sequence, and the first slot of each pair is filled by a civilian figure. The second feature stabilizing the incipient civilian-military dualism is that of hierarchy. The demonstration of hierarchy, including the subordination of the military to the civilian sector, is most evident in the spatial alignment during the kindling of the flame and the President's speech.

In its first minutes the entire thrust of the event is laid out along its east–west axis. From east to west along this axis are aligned the following: Wall, flag, memorial flame, President, Chief-of-Staff, and at the plaza's western edge, bereaved families, and behind them, spectators. Flame, flag, and Wall are imbued with eternality. The flame separates the eternal from the transiency of the living. Flame, flag, and Wall nest within one another, in accordance with 'encompassment.' The imaginary of people-hood (signed by the Wall) generates the State (signed by the flag). The imaginary of the State generates the soldiers who sacrifice their lives (signed by the flame) for the state. In the reverse direction, these soldiers are encompassed by the State, as this is encompassed by the people.[11]

On the side of the living the complex relationships of encompassment become simpler ones of rank. The President, the first citizen, is ranked higher than the Chief-of-Staff, who is first a citizen and second the commander-in-chief. The latter, at whose command the fallen entered combat, ranks higher than the bereaved families. In their sacrifice of their sons, the bereaved families exemplify the highest virtues among the rank-and-file of the people, who stand behind them. During these minutes the entire length of the east–west axis is constituted through principles of hierarchy, first of encompassment and then of rank-order. On the side of the living, this elongated alignment vividly shows the hierarchical relationship between the civilian and military sectors, that is continued through the alternation of discursive practices.

Lighting the memorial flame, the President articulates the living to eternal verities. We called this the moment when the living reach out to touch the dead. At the close of the President's address the lineal hierarchy is severed at the juncture between the living and the eternal. The President sits among the bereaved families. The first among the people is the first among mourners. For the remainder of the occasion the center of the plaza remains dark and vacant, separating the living from flame, flag, Wall. The living have drawn back from the eternal, and further activity is more distant from the flame, conveying reflection and contemplation on duty, heroism, loss, afterlife.

The most striking feature in the forming of this event is its monolithic shaping of unity through singularity. The singularity of theme is self-evident: architectonics, actions, utterances highlight the same focus of sacrifice, loss, mourning, and the meaning of heroic death for the continued existence of State and people. Yet singularity is prominent too in the ensemble of categories, in that there is but one of each: one Wall, one flag, one flame, one president, one chief-of-staff, one rabbi, one cantor, one bereaved male, one bereaved female, one female soldier (and the one language, Hebrew, is used throughout). Each category signifies a multitude in its typification, but each is one: the Wall signs all of the people, the flag all of the State, the flame all of the fallen, the President all of the citizenry, the Chief-of-Staff all of the armed forces, the bereaved male all bereaved males, the bereaved female all bereaved females, the female soldier all female soldiers. Each signed multitude is as one, a multitude of homogeneous equivalences within each category, unchanging throughout the occasion.

This oneness of semiotic condensation returns us to the principles of hierarchy informing the event. Once more the categories collapse, accordian-like, into one another in increasing orders, first of magnitude and then of encompassment. Through this extreme condensation the Jewish State stands as one.[12] In part, oneness stems from the inclusion of singular characters who can neither be duplicated nor varied: there is only one president, one chief-of-staff. Nonetheless, other signs (flag and flame, bereaved mother/widow, bereaved father, female soldier) easily could be multiplied, either in kind or in accordance with cultural codes of variation on a common theme. Yet throughout the occasion there is the decisive semiotic equation of oneness and unity.

The event is produced by the Ministry of Defense, and its forming owes much to this provenance. The lineal ordering of signs during the lighting of the flame has substantive affinities to military forms of monothetic ranked order, as discussed in Chapter Six.[13] Yet this hierarchical ordering is predicated not only on ranking and bureaucratic logic, but also on the encompassing capacity of higher-order signs to absorb those of lower order, and so to generate the latter. Hierarchy here depends on rank-ordering in the realm of the living, and on encompassment in the realm of the eternal, so that the latter encompasses and generates the former.[14]

The version of moral and social order presented through this event is marked by a sparseness and singularity of signs, by a homogeneity of membership, by a single-mindedness of intention, and by a oneness of being – of everything in its place in a continuous hierarchy of heritage and legacy, of the human and the super-human. An extremely holistic unity, in which each component imparts its sense of purpose to the one beneath, with no overt strain or competition.[15]

The occasion imparts an ordering of the national that is familial. At memorial services and festive gatherings alike, past and present members of armed forces units are called 'family.' On Remembrance Day the people are called the bereaved family. The Family metaphor has powerful associations: of common ancestry, of a close relationship between kinship and membership, of the warmth and support of kin relations, of the oneness and protectiveness of family spirit, of the relatively small number of kin roles that family structure offers, and of an inter-generational structure projecting itself into the future.

This atmosphere of familism is present in the lighting of the memorial flame. The fire is lit by the President, who structurally is a father-figure. He is aided by a bereaved woman. Together, the couple tend to kindling the memory of their dead sons. The older woman is escorted by a young one doing her national service. In terms of age and task, she fits the position of daughter, and of younger sister of the deceased. The flame is protected by an honor guard of four young male soldiers doing their national service. They fit the position of younger sons, and of brothers of the deceased. Behind the father President stand the two senior officers, fitting the position of older brothers of the deceased. A tightly-knit group within which the 'parents,' having procreated the sacrifice of their offspring, now procreate his memory, surrounded by living offspring with the potential to procreate the future (that may make of them the sacrifices of future wars). The grave is the cradle of the nation (see Zempleni 1999). Following his address the President sits with his wife among the bereaved families. They together with the others are the 'bereaved family,' the family-in-arms, indeed the family in-its-own-arms, embracing itself.[16] Is this 'family' a Jewish one? Without doubt. Though the occasion is one of mourning for all those who fell in the wars of the State (including Druze, Bedouin, and Circassians, all of whom have their own memorial occasions), the major signs are Jewish and the genres of mourning are those of Jewish liturgy. This event is closed and inward-looking, contemplative, reserved for members of the immediate family.

The major occasions of Remembrance Day itself are smaller-scale renditions of the opening event. Early that morning at an appointed hour a memorial flame is kindled in all military cemeteries, and memorial services are held in synagogues. In mid-morning, again at the appointed hour, sirens moan throughout the country for two minutes. This signals the beginning of memorial services in all military cemeteries. Synchronized with this, members of youth associations pay their respects at numerous memorial sites and markers. In this multitude of occasions, replicating the singular thematics and signs of the opening occasion, the dead are re-membered through their more particularistic affiliations: by region, community, locality, and military unit. Allowing for local variations, these occasions evince the remarkable degree of extreme unification of the national evident in the opening event.

Opening Independence Day, Opening the National (Somewhat)

> And the land is divided into districts of memory and provinces of hope,
> And its inhabitants blend with each other
> As people returning from a wedding merge with those returning from a funeral.
>
> Yehuda Amichai (1995: 338)
> With permission of HarperCollins Publishers

The event that closes Remembrance Day and opens Independence Day is held at Herzl's tomb, on the summit of his mountain. The architectonics of this occasion are radically distinct from those that opened Remembrance Day. We begin by discussing space, since its forming (like those of the openings of Holocaust Remembrance Day and Remembrance Day) encodes the version of moral and social order elaborated through performance. We then discuss the event, that falls into three segments. The first segment closes Remembrance Day. The second – composed of readings, songs, and the address of the Knesset Speaker – is a brief transition between the two Days. The third – the lighting of beacons and a military tattoo – celebrates the beginning of Independence Day. The entire occasion takes some forty minutes.

The spatial layout is orientated to a center, Herzl's black, basalt tombstone, encircled by flower beds. Before the tombstone is an open plaza, bounded on all three sides by

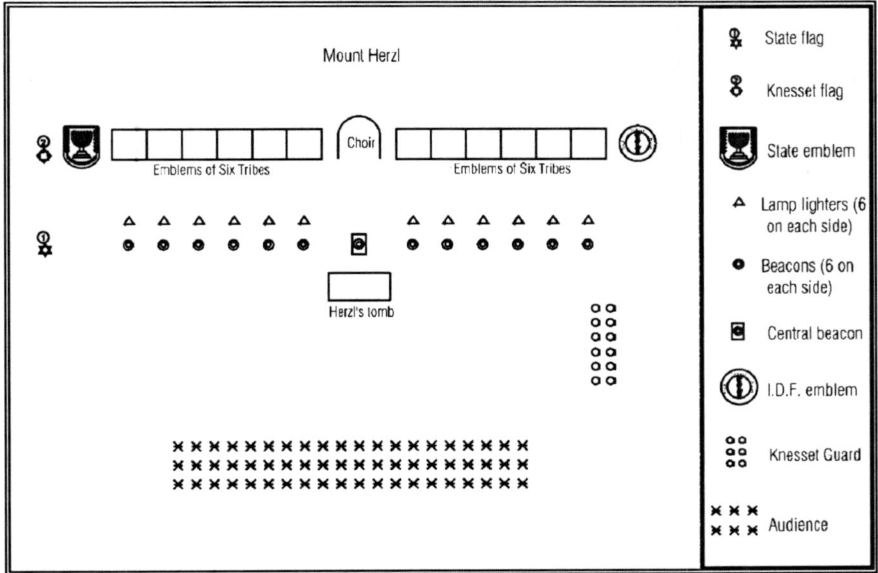

Figure 4 The opening event of Independence Day, spatial layout.

temporary bleachers for a diverse audience, including tourists from abroad and foreign diplomats. Behind the tombstone is a large circular, unlit beacon (see Figure 4). To each side of this central beacon is a row of six smaller, unlit beacons. Behind each set of six beacons are the painted emblems of six of the tribes of ancient Israel, again twelve in all. Below each emblem is inscribed the name of its tribe. Between these sets of beacons and emblems is a half-shell within which the choir stands. On the upper arch of the half-shell is inscribed a motto enunciating the theme of that year's Independence Day. To the north of the northerly set of tribal emblems is the official emblem of the State (the menorah, or seven-branched lamp). Immediately north again of this emblem is the flag of the Knesset. In front of this flag is that of the State, now at half-mast. To the south of the southerly set of tribal emblems is the emblem of the IDF. The circumference of the plaza is decorated by state flags. Next to the state flag is a small IDF honor guard. Announcements of what is to occur are made in three languages: Hebrew, English, and French.

To this point we note the following on these architectonics. In the pantheon of Israel, Herzl is the visionary of the Zionist state. But his figure is not one of encompassment. Herzl's figure is more the nexus of the national, of people and state, than it is one of hierarchy. Similarly, the other major signs and symbols of the event take their orientation from his tomb, but more in a formation of centricity and semi-clustering, than one of lineal, ranked hierarchy. In this formation the tomb is more pivot than apex, and any sense of hierarchy is more flattened than vertical.[17] The same holds for the central east–west axis of the event (tomb, central beacon, motto). Balanced to each side of the central axis, are equivalent sets of signs of the State (the beacons) and the people (the ancient tribes). All twelve beacons are equivalents of one another, as are all twelve tribes.

At its northern and southern edges, this ensemble is framed and contained by signs of the State: to the north by its emblem, Knesset flag, and national flag, signifying political autonomy and legislative authority, and to the south by the emblem of the IDF, signifying legislated might. The north–south axis (beacons, tribal emblems, signs of the state) is an expansion and elaboration in breadth of the values encoded in the central east–west axis (tomb, central beacon, motto). The overall forming is one of the state containing those who constitutes it, its citizenry and people.

From above, this semiotic space is formed as a broad, flattened triangle, anchored at its base by the signs of legislative authority and legislated might, and at its apex by the tomb of the visionary founder. The content of this horizontally inclined triangle is very much what this event, this imaginary of the national, is all about. Here the shaping of space depicts frontally a sense of breadth rather than of length, in contrast to the event opening Remembrance Day. The heterogeneity of signs in this event, including the composition of the audience, points to the relative openness of its boundaries, in contrast to the inwardly focused 'bereaved family' of Remembrance Day.

The announcer declares the event open, locating it in relation to Herzl's tomb (by stating that the assembled are 'facing the tomb of the visionary of Israel'). The lighting is indirect, the plaza dark. The Knesset Guard enters, filling the central space in close-order drill, taking up position in serried ranks at the southeastern edge. The Guard, commanded by the Knesset Speaker, is charged with security, protection, and order in the Knesset compound. The Guard's transposition to Mount Herzl signals major themes in this event.

The Speaker enters, flanked by two senior IDF officers. The three sit just in front of the first row of spectators at the western edge, facing the tomb, but rise immediately as a soldier marches forward, telling the Speaker the event is ready, asking his permission to proceed. The Speaker assents. The occasion is enacted under the auspices of the Speaker. Elected by the Knesset from among its membership, the Speaker is the head of this assembly, charged with numerous tasks of adjudication and mediation in its functioning. Though a representative of a political party, he is expected to become more apolitical. Of the 120 Knesset members, the structural equivalents of one another, he is the first among equals. Just as the President officially is the first citizen of the state, so the Speaker is the first citizen of its parliament. There is a direct structural link between the offices of President and Speaker. Should the President be unable to carry out his duties, the Speaker becomes President *pro tem*. In this occasion, through the agency of Speaker and Guard, Knesset values of legislative democracy and egalitarianism are transposed to Mount Herzl. As in the previous two Days, the openly partisan, political leadership of the country is conspicuous by its absence from active participation.

The *yizkor* memorial prayer follows, asking the people of Israel to remember their war dead.[18] The prayer is the final act of Remembrance Day, and its note of civil rhetoric is unlike the ritual liturgies recited during the event that opened this Day. This prayer shifts focus from the level of the eternal to that of the human and the celebration of State and people. As the state flag is run to the masthead, accompanied by bugling, the announcer declares the end of Remembrance Day. The shadowy sadness of darkness lifts as the plaza is illuminated, and the full panoply of varied and colorful signs is fully revealed. Some seven minutes of the event have elapsed.

The second segment consists of alternate readings and songs, closing with the address of the Speaker. The readings convey a mood of historical transition, paralleling the shift from one Day to the next. The first reading typically is from the biblical books of the Prophets, giving voice to the ancient tie between the people and the land. The following readings take up the modern legacy of ancient longings, the ingathering of the exiles, the people returning to their land. The songs, spirited and tuneful, are modern folk-songs (often called in Hebrew, 'songs of the people'). The choir is an amateur group, composed of persons whose song is vocation, not profession. They sing out of affection for the music and the love of the land that it expresses. These values of free choice and vocation characterize all of the civilians who hold center stage during this event.

These readings and songs are mood-shifters between the two Days. The few minutes of their performance are the sole acknowledgement of the existential difficulty of switching abruptly from mourning to celebration. This brief period changes the focus of occasion in another way. Remembrance Day is preoccupied with the duty of the people to the State and the obligation to remember the fallen. But this period of reading and song introduces the spirit of voluntarism, and its centrality to the free and independent people and State. Readings of biblical prophecy, fated and deterministic, give way to the free-spirited pioneering of nation-building. Above all, to the desire of choosing freely to return, echoing the romanticism of Herzl's most quoted words: 'If you will it, it is no dream.' Moving into Independence Day, the embrace of vocation comes to the fore, giving full expression to the architectonics of this occasion, leaving behind verticality and determinism. This intermediate segment is closed by the address of the Speaker, standing next to the tomb. This is the sole niche in all three opening events in which a participant is quite free to express himself as he wishes, as citizen and individual. Some Speakers treat their address as a stocktaking, sometimes critical, sometimes laudatory, of the moral condition of the State during the previous year. Others ignore, for example, issues of racism, violence, and other dangers to democracy.

The opening event of Remembrance Day is monolithic, singular, evoking a monochromatic mood of subordination and sacrifice for the sake of the national whole. No doubts or questions are even intimated. Moral and social unity are presented as harmonious from top to bottom, without the slightest cracks in public opinion. The event opening Independence Day demands unquestioned allegiance to the State, yet proceeds to enumerate various aspects of the body politic, like and unlike, sometimes showing their integration to be imbalanced and imperfect, at least here and there. The Speaker talks as the first among equals, close to his fellows, with a minimum of ritualized rhetoric. The message often is one of the individual's responsibility for a society continuously in the making, changing in its contours from year to year. The design of this event contains this small window of opportunity to evoke greater reflexivity towards moral and social order.[19]

At the close of his address the Speaker declares the beginning of Independence Day celebrations, and lights the central beacon. The lighting of the beacons is the highlight of the occasion. The entire event sometimes is called 'the lighting of beacons on Mount Herzl,' and these have been kindled on this mount since 1952 (Levinsky 1957: 501; Don-Yehiye 1984: 15). The number of beacons is identified explicitly with the twelve tribes of the ancient people. In the early years the beacons were lit by twelve new immigrants from different countries, embodying the 'ingathering of the exiles,' moving from the foreboding darkness of the diaspora to the light of Israel on the mountain top, kindled anew by the efforts of those who ascended there.

The template of twelve tribes, twelve beacons, is a horizontal taxonomy, a plural formation whose categories (the beacons) turn any content within them into an egalitarian vision of social order. This is in distinct contrast to the vertical, singular formation of the Remembrance Day occasion, that admits no variation. The Independence Day formation plays on what Nathaniel Tarn (1976: 28–9) calls detotalization and retotalization. These two aspects are combined in presentation – the whole and its parts are simultaneously on view and open to inspection, continually constituted through one another in the vision of viewers.

The motif of the twelve tribes is the key to how this occasion expands out of the monochromatic singularity and hierarchy of Remembrance Day. As this commonly is understood, the twelve tribes were the offspring of the Sons of Jacob: the people were divided into twelve different units of affiliation, in principle the equivalents of one another. Added together, these units formed the entire people. Nonetheless, each tribe had its own identity (as its emblem implies), different from every other. Therefore the twelve included diversity within their egality, heterogeneity within their equivalency. This is consonant with the Zionist vision of relationships among different Jewish ethnicities, discussed in Chapter Three. The imagery of the ancient tribes presents the entire people in the mold of pluralism and equality. The analogy of the tribes to the modern people casts the latter in the same mold, retaining their mythic relationship of forebears and descendants. The people are the Jewish State, with both presented here in the mold of egalitarian pluralism. Any non-Jew (Druze, Palestinian, Bedouin) within this national template is present as an honored guest, but a guest nonetheless.

This public event is keyed to a dominant theme chosen annually. The theme is enunciated in the motto, is evident to a degree in the Speaker's address, but is highlighted especially in the choice of the lamplighters. The theme is chosen by a committee of public figures and educators. Every second year the choice of theme is coordinated with one promoted by the Ministry of Education in the country's schools. As in the past, the event is intended as didactic (Don-Yehiye 1984: 12). In contrast to the eternality of Remembrance Day, this opening event is made a bit more dynamic, attuned to changing national moods. Thus the theme may be intended to advance trends perceived as positive, or to counter destructive ones.[20]

The twelve lamplighters are chosen (by committee) because their lives, deeds, or affiliations are thought to exemplify or embody that year's theme. The Speaker lights the central beacon, delegating the others to follow suit. The first among equals passes the torch of renewal to people who are the full equals of one another. The beacon lighter is flanked by a young male soldier who holds a lit torch and by a young female soldier who holds out a microphone. The lighter, on a podium, is raised above the flanking military pair. Before each kindling, with stirring music in the background, the lighter dedicates the beacon in terms of that year's theme. The dedication itself is formulaic: I [full name of the lighter], the son/daughter of [the names of his/her father and mother], [followed by the title, position, or dwelling-place of the lighter], am honored to light this beacon, to the [numbered] year of independence of the State of Israel, in honor of [there follows the recitation of social categories, sectors of population, institutions, regions, deeds, and so forth, that the lighter is representing], and to the glory of the State of Israel.' The lighter accepts the torch from the male soldier, lights the beacon, and the focus shifts to the next.

The following points emerge from these practices. The Speaker, the elected first among equals, represents the Knesset of 120 elected members, just as they together are the legislative body of the entire citizenry. Analogously, each of the twelve lamplighters is here the 'first among equals' of that segment of the population he or she represents in the event. Together, the lamplighters (overwhelmingly Jewish) represent the entire citizenry, as it is organized taxonomically by the theme of that year's Independence Day. In the event, the speaker plus the twelve lamplighters are the metaphor for the elect of the Knesset in the daily life of the state. The first words of the formulaic dedication of each beacon (I, [name of lighter], the son/daughter of [name of father and mother]) are similar to the first words of the swearing in of a new Member of Knesset.

As is frequent in Zionist cosmology, signs in the present are made to play on and evoke what is perceived as the ancient past. In Zionist cosmology the recent and distant pasts are 'hot chronologies,' 'those of periods where in the eye of the historian numerous events appear as differential elements' (Lévi-Strauss 1966: 259). These are the periods full of occurrences of national import. Since the distant past is perceived as a spiritual ancestor and spatial precursor of the present, metaphors of their temporal continuity are elaborate.

Continuing for a moment with these temporal analogies, one of the meanings of the word, knesset, is that of 'The Great Knesset' (*Knesset Hagedola*), the Council of Sages, 120 in number, and ruling body of the people during the period of the Talmud. The Knesset takes the number of its members from this ancient body. Another meaning of the word, knesset, is that of the 'Great Assembly of Israel' (*Knesset Yisrael*), that during the talmudic period was used analogously to the 'Whole of Israel' (*Clal Yisrael*), a term that was equivalent to the People of Israel (*Am Yisrael*). In the present day, deliberately echoing these textual sources, the Speaker represents the parliament of Israel, the Knesset, that represents the People of Israel in their modern reformulation as the citizenry of the Jewish State, the whole of Israel. Similarly, the twelve lamplighters represent the citizenry of the Jewish State, again the whole of Israel. The signs of beacon lighters and Speaker resonate strongly with one another, as do the collectivities they respectively represent, the Jewish national and its Knesset.

In turn the lamplighters recall the twelve tribes, with whom they are paired and whose emblems stand behind the former. The twelve tribes were the primeval people led out of ancient Egypt in the exodus, to become the People of Israel in Sinai. In a later era, the People were governed by the Council of Sages, 120 in number . . . These temporal cross-references are teleological in their sentiment, chronological in their historicity. Their intent is to sound the 'hot' past for recurring echoes of the present, grounding historical progression, the 'march of history,' from the former to the latter. In this semiotic there is the deliberate knotting together of timelines and place markers. This encourages collapsing time, so that present is identified with past in the same space, and, too, the elongation of time, drawing out the long strands of continuousness between present and past, again in the same space. The relationship between now and then is metaphorized as so very lengthy, yet so immediate. Yet foremost, the beacon lighting foregrounds relationships in the present: the metaphoric delegation of peoplehood and its representation, from Herzl (the modern vision) to the Speaker (the democratic parliament), to the twelve lamplighters (the free and independent Jewish citizenry) who reflect continuity with the ancient twelve tribes (ancestry, identity, history).

The dedication of beacons spells out the plural version of moral and social order by articulating personhood, a sector of society, and the 'glory' of the state. Lamplighters identify themselves by name, parentage, and location in society. Each is not only a (Jewish) citizen, but also a named individual with a personal history, appearing in the event voluntarily. This individualization of the beacon lighters is signed also by their dress. In contrast to the uniformity of the military and Guard, the lighters dress as they please. That of the men varies from open-necked shirt or sweater and trousers to suit and tie; that of the women from fancy dresses to blouse and slacks. Through their self-adornment they embody their own individuality (though this may be stereotypic). The Jewish State is presented as composed of autonomous individuals, each signing more than his or her self, and each dedicated to a common thematic and to the greater good of the national.

Depending on choice of theme and lamplighters, the national vision of the event may be one of the harmonic integration of a complex heterogeneity of identities, often at odds in the social world beyond the occasion. In one particular year, for the example, the kindling of beacons brought together a diversity of persons who in the usual course of living would have little or nothing to do with one another. Their number included a kibbutz member, a resident of an economically depressed town, a Druze soldier, two rabbis (one Sephardi, the other Ashkenazi), the wife of a Yemenite rabbi, a Muslim Palestinian teacher of Arabic, and new Jewish immigrants from Iran, Ethiopia, Russia, and the United States. In daily life the lines of potential cleavage among these marked identities approached the exponential. Within the event, these identities coexisted in their common cause of kindling the beacons.

As in the opening event of Remembrance Day, here too the monothetic taxonomies (the twelve lamplighters, the Twelve Tribes) are Jewish and national – semiotically, historically, mythically. The project of making citizenship national continues. Though there are contradictions of citizenship, nationality, and religion when a non-Jewish lamplighter stands in front of the totem of an ancient Israelite tribe, while lighting a beacon to the glory of the Jewish State, the problem is more the lamplighter's. Whether this lamplighter is mediating changing conceptions of nationhood and citizenship, is an 'honorary Jew' in the Jewish state, or is a powerful magnet for conflicting claims cleaving the country outside of the occasion, he is the one in ambiguous synchronization with the event. The event is not of out of synch with the lamplighter. The national is Jewish.

Until the early 1970s lighting the beacons ended the occasion. Then a military tattoo was grafted onto the event. The foci of the tattoo are the official flags of the State and the IDF. During the preceding year the flags were entrusted to one branch of the armed forces. During the tattoo these flags are given over to the safekeeping of another branch, until next year's Independence Day. In this closing phase the national is summarized in its most popular of signs, the flag, given over to the protection of the armed forces. The tattoo is colorful and full of disciplined, rapid movement. The music is martial, the armed forces dominant. This shift to the tattoo effaces the voluntarism of diversity brought to the fore by lighting the beacons. Regimentation of difference (the colors and uniforms of the participating units) and closure of ranks, dominate. The Jewish State is again taxonomized rigidly, its borders hardened. The addition of the tattoo juxtaposes two alternative endings to the overall narrative sequence of the three Days. The most popular is perceiving the beacon lighting as climactic, the tattoo as a colorful show. Still, these versions – Jewish democracy or disciplined nation-in-arms – interact continuously since the State's founding to gladden, bewilder, and frighten people.

The shift from Remembrance Day to Independence Day complements the shift from family loyalty to national allegiance, discussed in Chapter Four. In the kindergarten the shift indexes the maturation of the little child. Here the shift indexes the maturation of the family through the sacrifice of its children to protect and regenerate the holism of the national. The loss of the child is the birth (and rebirth) of the State. The national, the Jewish State, is the offspring of its people, then maturing to exist in its own right. The classic poem of sacrificing the child to the national in Palestine was written in 1947 by the poet, Nathan Alterman, and entitled 'The Silver Platter'

(*Magash Hakesev*). Alterman envisaged the death of a generation, whose bodies are the silver platter upon which the yet unborn state would be given to the Jewish people. Three decades ago the playwright, Hanoch Levin, in his satire, *Queen of the Bathtub*, savaged this idea of sacrifice:

> Dear father, when you stand over my grave
> Old and tired and very much alone
> And you see how my body is interred in the earth – ask my forgiveness,
> my father.[21]

The public was outraged, the project of making citizenship national continued. The semiosis of family and family-in-arms, so powerful if implicit in the opening events of Holocaust Remembrance Day and Remembrance Day, is completely absent from the opening event of Independence Day. The family-in-arms nurtured by the national into begetting the State disappears as the State fully matures into the entity that rules itself in its own right.

The event ends formally with the national anthem, not sung at the close of the opening of Remembrance Day, indicating again the intimacy between these occasions.[22] Just as the Remembrance Day event begins with the kindling of a single flame, so that of Independence Day climaxes with the lighting of multiple flames, signing without contradiction the originary source of both national sacrifice and national rebirth. In the spirit of its opening event, Independence Day offers an elaborate variety of activities, planned and informal. Like its opening event, this Day tries to offer something to the bulk of the people. Among these activities are an international bible quiz for youth and the awards of the Israel Prizes. Both are televised live. The Prizes are the highest public accolade that the State offers to the life works of its living scholars, writers, and public-spirited citizens. This Day celebrates the excellence of achievement by named individuals through the competition of youth and the capping of careers. To the close of this Day, the Jewish national is cast in a more plural and egalitarian vision, here of the achievements of mind.[23] Just as the monolithic singularity of Remembrance Day is opened by the President, so the closing of Independence Day, the awarding of the twelve Prizes, is held in his presence. The vision of each Day keeps its integrity, just as the two are joined in their completion.

National Cosmology and the Encoding of Rhythmic Time

> The past throws stones at the future,
> And all of them fall on the present.
>
> Yehuda Amichai (1995: 465)
> With permission of HarperCollins Publishers

Chapter Five commented that the lineal encoding of time creates sequential narrative, generating cumulative and climactic story-lines. These story-lines are progressions, similar to those we call 'history.' In this section we argue that the commonsensicality for Israeli Jews of the national sequence of Holocaust Remembrance Day, Remembrance Day, Independence Day, and the story-lines this sequence generates, are grounded in and empowered by axioms of time in general Jewish culture. As we noted earlier in this Chapter, these axioms are rhythmic. They pulsate an impetus through Jewish cultural time, though without forming the contextualized interpretations attributed to temporality, whether as history or myth.

We begin with properties of time self-evident to Israeli Jews, turning then to a more developed interpretation of the national narrative, whose practice receives especial elaboration through the sequencing of these three Days. We argue further that this narrative encodes the story-lines it does because its sequencing reproduces experientially the rhythmics of time referred to above. Therefore we discuss this rhythm, and some of the durations through which it is encoded and practiced. In conclusion, we return to the sequence of the three Days, and to time as the blueprint of history.

The self-evident encoding of time in Zionism is summarized succinctly by Lewis (1985: 138–9): the 'existential thrust [of Zionism] is deeply rooted in the ethnohistory of the Jewish people. In this, it adopts a conception of time implicit in the Bible, a view that suggests that the meaning of the Jewish people is intimately bound up with the working out of Jewish history.' Religious thought commonly links the ingathering of the exiles to the onset of redemption for the people, and to the enhancement of their spiritual perfection, increasing the likelihood of God's intervention in history to end time, beginning utopic existence. Zionist time adopts and adapts the idea of the ingathering, making the viability of the Jewish State contingent on this. The national becomes the means to the physical and spiritual unification of the people and their moral purification and renewal. The rational national will bring about the redemption that Ben-Gurion called, 'a model people and a model state.' Yet this attainment depends upon a metaphysic of Becoming: exile, return, redemption. Achieving utopia denies yet embraces a temporal rhythm of Jewish cultural time.

The encoding of time as a metaphysic of Becoming is essential to the sequence of the three Days, experienced as temporal progression. To give meaning to time is to generate history.[24] History concretizes the temporal continuity within which the three opening events become phases. Yet the temporal rhythm of these three events is akin to a musical scale of three ascending tones, and so too is the history this rhythm encodes.

The opening event of Holocaust Remembrance Day commemorates the horrific destruction of European Jewry, the destruction of the Diaspora. More abstractly, the Holocaust signifies the rupturing of Jewish humanity: disconnection of all vital values, uncoupling of all essential relationships, dismemberment of all community and collectivity, of social body and human body, inevitably leading to death. Through its absolute negation of the human, the Holocaust is ramified destruction on the cosmic scale, a huge death-world in Wyschogrod's (1985) phenomenology, organized teleologically to take life deliberately from the living, and for Jewry, the experiencing of the primeval extinction of cosmos.

The opening event of Remembrance Day practices the polar opposite of the destruction of presence, utterly negating this. The national replaces the diaspora. The event presents the Jewish State as the moral order of a monothetic taxonomy of ramified hierarchy. Every element of the social has its proper place and is located there, while all elements are interrelated in principled ways within rigid, inward-looking borders, inclusive and exclusive. The event practices unity, yet a unity verging on encompassment; and encompassment in its primordial, mythic agency speaks to the creation of cosmos from absence, in Judaic cosmogony. This event is a statement of severely sinewed integration, of a total cosmos of extreme order made from primordial chaos through sacrifice – itself an ancient mythic theme of cosmogenesis – and itself forming presence from absence, creation from extinction. Every (war) sacrifice continues primordial themes of cosmogenesis.

The opening event of Independence Day celebrates the fruition of the living Zionist cosmos, the Jewish State. On the foundation of its exacting certainty and ordered solidity, the external boundaries and internal sinews of the Jewish cosmos are relaxed, integration is decentralized, pluralism (within taxonomies of the Jewish) is extolled, variance in ways of living is more tolerated, individual will and creativity are encouraged.

This practice of cosmogony echoes Zionist allegories of biblical and liturgical process. This cosmogony is a story-line of Becoming, elemental to Zionist credo, a forming of form taken for granted and practiced over and again in public and private acts, as a schema for in-forming the world with significance and meaning. In keeping with Ricoeur's (1984: 206–25) understanding of Judeo-Christian narrative, if this story-line did not exist, neither would Zionism as we know it. Yet in-forming the world with sense is what any principled practicing of cosmologic is about. Here the force of practice is augmented by its embeddedness in the cosmology of the national, this modern imaginary of power enshaped, but monothetically, through the forming power of bureaucratic logic. We argued that the narrative structure is encoded and practiced in the scheduling of Days, in their topological inscription, and in the events that activate, practice, and unify these matrices of time and space as chronological history. The practice of this cosmology of the national is characterized by extreme redundancy, of the same set of messages encoded through numerous media.

These three national days encode narratives like the cosmogonic because their sequencing is the experiencing of an elementary rhythm of time in Jewish culture. How to explicate this rhythm?[25] Zerubavel (1985: 115) comments that the Jewish week is characterized by a peak day, the Sabbath, imparting a 'beat' to the week. He continues: 'The experience of beat is essentially a sensation of a throbbing pulsation.' The Jewish week is a unit of cultural time that pulsates in accordance with a certain beat, or impulsion.[26]

This rhythm of temporal pulsation is embedded deeply in numerous units of time in Jewish culture. Once more, this pulsation is a beat from lower to higher, from ordinary to extraordinary. The rhythm is climactic, the impulsion coding movement from the less valued to the highly valued. This impulsion also may be experienced as movement from fragmentation to unity, integration, holism. In keeping with this climactic pulsation, the abstract forming of time is, generally speaking, that of cumulating directional development and collective becoming.

As important for our purpose is the premise that the movement of time, the fixing of times, are imbued with the moral valuation of the human condition (Kaufmann 1972: 73). Becoming is in the first instance (and in the last) a moral problem; and time, the medium of becoming, is necessarily the moral ordering of existence. The pulsation of Jewish time was and is the forming and encoding of the impulsion of moral order, through different durations.

In the biblical myth of cosmogenesis the creation of time, the separation of light from darkness, day from night (Genesis 1: 3–5), is almost isomorphic with the onset of cosmic creation (and with the initial forming of cosmic taxonomy), while the entire creative process is encoded by consecutively numbered days, culminating in the seventh, which God blessed and made holy. As the medieval philosopher Maimonides (1956: 171) stated, 'Even time itself is among the things created.' Whereupon he added (for his own purposes) that the 'true and essential condition' of time 'is not to remain in the same state for two consecutive moments.' Time is inherently processual.

That time has a special status in Jewish thought is not in question. Heschel (1951: 8) writes that, 'Judaism is a religion of time . . . The main themes of faith lie in the realm of time.' The nineteenth-century Orthodox thinker, Hirsch (1985: 41) stated that,'The catechism of the Jew consists of his calendar.' Once time is created, everything else (with the exception of the Creator) happens within and during continuous time. Heschel (1951: 100) argues that 'it is within time that we are able to sense the unity of all beings.'

This evokes a crucial characteristic of this temporality. Time is continuous with cosmos. Moreover, time is the one matrix of cosmos that never falters, that never loses its continuous self-coherence, integrity, unity. Time is not entropic. By contrast, space is alienated (by expulsion), fragmented (by destruction). Desired space at best is the promise of time: elsewhere, attainable only through the coherent continuity and integrity of time. People are perceived over and again as dissipating their moral virtues, shattering their collective endeavors, dislocating in space, suffering dispersal. All strivings for utopic perfection, for the unification of people and place develop within and through the pulsating rhythms of time, encoded as a moral order of becoming. The eschatological visions of traditional Judaism, of God intervening in time to end time, point to the essential integrity of this matrix. Time ends when it is no longer necessary – when its processual shepherding of Becoming is completed.

The matrix of time (and texts documenting 'times' and 'timing') holds everything together in the Jewish phenomenal world.[27] As Newton-Smith (1980: 88) comments, 'relative to our system of beliefs, non-unified time is a much more outlandish possibility than non-unified space.' In secular Zionist discourse, ethno-history has pride of place rather than time. Yet to appreciate the practice of this ethno-history one must recognize that its 'sensible' interpretations are harmonics resonating with rhythms of cultural time, whether perceived in secular or in religious terms. In a phenomenology of Jewish life, time is a root metaphor expanding into three dimensions of existence.

First, time expands into the continuous totality of the world, never shattering, never losing its resilience or integrity. This view of cultural time is akin to what Wittgenstein termed 'logical space' – determining nothing, yet suggesting which combinations of elements are possible. Second, time signifies movement towards (and away from) the actualization of moral unities or completions within this totality. Third, this movement often is encoded in terms of the rhythmic pulsation of duration we sketched earlier. This rhythm of pulsation – low to high, morally inferior to morally superior – beats through different durations of Jewish time, from the short to the lengthy.

Consider the pulsation of the Jewish twenty-four hour day. In the phrasing of Genesis (1: 5), 'And the evening and the morning were the first day.' The Jewish day begins in darkness and moves into light. Light has more valued connotations of morality and capability, than does darkness. In a simple yet ever-continuing way this night-day (Hirsch 1985: 42) condenses and practices the momentum of cosmogonic and existential movement.

Consider the pulsation of the Jewish week. It moves through six ordinary days, peaking at the extraordinary seventh, that Heschel (1951: 14) calls 'the climax of living,' with its own distinctive, superior character (Zerubavel 1985: 113). In the biblical text, 'the Sabbath commemorates the creation' (Kaufmann 1972: 117), again practicing that elementary momentum.

Consider the pulsation of holidays like Purim, Passover, and Hanukkah. Purim is preceded by a fast day, commemorating the period of trepidation and repentance when the Jews of Persia were under dire threat. On the eve of the holiday the story of their salvation is read. The following day is one of celebration and jubilation. Passover is preceded by a fast day, commemorating the time of trial when the first-born of the Egyptians were slain while those of the Israelites were protected. On the eve of the holiday the story of the exodus is read. Hanukkah too is a tale of trial and triumph. The beat of all these holidays moves from the low of tribulation to the high of triumph. But their peak, like that of the Sabbath, is celebrated during their eves, in darkness. The reversal of the usual night-day significance ushers in their special climactic beat, as darkness is eclipsed, turning into the height of light.

Consider rhythms of longer duration. Every Sabbath service includes a reading from the Torah (the Pentateuch), concluding with a reading, called *haftarah* (literally, 'conclusion'), usually from the books of Prophets. Exegeses tend to link the meanings of these sets of readings, of a given Sabbath. Consider the rhythmic pulsation of the readings, in Ashkenazic tradition, for six Sabbaths that fall in sequence between the end of the Hebrew month of *Shevat* (February–March) and Passover (March–April).[28] Here we review this implicit rhythm in brief, without discussing substantive details (texts and commentaries are available in Hertz 1938).

The first of these Sabbaths is called *Shekalim*. The Torah reading tells of the obligation of every Israelite to contribute a half-shekel towards the upkeep of the Temple. This has been interpreted as an annual renewal of collective membership (Hirsch 1985: 323; Vainstein 1953: 139). The associated Haftarah tells of revolt against foreign idolators, of the enemy within and of their destruction (Hertz 1938: 954). The second, called *Zakhor* ('remember'), precedes Purim. The Torah reading recalls the unprovoked, vicious attack of Amalek on the Israelites, following the exodus. The Haftarah tells of Saul's extermination of the Amalekites. Both readings relate to the destruction of the enemy without. Haman, the arch-enemy of the Jews of Persia who is destroyed at Purim, commonly is assimilated as a descendant of Amalek.

The third of these Sabbaths is called *Parah* ('heifer'). Its readings are on themes of purification, bodily and moral, and on renewal of the nation from within, preparatory to the fruition of the desolate land (Hertz 1938: 961). The fourth is *Hakhodesh* ('the month'). Its Torah reading describes preparations for Passover, the festival of the exodus. The Haftarah is part of a prophecy of the New Jerusalem, arising when exile is ended. The fifth, *Shabbat Hagadol* (Great Sabbath), is the Sabbath prior to Passover. The Haftarah concludes with a vision of the coming of the Prophet Elijah, in religious tradition the herald of redemption who would appear at Passover-time (Hertz 1938: 967). The sixth of these Sabbaths falls during Passover itself. Its Haftarah is Ezekiel's great vision of the dry bones returning to life, of resurrection and redemption: 'I will open your graves, and cause you to come up out of your graves, and bring you into the land of Israel' (Ezekiel 37: 12).[29]

The sequence of these Sabbath texts encodes crescendo, including the peaks of Purim and Passover. The sequence begins with the corruption from within, its expulsion, and the renewal of collective identity. It continues with the collective response to evil from without; and then with themes of purification and cleansing from within. The subsequent texts relate to visions ending fragmentation and exile, and to the onset of reunification and perfection, climaxing during Passover, itself identified with the primordial coalescence of the Israelites in their collective deliverance from oppression.

Consider the period of fifty days (seven weeks of seven days, plus one day), called Counting the Omer (*Sefirat Ha'omer*). This begins on Passover and continues until the holiday of Shavu'ot, identified with first-fruits and with the giving of the Torah, the voluntary surrender of freedom in contractual relationship with God. This period is one of quasi-mourning, broken once by the holiday of Lag B'omer. In traditional exegeses, this sad period has assimilated numerous catastrophes, most recently that of the Holocaust (through the timing of Holocaust Remembrance Day). However the Chief Rabbinate proclaimed Independence Day, occuring during this duration, a time of rejoicing, thereby likening it to Lag B'omer (Vainstein 1953: 156–60). Thus time beats in diminuendo, rising to the minor peak of Lag B'omer, and then to the climax of Shavu'ot.[30] The sequence of Passover (the struggle for freedom from slavery) to Shavu'ot (the contractual surrender of freedom) has its own analogies to the sequence of Holocaust Remembrance Day (oppression, annihilation, struggle), Remembrance Day (the cohering nation continuing the struggle for freedom), and Independence Day (the voluntary, contractual relationship between Jewish citizen and State).

Consider the lengthiest duration of Jewish religious time, the eschatological. Whether progressively incremental or apocalyptic, time pulsates towards the climactic and utopic, towards the moral unification and perfection of the cosmos.

In sketching these durations of this ethno-logic of time, we avoided discussion of specific cultural substance – whether this logic is peculiar to Jewish (and Western) cultural rhythms, and whether time can be ordered, lived, and anticipated otherwise (the likelihood is that it can). We addressed a certain ordering of time and one of its prominent rhythms, that of climactic pulsation through various durations nesting within one another, overlapping and practicing one another. There is change in particular referents and interpretations of time, yet its elementary rhythm and phenomenal experiencing remain – whether for secular, traditional, or orthodox Jewry.[31]

This rhythm of time – pulsating and climactic, felt morally, lineally moving from low to high, holding within itself impulsions from fragmentation to unification – shares much in common with visions of progression in secular Zionism. The proviso is that here time is not perceived as teleological. These secular visions of progress are old-fashioned in the uncertain postmodern era, yet still operative in common sense, for all that. Remember that the State of Israel officially adopted the Hebrew Calendar, the Hebrew Sabbath as the weekly day of rest, and much of the annual cycle of holidays, thereby attuning the existence of the State to these temporal pulsations. Secular Zionists sloughed off the strictures of teleological religious tradition. Yet secular and religious alike continue to have in common the rhythmics of time and what constitutes a proper narrative structure.[32]

The sequence of the three Days reflects the significance accorded to the encoding of cultural time, and a plethora of examples could be adduced. The cosmology of Zionism depends on its practice, control, and elaboration of time – on the forming of temporal sequence and process. The forming of national history is generated through temporal rhythms, and within this ethno-history the Jewish State is legitimated to itself. This hegemony of ethno-history constitutes a moral economy of time, one keyed to innumerable injunctions to remember.

The ordering of Days is formed through the cultural rhythms of time, and this sequence is itself constituted to encode other durations, themselves the formations of these rhythms. Thus the narrative structure of the Days enables the encoding of Zionist temporality on different planes of abstraction and time scales. The most abstract plane is the encoding of cosmic process, of an implicit narrative of creation, from absence to cosmos. Its temporal scale, grand and mythic, is a cosmic root-metaphor. The temporal momentum of this plane is one of unidirectional coalescence and progression.

The second plane, in keeping with Zionist 'hot' chronologies, encodes time as modern history. Its scale is roughly the twentieth century. This plane explicitly tells the narrative of the Holocaust, the death of Diaspora, the birth of the State, within which peoplehood is again made viable, progressing towards the utopic vision. Its temporal momentum is again one of unidirectional progression, echoing the cosmological.

The third plane encodes time as a more immediate, shorter duration. Its temporal scale is that of Israel from independence through the present. Its markers of chronological division are those of 'the interrupted system' – of war and peace, crisis and relative normalcy (Kimmerling 1985). By Israeli reckoning, Israel has fought six wars and two Palestinian uprisings since the declaration of independence. Each of these (apart from the Lebanon War of 1982) is characterized consensually as a war of defense. Each demands the mobilization of the people. Every mobilization shifts social order from a plural vision to a singular one, from personal autonomy to the duty of the nation-in-arms, from free will to the constraining intimacy of the family-in-arms and the mourning family, from egalitarianism to hierarchy. Every crisis footing (including the current Intifada) practices the extreme unification of order informing the opening event of Remembrance Day; while relative normalcy practices the pluralism of the opening event of Independence Day. On this plane of encoding, the narrative of Days becomes the relationship between a closed and an open society, and of the dependence of the latter for its survival on the former. The only alternative offered is the descent into chaos and absence, and Holocaust Remembrance Day girds consciousness with the borders of Auschwitz as national pulsation and terrain are shaken.

On this plane, temporal momentum is asymmetrical (depending on the chronology of war and crisis) and oscillating. Oscillation is embedded deeply in Israeli Jewish perception and sentiment, though not a necessary feature of this cosmology. Oscillation is an emergent property of Israeli Jewish practice and experience understood through cosmology. Israel's major wars are moments of creation, since the conditions of viable national survival are put to the question. The alternative is akin to the annihilation of the Zionist cosmos. Victory is perceived as re-creation, as the moral moment of the high amplitude of Jewish time, resonating with all other high amplitudes. Making war is re-creating order out of the threat of the chaotic, with all that this entails (see for example, Greenhouse 1989).[33]

Every war evokes the temporal logic of planes of lengthier duration. Yet the emergent, oscillating momentum of this most immediate temporal plane also threatens to encode a sense of circular inevitability into the relationship between crisis and normalcy. This coding of temporality is dangerous yet prevalent, since it changes the valence of its poles of oscillation. In Zionist linear history, it is Independence Day, its relative democracy and humanism, that signify the climax of temporal progression, and not the catastrophe and violence of Holocaust Remembrance Day and Remembrance Day. Yet, coded as oscillation, the autarchic imaginary of these Days rises, becoming symmetrical with or overriding the imaginary of Independence Day.[34]

The fourth plane encodes this temporality most overtly, in a still shorter duration, that of the year, annual and cyclical. On this plane the Days monitor the Jewish State in close dialogue with itself about the meaning of its own history, and the relationship of this to the present ceaselessly becoming the uncertain future. On this plane, Holocaust Remembrance Day reflects on the chaos that was, and warns against present-day dangers presaging this descent into nihilism. The boundaries of the people, the terrain of the State, the pulsating of time, are all signposted with danger. Remembrance Day reflects on the battle and sacrifice to form and keep the Jewish State. From this the people are made whole; the borders affirmed and manned; the pulsation of time directed upward. Independence Day celebrates the fruition of this temporal progression in the present.

The encoding of national history on these different temporal planes has two significant consequences for national cosmology. First, the narratives encoded by public events telescope into and expand out of one another with little contradiction, since these narratives are harmonics of, and resonate with, analogous pulsations of temporal rhythm. Second, these planes together encode narrative through various modalities of time – lineal, oscillating, cyclical. Together, resonance and modality enable the multidirectional, perhaps musical cross-indexing and cross-referencing of lengthily separated periods and events. The result is a complex temporal grid of the mastery of time, a score of rhythms and tonalities helping to shape the meanings of national history and interpreting ongoing, national existence through the perception of such temporal processes. On all the planes of encoding temporality, its pulsations are crucial to making citizenship national.

Part IV
The Holes of Absence

Prologue

This is the land whose dead are in the soil
Instead of coal, gold, and iron,
And they are the fuel to bring Messiahs.

Yehuda Amichai (1995: 239)
With permission of HarperCollins Publishers

In principle no modern nationalism has relinquished warfare. The national practices itself into presence through the celebration of sacrifice. National death makes the absence that opens the future before the living. Filling the absence through commemoration, the living move into this future. Commemorating the national dead makes them present in the future, filled by the living practicing this memorialism. The national dead are pioneers of a sort, braving the way to life through death, through the death of their own future, towards the eternal. Therefore the future of the living is the presence of the dead. Making the national dead present is the sign of the future for the living national. This is why nationalism cherishes making and experiencing absence through sacrificial violence. The invocation of sacrifice leads inevitably to filling its holes with a sense of presence, felt as holistic, and therefore including the future into which the living are moving.

Bureaucratic logic, on the other hand, is obsessed only with presence, with knowing the presence of every person, every item, that is made relevant to its domains of classification. No detail can be left as an emptiness – the formulation itself is paradoxical. Unlike nationalism, bureaucratic logic does not create absence in order to form the holism of memory. Nonetheless, while nationalism opens holes in the social fabric, bureaucratic logic insists on filling these holes. Though far from unique in how they work on and relate to memory, the national and bureaucratic logic interact synergistically in the modern state to fill death with national presence. In phenomenal terms the effect of this synergy is, 'the filling of a void, whose emptiness had exercised diverse collective memories, [yet that] ends by excluding all but a single dominant one' (Forty 1999: 10).

What are the violent, sacrificial tears in the social fabric filled with? Filled to what degree? Filled with what significance? Not all holes of absence are privileged to the same extent. These and other issues are addressed in the chapters of Part IV. In Part III, time, the rhythms of time, were privileged over space in understanding how national sacrifice raises duration from the pit towards the heavens. The sacrifice that was (Holocaust Remembrance Day), reborn as the sacrifice that is (Remembrance

Day), moving still higher in the utopic imaginary, yet also towards the sacrifice to come within these encodings of time. Yet what of the encodings of sacrifice and absence in the space of the Jewish State?

The ways in which absence is opened through sacrifice, and filled and made present in space through memory, is the subject of Part IV. Chapter Eight addresses how the land is shaped through memorials of sacrifice – the military gravesite, the military memorial, the Holocaust memorial – and the significance of the body of sacrifice in fertilizing and sowing the space of the national. Chapter Nine then takes up an aspect of the great rise to prominence of Holocaust remembrance in Israel – how survivors are taught to tell their stories, thereby sprouting above the surface of the land, changing its contours, and turning themselves into their own living memorials.

–8–

The Presence of Absence: The Memorialism of National Death

[This chapter was coauthored by the late Lea Shamgar-Handelman.]

> And the land is a package land.
> She is neatly wrapped, everything inside, well tied
> And the strings sometimes hurt.
>
> Yehuda Amichai (1995: 338)
With permission of HarperCollins Publishers

> Sometimes as Momik lies on his stomach . . . he sees
> the tall smokestack of the new building they just
> finished over on Mt. Herzl, which they call Yad Vashem,
> a funny sort of name . . . and he pretends it's a ship sailing
> by, full of illegal immigrants from Over There that nobody
> wants to take in . . . and when he asked his old people what
> the smokestack is for, they looked at each other, and finally
> Munin told him that there's a museum there, and Aaron Marcus,
> who hadn't been out of his house for a couple of years, asked,
> Is it an art museum? And Hannah Zeitrin smiled crookedly and
> said, Oh sure it is, a museum of human art, that's what kind of art.
>
> David Grossman (1990: 55)

The spaces of modern states are contoured and furnished as national landscapes, molded with meaning and sentiment through ideological claims, historicist ethos, and political strategies (Williams and Smith 1983: 504; Cosgrove 1984: 13).[1] Making citizenship national entails enabling people to have morphic affinities with national landscapes, feeling themselves emerging (naturally, historically, mythically) from the land. When territory is contested space, the presence of the national must be embodied, made visible and empowered by artifacts having their own affinities to the land.[2] In the romanticism of the modern state, territorial boundaries are borders of being within which national landscapes are sown with collective memory. Of central importance to the production of claims to natural territory is the planting of death that has national import. The sowing and commemorating of national death is central to holistic collective memory in numerous states (Shamgar-Handelman 1986; Mosse 1979; Ben-Amos 1989; Tumarkin 1983; Kapferer 1988: 149–67; Ingersoll and Nickel 1987; Bilu and Wiztum 2000).

Death transforms presence into absence.The immediacy of death is the absence of presence among the living – the imploding black hole, sucking in being, nullifying presence in the absolute density of vacancy. In official discourse the dead soldier is referred to as a *noffel*, one who fell, or as a *khallal*. Khallal is empty space, connoting one who abruptly departs, leaving behind vacant volume. If the shape of this volume is not filled, not made to keep its dimensional shape in memory, then the implosion is complete, the shape of existence disappearing. The khallal becomes the shape of space the soldier leaves behind. Memorialism embodies the shape and texture of this imprint on emptiness to create the presence of absence. Without this the dead soldier falls into the vacancy of own death, disappearing.

In the moments following death, individuals have memories of the dead, yet these rarely are cathected with wider penumbrae of meaning, making their death significant to greater numbers. The extension of these penumbrae is a kind of second-hand death – people who knew people who knew the dead; people who know people who know people who knew the dead; knowing the dead through the mass media . . . Memorialism has an unusual task – making this absence present so that it serves the agency of the living (Handelman 1985; Huntington and Metcalf 1979; Bloch and Parry 1982). This is at the heart of practices of commemoration, of making citizenship national. Memorialism succeeds when the absence of presence is turned into the presence of absence; the nullity of the dead transforming into feelings, topoi, and durations of their absence.

The relationship between the grounding of being in place and the motility of its horizons of memory through time is intimate. Place and memory seem to seek, select, and shape the perception of one another, so that 'a given place will invite certain memories while discouraging others,' while 'memories are selected for place: they seek out particular places as their natural habitats' (Casey 1987: 189). Perhaps this is one way through which dreamscapes are turned into landscapes (Ezrahi 1992: 482), to the extent that signs of place substitute for the self in remembering:

In the landscapes contested by Jews and Palestinians, it is violent death that is understood as national sacrifice. In its religious senses, sacrifice is violent death in which the body is rent, life torn from its remnant, transforming or preserving other life (Hubert and Mauss 1964; Smith and Doniger 1989: 224; Herrenschmidt 1978). Metaphors of sacrifice in national discourse signify the willingness of the individual, the part, to die on behalf of and therefore in place of the whole. The place in which this sacrifice is memorialized substitutes for and becomes the national whole. This is especially powerful when the body of sacrifice, perceived to embody the national whole, is itself in the place memorialized. The national practices itself into being as an imaginary perceived as whole through offerings of death that open holes, absences, crying out for their own disappearance.

Sacrifice here is the making of order through destruction, filling absence with presence. For more than a few states making war is making order, indeed, moral order (Greenhouse 1989), so that the continuousness of war is no less that of continuously making order. In this regard, war has cosmogonic properties, especially through sacrifice. The sacrifice in the first instance makes destruction, loss, vacancy, emptiness. This disorder is classified, reified, generalized, given value, presented as absence. Done this way, absence is fillable, this disorder ordered through memory work that remembers the presence of the sacrifice. Those who remember take the absence, the disorder, into themselves, validating and controlling it, thereby overcoming the absence through its existence within them as presence. Making war may order through remembering the resultant disorder as order, turning the absence of the dead into their presence among the living.

This chapter addresses national death through its memorials.[3] Mosse (1990: 36) calls such memorialism the nationalization of death. Like land, death is co-opted by the State for its purposes. The sacrificial death emplaced is 'public,' an event in its own right, with many publics. Different publics claim rights to use this death: to explain the intentions of the dead in their dying; to speak in the name of the dead; to give meanings to these deaths; to make relevant the multiple affiliations of the dead to place and population. More generally these memorials are intended to evoke national identity and common goals (Halbwachs 1992), shaping the national as materializing, solidifying, and keying the national into the land through the construction of collective signs signifying through death the especially intimate link between individual and collectivity, nation, land. This is the national landscaping of commemoration. In particular we are exploring the degrees to which memorials are elaborated as signs on the surface of the land, where surface is intended always to index deeper significance for the national. These memorials are intended as icons of national topoi, rooting ideology in the originary land, such that these icons signify the cosmogonic emergence of the people from the land.

Kuchler (1993) distinguishes between landscapes *of* memory and landscapes *as* memory, attributing the former to Western perceptions. The landscape of memory is a picture of landscape, a static surface to which memories are affixed and labeled, and from which the referents of these memories are read off. Landscape as memory indexes landscaping, the practice of landscape as memory-work, unceasingly re-forming the shaping of its own significance. The distinction is useful, yet overly rigid. Memories and landscapes of national death increasingly mutate (and migrate) in order to continue to be perceived as eternal. The landscape as memory produces the landscape of memory, and their relationship is processual, as the work of Henri Lefebvre suggests (Shields 1991: 50–6). What Lefebvre (1991: 41–2) called representational spaces open up spaces of representation, configured into national landscapes. The cultural encoding of ideology, history, knowledge, practices the imagining of lived spatializations that reproduce and critique dominant social orders. In terms of native perception and aesthetics, the encoding is iconic, not representational, yet this works best only with the body of the sacrificial dead planted in the land – in the military cemetery.

But there are two other kinds of place that articulate the relationship between sacrificial death and the land – the relationship that embodies and empowers the land with the presence of absence. These are the military memorial and the Holocaust memorial.[4] Each of the three kinds of place visualizes the relationship of the dead to the land, thereby constituting claims for the landscaping of sacrifice. In the instance of the military cemetery the relationship of the dead to the land is more iconic; while in the other two kinds of place the relationship is more representational.

The contrasts are related to the degrees to which the dead sow the land with the presence of their absence. The highest degree of presence is in the military cemetery, where the body is in the land. The lowest degree of presence is in the Holocaust memorial, from which bodies and significant places of death are absent. In between is the military memorial, articulating dead and living in relation to places of significance to both, though the bodies of the dead are absent there. The greater the presence of the sacrificial dead, the more powerful is this presence for the national, and the less problematic is this relationship between living and dead.[5]

The Military Cemetery

> And memorial tombstones everywhere, are weights
> To keep the history of the country from flying off
> Like papers in the wind.
> Yehuda Amichai (1995: 393)
>
> With permission of HarperCollins Publishers

The military cemetery contains the body of sacrifice, embodying the full fruition of sacrificial death. The military cemetery is the exemplar of the presence of national death. The graves of soldiers are set apart, located either in a military section within a civilian cemetery or in a cemetery given over wholly to military death. An intimate relationship is struck between the body of the dead soldier and the substance of the land he defended (Mosse 1979, 1990). As he sacrificed himself in life for the living land, so in death its earth takes him in, his presence propagating the intimacy of their relationship. The body belongs to the land, while the land is felt to acquire contours resonating with the bodies buried within it.[6]

Our discussion refers in particular to the military cemetery on Mount Herzl, discussed briefly in the Prologue to Part III. The graves – over four thousand – begin within a few dozen meters from the plain arch of the entrance. Unlike the largely barren terrain of the Jerusalem hills, the cemetery mountainside is forested. The trees, mainly pine and cedar, were planted when the space was developed as a cemetery. This side of the mountain is heavily terraced, shaping small islands of level ground at different heights and angles of perspective, embedded in the slope of the mountainside. The graves are placed in these small clearings. Clusters of trees and other vegetation separate the levels of terraced clearings from one another. At each level the terrain is formed into a series of shady groves, connected by pathways and steps.

From no vantage point in the entire cemetery is it possible to see its whole landscape of death. One's perspective is foreshortened and enclosed by the trees and the rounded slopes, and one's gaze is drawn into the clusters of graves in their terraced groves. Soldiers who fell in the same war or action often are buried in the same area. Here the constitution of the national is that of small communities, whose inhabitants are the dead, set deeply and intimately within the natural landscape. These communities of the dead look out and down at the vista of city and more distant hills. Here the dead in their place are elevated above the living, and sacrificial death is shown as a hermeneutic of the presence of and feelings for the dead.

By law, in Israel the disposal of the corpse must be in accordance with religious tradition. In Judaism the presence of the corpse is of extreme importance, since the body is to become the site of resurrection and redemption at the End of Days, the end of time. Following military actions every effort is made (even years later) to retrieve the remains of soldiers for proper burial. The gravesite, iconic of the presence of the dead body, is of major significance. The military gravesite is shaped by regulations of the IDF. All graves conform in general to army regulations, and are similar in composition. Each gravesite contains a holder for a memorial candle. The headstone is of local stone; the body of the grave consists of a rectangle of stone raised above the surface of the ground, and covered by earth planted with the evergreen shrub, rosemary. The effect is that of the body within rock and earth vital with life. The dead not only rest, but nourish the living earth of the national landscape with their last remains. The memories of death evoked here are close to images of life. Each gravesite embodies the intimate relationship between the dead and the land, while the entire cemetery landscape itself resembles a natural extension of the land that is cared for carefully and especially well. This careful cultivation of the cemetery accords with the Zionist vision of the reclamation of wasteland (but also with changing conceptions of cemetery landscaping, influenced by the Enlightenment romanticism of nineteenth-century Europe; see Mosse 1990: 4–45.)

Each self-sacrificed body put into the soil practices the nationalist vision of the state and its territory. The body is the authentic witness to the conjoining of intent and action in self-sacrifice, enabling gravesite and cemetery to signify the holism of the national. Just as the military cemetery is a version of the entire national territory in the idiom of self-sacrificial death, so too each military gravesite, the equivalent of every other, is a microcosm of the entire nationalist landscape of self-sacrifice. Through this synecdoche the relationship of the military gravesite to the territory of the state is metonymic. Even a single gravesite with the appropriate headstone is sufficient to recall the topos of national death, bringing into temporary existence an entire landscape of place and narrative. The gravesite of self-sacrifice creates a center both personal and national, 'against which all future will be made' (Golden 1990: 17).

> As a child he would mash his potatoes
> to a golden mush
> And then you die.
> A living child must be cleaned
> when he comes home from playing.
> But for a dead man
> earth and sand are clear water, in which
> his body goes on being bathed and purified forever.

Yehuda Amichai (1986: 92–3)
With permission of the Regents of the University of California

According to the information on the headstone (sometimes referred to by bereaved parents as 'the little head pillow'), the sacrificed body has a personal identity (the name of the dead), an age (date of birth, date of death), a genealogy (names of parents), and a place of origin. The date and place of death deliberately articulate the deceased with the history of the state (and in some instances, pre-state history), and the struggles for survival.[7] The text also articulates the dead to the State through the symbol of the IDF, and through the military classifications of army number and military rank at death. The context of death in the inscription invokes a taxonomy of the degree of sacrifice of the dead. In descending order of prestige, the categories are: 'fell in battle' (telling the reader of the conscious intentionality of self-sacrifice), 'fell while doing his duty' (while on some kind of active service), and 'fell during military service' (covering all other instances of death while on active service, including traffic accidents, and so the most ambiguous of these categories).

In terms of these coordinates, gravesite and body belong fully to the land that enfolds them, but that also is made over – in-bodied – by the presence of the dead beneath the surface. And whatever the stories (Berdoulay 1987) generated by the headstone text and the memories the grave evokes, they tend to be more intimate tales, easily articulated with greater national landscapes, as is the corpse that gives them birth. The typification of the dead as national sacrifice virtually ensures that these intimate narratives will be articulated in some way with national aims (see Katriel and Shenhar 1990). The centrifugal currents of sentiment generated by each body in the military cemetery conversely pull in the living, in private acts of remembrance, care, commiseration, or during events of commemoration. These are the living who belong to the dead, since they continue to exist through the sacrifice. Through the semiosis of self-sacrifice, bereaved fathers become the offspring of their dead, heroic sons. In keeping with the concluding discussion of Chapter Seven, these moments through which the living are cast back in time harmonize them with the nadir of catastrophic moments, from which they ascend to the apogee of triumph in the present, the times of commemoration, the embodying of presence. Living through remembrance is in itself a kind of self-sacrifice through which the living experience the self-contraction of pain and suffering on behalf of the dead, but through the rhythm of ascending time.[8]

A man whose son died in the war
walks up the street
like a woman with a dead fetus in her womb.
"Behind all this, some great happiness is hiding."

Yehuda Amichai (1986: 96)
With permission of the Regents of the University of California

The body of sacrifice is the most powerful presence of national death in Israel. Though its placement requires consecrated ground, this venue could be located almost anywhere on the land. The body of sacrifice is at home everywhere in the land. The body is the authentic witness to the sacrifice through which national contours are re-formed. Given the metonymy between the dead soldier and the land, the gravesite is more iconic than metaphoric, and so the military cemetery contains little representation. The land is in-bodied with the sacrificial dead, covered with a plain marker and a simple text. This is where the sacrifice is. Here the logic of forming form and its aesthetic of place near the self-explanatory.[9]

The Memorial Place

Let the Memory Mountain remember instead of me,
That's its job. Let the Garden-In-Memory-Of remember,
Let the Street-in-the-Name-Of remember,
Let the famous building remember . . .
Let the memorial remember. Let the flags remember,
History's colorful shrouds: the bodies
They wrapped turned to dust. Let the dust remember.

Yehuda Amichai (1995: 241–2)
With permission of HarperCollins Publishers

Apart from military cemeteries, hundreds of memorials to self-sacrificial military death incise, chisel, and form the landscapes of the country.[10] Some signify where sacrificial death took place, stressing that 'it happened here.' Others commemorate the dead of military actions, and are placed within the locale of theaters of operation. Many others emblazon the local provenance of the dead, and are located in or near the communities the dead belonged to. Still others highlight the membership of the dead in particular military units, and are placed accordingly. Some memorials commemorate hundreds; others, a single individual. The generic word for these memorials is *gal-ed*, in biblical terms (Genesis 31: 48) signifying a heap of stones as an eternal sign, as witness to a covenant. In military memorialism the sign is a witness left on the land, in place of the dead who are not in the land.

These memorials are thought to share a common orientation to the land, one enunciated clearly by the murdered prime minister, Yitzhak Rabin (1989: 7): 'We build neither arches of triumph nor palaces of heroism. No one knows as we do that wars . . . are lengthy journeys in pain and bereavement . . . The little with which we, the living, can reward our dead friends is with the memory that follows them and is with us . . . The memorials are signposts (*tziyunei derekh*) of the historical and geographical map of the wars, actions, and accidents . . . The history of this land is carved in the memorials of wood, stone, and iron.' These memorials place the memory of self-sacrifice on the land, shaping its contours of national death. The land is signposted in space and time, in coordinates of national sacred geography, history, myth, the signposts carving the landscape with remembrance.[11]

These memorials share another attribute: the absence of the essential witness to self-sacrifice, the dead body that is its transcendental authentication. This absence is crucial for the extension and substitution of memorialism. Unlike the military cemetery the memorial is a number of removes from 'the presence of absence,' teetering closer to 'the absence of presence.' In the previous section we argued that the presence of the body within the land is paralleled by minimal representation of its presence on the surface. Where the body is in the land, there is little monumentalism on the surface. The presence of the body in-place is near the self-explanatory.

In its absence the body cannot be replicated, but only represented in various ways. The absence of the iconic body creates a dynamic of representation to fill that emptiness with presence, the presence of absence. Then this absence can be reproduced endlessly, in ways that the presence of the body cannot. The presence of the body speaks to the uniqueness of authenticity; its absence, to Baudrillard's simulacra, to the multiplicities of reproduction.

This helps explain the profusion of memorial places in Israel. The absence of the body of sacrifice enables the memory of the dead to be related publicly to numerous categories of the living. In this way many publics partake of and use the memory of the dead for their own purposes; and the dead acquire numerous identities linking them to locality, community, social group, historical period, military action. Moreover the absence of the body gives to many others greater freedom to speak in the name of the dead. The presence of absence is more variegated and contradictory within the multiplicity of memories evoked by the memorial. Memorial places parcel out the ownership of the dead as the cemetery cannot.

A spate of private memorials erected primarily by comrades-in-arms and kin of the dead follows every war. Early on the State organized memorialism from the top.[12] The desire of parents to memorialize their fallen offspring clashed with the capacity of municipalities, army units, and the state itself to honor individually each of the dead. State intervention in memorialism arrogates ultimate authority to the greater collectivity – the nation-in-arms, the family-in-arms – at whose command voluntary self-sacrifice is practiced in battle. This is the semiotic complement to the singular body of the military dead becoming the synecdochal whole through self-sacrifice, for here the national whole reabsorbs all of its human parts, dead and living. Here, the visual shaping of memorialism gives a common national identity to the dead by making them equivalents of one another – by standardizing name-plaques, by grouping the dead on such plaques according to military units, and so forth. Here bureaucratic logic again intersects powerfully with nationalism, enabling the uniqueness of the individual dead to be substituted for the uniqueness of any other, since all are ultimately equal members of the Jewish State.

The State worries about over-commemoration, about a profusion of privately erected memorials placed willy-nilly in the national landscape of sacrifice, altering its shaping (Azaryahu 1992: 69). These more singular and spontaneous expressions of comradeship and family, often excluding explicit recognition of the State, would form a littered landscape of national sacrifice (the detritus of family outings), in place of the ordered landscape envisaged by the State, reflexively indexing its 'natural' appearance. Various compromises emerged. Some private memorials were moved, others reshaped, others became part of more collective memorializing, and still others were left as they were, in return for receiving official recognition.

The great majority of memorials stand on the land, open to the sky, many constructed of stone. Many are continuous with the natural landscape; others appear to sprout or thrust from this. For example, the memorial to General David 'Mickey' Marcus, killed in the 1948 War, is an irregular, elongated, pyramidal shape standing high in the hills in the vicinity of Jerusalem. Erected in 1957 the monument is close to the place where he was killed, constructed of stone from the locale. The memorial belongs to the place, through its location and the materials of its construction. The memorial is native to the place, as is the place to the broader landscape. The monument is formed as a common visual analogue of courage and bravery – its tapering height reaching towards the heavens, its bulk impressed firmly on the land. Given the absence of the self-sacrifice, the body is metaphorized, made into a certain shape of memory giving form to the space into which its dimensions move, larger and more powerful than human life.

Other memorials of natural stone hug the ground, inverting the power of the absent sacrifices, representing above ground their powerful intimacy with the land. Still others confront and dare the elemental in their design. The memorial to those who broke the months-long siege of Jewish Jerusalem in the 1948 War, tears at and pierces the naked sky. Six rugged, irregular lengths of sharp corrugated iron, the longest twelve meters, are extruded by the rocky hillside at a forty-five-degree angle, pointing in the direction of Jerusalem. Here human (perhaps male) qualities of desire, focused intensity, effort, are metaphorized through positioning, shape, angle, texture.

The absence of the body enables the same sacrifice to be memorialized in different places, through different signs, each commemoration given a different affiliation yet the same value. Northwest of Jerusalem a small plaque screwed into stone commemorates six soldiers who were killed in the capture of Radar Hill during the 1967 War. Following on the names of the six, the brief text reads: 'From their friends in the *Portzim* [Breakthrough] battalion.' Battalion members placed the plaque on the hill near the location of their comrades' death. The names of the six also are included in the memorial lists of the dead of the Har-el Brigade, to which the battalion belongs. The presence of the six is copied from location to location, once signifying the place of sacrificial death and once membership in a more inclusive military unit.

Such substitutions are commonplace, demonstrating in the absence of the authentic body of sacrifice the metaphorization of name, place, memory. The basic point derives from Walter Benjamin's (1969: 220) argument that the authenticity of a work of art requires its singular presence in time/space, 'its unique existence at the place where it happens to be.' Its authenticity is its ultimate authority (to appear in its own right, to be seen for itself, as that which it is and nothing else). The authentic work of art exists only at a single set of coordinates of time/space, occupying only a single place shaped in keeping with its authentic form. The authentic work of art is akin to the military gravesite whose form (headstone, body) is more literal than figurative, approximating the shape of the human body on its back, at rest. But the absence of the body generates complex metaphors of substitution in the placing and shaping of memory on the surface of the land. Regardless of how elaborate these metaphors become, their presence points over and again to the absence of that which they represent. These body-substitutes are not Baudrillard's simulacra, rendering reality as collaged copies of itself, and therefore inauthentic, in the terms of this Chapter. Nor are these body-substitutes 'floating signifiers' (Poster 1990: 63), cut adrift from their referents to be moored to any number of possible signifiers, thereby creating imaginary worlds. Foregrounding the presence of the absent dead in these war memorials is the cultural authenticity of their sacrifice, the powerful existential reality of their being, of their being dead.

Place may be metaphorized, its significance shifted from one locale to another. Metaphorizing presence often drives fragments of authenticity of the immediate place of death into memorials (Azaryahu 1993), thereby creating relics (not of the body, but of the space of death). A memorial in Ophira, in Sinai, commemorated the deaths of five members of a radar unit killed by an Egyptian missile in the first hours of the 1973 War. The memorial was constructed from pieces of radar equipment damaged in the attack. Following the Israeli withdrawal from Sinai the memorial was moved to the Judean hills within green-line Israel, but placed on a base of stones brought from the area in Sinai where it was first erected. A bit of the authentic place of death was reconstituted within Israel through the metaphorization of space as place. Memory was brought home, the now alienated territory of Sinai embedded in the home landscape.

Such fragments are authentic pointers to the absence at the broken heart of the sacrifice. The relics or other found objects 'were there.' Through these parts, the enveloping context of battle, the moments of death, are metaphorized as *lieux de mémoire* (Nora 1989). The living reach out to touch, not the place of the dead, but a substitute in touch with their presence.[13] The use of relics abounds, and here a few illustrations suffice. The memorial to a tankist killed on the Golan Heights during the desperate blocking of the Syrian breakthrough at the outset of the 1973 War includes two sprocketed tank wheels and a short section of tank tread. A lengthy section of tank tread, lying on its side in a three-quarter circle, demarcates a memorial to three tankists killed in Sinai during the same war. The centerpiece of a memorial to fifteen scouts of a paratroop battalion killed in the 1973 War is a halftrack, its tread passing under and caught by the living rock. A plaque on a decapitated jeep is the memorial to a soldier killed in the 1967 War when his jeep exploded a mine. A memorial to paratroopers is a damaged aircraft of the type they parachuted from. Outside, a plaque asks the visitor to enter the body of the plane, concentrating memory on those who fell.

Many of these memorials are highly personalized artifacts, put together to represent affinities to particular landscapes, their histories, and certain categories of people. Numerous memorials, as noted, are designed at the behest of people who are kin, members of the same community, comrades-in-arms. During the 1948 War, Hill 69 guarded against the route of the Egyptian advance. Twenty soldiers were killed there. In the 1950s at the initiative of the bereaved families an elaborate memorial was erected there. The text of the memorial plaque reads in part: 'Here on Hill 69 . . . in bitter battle with the Egyptian invader, they gave their life defending their motherland . . . Their name will stay with us forever.' The Pilots' Forest consists of small groves containing numerous plaques and some memorials in memory of air force pilots. These memorials often contain pieces of destroyed aircraft. Plaques and memorials were done at the initiative of family and friends of the dead. For example, one memorial was erected by friends and dedicated on the dead pilot's birth date. Such memorials belong first and foremost to these people.

The relatively elaborate representation of death in memorials is related to the absence of the authentic body of sacrifice below ground and a corresponding metaphorization of body and place above ground. Two other aspects need mention. One is the relationship between the scale of memorialism and the totality of its representation. The other is the linking of military memorialism in Israel to Jewish armed resistance during the Holocaust.

Generally, the representation of military death in Israel increases in scale and elaboration when the size of the units and the numbers of dead greatly increase. A prominent example is the memorial in remembrance of the dead of the steel division of the armored corps in the 1967 War. Erected first in the town of Yamit in Sinai, the memorial name plates were moved to Israel following the withdrawal. In the desert area close to the Gaza Strip an identical (though expanded) monument was built, covering almost four acres. In the center of this landscape is a tower, twenty-five meters high, constructed of five half-cylindrical columns supporting an observation platform. Radiating from the tower, spread over the landscape, are 400 concrete pillars of varying heights. Atop each pillar is a damaged part of an armored corps vehicle or weapon. Each pillar symbolizes the Pillar of Fire (*Amoud Ha'esh*), the heavenly sign of the Exodus that led the Israelites out of bondage from Egypt. In this memorial the militarized pillars of God stand guard, defend the land, and are elevated in value. But the pillars also represent the sacrifice, each holding up towards the heavens a relic of battle. These relics were operated by soldiers who (as pillars) are metaphorized as larger-than-life, in height, strength, vision. At the base of the observation tower there is a memorial room containing the bronze name-plaques grouped by unit.

This monument departs from the others we have discussed. Though the memorial is open to the elements, it shifts towards the forming of a total environment through monumentalism. Its pillars are not only abstract but also bear a limited relationship to the surrounding desert. Rebuilt from scratch, the memorial turns in on itself, holding and enclosing the names of the dead, returning to its sacrificial origins. This monumental copy of the Sinai memorial contains its own sacrificial core, the original name-plaques, themselves representations of the dead. The inner core of the monument is itself a smaller-scale total environment, sealed from the surrounding landscape. Impressive in scale, bulk, conception, the overall effect nonetheless has something of an imposing and imposed alien presence in the land. The pillars stride over the earth, totalizing it into a cyberscape.[14] These kinds of representing and elaborating absence are more distant from the memorialism of the military cemetery, moving closer to Holocaust memorialism.

> Dicky was hit.
> Like the water tower at Yad Mordekhai.
> Hit. A hole in the belly. Everything came flooding out.
>
> But he has remained standing like that
> in the landscape of my memory
> like the water tower at Yad Mordekhai.
>
> He fell not far from there,
> a little to the north, near Houlayqat.

Yehuda Amichai (1986: 94)
With permission of the Regents of the University of California

At Kibbutz Yad Mordekhai, near the Gaza Strip, a ruined water tower stands overgrown by foliage, its concrete walls torn by shell holes. The tower was left as a memorial to one of the fiercest battles of the 1948 War, the repulse of an attack on the kibbutz by a large Egyptian force. The water tower is in keeping with military memorialism: it is native to the place, integral to the landscape, a relic of the battle. In front of the tower is a heroic figure with grim visage, his shirt torn open to the waist, exposing a powerful chest. One strong hand clutches a grenade at the ready.[15] The statue, put in place in 1951, is that of Mordekhai Anielewicz, in 1943 the commander of the Warsaw Ghetto uprising. In that year the kibbutz was renamed in his memory. The juxtaposition of water tower and statue is significant. The figure was intended to signify the antecedents of the 1948 fighting, and the tower the continuity between heroic Jewish armed resistance in World War II and that of the kibbutz fighters in the War of Independence.

Especially interesting is the Ghetto fighter in the shape of Anielewicz. Here, representing a faraway location, the presence of the body returns. This figure is neither an abstraction of the heroic body nor a relic of sacrifice. It is a copy, the style in keeping with the social realism adopted by the sculptor. The sculpting of the realistic human body is comparatively rare in Israeli memorialism of military sacrifice. In general this kind of copy is associated with an even greater degree of absence, of both the authentic body of sacrifice and the place of sacrifice, typifying Holocaust memorialism. The memorial at Yad Mordekhai demonstrates the difference between memorializing the sacrificial body through authentic place or relic, and that which depends entirely on copies. In the latter instance the realistic body returns, but as an elaborate copy, above ground.

When the body of sacrifice is absent it is the memory of body through memorializing place, and belonging to place, that rises into prominence. In the main these places of memorialism are continuous with the landscapes of Israel. They are in place in this terrain, culturing this naturally. However, there is greater elaboration in representation as the absence of the body is filled with metaphoric allusions to its presence. As in cemetery memorialism, here too there are kin, intimates, comrades, who constitute a personal public attending the military memorial. These patterns alter drastically in Holocaust memorialism.

The Holocaust Memorial

The slaughtered children are heaped in a big stack, they are added, thrown onto the pairs of adults. Each corpse is laid out on an iron 'burial' board; then the door to the inferno is opened and the board shoved in. The hellish fire, extending its tongues like open arms, snatches the body as though it were a prize. The hair is the first to catch fire. The skin, immersed in flames, catches in a few seconds. Now the arms and legs begin to rise – expanding blood vessels cause this movement of the limbs. The entire body is now burning fiercely; the skin has been consumed and fat drips and hisses in the flames. One can no longer make out a corpse – only a room filled with hellish fire that holds something in its midst. The belly goes. Bowels and entrails are quickly consumed, and within minutes there is no trace of them. The head takes the longest to burn; two little blue flames flicker from the eyeholes – these are the eyes burning with the brain, while from the mouth the tongue also continues to burn. The entire process lasts twenty minutes – and a human being, a world, has been turned to ashes . . . The fire burns boldly, calmly. Nothing stands in its way, nothing puts it out. Sacrifices arrive regularily, without number, as though this ancient, martyred nation was created specifically for this purpose.

Zalmen Gradowski, 'The Czech Transport: a Chronicle of the
Auschwitz Sonderkommando (March–April 1944)'
(in Roskies 1988: 563–4)

Zionist ideologies imagined a Jewish homeland in Palestine as the antithesis of Jewish life in the European diaspora. The new Jews were to be everything their diasporic counterparts were not. These sentiments were given acute if ambivalent expression in responses to the Holocaust following the founding of the State, though these meanings have undergone major changes since then (Segev 1993; Ezrahi 1985–86; Friedlander and Seligman 1994). After World War II there were strong proclivities to characterize the behavior of European Jewries during the Nazi period in negative terms, as that of persons who responded passively to their own destruction, as 'sheep led to the slaughter.' Two developments modified this denigration.

One emphasized the flare-ups of armed resistance to oppression and extermination. As in the memorialism at Yad Mordekhai, active resistance was made to bridge the abyss between European and Israeli Jewries. So, just as some Jews in Europe became heroic, many, many more practiced heroism in the homeland. The second development complemented the first, positing the theme that so many of the European Jews who died did so, wittingly or not, for the Sanctification of the Name (*Kiddush Hashem*); dying for the sake of their Jewish identities and Judaism. Still later, all Jewish Holocaust death was referred to in this way. In religious terms this kind of death indexes 'martyrdom,' joining the 'martyrs' to all those other catastrophes through the ages in which Jews were oppressed, menaced, killed, because they were Jews.

The shaping of these narratives is complex, in both religious and secular terms. In religious terms these narratives raise issues of divine patterning or plan, of the motivation of God and of the possibility of divine punishment and the unwitting role of the Nazis in this.[16] In secular terms the idea of divine intervention and martyrdom is understood as allegory, expressing the immensity, tragedy, and horror of the life lost. Even if one accepts that there is sacrifice embedded in this martyrdom, it is difficult to find the conscious willingness to self-sacrifice in this, paralleling that applied to heroic military death. The religious narratives also complicate the value of the heroic, secular response to oppression in the Diaspora.[17]

The consensus among Israeli Jews is that despite the lack of unequivocal documentary evidence the Nazis undoubtedly did plan the total extermination of the Jewish people (Taylor 1985; Lang 1990), and the Holocaust is understood as national death. In recent years the existence of the State is interpreted more as the answer itself to the Holocaust (Friedlander and Seligman 1994). Thus, through the rhythms of time, the national death intended by the Nazis helped produce the rejuvenated Jewish nation in its national home. So, too, runs the argument, had the state existed with the rise to power of the Nazis, European Jewry would have had the refuge denied them everywhere else in the Western world. This is in keeping with the ideological tenets of Zionism that the State is the homeland of all Jews, who have the legal right to return there; and that Israel is the sole guardian of the interests of Jews as Jews everywhere in the world, defending Jewry wherever it is threatened.[18]

In these senses the Holocaust dead are of the remarkable kind that belong to the State. Yet this belonging is more problematic for the Holocaust dead, as they lived and died elsewhere. One difficulty concerns the meanings attributed to their death, the other, the relationship between their death and the State. In the first instance, to argue that their deaths were those of intentional self-sacrifice is convoluted, though it is existentially devastating to claim that they died for naught. The argument that they died for the Sanctification of the Name gives the meaning of faith to their death. But in contrast to the military dead, the Holocaust dead have a more tenuous articulation to the Israeli landscape. This is expressed in the construction of their memorialism.

Unlike military memorialism, that of the Holocaust is spread neither widely nor densely over the landscape. Instead it is concentrated more in centers that specialize in this kind of commemoration, of which Yad Vashem is the national site. This speaks to the more difficult relationship of Holocaust memorialism to the landscapes of Israel. Yad Vashem means 'a place and a name,' taken from Isaiah (65: 5), in which God states: 'I will give in my house and within my walls a place and a name better than of sons and of daughters: I will give them an everlasting name, that shall not be cut off.' This immediately implicates the problematic relationship alluded to above. On the one hand, Israel is conceived of as the land of the Jews. On the other, in the perceptions of Israeli Jews the Holocaust could not have happened within the landscapes of Israel.

Following the State's founding, commemoration of the war dead was taken for granted. But perceptions of Holocaust remembrance were quite different. Thus the 1953 Knesset law establishing Yad Vashem defined the mandate of this institution as to 'gather, study and publish the entire testimony concerning Holocaust and heroism and endow the nation with its lesson; [to] . . . foster an atmosphere of unanimity in memory' (*State of Israel Yearbook* 1954: 250–1). In Israel, knowledge of the Holocaust had to be cultivated deliberately in order to turn this into memory cathected with feeling shared by the populace, because this consensus was lacking.[19] The presence of the Holocaust dead was absent, despite the large number of survivors who settled in Israel. Often those who survived nonetheless were absent as survivors from Israeli landscapes – this problematic is the subject of Chapter Nine.

Holocaust memorialism does make present the absent dead. It gives them identities and makes place for them within the Israeli landscape. Yet to do this, highly specialized places must be constructed for Holocaust memorialism; and in their composition these places are made to be discontinuous with the surrounding landscapes. Within these modes of commemoration the bodies and the places of Holocaust death are absent, as they are from the entire landscapes of Israel. Present is the memory of the dead, yet to fix memory within the presence of such absence is a complex matter.

Within the distinctive environments of Holocaust memorialism there is only representation elaborating representation. Present are the disembodied names of the dead, the signs of distant lands, and the memories and metaphors they evoke in others. Unlike military memorialism, Yad Vashem builds its presence wholly upon absence. Within the Israeli landscape Yad Vashem transforms the absence of the Holocaust dead and their places of death into presence, yet at the heart of this presence is the absence of the authentic bodies and places of sacrifice. The extent of this absence is reflected in the extent of the metaphorization and reproduction of that which is absent.

The entry to Yad Vashem (facing away from Mount Herzl, towards the sea and Europe beyond) is a voyage to otherness – not to another Israel, but elsewhere. The monumental gate at the border has qualities of a checkpoint. The parking area follows, and then beyond this another border, though it is not called this. Yad Vashem is built along the top of a ridge. Most of the major edifices front along the southern exposure of the ridge. The outermost path running from the parking area along the southern edge of the ridge is called, The Avenue of the Righteous Among the Nations. On either side of the long pathway are carob trees, planted by gentiles who saved Jews during the Holocaust at risk to their own lives. This risk-taking is a condition of recognition as a righteous gentile. In front of each tree is the name-plaque of the gentile so honored, and the name of that person's country.[20] Within the Israeli landscape the voyage to Yad Vashem is one through discontinuity, to a foreign land whose physical border is marked by gentiles, not Jews. These are the good gentiles; the evil ones are hidden from view, deep within this land.

The major memorial structures of Yad Vashem are of two kinds, closed and open. The closed structures are buildings enclosing space designated for specialized functions, named and furnished accordingly. Neither the functions nor the appurtenances of any of these buildings are identifiable from their facades. The innocent exteriors hide their interiors from the external gaze, as the killing grounds of the death camps hid themselves innocuously from outside glances. By contrast, the open structures are freestanding sculptures or monuments open to the sky, utterly exposed to the external gaze and natural elements of the landscape. The functions of the enclosed structures are most embedded in the commemoration of Holocaust genocide, while many of the open ones point more to the heroic, fighting response. The latter are closer to forms of military memorialism in Israel, the former, more distant. In Yad Vashem, evil is beneath the surface, not the heroic dead.

Yad Vashem is characterized by the presence of absence. Its built environment struggles through numerous media and perspectives to give shape, meaning, significance, to this absence – historically, pictorially, textually, statistically, metaphorically, allegorically. Commemorative ceremonies are held in the Hall of Remembrance (*Ohel Yizkor*), a cavernous structure of boulder-like stone walls, off-center concrete ceiling, and massive iron doors. In the mosaic floor are inscribed in Hebrew and Latin script the names of the twenty-two largest Nazi concentration and death camps. In one corner is the Eternal Flame. In front of this is a raised, covered, rectangular receptacle, within which are interred the ashes of bodies destroyed in death camp crematoria.

The Hall was inaugurated in 1961 with the interment of the ashes and the lighting of the Eternal Flame. With the participation of a unit from the IDF Rabbinate the area of the receptacle was consecrated as burial ground. In those early years this receptacle sometimes was referred to as the Tomb of the Unknown Ashes. To date, the ashes are the only relic of bodily substance in Yad Vashem.[21] The dark hall is perhaps the largest enclosed memorial in the complex. Within, the pervasive feeling is of the bursting emptiness of absence, contained by massive walls and ceiling, focused on the single flame and the imagery of ash, ephemeral dust. In order to shape this emotional space of foreign lands and the memories and imagination they evoke within the Israeli landscape, this local landscape, its sights and sounds, must be kept without. Were this memorial open to the sky and the elements, the wrenching emptiness of its internal space would dissipate, permeated and overwhelmed by the local environment.[22] Enclosed as it is, the Hall is metaphorized as sacred space, the ashes as sacred ash; every man entering is requested to don a skullcap, as he would in a cemetery. To our knowledge the only official visitor who refused to do so was Kurt Waldheim, while secretary-general of the United Nations.

The Children's Memorial (inaugurated in 1987) fills a dark void with a multitude of metaphorical images of light. The cavelike memorial, built into a hillock, commemorates the estimated million and a half children who perished in the Holocaust. Within, the only source of light is of five memorial candles. Through the use of mirrors their little flames are multiplied infinitely, over one's head, under one's feet, on all sides. Entering from the brightness of the natural landscape, one is abruptly suspended in a pitch black void ventilated by thousands of tiny lights receding to infinity, the only sound a disembodied voice reciting the names, ages, and countries of the dead children. One gropes blindly for the way through. With time and retinal adjustment to the darkness, the lights become merely reflections, artful representations; and then their presence evokes a terrible anguish of absence. There is indeed nothing – nothingness – behind the artifice except the machinery of artifice, no uplifting revelation, no moralistic liturgy. The sense of loss is overwhelming.

The Children's Memorial is the only site at Yad Vashem that works active, cognitive transformation into its design of experiencing: from representing the presence of absence to realizing that this absence is just that – nullity, the utter absence of substance, not the resistance of stone, the entanglement of text, nor the copied embodiment of photograph. There is no solace here, no narrative finally raising the spirit. Moreover this memorial works directly and immediately on the body of the visitor, effecting transformations in one's state of being regardless of whether the person cooperates or comprehends: endocrinal and kinesthesic changes occur in the body's response to darkness and sensory disorientation, just as they continue to occur as the body adapts to the darkness and the person sees more.[23]

In the Hall of Names the dead are represented by name. For each there is an information sheet, a page of testimony, which contains details given by relatives, friends, and others, registering the dead in the name of the Holocaust. Here the dead are individuated, their collective presence evoked by the very density and quantity of these sheets, packed tightly one on the other within file boxes. Collecting names began in 1955, and some three million have been recorded and filed alphabetically in the Hall of Names.

The Historical Museum represents the Holocaust and its dead pictorially and textually. To quote from the official guide to Yad Vashem, in the Historical Museum, 'the story of the destruction of European Jewry is told through authentic photographs, artifacts, and documents.' This museum exhibit was composed by historians as a book of history illustrated by photographic examples. The textual and pictorial narratives – the pages of this book of history – are ordered chronologically; and the visitor leaves the museum through a separate exit, preserving the historical coherence of the chronology. The photographs and texts stress the factuality of exact historiographic disclosure, highlighted by the contrast between the pedantic accuracy of the texts and the pain, terror, and torture of the photographs.[24] The narratives cover the Nazis' rise to power and the persecution of the Jews in the Third Reich; the mass killing of Jews; Jewish armed resistance; the liberation of the camps; and the successful struggle of many of their former inmates to reach the land of Israel, where the Holocaust is exhausted on the beach, in this version of the showing and telling of catastrophe. The section of the museum on armed resistance is entered through a tunnel, slanting upward, signing 'the sewers which served as hiding places and escape routes for Jewish fighters in the Warsaw Ghetto,' according to the official guide. In this section self-sacrifice in battle comes to the fore, and the visitor ascends from the pit to the surface, to the exterior of the Holocaust, as did the fighters and then the sojourners to Palestine.[25]

Through varied media these closed sites tell, reflect, and represent the stories of the inexorable destruction of Jewish presence in Europe. However, many of the larger-scale open structures – the monuments and sculptures – provide a contrastive emphasis. The open structures reveal themselves utterly to the external gaze, as proclamations on the land. The smaller of these tuck into the folds and curves of the cultivated landscape. They are more continuous with the theme of genocide. Appositely, the larger ones abruptly thrust up from the land, to hold gaze and dominate perspective. These open structures, geometric and figurative, are dedicated to Jewish resistance and heroism during World War II (Young 1989a, 1989b).

The three largest form a set of triangular coordinates corresponding geometrically to the shape of the ridge. Near the entrance to the Yad Vashem complex, the Pillar of Heroism (the 'smokestack' of Momik's epigraph to this Chapter), simple and severe in design, soars some twenty-one meters into the sky from the highest rise in Yad Vashem. Its inscription commemorates all forms of Jewish rebellion and resistance during the Holocaust, including those who died sanctifying the name of God. The other end of the long ridge is dominated by the massive monument to the Jewish soldiers, ghetto fighters, and partisans of World War II. It is composed of six oblong granite blocks, three on each side, that between them form a window-like space in the shape of a Star of David. This space is bisected by a gigantic, needled sword piercing the sky. The blocks represent the six million dead, the Star the Jewish people, and the sword the fighting opposition to the Nazis. Almost equidistant between these two memorials, and forming the third angle of the triangle, is the powerful, larger-than-life monument to the Warsaw Ghetto uprising, discussed in Chapter Six.

Recollect that the outermost path along the southern edge of the ridge is a bulwark dedicated to the Righteous Among the Nations. Following on this, the symmetric triangulation of the three memorials to heroism constitutes a second bulwark within the outer one. Inside this space of representation is constituted the absence of place and bodily substance of the Holocaust dead – through emptiness, ash, reflection, photos.

Within the landscape of Israel, Yad Vashem converts the absence of presence of the Holocaust dead into the presence of their absence. Yet this utter absence means that its presence can only be alluded to, metaphorized, allegorized, through various media. The use of these media signifies degrees of reproduction, illusion, distance. The problem of the utter absence of the Holocaust dead and their places of death is insoluble. This is indicated by how the memorializing of these dead is done. First, the presence of this absence is constituted through various media. Yet the presence of this absence generates attempts to fill the void made present, and the very media substantializing and excising the void are themselves only copies, continually reconstituting the presence of absence. Thus the dynamic set in motion by the absence of body and place generates the ongoing and increasing representation of memorialism.[26]

We stated earlier that the journey to Yad Vashem is a voyage to a foreign land within the Israeli landscape. To this we add that Yad Vashem builds Europe within Israel in order to convey the Holocaust.[27] Only this totalizing, highly specialized simulation, discontinuous with and alien to the Israeli landscape, can memorialize the utter absence that is the heart of the Holocaust. Yet then there are consequences for memorialism and the constitution of place. Despite the collection of their names and details, the Holocaust dead are quite anonymous at Yad Vashem, and their relationship to the living is problematic. The Holocaust survivors diminish with time. Unlike military memorialism, revitalized continuously by ongoing warfare, the Holocaust continually recedes from the present.[28]

The memory of the Holocaust must be kindled in the offspring of survivors, in their children and in numerous others, for Holocaust memorialism to survive (see Kidron 2000; Feldman 2000). While military memorialism is the intimate preserve of kin and comrades, of those belonging to the dead, Holocaust memorialism is thrown open to everybody (to the living 'every body' paralleling the anonymous 'any body' of the incinerated Holocaust victim). The vast majority of visitors are strangers to the dead. Foreign dignitaries visiting Israel are taken to Yad Vashem at the beginning of their itineraries, to be guided through the Historical Museum and then to place wreaths on the anonymous ashes in the Hall of Remembrance. This sequence is important: these visitors first learn of the Holocaust, studying it, as it were, from an Israeli Jewish perspective. For these visitors this act turns the absence of presence of the Holocaust dead into the presence of their absence; and then this presence of absence is ritualized and memorialized – semiotically, these dignitaries cross the border into Israel through Yad Vashem. Ironically, within the totalistic environment of memorialism constituted there from stone, metal, glass, flame, paper, it is the living trees of the righteous gentiles that take root, live, and grow in the soil of the land of Israel.

The Presence of Absence: Counter Cases

> Spilt blood isn't roots of trees,
> But its the closest to them
> That man has.
>
> Yehuda Amichai (1971: 93). 'Jews in the Land of Israel,' in his
> *Selected Poems*. Harmondsworth: Penguin Books.
> With permission of Hana Amichai

A crucial problem of memorialism in the modern state is how to turn the absence of the self-sacrificial dead into the presence of their absence. The Israeli materials suggest an inverse relationship between the presence of the dead within the land and the absence of their representation on the surface. The less the degree of presence, the more elaborate the representation.[29] This aesthetic of elaboration substitutes for the presence of the dead, visualizing and shaping their absence, thereby turning this into the presence of absence. The presence of absence evokes the consuming self-sacrifice that is essential to modern nationalism.

In this section we discuss instances that seem to contradict the relationship between absence and representation. In the concluding section we argue that this relationship is significant for the Israeli Jewish national, because it focuses attention on the importance of part-whole relationships in nationalist ideologies. A number of monumental structures of representation stand within the military cemetery on Mount Herzl, seemingly in contradiction to the inverse relationship. However, these memorials are constructed in memory of the absent body of sacrifice. One monument commemorates the volunteers from the Jewish community in Palestine who were killed in World War II. Its centerpiece is a large boulder set onto the rocks of the mountainside. The boulder is pierced clear through with the sign of the Star of David. The Star is shaped into and through the natural land. One's gaze through this hole in the boulder is molded by the shape of the Star, itself given form by the natural stone that holds it together. The absence in the emptiness within the Star signifies the loss driven into the substance of the strong, firm land (the boulder) by these deaths; the shape of the Star signifies the presence in the land of the national imaginary, carved out by the self-sacrificial absence. The monument metaphorizes the presence of absence in the shape of the national, but an absence integral to the forming, to the presence, of the land.

Other monumental structures in the cemetery are given forms metaphorizing the shape of place or location of death. The memorial to 140 seamen lost in the sinking of their vessel by the Germans in World War II is constituted as a reflecting pool, with a structure at one corner resembling a ship's superstructure. The four sides of the bottom of the pool are lined with name-plaques for each of the dead. This extended visual metaphor constructs sea, ship, and the drowned dead, all within the cemetery. The memorial to the sixty-nine submariners lost in the disappearance of their vessel, the *Dakar*, is constructed as a massive submarine-like shape with a rudimentary conning tower. The memorial is partially sunk within the ground, and encloses an interior memorial chamber lined with name-plaques of the dead.

Within the cemetery, as outside it, where the bodies of the sacrificial dead are absent, their presence is made tangible through more elaborate representation. In some of these monuments this representation approaches the simulation of totalistic environments (ship, sea, the water bottom; the interior of a submarine-like structure) within which the distant locales of death and traces of the dead are made explicable. Of particular interest in this regard is the memorial to those who were killed defending the besieged Jewish Quarter of the Old City of Jerusalem during the 1948 War. During the siege the dead were buried in a common area within the Quarter. After the Quarter fell to Jordanian forces, it was not possible to retrieve the dead. In 1957 the memorial to these fallen sprouted in the Mount Herzl cemetery. Partially below ground, the long, covered structure is intended to resemble an alleyway in the Old City. Covering the walls of the low thoroughfare are the name plaques of the memorialized dead. After the Old City was taken by Israel in the 1967 War, the remains were moved to ordinary graves in the cemetery. The absence of the sacrificial body produced a representation in the cemetery of the presence of the place of sacrifice. This creation of context contained representations, names, of the dead. However, when the bodies of sacrifice were buried permanently, simple gravesites with minimal representation above ground were sufficient.

Some years ago Yad Vashem completed its largest memorial to destruction in the Holocaust. In contrast to the major closed structures commemorating genocide, the Valley of Destroyed Communities is in the open air, seeming to contradict our analysis. The Valley is located on some six acres of flattened rocky hillside immediately below the massive monument in the shape of the Star of David, commemorating Jewish armed resistance during World War II. This monument immediately becomes the guardian of the Valley, marking architectonically the visual contrast between the heights of heroism (the monument) and the depths of destruction (the Valley). The Valley commemorates the 5,000 Jewish communities destroyed in Europe. The Valley is blasted and carved meters deep into the living rock and earth of the land of Israel. From the hill above, the Valley is intended architectonically to resemble a schematic map of Europe, cut into the landscape. From within it has the vision and feel of a labyrinth; only the sky and the massive, sheer walls are visible, as the Valley floor turns this way and that through the schematic contours of the map. Incised in the rock faces of these cliff walls are the names of the communities, grouped together in locations that correspond to their approximate positioning on the map.

The Valley is a place of desolation without redemption, the Holocaust vision of Europe. To know the Holocaust one journeys to Europe, entering into the entire space of its map. There, within the absence of presence, one learns the stories of the presence of absence. Although the site is outside, under the sky, one must enter it to know it; and from within it is a sealed, totalistic environment, no more open to the Israeli landscape than the other closed memorial structures. Although the intention is to make this site an integral part of the broader national landscape, the Valley is a deep brand of elsewhere burned into the flank of the land. Once more, this site makes its place within Israel by making a part of Israel into another place; and in so doing, Holocaust memorialism differs radically from that of military death.

Memory, Metonymy, and Metaphor in National Memorialism

> To know everything it's possible to know,
> and that's everything
> because it's impossible to understand.
>
> Israel Radio advertisement for *The Encyclopedia of the Shoah*,
> whose publication was co-sponsored by Yad Vashem

The elaboration of absence signifies the importance of part-whole relationships in nationalist ideologies. Ideally these relationships are intended as metonymic. This is especially problematic with regard to Holocaust memorialism, and foregrounds how Israeli nationalism would have to change in order to fully absorb the Holocaust into its narratives of national identity and solidarity. Yet it is precisely through its disjunctions with the Israeli landscape that the Holocaust Memorial tells us more than do others about the process informing all memorialism of national death in Israel – how the absence of presence is filled with the presence of absence. Absence in Jewish national memorialism is rarely permitted to become a zero signifier, a sign deliberately left vacant, empty of specific meaning yet full of a virtual infinity of potential meanings with the capacity to reorganize whatever composition it is a part of (see Ohnuki-Tierney 1994). The indeterminacy this emptiness generates is anathema to national symbolism (as it is to the bureaucratic logic shaping the national) (Handelman and Shamgar-Handelman 1990, 1993), and perhaps also to Judaic traditions in which the injunction to remember exactly is central.

How is the absence of presence dealt with? Memorialism of a past one has not experienced depends on the paradox of memory constituted by information that is wholly in and of the present. This is paradoxical because 'memory' and the 'present' are simultaneously active while negating one another.[30] This is memory related to a past the present can never reach and experience directly. One way of solving this conundrum is by furnishing memory in and of the present with images of the past, representations of which the person perhaps knows little or nothing about. Through this substitution these images of the past are implanted and cathected in memory of the present.

As these images of the past are made integral to the present, the memory of these images becomes part of the person's past. Memory and image change places. Images of the past shown in the present constitute the absence of presence. Thus in the present there is memory of images of the past. Yet then these images become memories of the past – the presence of absence. In this way, memory in and of the present – memory of images of the past – is turned into images in the present of memories of the past. The person experiences present as past, and remembers this past in the present. The absence of presence is filled with the presence of absence. This is the process by which 'collected memories' (Young 1993) become collective memory. In terms of the kinds of memorialism discussed in this Chapter, this process of forming absence and then filling it with the presence of absence is most prominent in Holocaust memorialism, because of its simulation of totalizing worlds of experience that are foreign to the Israeli landscape.

We commented earlier that a single, simple military gravesite is sufficient to awaken the self-sacrifices sustaining the entire land and people. In the nationalist imaginary the place of burial is the synthetic conjunction of space/time. Nationalist dreamscapes pursue the seamless holism of people in place through time. The self-sacrifice becoming integral to the land is perceived as proof of the complete identification between people and place. The gravesite is a part signifying the entirety of national holism. The dreamscape of the synthetic holism of people in place through time is retrievable time and again from a single military gravesite, just as this holism signifies all military gravesites as integral parts of the national entity. The military gravesite is a metonym of the holistic vision of people in place through time.

However, once body and place are separated, disjunction enters metonymy, and processes of metaphorization set in to reconstitute the loss of synthetic holism. Thus representation marking place in the absence of the body becomes more elaborate. Just as metonymy thrives on continuities among the parts of a whole, their absence or disjunction generates metaphor, striving to reunify holism (see Eco 1985). In memorializing Holocaust death in Israel, disjunction, the metaphorization of absence, and the need to fill this absence with unconsolable presence, reach their apex – and the presence of absence slips and slides over and again into the absence of presence.

Neither the Holocaust dead nor their places of death are native to the Israeli landscape. The dead are neither in place nor in memory. Their time and temporal experience are not those of the Israeli Jewish vision. Belonging elsewhere, the Holocaust dead can be synthesized into the national dreamscape only by making disjunction integral to this holism. Then the powerful metaphors and allegories generated by these contradictions can be used to articulate the Holocaust dead to the land of Israel. The temporal becomes crucial to this endeavor. Linear time depends upon sequencing, on ideas that connect before and after. Time enables narrative, narrative enables lineal history and its telling, in Judaeo-Christian tradition (Ricoeur 1984). Holocaust memorialism in Israel is first and foremost narrative, often metaphorical and allegorical even as it historicizes. These stories strive to form a narrative incorporating into a greater synthetic whole the disjunctions between the Holocaust dead – elsewhere, elsewhen – and the land of Israel. Most showings of the Holocaust in Israel are also organized as tellings. However, because of the disjunctions between the Holocaust and Israel, each telling must be holistic.

Each military gravesite is the coded narrative of the metonymic whole. Each grave condenses the whole national story over and again, because that metonymic whole is constituted by the landscape of people in place through time. Under ordinary circumstances these stories do not need elaborate representation in order to signify the holism of the national entity. By contrast, each viable Holocaust memorial must once more simulate an entire context constituted of implanted memory, history, and narrative that bridges and articulates the disjunctions. Only within this simulated whole – Europe through time, in Israel through time – do the various parts of the Holocaust acquire their fuller, awful significance. Ironically, these disjunctions are not erasable, for they are essential to the historical narratives that strive to bridge the absence of the diaspora in Israel. And, so long as Israel is not made into the diaspora, these disjunctions will continue to generate sentiments of ambivalence and compassion, alienation and identification. These are the sorts of ambiguity diagnosed by our surface reading of the absence and presence of representation in memorials of national death.

> Is all this sorrow? I guess so.
> 'May ye find consolation in the building
> of the homeland.' But how long
> can you go on building the homeland
> and not fall behind in the terrible
> three-sided race
> between consolation and building and death?

Yehuda Amichai (1986: 94–5)
With permission of the Regents of the University of California

–9–

Absence Rising: Telling Little Holocaust Stories, Shaping the National

That voiceless combination, again trying to escape,
as it had every time Death confronted me in Auschwitz;
that mute combination getting no further than my
clenched teeth denying it exit. The secret of its omnipotence
was that it outdid vocalizing . . .

K. Tzetnik (1988: 325)

(To paraphrase Kafka)
The narrative is the axe for the frozen sea within us.

At the close of a workshop on how to narrate their own Holocaust experiences the narrators tell one another how it felt to speak. Here are the comments of five, women in their sixties, sitting around the table.

Says Ruth: 'All my life I avoided talking about this, even with a good friend who was in the camp with me. This is the first time I was given the opportunity to talk.'

Echoes Brakha: '. . . Everything was locked up inside me . . . we were freed a little, at least myself. I can talk a little more easily . . . [But] those points that until now I was frightened of, I couldn't get out, I still can't. I was frightened. Simply a very dangerous grenade [inside me]; it'll explode and take me with it . . .'

Adds Clara: '. . . There's a question . . . about whether we told [about our Holocaust experiences] to family, children, and so on. I never told, but I cried a lot, I cried a lot every time I saw pictures or a movie, I immediately became upset . . . we must talk . . . we must speak, to tell the coming generations . . .'

Confirms Hadassah: 'I didn't get any particular encouragement at home. "Why start the whole thing over again, opening up wounds; what'll it get you?" But I'm stubborn and I said I've got to participate [in this workshop] . . . I was too closed . . . Now its important for me to leave something to the next generation, even to my grandchildren. I'm more open now . . . because one doesn't want to talk, doesn't want to bother the children . . .'

Agrees Lea: 'I went through a great deal in the Shoah. I never distanced myself from any of this. But after the first day here [in the workshop] I returned home feeling heavy, and I couldn't explain it. I hid my feelings from my husband because he's a sensitive person and I was afraid he'll say [she slaps the table hard] "No more, its over." I did everything [that evening] so he wouldn't feel anything [about this]. I read a lot because I couldn't fall asleep. When I came here the next day and my friends here started telling, I saw a little of myself in every story. So I said to myself, what am I trying to run away from? From myself? . . . We need to know exactly what was done . . . I'm so fulfilled that I had an opportunity to get something out.'[1]

These women and other of the participants perceive themselves as moving from deep within their selves outwards; from the practice of sealed self-closure to some degree of openness that is connected to telling; from being victims of social practice to becoming their own agents. Each buried within herself, an unmarked memorial, is now rising to the social surface, to be recognized and respected as one who lived through the Holocaust as a youngster. The Holocaust self, made absent from the lived-in world, is now rising into presence, a presence carrying with it a virtual infinity of absences – of destruction, degradation, death.

I use the term, surface, to foreground the Holocaust self by reducing the depths and complexities of social order to flatness, thereby giving the self greater depth below the surface. So I will say that the Holocaust self is buried below the surface of the practice of everyday life, rising to the social surface during the special condition of telling. The surface also becomes that of the Holocaust self as it appears.[2]

The relative absence and presence of self is a critical shaper of the social and emotional contours of being in the world. Absence and presence, as discussed in Chapter Eight, are not a binary distinction, but positionings, enjoining a broad spectrum of engagement with the social. At issue here is not healing, not authenticity, but how persons weave their difficult selves into procrustean social worlds in which the national often is dominant, and in which the Holocaust increasingly assumes a central position. Despite their being guided to a degree, the stories victims learn to shape are malleable, with far more personal agency than that of participants in other of the public events discussed in this book. In Holocaust remembrance there are two kinds of absence to be considered: one is the personal absence of the living victim from many of the social worlds of Israel; the other is the absence that the doers of Holocaust perpetrated. The living victim must turn her absence from the social world into her presence, as she rises from within herself to the social surface – to the interface of selfhood and social order. In doing so she brings with her the great absences of the Holocaust. Through turning her personal absence into social presence, the victim foregrounds the presence of absence that is the Holocaust, and contributes in her small but powerful way to shaping the national.

Following on the argument of the previous chapter, for memory (experiencing the past), for pastness (feeling that the past has passed), and for memorialism (publicizing the past in the present) to exist, the absence of presence must be turned into the presence of absence. The presence of absence indexes the per-durance of memory, and often the memory of memory (Casey 1987). This interior lurch is done most feelingly and effectively when the presence of absence is embodied, for example, in the presence of the living victim.[3]

During the workshop (for a time held annually, and sponsored by a major institution of Holocaust memorialism), victims are taught to tell stories – each of a few minutes duration – on their experiences in the Holocaust. Later on, those who are willing tell their stories to pupils in their classrooms (and to youngsters in other venues, including the army). The length of the story – a brief sight-and-sound bite – is that which younger children in particular are thought capable of absorbing, given its subject matter. These stories are intended to sensitize Israeli youngsters to the Holocaust (and not all the stories are tragic or sad, despite their venues). The narrators who speak here – in their sixties and early seventies when they learned to tell these stories – were children or teenagers during World War II. One woman said poignantly that these memories were not of childhood, because these children, '. . . never had any childhood, ever. They had to look after themselves and they lost something that they can never have again, never. Adults could remember better days. They knew if they lived, if they got through the war they'll, they could describe to themselves, maybe they'll get there and it'll come back to them. Children don't remember anything at all. They didn't know didn't know in what in what direction to go. And what awaits them.'

The authenticity of the stories is not questioned. The stories are rooted in embodied experience that must not be denied. One of the organizers, herself a survivor and psychologist, said at the opening of the workshop that many professionals deal with the Holocaust, 'but their knowledge is limited because they weren't there. We, the survivors, represent the testimony of the last ones. The knowledge of the researchers is based on our experiences . . . It's sufficient that we are living witnesses to the horrors of the Shoah . . . Our stories and our experiences are *always* authentic.' An administrator of the institution responded by raising the problematics of memory, yet he immediately qualified this: '[But] there's a difficulty, because their [the survivors'] memory is not what it was; they also read books, saw movies, learned from others, and there are already uh uh problems – *not that they don't speak the truth* – but there are things that are blurred. That's that's clear. Here we try to help each of you to bring out your own authentic voice which is different from every other. There are no two similar stories, no two experiences.' If every experience, every story, is different from every other, then the final authority on authenticity (and perhaps also on truth) is the narrator, not the historian.

This introduction discusses one story that raises the absent Holocaust self. The section after addresses how the Holocaust self is made more fully present in the telling of stories. The penultimate section points to the relevance of prospective audiences for the construction of stories. The closing section takes up how these little stories are related to the national.

Consider how in the following story (of some four minutes' duration) the Holocaust self rises into presence, phase by phase, bringing with it absences that in telling are at the core of this self. These absences are made present through increasing shifts from presence to absence in the chronology of the story. Absence and presence, presence and absence, generate one another through loops of being that turn into becoming and loops of representing that reveal themselves as being. The narrator is Nekhama (born in Munkacs, and sixty-three at the time of this telling). She stands behind the table at the head of the room, her arms spread, leaning forward, fingers splayed on the tabletop. I do not quote the entire story verbatim.

Nekhama tells that she was one of a family of twelve, from whom she was separated at age fourteen. She states that she is going 'to condense . . . a few scenes that are very moving.'

> The first scene: a few days before the family was moved to a ghetto, the gentile woman doing the packing came to their home and told Nekhama's mother: 'Mrs F., I want to hide your daughter, Nekhama, until you go through this critical period.' Nekhama's mother was shocked, and didn't reply at once. Then, 'She stood and said: "I won't desert my daughter. She'll come with us to wherever all of us will go".'

> The second scene: 'Now there's the second scene. From the factory from which they take us to the Transport [the cattle cars], I have a picture that's very hard to free myself from. Very hard. A long line of people, with hats, grey, each with his personal belonging, walking to the train. This is a picture that its very hard to be free of, even after forty years, it will hound me for as long as I live.' [She raises her hands from the table and turns them over, empty-handed.]

> The third scene: 'We arrived at Auschwitz and there we got down from the from the from the train. My mother was with the [my] four little sisters. I took two from her so it wouldn't be difficult for her. At the last moment my [older] sister came to me and said, "Nekhama, give the two [little] sisters [back] to mother, and we'll go on together." So that's what I did and my mother and [my] four [little] sisters [were sent] to the left side to the fire [the crematoria] and I and another two sisters to the right side. And here I was saved from death for the first time. We move on together and we see a big heap. I look at the heap, people alive, thrown away [in a heap], old people and sick people; in the middle of the heap [I see] my uncle's head [she stops speaking and raises her right hand to feel her face], and above, on the top [of the heap] there was my brother, thrown away; with his head, we separated with [our] eyes.'

In the first scene the family is separating from home, from place. Mother has agency; she keeps the family together despite the gentile woman's very generous offer (one likely dangerous to herself) to protect Nekhama. Indeed she is shocked into silence by the abrupt clarity of the offer. In all this there is a hint that neither mother nor the rest of the family really comprehend the precariousness of their situation, nor do they anticipate the horror inevitably approaching. Nekhama will stay within the bosom of the family because the family with agency sticks together. Their absence from one another is not an issue, is not even conceivable, even as they separate from home. Wherever they go they will remain united.

In the second scene, a river of greyish-tinged people are moving silently to the cattle cars. Presumably Nekhama and her family are among them – yet these people are indistinguishable from one another. They are on their way to becoming ciphers – a flow of fedoras. They appear to move of their own volition, but agency is denied them. As Nekhama makes herself present in her story, the narrative becomes one of absence.

In the third scene, the family is ripped apart in the Selection that was done immediately to new arrivals at Auschwitz. Those ordered left walked directly to the gas chambers. Nekhama's mother and her four little daughters are murdered. Those ordered right walked into life and hard labor, though their lives often were short and dirty. Nekhama and her two older sisters go that way. Two fateful, diverging paths with no choice. Agency is now wholly external to the family, dividing and redividing these passive victims over and again (on this theme of division, see Wyschogrod 1985). But Nekhama has not yet left her family – they still await her on the way right. She comes upon a heap of people piled helter-skelter atop one another, bodies still alive, dying or waiting to be murdered. In the middle of the pile, her uncle's head protrudes, and on the very top, her brother's. An axis of ascending absence in terms of genealogical closeness. The inverted axis of loss and pain that was driven deep within her from then on.

As she sees her uncle's head she stops (speaking, walking) and touches her face (at the seminar table, on the way in Auschwitz). Where is she? Who is she? As the loss of agency and the absence of persons close to her rise within her story, she embodies herself with feeling in the present.[4] Telling this agonizing part of the story she stops talking, momentarily mute, but holds her face, affirming the firmness of her presence, feeling in that instant her most outwardly expressive and exposed body part. As the presence of absence rises through the story, the victim's presence is vividly solidified on the social surface. For the moment at least, Nekhama is no longer a passive, muted victim. On the social surface she is now a survivor [fem. *nitzola*], speaking of the Holocaust and making her presence known and perhaps forceful.[5]

One of the major ideological changes of recent years in Israel is this turning of the living Holocaust victim (a product of historical practice in Israel) into the Holocaust survivor (related directly to the appearance of the performing Holocaust self). The increasing outspokeness in Israel today of persons who lived through the Holocaust has virtually eliminated the term, victim (*korban*), and made that of survivor (masc. *nitzol*) popular. Survivors who become witnesses (masc. *edim*) by telling personal stories and by giving eyewitness accounts are the most empowered of those who have lived through the Holocaust. Embodying survivorship, the Holocaust witness is today given a major performative role in making citizenship national by carrying the terrors of Europe and the failure of the Jewish diaspora into Israel, far more powerfully than the yishuv pioneers were able to do. In this regard the chronoscape of the survivor is especially valuable, since it simultaneously witnesses both ends of the national progression from catastrophe to redemption.

Absenting Presence

The Israeli social surface has been difficult terrain for numerous Holocaust victims, driving them underground into absence. Absence secretes hiding places below the surfaces of social life – and into these holes tumble memories, pasts, places, many of the dead, sometimes the living-dead, perhaps never to be unearthed. These are unmarked graves of the Holocaust self, metaphorical and real, generating the absence of presence, the absence of memory traces on the social surface (Straus 1966; Sturken 2001).

If the absence of presence is turning into the presence of absence, then the least acceptable absence is refusing to attribute existential meaning to Holocaust experience, to the Holocaust self – rejecting the making of a story of what is not a story (Greenspan 1992: 145–7). This kind of absence is the furthest, the most alienated from the national meta-narrative of redemption, with its rationale of making citizenship national. In the following story, Moshe rejects even his few minutes, ending minimally within forty seconds. He sits behind the head table, balding, wearing glasses, a light polo shirt and a heavy, blue zip-front sweater open to the waist. Throughout he speaks at a steady pace, in an even voice that neither rises nor falls.

> 'I'll tell you about what gripped us from the moment we entered the camp until the end. Fear, hunger, and uncertainty. At the [camp] entrance, after reception, fear struck us and was with us all the time. We went to sleep with hunger and we awoke with hunger. And uncertainty, because we didn't know when the end will come, until when we'll last. There's no way of knowing or weighing how to evaluate these things.'
> Impassive, he nods his head in agreement with his voice.

Absence barely rises towards the social surface, and in this sense this is a non-story, perhaps an un-story, one that undoes narrative. The contextualization is minimal; nothing happens (except that what is, is utterly overwhelming); and the account is depersonalized – an anonymous camp, together with powerful drives (fear, hunger, uncertainty), yet all referred to in the first person plural. The speaker seems hardly involved. He closes with, 'There's no way of knowing or weighing how to evaluate these things.' A statement about an existence that could continue this way until death. The feeling tone is Kafkaesque – the subject is gone. A condition of existence without meaning except for the directness of feeling, yet feeling is objectified as part of the missing subject. An un-story that shuts off development and closure – conditions are plainly as terrible as they are. The speaker's final utterance states bluntly that there is no way of understanding the concentration-camp existence, no way of making sense of this imponderable. His un-story rises towards the social surface, but there is no hospitable response there, perhaps because the Holocaust self does not rise through the un-story.[6] Given the social stress on meaning in Holocaust experience, this teller might as well be stuck forever in a half-buried grave, still feeling fear, hunger, uncertainty, still insisting on their inexplicability in that alien place.

> As the speaker finishes, the instructor's immediate response is: 'I don't understand. Is there someone else [here] who doesn't understand? [A hubbub of voices breaks out] Or is it only me?'

The instructor's response rejects non-meaning (or rather, un-meaning) that obliterates Moshe's undoing of story (the un-story). Moshe may speak in an authentic voice about the existential reality of the camp, but this voice is subversive to the workshop, where accomplishing meaning is essential. The essence of meaning here is that the story does something to the horizons of the teller (and listener) – the horizons should not freeze, forcing a reality without movement, without climax. The story should shift horizons, and so the capacity of the teller to imagine different possibilities of existence. These may be tragic and horrific, romantic or upbeat, but by existing they engage the teller in the world as a feeling subject (and, so, open affect within the listener). By contrast, Moshe disembowels himself with the axe of narrative.

The presence of meaning depends on the presentness of the feeling subject, even though the narrator depicts himself as an anti-hero, as in Aharon's story. Balding, wearing an open-necked white shirt with pen in pocket, Aharon speaks in a matter-of-fact staccato voice (something like Moshe's).

> As a young teenager, Aharon escaped the Warsaw Ghetto. Looking for work he came to the farm of a Ukrainian family in Tarnopol (Eastern Poland). So that the farmer would not suspect he was a Jew, Aharon insisted on Sundays off to go to church, and he refused to sleep in the same room with the farmer (because he shouted in his sleep in Yiddish, his mother tongue). Aharon slept in the cowshed. Then came the final *action* against the Jews of Tarnopol.

> 'The Ukrainian called to me and said, "Come, let's go and see how they kill Jews." And of course I agreed. But the next morning, in my sleep I suddenly heard noise in the cowshed and that, I see a boy. He was about two years younger than me. So I said to him, "What are you doing here? Run away," or something like that, and he said, "Look, I don't want to run

away," I've had it, there's nothing more to do, I'm staying here." In the meantime my boss came, because I was the servant there, the boss came and asked, "Who's this, now?" I said I don't know. He asked the boy, he said, "I'm a Jew." [The narrator shrugs]. He [the farmer] said, "Should we protect him?", and left the yard, and I had a lot of Ukrainian friends, and he left the yard and around an hour later he returned [the narrator pauses] and brought two Ukrainians with him [the narrator swallows, his voice drops into the space of the narrative] and they killed the boy in the yard and I buried him. [The woman sitting next to the teller looks up at him and lets out a long sigh.]

The Russian troops arrived. 'A week later I went to the city and entered the police station and I said, I met, I saw one Jewish guy there and I said to him, "Listen, I've got a story, but because I'm not sure that I'm free, I'm going back to where I'm working, and this is my story, like this this this and this. But I don't want them to know I informed on them. The next morning two Russians arrived on horseback and called him out . . . and they called him out and said, "You did this and this and this." He said, "I never did anything like that, I have a witness. [The narrator points, holding out his right hand, palm up]. My servant will tell you it's not so." They called to me and I said, "That's right, it's not so." And they said, "We'll check into it." And they took him. And afterwards I learned that they killed him.'

Unlike Moshe, Aharon knows how he survived. And unlike the young boy declaring himself a Jew and depending for survival on the goodwill of gentiles, Aharon practices and hones his survival skills. Thinking through every move and its consequences, camouflaging himself as a gentile even as Jewish blood flows around him, and never, never, breaking role in the vicinity of his enemies. He is the agent of vengeance, yet this too is situational, taking advantage of changing circumstances. The intentionality of his Holocaust self is diamond hard, eschewing any form of heroism in favor of deceit in his struggle for survival. His narrative is pervaded by the significance of self-discipline and self-control over mind and body, the meanings he made for himself as a boy.

When the Holocaust self is made to disappear from the social surface (as in Moshe's un-story), then the voice of the victim is buried within himself just as he is buried below the surface of society. Through this interment within interment, social order loses the traces of the Holocaust self. Even the semiotic signs of human presence in the present lose their shape and drift away. To turn absence into presence, to make victim into survivor, the voice of the victim must be made more performative, emerging from the prison of its embodiment, speaking through the body in the name of the embodied Holocaust self. As voice emerges, self rises. The pain of this tortuous historical journey, the distance from heart to throat, from Jewish Palestine to the social surface of the present, emerges in the three-minute story of Yael.

Yael was born in Prague, and liberated from Bergen-Belsen by British troops. She was a *muselmann,* one who had lost all will to live, socially invisible, present yet absent, a vacant presence, one of the living-dead.[7] Yael had to be taught to walk anew. All members of her family were dead. She arrived as an illegal immigrant in British Palestine in 1946, coming to her older sister who was then thirty. Yael was then sixteen. (From here on, much of what she says is through tears, standing behind the head table and wiping her eyes with a tissue.)

'. . . and I thought, finally finally, I can open my heart and tell about what a hell [*gehenom*] I went through, its impossible to describe, I was only ten when I entered the camps
[Her voice breaks, she wipes her nose with the tissue, and holds it to her throat, the locus of outward passage. She is crying; she tries to speak but can't. Others begin talking; she waves them off but cannot speak herself]
Instead of this, no reaction, no-one asked me anything. Nothing. Nothing. My sister never asked me anything. The opposite. She always said, "Oyh, what do you know, we suffered here; it was so hard for us." And it [the silence] stuck inside me. So it grew here [She touches her throat], the silence, like like, excuse me
[She bows her head, covers her face with her hand, then with both hands]
Like explosives it grew in me until I really got serious depressions . . . I had to be in psychiatric treatment because no one asked me, everyone just said how bad it had been here, and how much, and here too they were hungry, and here too, and here we worked in the orchard [and] we could eat as many oranges as we wanted, but not to take them away. So I say but that's not hunger, eating oranges till you're full, that's not hunger. And they shut me up, "What do you know about how we suffered?" Afterwards my sister married me off at a very young age, I was already married at seventeen, and now the same thing with my husband. He also said, "Here we also suffered hunger, we were hungry here." [She touches her throat, now with the fingers of her right hand.] Until I got strong claustrophobia. I couldn't stand being in a closed room because I was cut off from everything. And again psychiatry, and again pills, nothing helped me. And no one asked me . . . For decades I didn't talk. And now when I have the opportunity, in front of soldiers or other people in public, it pours out of me like rain I've been waiting for for forty years, that I should be asked something. [She begins to cry again and wipes her eyes.] And I can talk only in this kind of forum. [Her head bowed, she covers her face with her hand.]

> Responding to a question from the instructor, she adds that though the speakers were permitted to invite guests, she invited no one, not her friends, not her husband. Since they had asked her nothing of the Holocaust during all these years, why should they hear her anwers now?

Yael initially undergoes a sort of revival. Freed from the camp, she is a muselmann, a vacant presence. She must be taught to walk anew, to climb up again to the bipedal posture, the vantage point that expands horizons, distinguishing the human from the animal (Straus 1966). A child when she entered the camps, evil has taken her maturation, perhaps her capacity to grow. The sole remnant of her family in Europe, she seeks to relocate herself within the nurturing matrix of family and collectivity, and sails to her older sister in Palestine.

She desperately desires to relate what has happened to her: '. . . and I thought, finally finally, I can open my heart and tell what a hell I went through . . .' But against her will her Holocaust self is shut up, shut off, and sealed deep within herself by Jews struggling through their own tribulations to create their own social surfaces and selves as distinctive and distinct from those of European Jewry. Her suffering would send them back to Europe, perhaps to reconsider their closeness to the diasporic past. Instead, their trials displace hers.

As her silence sticks in her, growing in her throat 'like explosives', she touches her throat, chokes, and loses her speech in the seminar room. As she weeps, the explosives detonate. Her body opens, her voice returns. She is 'married off' at seventeen, an apt description of her self as passive, victimized. No one here is ready to listen to her Holocaust self – not sister, not husband, not friends. Until recently she is locked away within her own sealed, claustrophobic space. But now she tells of her experiences in public (and she can only speak of these in public), and the Holocaust 'pours out of me like rain I've been waiting for for forty years.' Tears fertilizing her Holocaust self as this rises towards the social surface, in her view sprouting fruitfully there, yet perhaps her pain spilling corrosively, now deeply pitting and scarring this surface.[8]

From the victim's perspective, present-day Israel may be an extension of Holocaust Europe, especially if she is muted. The passive victim is an absent survivor. The victim's heart made claustrophobic within the body to which it pumps life. The heart at the bursting point – the near collapse of embodiment, perhaps a form of suicide. The victim shut up and shut off within her self is one who, potentially, can climb out of the hidden Holocaust hole as a survivor to spill her experiences corrosively across the social surfaces of the present, thereby telling of a past-ness of the present, a present-ness of the past.

Holocaust victims were often expected to be muted (if not mute) in relating Holocaust experiences. They were hidden away in the folds and holes of the positivist, futurist national edifice. They were seen as ambiguous beings, lacking the positivist, redemptive core, sometimes as tainted, as Yosef tells in this excerpt from his story:

'One sentence of what I didn't tell. I had a sister who was in Auschwitz. She had a number here [He gestures to his forearm] and for many years she wore a plaster [over the number]. [The woman sitting on his right is wiping her eyes.] Why? Because one day she walked in the street and she heard an American Jewish couple who spoke English to one another, Jews, but she knew them from the neighborhood, and he [the husband] said to her [his wife], 'That number is worth a lot of money.' [He points to his forearm.] When she [Yosef's sister] heard that she said [His voice falters, rises, chokes; the woman on his right holds his shoulder with one hand and pats it with the other.]⁹

Yosef's sister erases the sign of her disparaged Holocaust self from the social surface of Israel, hiding it under a second skin, within her skin, within herself. The sign is numericized twice over – once the Nazis quantified her soul, and now her fellow Jews dissolve her in the flow of money. She masks the sign with another, yet this sign is visible. Covering the number with a plaster, she draws the gaze of others to a festering wound that will not heal, while not permitting the gaze to see the nature of the wound. In another sense, her Holocaust self, so present to herself, is hidden on her very own surface, her skin, as together they move across the social surface under the unseeing eyes of onlookers. She remains a victim until death buries her remains.

Yet, as in the following story, the victim may encode the deep meaning of his survival through a semiosis openly present on the social surface, but silent unless one has the key. The teller, Avram, describes in a matter-of-fact tone how he escaped from France through the November snows of the Pyrenees, and then to Palestine where he joined the British army. He continues:

'. . . my story is one of Shoah and re-birth [*laida mekhadash*]. I don't use the words arisal [*tekouma*] or resurrection [*tekhiya*]. Re-birth, in the symbolism of my daughter. Her name is Shai-Ela, Gift of God. The [letter] *shin* is for the name of my sister Sarah. [His voice wavers, chokes, blocks. He sips water.] The [letter] *yod* is Yehuda, the name of my father. [He stops again; his voice becomes thicker, rougher, then higher, more clipped, each word chipped off as it leaves his mouth.] The [letter] *aleph* is Esther, my mother. The [letter] *lamed,* Lea and Leib, my grandparents, and [the letter] *hei* is 'The Name [God] will avenge their blood' [*HaShem incom bidamam*].

Embedded in his daughter's name, entirely constituting this name, are the three generations of his family, dead in the Holocaust, and the vow to avenge them. The dead are re-born through his child, herself born in a new land, distant from the European landscape smeared with the blood of his family. Whether or not Avram had spoken out about the Holocaust, he has externalized its absences from deep within himself, his Holocaust self rising to the surface in the form of new life. Yet the dead are dead; they died as they did. When Avram sees or feels his daughter, does her presence also carry the absences of the dead embedded within her, but always on the (social and personal) surface whenever one calls (or thinks) her name?

For many victims, decades passed before those still alive found their voices (like Yael), turning into survivors insisting that their own experienced Holocaust was of direct ideological and political relevance to the metaphysical and historical foundations of the Israeli state – that the existence of the state was an answer to (and so depended upon) the realities of the Holocaust. Promotors of Holocaust memory continue to argue that the catastrophe is a founding and foundational event shaping Israel's identity as a viable Jewish state whose people emphasize in their remembering that the dead, regardless of generation and age, are the ancestors of the living. Many of the stories told in the workshop are linked affirmatively to the State in ways that echo this theme. Forming Holocaust catastrophe into the viability of the Jewish state has a climactic character, resonating with the rhythms of time discussed in the concluding section of Chapter Seven.

The struggle to capture absence, to cherish absence, to make something of absence, to turn absence into presence, is central to many of these stories. The dead are absent, the camps are absent, the victims live with their memories, seeking to fill the absences within themselves and by so doing to entrench these absences within the social surfaces of Israel. They seem to be exclaiming, let these absences, these holes in our private and collective being, take root on the surface as we turn ourselves inside-out, turning our insides, our Holocaust selves, into the landscapes in which all of us (you included) live. Let the pain in our entrails shape your lives. This is the purpose of the workshop – shaping the stories to be aimed at the young, emotionalizing their perceptions of the Holocaust in relation to Israel. The young Jews are to be the direct descendents of the Holocaust dead.

Telling Stories

Telling stories is a way of performing, a way of practicing the awakening of critical capacities of selfness. As one critic of theater comments, '. . . what is universal in performance is the consciousness of performance' (Blau 1990: 259). The criticality of the Holocaust self, buried beneath the surface, rises into presence through sensuous telling. The workshop gathering is one of sensuously performing survivors, not muted victims. And as most speak they mutate from survivor to witness – witnessing as the authentic testament of embodied experience that is not taken as representation. The self of the witness enacts the presence of absence. The rising Holocaust self riven with absence raises absence, and this absence is sensuous in remembering sharpened spikes and edges of pain, the hooks of memory embedded in shadows, echoes, shapes.

The witness performs the presence of absence, raising absence within herself, within her embodiment of this absence, from experience, psyche, and bodily knowledge, activating throat, vocal cords, the voice that speaks in one direction and chokes in another; in tones, registers, pauses; in the softness of tongue and hardness of teeth; in tearing ducts and eyes that see in both directions (interiorly, exteriorly) and none; in obsessive, spasmodic movements of fingers, hands, shoulders, feet. These and more are a choreographing of being there while here, an orchestrating of bringing here to there and here once more, all in the now. Yet the absence made present through performance is itself so often about the nullification of presence through degradation, destruction, death. In today's political discourses, making these absences present, empowering their presence, turning their presence into new practices, are all integral to the struggle to alter foundational myths and histories of people and state by making the Holocaust a tortured pillar of people and state.

The shift into telling contains revolutionizing potential. Rising towards the social surface, the Holocaust self puts into question the routine grounds of the everyday. The absences the Holocaust performs within Israeli Jewish imaginaries, and the reasons given for these absences (the hatred of Jews, everywhere, nowhere; the unique intentionality to exterminate all Jews) contain this revolutionizing potential. The little stories and their intended impact on the young, are but one example among many. The performance of Holocaust absences gives way to their unquestioned practice through the routine grounds of the presence of absence. Then the effects of this catastrophe are practiced with little or no critical exegesis.

Practicing the absence of the Holocaust on the social surface during the first decades of Israel's existence is producing countervailing efforts to heighten consciousness of this catastrophe by performing aspects of Holocaust history, memory, theology. As consciousness of the Holocaust rises towards the existential surface, its practice becomes highly self-conscious, pointing over and again to absence (death, loss, sorrow). In the first decades, the performance of Holocaust (the Kastner trial, the Eichmann trial, Holocaust Remembrance Day, the built memorials) did not articulate well with the positivist ethos of Israeli nation-building. Today the performance of the Holocaust self enters the taken-for-granted practices of the everyday and, in times of peace, Holocaust loss and absence compete for attention in the public domain even with the the army dead.

The routinization of performance essentializes the authenticity of Holocaust absence in everyday Jewish consciousness. But this performance of Holocaust is not due solely to the desire to reveal the murder of European Jewry, the suffering of survivors in Israel, the human dimensions of slaughter and sorrow. The essentializing of Holocaust absence is due also to the prospering of Israeli Jews at the expense of their pioneering ethos (thereby inflating the symbolic capital of the absence of substance, and contributing to the growth of celebratory historical museums [Katriel 1997]); to the claim of the State to represent all Jews, the living and the dead; more implicitly, to the oppression Jewish governmentalities practice against Palestinians (related directly to the prospering of Israel) and to the need to justify this by essentializing it; and, yet more implicitly, to the ethnic battles between Jewish Easterners and Westerners over who has accumulated the greatest heritage of suffering in the immediate past – the Easterners who say that they were eviscerated as their native cultures were torn out of them and obliterated after their arrival, or the Westerners whose family and kin were exterminated in the Holocaust. Benefiting is the growing business of advertising and marketing Holocaust absence and its memorialism, a circus of ashes.

Doing the Presence of Absence

Before a speaker shapes a story, she is subjunctive on the social surface – the performance of the yet-to-be (but on-the-way) self through the yet-to-be (but on-the-way) story. The agency the speaker discovers in shaping a story shifts her into performance, exteriorizing a part of her Holocaust self. The story may be one in which she is embedded as a character, as it and she are taken in, digested, by others (see Rimmon-Kenan 1984; Handelman 2000). The shift to performance may also be an ordeal. If the buried, muted fragment is not to remain the victim, then she must be unearthed, entering the agency of a survivor, one who has endured. If she becomes an active agent, especially through telling, then she turns herself into a witness (fem. *eyda*) mutating the made absences of the past into the social practices of the present, reshaping the contours of Israeli Jewish imaginings.

The ordeal of performing the Holocaust self is managed in various ways. Body may shut down voice and continue the performance; or, the teller may distance her self from the experience. To witness, the victim must give voice to her voice, to the Holocaust self rising through heightened consciousness towards her exterior. She hears herself shaping her self in the thrust of the arrow-like moment of self-exposure, perhaps in the last second to shut down her voice and stab herself in the throat. This is perhaps the most explicit moment of the ordeal in making absence present through witnessing. The Holocaust self batters and shatters against its embodiment, against the simultaneous desire to open up and to shut down the body that enables and prevents the exposure of the victim. But the body in pain, the embodiment of Holocaust experience, may not only shut in the mind, it may also shut the mind down. This is the 'break' – the physical inability to continue telling – that characterizes numerous efforts to narrate. This is Shulamit's condition as she begins to tell. A tallish, slim woman in an open-necked checked sport shirt, she stands behind the head table, resting her splayed fingers on its top.

> Shulamit: 'I was born in Poland. Kracow. I couldn't make up my mind about which story to tell and I decided [She pauses, picks up the water cup] water helps [She drinks] to tell [She pauses, her right hand

touches her chest, and then moves out towards her audience and then upwards, thumb up; she slaps her open hand on the tabletop, looks away – the opening of a connection and its shattering – and] I'm angry [she whispers].'

Instructor: 'Continue. Now you're not in the introduction [practicing an introduction]. You're in the real part.'

Shulamit: [A long pause. She pulls the table towards herself with both hands, as though pulling herself upright by pulling closer the task at hand; or perhaps pulling herself into her own tale world.]

Instructor: 'Stop for a moment. Sorry that I'm allowing myself this [interruption]' [Shulamit indicates that the interruption is in place with an inviting wave of her right hand]

Shulamit: [She interjects, but it is inaudible]

Instructor: 'No no no no are you following me?'

Shulamit: 'Yes.'

Instructor: 'Perhaps you'll tell another story? A story that's like, in our bones, that we choose very carefully who to tell it to because its intimate. You're going to tell this to an audience of elementary school kids whom you don't know. Isn't that suicide?'

Shulamit nods.

Instructor: 'So I'm asking, it's not part of your [allotted] time; perhaps you'll make a "switch" [in English]? What do you think? Another story that you'll get out of yourself more easily. Maybe this one in another two days [later on in the workshop].'

Shulamit nods.

Instructor: 'We'll begin again.'

Shulamit: [It's not clear if this was the originally intended story] 'We didn't succeed in staying in the ghetto. We went to a place thirty kilometres north of Kracow. In August 1942, when the extermination of all Galician Jews was decided on, we received an order to leave the town and go to the main city of the area, where the famous salt mines are. Every Jew was allowed to rent a horse and cart. We did the same. A long convoy of carts loaded with baggage, packages. Every Jew was allowed to take a table or a cupboard . . . People, Poles, stood on both sides of the road because there were no sidewalks, to see the Jews leaving the village. And then a woman suddenly came up to my mother, a peasant, *goya* [female gentile], the wife of the goat-keeper, she came up to her and grabbed her here [Both fists grab her own shirt-front; she whispers, her voice almost silenced; she stops, and takes a drink of water. Murmuring begins around the table, accompanied by a loud, 'Shhhhh'] and she said [Now on the verge of tears, whispering, her utterance partly inaudible] ". . . you won't get out of this".'

Shulamit breaks at outset and end. Witnessing the presence of absence, her rising Holocaust self cannot find any purchase on the surface, sliding, slipping, falling again into the holes within herself, into the vastness of genocide containing her, that at certain moments she can only whisper out of, as her body, her throat, her lungs, enclose and constrict her within herself. Embodiment is the container of genocide, of absence and emptiness, the body the (last?) bulwark against their escape onto the slippery, uncertain, social surface on which meaning is continually negotiated, where their reception is ambivalent.

Helmuth Plessner argues that bodily constriction, convulsion, crying, 'make their appearance as uncontrolled and unformed eruptions of the body, which acts, as it were, autonomously. Man falls into their power; he . . . lets himself break – into tears . . . He responds – with his body as body, as if from the impossibility of being able to find an answer himself' (Plessner 1970: 31). When one cries, 'the body, so to speak, takes over the answer for him' (Plessner 1970: 33). Yet in this and other instances, choking and crying are also the performativity that the body, as embodied experience, allows to the mind as embodied experience. As the mind surrenders to the body, in Plessner's terms, the body continues the performance through its own kinesthetics. The body's powerful appearance in such conditions of great distress is then not quite a 'dys-appearance, a bodily alienation or absence' (Csordas 1994: 8). Rather, the body enacts its embodied experience, the pain of its own embodiment, its very being as body.

In this culture losing voice is losing articulated meaning, yet not necessarily losing the significance of meaning that an articulate voice enunciates but also masks and hides (since speech must be interpreted). The body in pain unmasks and reveals this significance of meaning. The appearance of the body in pain (despite the subjectivity of pain [Scarry 1985]) compels attention (or deliberate inattention). If the speaker can overcome the pain of embodied experience, or time its appearance, the story may well gain added power. In any case the body is present, enacting its own embodied experience.[10]

Shulamit, her Holocaust self imprisoned within her body, surrenders to the body's answer – the body in pain constricts, twists, grasps the social surface, chokes, cries. An answer but not quite a complete story in words – the initial portion of Shulamit's final utterance is lost in whisper. Nonetheless as mind surrenders to body and body takes over performance, significance does emerge on the social surface, the significance of Holocaust absence enacted by the paining body. Whether the body in pain aborts the telling depends on where in the narrative this continuation of performance by the body occurs. Shulamit aborts her first attempt to tell, and despite her body's enactment of its deeply embodying pain, that story is dead before it begins.

Witnessing the Holocaust invokes sacrifice. The Holocaust dead leave the silence of absence in their wake, and witnessing demands that the living victim exorcize this absence, this frozen silence, from within himself. The axe of narrative may be the medium. Yet the axe is double-headed, double-edged, cutting both ways. Telling the story, getting it onto the social surface, turns the narrator into a sacrifice, a self-sacrifice to the remembrance of the dead for the benefit of the living. The self-exorcism is the performing of self-sacrifice. This is especially strong when the narrator enters as a character into her own narrative space, the story world opening through her telling. McNeil (1992: 118–19) and Young (2000) argue that the size of the narrator's body varies with its relative presence within its narrative space. In my terms, the sense of self-sacrifice expands when the narrator enters into and is enclosed within the space (gestural, narrational) that she opens before her as she tells. Inside her own narrative space, the narrator's body diminishes in size, while its sense of loss grows. The sense of self-sacrifice is less when the narrator distances herself from her own story world as she tells. Then her body increases in size, enclosing her story world.

The sense of self-sacrifice is pervasive when the narrator 'breaks' entering into or navigating within her story world, and is broken within it, by it. The narrator sacrifices silence, the silence of her fracturing as victim, but too, the silence of the dead. The rising and shaping of voice and gesture from within embodiment, the telling voice, becomes the moment of self-sacrifice, the private interior exorcized on the social exterior. The sacrificing of the silence – the silence keeping the unsayable within oneself, postponing the telling. In sacrificing silence the narrator's body size alters – a lot, a little, positionally – in relation to her story world. The more the narrator is a character in her story world, the greater the sense of self-sacrifice as she makes known the interiors of her embodiment, her narrative entrails falling across social space, dissected and reshaped by the agencies of the social.

Some narrators witness by avoiding the confrontation of psyche with its embodiment. In this respect, irony is a powerful device of distancing. Thus a woman is telling, like Yael, about the difficult reception she and her husband received in Israel from his two sisters and others: '. . . They told us not to talk about the Shoah because it's not acceptable, not important . . . Because we're losers; we lost. Because if we survived, for sure we paid money or we robbed someone or we didn't behave well. So it was forbidden to talk about this subject . . . I had an address of an aunt in the United States, we wrote her a letter. I wrote her that it was difficult here *because the locals didn't understand us.* A month later I received a package. Opening the package I found a dictionary, with love, and she hopes this will help me [quiet laughter in the room]. *It was a Yiddish-Hebrew dictionary*' [guffaws of laughter]. Through distancing, the Holocaust self is buffered and protected in the story, while the body is given autonomy of action. The self unthreatened, the body does not commandeer the performance.

In the following narrative, Malka distances her Holocaust self simultaneously from her body in the story and in the workshop. This distancing and autonomy of the self from its embodiment generates an ironic and surreal perspective on surviving.

Malka, born in Warsaw, is telling of the way to Maidanek after she, her family and friends were taken from the bunker in which they were hiding.

'. . . I very much would like to talk about my home, [my] parents, but I'm not able to . . . So I'll tell about an incident that until today, I can't say that it pursues me, but I remember it until today – the way to Maidanek in the railway [cattle] car . . . Most of the [my] family went in, including among others the family about whom I want to tell: father, daughter, and son. The son was about my age, a boy, a Polish gentleman . . . In the railway car there were, its difficult to tell [you] what there was – crowding, the head, the the the emotion. It was terrible. This boy that I knew, he was a relative, he had a suitcase. He put it down and sat on it. I stood next to him and I felt I couldn't [stand] anymore. So I said to him, "Marek, let me sit for a bit." He shook his head, he can't. In the meantime people were crying and yelling, "water water." So his sister, she limped and was a doctor, said to me, "Listen I'm telling you, I'll give you a little urine, and drink it. I also drank it." And it helped me. In the meantime from the screaming the evening had come, anyway it was dark. I stood next to Marek's suitcase and so I wouldn't fall I leaned against the wall and hung onto a nail. [She shows how with her right hand]. I don't know how long I stood like that – either I fell asleep or I fainted, but at a certain moment I woke up and I started to step on something soft, like a mattress. Mattresses? How can it be? I stepped and it was soft. But it was dark. And I check it every time and I wonder, for what did they give us mattresses? It's so crowded. The yelling and the crying, by the way, there was one who went crazy and grabbed me and started and started, I won't. And when they opened the doors [at Maidanek] and there was light I saw that I was standing on Marek's stomach. He fell exactly next to me. And I didn't know, I thought it was a mattress. When we went out, half the railway car was dead. His father and sister who limped, they went straight to the crematorium.'

In Malka's story the Holocaust self retreats from its own pain. She will not talk about her family; and she immediately pulls back when her voice begins to tell about being attacked in the cattle car. Refused a little succour, a little mercy, by the boy, her mind or psyche insulates itself from the horror and terror around and within her. Her body does her surviving. The boy's sister, a doctor, shares urine with her and she, her body, drinks it without question, without revulsion, without asking whose urine her body is taking into itself. Her mind distances itself, fainting, sleeping. She awakens to her body standing on softness. As she discovers, her vertical, living body is standing on the boy's horizontal corpse, supported by its soft stomach. Her body objectifies and stabilizes her relationships with the environment: whatever her body is doing – drinking urine, hanging onto a nail, standing on the boy – it is protecting her survival. So, too, there is nothing in her uttering threatening to her self; and her body does not interfere, does not constrict or choke off her voice.

The story of her body's actions is ironic – distancing, self-protective – as she stands on the pliant surface of a corpse in the hell of that cattle car on her way to the death camp. Her Holocaust self is somewhat detached, rising to the surface – now – by telling about her somewhat detached body's relationships to others – then. This body does not enact pain, nor does it continue the story. The mind is free to tell a curious tale, one seeming hardly to involve the narrator – as she states at the outset, this is not an incident that has pursued her.

In the following example, Mina's mind controls her body until after she utters the climactic moment of her story. She is seated behind the head table.

> '. . . Plascow was a work camp [and later a concentration camp]. We carried big rocks. We worked hard. Transports came and came. I waited for my mother and sister, I separated from them during the Selection in Auschwitz. I prepared for their coming and collected pieces of bread, hid them under my mattress, and I got to six pieces. The first thing I did after work, I checked my treasure. [One day] as I always did I checked under the mattress and the treasure was gone. There was no bread. I felt so sorry, but the pain is still with me. I never saw my mother and sister again.' (She begins to stand, slowly, sitting again as one hand rises to cover her crying face. Some ten seconds later she wipes her eyes with her fingers, saying, 'Excuse me,' takes a drink of water, and leaves the table).

Mina painstakingly and lovingly collects and secretes the bread to feed her mother and sister. The bread is stolen, her mother and sister never reappear. As Mina joins the disapearance of sustenance to the disapearance of nurturance, her body breaks in pain, unable to stand, hand covering the surface of her sacrificial Holocaust self, weeping. A living self-sculpting of embodying pain. Without sustenance, without nurturing closeness, hers is a broken being in the workshop. Yet she has told her story before her body shuts down her voice. Moreover, her break is climactic, coming precisely at the moment that stresses the full emotional resonance of the story's agony. Only the self embodied, the self given over to the body's judging, can perform sacrificially.

However the survivor organizes her performance, she is a witness, an I-witness, an eye-witness, and an aaaiiyyhh-witness to the events she experienced; though the scream is quiet, it reverberates throughout her existence. Unlike the muted victim who can easily be molded as representation, as a symbol of times past relevant (or not) to the present, the survivor is the witness to the past living into and shaping the ongoing present. The survivor's embodiment – now – in the present incorporates her embodiment – then – of the past. In a sense one body one tense. Stating that the survivor tenses is simply to say that he is embodied, and that his body is memory memorializing – his body remembers, responds, acts in the world. The tensed body of the past tenses apprehensively in the present of performance. The same body then and now and so perhaps the same tense(ness) – a presence everpresent, one not to become absent even as it experiences overwhelming absence.[11] Being here/now in the flesh remembering (the eye-witness) being here/there (the I-witness) in the flesh (the aaaiiyyhh-witness) – for some survivors there often may be little distinction between 'here' (present-day Israel) and 'there' (Europe of the Holocaust), between 'now' and 'then' (Langer 1995), between one's self as subject and object. Most of these Holocaust stories abhor the absence of presence, and strive to sacrifice silence by self-sacrificing their narrators. First and foremost, this power to evoke presence from absence on the social surface is important to the narrators as survivors and witnesses. Yet the effect of this affect on their audiences is no less crucial to the entire project of sensitizing the young (and others) to the Holocaust catastrophe.

Stories and Audiences

Central to this project of shaping narrative is the suitability of the stories for the hypothetical audiences they are crafted for. Despite the Holocaust's increasing breadth of presence, the premise is that listeners will not empathize with the experience told them unless it is turned, moebius-like, from the external and distant to the internal and close. In the workshop shaping of narrative, barriers to identification among Israeli Jews are removed; while the monothetic division between Jews and gentiles (and within this, between Jews and Israeli Palestinians) is stressed. The following example relates to the erasing of boundaries to enable broad Jewish identification; the second and third examples relate to the categories of Jew and gentile within these stories; and the fourth, to the extraordinary human qualities that in the eyes of Jews elevate the gentile above him- or herself.

> The barriers effaced in the first example are of the kind of language used. The narrator is asked to prepare her narrative for a school class composed mainly of children whose parentage is North African, and who have no direct experience of Holocaust survivors. These children live in a town built to house (and often to warehouse) their parents' generation. In beginning her story the narrator uses foreign words: 'The three of us [three sisters] got to Auschwitz and we immediately decided to be in the *Hofkommando . . .*' The instructor interjects: 'Madame, don't speak German here, we don't know German.' He does not interrupt again, despite her interspersing German terms throughout her narrative. But as she runs out of time, he stops her and continues his critique.
>
> Instructor: 'Time's up . . . I'll take the gloves off. There's a problem . . .
>   This isn't a piece for the audience you've been given.'
> Narrator: 'Not a piece.'

> Instructor: 'Sorry, you have, first of all, I don't like this kind of theater
> where I toss in an aside [as if] from someone in that audience [as he
> did at the outset of her story]. German in a development [new] town.
> Not only are you a blonde *vus-vus*, a *Shoah* survivor from the Northern
> North talking German, do you want to shut their ears completely?[12]
> Start preparing a piece in which there won't be a single foreign
> word.'[13]

Inadvertently using German words, the narrator gives the (correct) impression that the Holocaust was experienced primarily by Ashkenazi Jews. The worry is that this would reduce the willingness of children of Easterner parentage to identify (through the narrator) with the destruction of European Jewry (and so to take upon themselves the burden, but not the directing, of Holocaust memory). Moreover the narrator looks and sounds Ashkenazi – a Central European accent, her skin and hair light-colored, clothing and accessories stylish, expensive. By insisting on Hebrew only, the instructor points to how the national language embraces Easterners and Westerners alike.

In more advanced stages of storytelling, rehearsals may be done before a live audience. In the following instance, the narrator is addressing an audience of Jewish religious teenagers, telling why she began to talk to various groups about her Holocaust experiences, about her past in Europe, about the difficulties of being 'absorbed' in Israel, arriving in the present: 'The Shoah is working today too. (Her strong, clear voice takes on a higher pitch, wavers, breaks. She pushes her fingers back through her hair and takes a drink of water). The children of Sarajevo have nowhere to live.' (She cries and wipes away her tears). The instructor interjects: 'Excuse me for stopping you. The guys [*khevra*] have been sitting here with us for close to an hour. They're very polite. You're beginning a story it would be very good to hear on a different occasion.' Silenced, the narrator sits.

As the narrator journeys in her story from Israel to the former Yugoslavia, she crosses the border between Jew and gentile. The stories told in the workshop are intended primarily as stories of Jews for mainly Jewish audiences. The universality of the stories is in their Jewish suffering, but not in deliberately inflicted, mass human suffering. As the narrator begins to speak of the homeless gentile children of Sarajevo, her crossing turns into a taxonomic transgression – from the outset she has conflated gentile with Jew, in stating that, 'The Shoah is working today too.' The *Shoah* is Jewish, belonging to the suffering of past, the fear of future.

So, too, in the following example (much closer to home), the border between Jew and non-Jew is maintained, perhaps even strengthened. The hypothetical audience in this instance is one of Palestinian Israeli schoolchildren. The narrator tells of her growing affection, as a fifteen year-old in Bratislava, for a boy her age, a Jewish refugee from Vienna. They speak of many things, sitting on the front stoop because he is afraid to go into the street, frightened of recognition as a stranger. He is the first to tell her of (and to arouse her interest in) the land of Israel that he wants to help build. She falls in love with him. But one day she searches for him in vain – he and his family have been deported back to Austria. She says in conclusion that by coming to Israel after the war she realized their common dream.

The instructor asks her to add a final sentence: 'To summarize for this specific [Palestinian] audience – do a closure,' though he does not lead her into what to say. The narrator adds: 'What did I want to tell you in this story? Our dream was always to live here together with the people of Israel but also with you. And I think, I believe that both of us can live nicely together in this big and nice land. And, there's room for us to live together.'

A love story between Jews, with gentiles the enemy, just as Palestinian Israelis are perceived as the enemy by so many Israeli Jews. Speaking to a Palestinian audience, the narrator does not mention them. Her story leads directly (perhaps causally) from Holocaust to Zionist settlement. The story is irrelevant to her audience; or perhaps especially relevant in disadvantaging them in relation to Israeli Jews. The instructor, well aware of the story's irony for an audience of Palestinian children, asks that the story be made relevant for them ('to summarize for this specific audience'). From the Holocaust perspective the story empowers the divide between 'us' and 'them;' but here, 'they,' the Palestinians, are not distant in time and place – they are immediately present, the narrator addressing them. The irony of the target audience deepens with the narrator's summation. She focuses on the dream of Zionism – one people in place together through time – making room in this for the Palestinians ('but also with you'). This phrasing does not include them in this dream – but the narrator expands the cramped space of Israel into spaciousness ('this . . . big land'), within which two peoples can live side by side. The place of the foundational dream is in this space. There is also room for those others who are present as a practical given (they do not seem to dream).

In these stories the gentile as a positive presence in the Jewish Holocaust depends on this person displaying an extraordinary preparedness to sacrifice his or her life in order to save a Jewish one, transcending the extermination inflicted by non-Jews. These stories are desirable, showing what the agency of the gentile could accomplish, were there the desire and the will. In counterpoint these stories make the case for the baseness of the gentile, yet for the bounty of the human spirit. The instructor alludes to the latter in his own way, in responding to the following story.

The speaker is Adina, tall, well-dressed in a colorful sweater and dark trousers. She wears dark glasses. Earlier she had told the workshop that she had spent the war years with Christians, who had saved her.

> 'I'll tell you a story about a nun, one of the Righteous Gentiles. This woman is now eighty-one years old, a resident of Warsaw. For sixty-two

years she works in an institute for blind children. In the year 1942 the Germans heard that in her convent there were three Jewish nuns – that is, three women of Jewish descent who had converted to Christianity even before the War . . . the Germans turned to the mother superior . . . and told her that if the women aren't turned over within twenty-four hours, "We'll go into the convent." And then Clara volunteered to save one of them. Three she can't, but one, she is ready. She took one with her to the Carpathian Mountains, to Bukovina, and told that she was ill with tuberculosis and needs fresh, invigorating air of the mountains, right? She rented a tiny hut meant for a shepherd. And every day she went out to work in exchange for food. And so they lived for three years. When the winter of 1942 came, in Poland in winter the temperature drops some-times to 30 degrees [Celsius] below zero. There is no work in the fields, what to do? Sister Clara decided to travel to Krakow to ask for alms (*livakesh nedivot*). There was one woman [also a nun] she knew [in Krakow], it wasn't the first time she went out to beg that winter . . . She came to her acquaintance, and the Polish woman opens the door, "God sent you." She sees the woman is trembling. Sister Clara asks, "What happened? What is it?" And the Polish woman said, "The Germans were just here, in the apartment opposite. And there was a Jewish woman living there, hiding, a neighbor, and I didn't know it. I heard shots, they left, but I don't dare go into the apartment there, to see what happened." Sister Clara said, "But there are screams coming from there, screams of a child".'

'. . . They went into the apartment and what did they see? A body fallen, stretched out on the floor, and in a large basin, the kind they had then, sits a little girl, perhaps three or four years old . . . Sister Clara dressed her . . . and said, "I'll wait until evening; then I'll take her to me, to Bukovina." She didn't dare travel by train. The girl clearly looks semitic. She took her in her arms [the narrator stops, drinks water] and started to march by foot. The march took three and a half days – it was a long distance, close to 100 kilometers. For three and a half days she marched on foot with the child on her back under the shawl. That's how they came to the second nun who supposedly had tuberculosis, and the little girl and the nun stayed there until the end of the War, till January 1945. After the War the nun went back to the convent and Sister Clara took the little girl to Warsaw.' [Loud applause.]

The instructor relates to this story as a parable demanding soul-searching on every-one's part. 'And I ask myself . . . What would I do if I were on the other [gentile] side? Would I be a Righteous Gentile? I have no answer to this, no one has an answer. Its its, I think, for me. This meeting. I feel we have to be worthy of someone like her. We have to stand up to the humanitarian test every day. Actually I'm saying something I hate hearing from others. Yes, we [Jews] have to stand up to the test that perhaps other peoples don't have to. Didn't . . . I feel, I, this meeting with the nun turned me [around], I have to be absolutely [*glatt*] kosher. I have to test myself more thoroughly. Because someone like that did that . . . it's watering the tree. It doesn't go out of my head.'

The instructor transposes himself to the gentile side, asking how he himself would behave. Then in more general terms he asks of himself and the others, how good a person is each of us, in practice, not theory? For a moment the workshop is recontextualized in terms of a humanity transcending the differences between Jew and gentile. But only for a moment, as the instructor reinterprets the humanitarian test as one with especial relevance for Jews rather than others. The deeper implication becomes the *sotto voce* challenge to the suffering Jew to behave humanely. If the nun can behave so righteously, how much more difficult (yet necessary) is this for the Jew. The humanitarian test is now specifically a Jewish one. By extension, on occasions of Holocaust memorialism, Righteous Gentiles often are made honorary Jews; or more ambiguously, made betwixt and between, leaving the monothetic gentile category, but not entering the monothetic Jewish one. Though Adina's story is a paean of praise to Sister Clara, the instructor subtly holds to the division between Jew and gentile, indeed to the division between survivor and Righteous Gentile.

Where do these stories lead, in relation to the social surfaces on which they appear? What is thought of here as a good story is one with a climactic ending, often redemptive in relation to the Jewish State. Redemption positions the Holocaust as the basis of the moral existence of the State, turning Israel little by little into more of a Holocaust landscape, foregrounding the national (without citizenship).

From Rising Absence to Redemptive Presence (and its Consequences)

Lawrence Langer who has looked intensively at videotaped survivor testimonies is scathingly critical of the tendency in Holocaust commentary to attach the 'grammar of heroism and martyrdom' to the destruction, degradation, and death of the Holocaust. He refers to Martin Gilbert's chronicle of Nazi atrocities against Jews in which the historian, '. . . records them [the atrocities] with a ruthless and unsettling resolve not to masquerade the worst, leaving the reader heavy-hearted and bereft' (Langer 1991: 162–3). Yet Langer is exasperated by the very final paragraph of Gilbert's lengthy book, in which the poetism of 'resistance' to oppression suddenly appears. Here Gilbert (1985: 828) claims that: '. . . Even passivity was a form of resistance . . . To die with dignity was a form of resistance. To resist the dehumanizing, brutalizing force of evil, to refuse to be abased to the level of animals, to live through the torment, to outlive the tormentors, these too were resistance. Merely to give witness by one's own testimony was, in the end, to contribute to a moral victory. Simply to survive was a victory of the human spirit.' Langer (1991: 165) comments that, 'The pretense that from the wreckage of mass murder we can salvage a tribute to the victory of the human spirit is a version of Holocaust reality more necessary than true.'

Langer's position is no less theological than Gilbert's. Should tellings and other expressings of Holocaust have certain closures rather than others in order to be faithful to Holocaust and its narrators? To be faithful to the social surfaces on which these tellings appear? To be faithful to the summations of Holocaust, enabling its discussion as a phenomenon done by human beings? Is it not awful (and awe-full) that genocide was and is done? Langer is suspicious of redemptive Holocaust stories. Yet his position no less is a version of Holocaust reality more necessary than true. The Holocaust was awful. The story is a medium that often is its message. The absence rising onto the social surface is filled with myriad interpretations. No one, no one can speak for the totality of the Holocaust without shaping, redacting, manipulating the realities they are bringing into existence, and those hardly are independent of efforts to give particular forms – moral, theological, historical (yet rarely ethical) – to these realities. Judgement is retrospective. Therefore we judge, temporally, historically. As someone commented, the present exists to distinguish past from future. Our judgements of Holocaust, of memories of victims, of stories that raise memory, are all predicated on this historicist premise. Since this premise shapes realities, it cannot be used also to excavate these realities from beneath the topsoil of past-ness. The realities of memory exist now, not then.

What of the Holocaust stories of this Chapter? Young (2000: 79) asks whether narrators express emotions they had during the occasions they narrate – back then, historically, judgementally – and so whether they represent their emotions of that time in the present? Or are they having the emotions they do as a function of the embodiment they experience during narrating? She raises the intriguing possibility that emotion is shaped 'by and for the narrative in the course of which it appears . . . narrative evocations are . . . authentic originary instances of emotion. Emotions are not being represented here; they are being occasioned' (Young 2000: 80). Perhaps the *feelings* of absence are deeply embodied in the victim, and are a criterion of victimhood, more generally; while the shaping of *emotion*, necessarily at the interface of person and social world, is occasioned by the narratives through which these emotions appear on the surface of the person. Above all, and unlike the public events discussed in earlier chapters, the telling of stories in this Chapter is an *emergent* process that takes form as it takes form. The shaping of these stories can be influenced, but they are not molded, not by the instructor nor by others. These stories are not teleological. What then of closure in these stories? An important form of closure is indeed redemptive: when the occasioning of emotion dovetails with national metaphysics that the existence of the State is the answer to the Holocaust. The narrators made their homes in Israel largely by choice, and have grown old in the Jewish state. They are not simply molded expressively by the State, though they may well become amplifiers of the national, and of the rhythms of time discussed in Chapter Seven.

In the metaphysics of the national there are no passive, slaughtered victims of the Holocaust. Every one of the dead is defined theologically as a martyr, and all instances of Holocaust death are perceived as a victory of the spirit.[14] In recent years, though there is no lessening of the centrality of heroism, the dead also are perceived in more moving, human terms. So, too, in rhetoric there is some blurring of the distinction between active and passive 'resistance.' The stories of Holocaust discussed in this Chapter are part of this social process of personalizing and humanizing the dead in public, and of exorcizing the living whose absence from the social surface was discounted, devalued. The stories in this Chapter (aside from that of Sister Clara) are not about heroism, nor of martyrdom in its theological and populist meanings. But many of stories do close on a register of redemption, dovetailing with the Zionist premise that the State proffers to Jews the redemptive moment in Jewish history, ultimately rescuing them from the evils of the gentile world. This is so in Dina's story (that in voice, drama, pointedness, content, and . . . closing, is virtually perfect as a little Holocaust story).

Dina speaks slowly, deliberately, with numerous pauses, in a low, clear, gentle voice. She tells of arriving in Auschwitz on a transport at night, in terrible conditions.

> 'The doors were opened onto the light of hell. Powerful lamps provided light. Shouts. Dogs. People dressed in strange clothing with stripes. A lot of Germans. We were ordered to stand in a line. [She sighs.] There were masses of people. Children. Little children. Whose crying tore the heart. The old people could hardly stand on their feet. Shouts. More shouts. The Germans demanded order. [Irony dwells on her tongue.] With their order they succeeded in killing so many. We were ordered to stand in a line. My mother, my sister and I marched forward. A man in a German uniform, and my mother and sister he sent to the left [now in a very soft and gentle voice] and me to the right. I tried to join them but the man in uniform prevented me, and in a pleasant voice he said to me, "[This is] until they've settled in their place. Tomorrow you'll see them." The man in uniform was Mengele. Do you know what, who Mengele is? [Her voice rises sharply, keening.] Mengele The Angel of Death of Auschwitz. With the movement of his hand he determined life and death. So began my way of suffering, hunger, and degradations. This happened when the Jews didn't have a state. The answer, when there is a state, is the Entebbe Operation. Only the State of Israel could defend us so there wouldn't be the Shoah.'
>
> [Applause.] The instructor's response, 'Wonderful.'

By contrast, in the following three instances each of the narrators has difficulty completing the story – embodied experience strangles the voice, perhaps the interiority of feeling blocks the exteriority of emotion. In each, the instructor persists until the teller accomplishes closure; and in each it is this redemptive moment that is performed as the end of the story. As in Dina's story the Holocaust is joined to national meta-physics, in keeping with statist aims – yet the Holocaust is also reshaping the premises of the metaphysics, re-forming the aims of the State.

The narrator tells how the Jewish police of the Vilna (Vilnius) Ghetto showed the Germans the place where her father and other men were hiding. She begged a Jewish policeman there to leave her father alive [she chokes, excuses herself, cries], but he refused to help, and she never saw her father again. She says, 'I can't continue any more. Thank you.' Getting up to leave the head table, the instructor tells her to sit down and drink water. She begins again: 'It's hard to believe but these are the facts of life . . . children, remember my story, and when you have fateful decisions in front of you, remember that your place is here so that the people of Israel won't go through another Shoah.' The narrator tells her imaginary audience of schoolchildren that as Jews they must remain in Israel, the sole defense against the repetition of the past.

The narrator tells how she was in the second grade in a Krakow school when war began. After the defeat of Poland, she along with all Jewish children was expelled from school. She felt shameful, unable to comprehend this action. She continues: '. . . from that day I started along my tortured path, that's, fact, that I was Jewish put me outside the framework of life.' She stops; her splayed fingers touch her face; she's trembling. The instructor tells her to take a deep breath. She takes a drink of water and starts again: '. . . always, somehow, I believed that I'll get through it so that I'll talk about it, and that's the purpose I'm fulfilling here. So that you'll know there were hard times, very hard times, but we got through that, and now were in a [school] class in the State of Israel and our pride is that we're Jews.' The narrator alludes to Israel as the answer to the catastrophe, contrasting the pride of being a Jew in Israel to the degradation of Jews in the Holocaust.

The narrator has great difficulty in speaking: '. . . actually, we're the last ones, the last of the survivors, the fragments [she shakes her head with a grimace, takes another drink of water, pulls up her sleeve, sniffles] . . . we're among the last of the survivors, you've heard me, that's what I've said. Actually actually today I'm pleased . . .' [She sniffles, sniffles, shakes her head, drinks water.] The instructor asks her what she's pleased about. She continues: 'Today actually I'm pleased that I'm here in the land of Israel because I see what we've built, what a beautiful State we have, what a beautiful people we have, and what wonderful generations [of people]. The people of Israel live and will live.'

The narrator closes with a paean of praise to the successful nation-building of Israel, declaring with certainty that the future of the Jewish people is secure in Israel. In this closing the narrator's singularity ('I') turns into a multitude with whom the narrator identifies ('we'), spreading across the generations in a chain of transmission, rising to a crescendo *as* the people of Israel, through whom the uncertainties of history are turned into eternal presence.

Each narrator speaks of the past with difficulty; her voice is closed down; her story ends. In each instance the instructor persists. And in each the narrator returns to speech with a more powerful, fluent voice, switching from the terror of the European past to extolling the glory of the present in Israel. Narrative space is given redemptive closure – survivors and youngsters live together within the Jewish state, protecting them by force of arms, enabling these survivors to witness their tragic past in front of these youngsters whose task it will be to ensure the survival of the state. The real or imagined presence of children gives the witness an imaginable future that includes these children. The tellings are inter-generational, dominated by the militancy of witnessing, the Holocaust self emerging above the social surface, remembering, and blocking forgetting and entropy, the forces encouraging the absence of presence. Someone says in the Claude Lanzmann documentary, *Tzahal* (The Hebrew acronym of the Israel Defense Forces), the sequel to his film, *Shoah*, 'Israel has always functioned as an answer.' But if Israel functions as an answer, one need ask, what is the question – and to this there may be too many answers.

The redemptive closing of these stories is a triumphal mode in which profound agony, loss, sorrow, are magically mutated into the victory of being alive within the state. Or, perhaps not so magically – choking off the voice before closure may embody and express the terrible rupture between living through the Holocaust and surviving afterwards. Returning to voice on the social surface practices living through this rupture, another kind of absence made present. The story also closes by embodying the state within the survivor. The victim who wails and screams below the social surface for her dismembered, destroyed family stands precariously on the surface of her self, joining herself through telling to the voice of the State as it proclaims itself the eternal answer to the threat to Jewish being. Doing this, her body is taken into the State, speaking through her. The story of the State acquires a speaker (Linde 2001). As she joins herself to the State her voice changes from hesitancy to certainty. Of more significance, the embodied experiences rising to the surface of her self through telling turn into the signing of these experiences on the social surface. She no longer expresses her story, her emotions, but becomes (or is made into) the living sign of herself. She is a sign, as she was in the past, only now a different sign – then a victim, now a witness; then told to shut up, now to shout. Is the survivor humanized for public consumption in this process, or is she typified once more to reflect (and make) a changing social order? If the existence of Israel is narrated more and more as a redemptive response to the Holocaust, whose (theatrical?) agency is at work, who is staging the performance?

One point is clear: in such stories the self-redemption of the Holocaust victim through narration reveals the State as the redeemer of the Holocaust self.[15] Many of the stories relate Holocaust to State. In this regard, becoming a survivor and a witness through narration in Israel is often a political act. And the act has strength, especially since 'the enormity of the event always precedes the individual story, so that every detail becomes portentous' (Kirmayer 1996: 192). Every act of Holocaust witnessing invokes the entirety of the atrocity. Every act of witnessing speaks on behalf of the entirety, a constituency that through the rhythms of time and their relationship to remembrance stretches far into the past, far into the future. The holism of Holocaust meets the holism of State . . . embracing one another in their mutuality?

The viability of any relationship between Holocaust and State depends on whether it is turning into the routine practice of the national in Israeli Jewish life. Not the banalization of trauma in daily life, but rather its theodicy, and so, its religiosity, as an insistent and insisting response to the embodied musics of absence often felt integral to Jewish existence in Israel. Yet to turn the relationship between Holocaust and State into everyday national practice requires its enactments, the most persuasive of which are still those of survivors. When the witness becomes the redemptive presence of absence rising, the lives of survivors become apt metaphors for attempts to shift the foundational myths of the State by maintaining that the Jewish national acquires its meaning and moral worth as the answer to the Holocaust. The ephemeral ashes of the crematoria are mortared as moral cement between the building blocks of the Jewish State. The Holocaust stories are one medium of many sifting these ashes, these absences, for the imagining of meaning for the present.

There are crucial issues largely ignored in the struggle to re-position the relationship between Holocaust and State. One is whether a (democratic) state can stay viable if it postulates its existence upon ruination and destruction. What sort of state and people grow from foundations that burrow incessantly into the nullities of absence and emptiness? Perhaps one answer is that of an expansive Zionism either holding on mightily to the substance of land through time, or being sucked into a black hole of national absence. Another issue is whether making the Holocaust the foundational meta-narrative of the State empowers the State to act with impunity to oppress others in the name of the Holocaust dead? Absence rising – the embodied experience of historical atrocity made into an adulation of the State in the present – provides the grounds for morality founded on absence, for morality that negates itself, instead of providing the grounds for the presence of a multiplicity of inter-subjective voices.

Epilogue: The Cyborg State

What animal would die of hunger in a river of milk? Man alone.

La Mettrie (1993 [1748])

In the Prologue to Part IV I suggested that bureaucratic logic and the national interact synergistically, filling death with sacrifice and presence. This claim needs qualification. Though synergistic, bureaucratic logic and the national torque together unevenly, their twisting into one another fraught with tension. This fragility pervades their relationship in public events, but no less so in their wider social orders. Torquing indexes the joining of phenomena where the jointure fits together partially and therefore discontinuously (Bunn 1981: 16–17). So bureaucratic logic may constrict, strangle, choke off the emotionalism of the national, and the enthusiasm of the national may rent, shred, overflow, swamp, the neat borders and divisions of bureaucratic logic. Yet the torquing relationship between bureaucratic logic and the national is also chiasmic, one of crossover (Merleau-Ponty 1968: 263), of their knotting and folding together (Bunn 1981: 72), of each turning into the other, of something else emerging. Chiasmic crossovers seem to come into existence where and when complexity and variety peak, though not necessarily in stabilizing ways. Chiasm opens vortices of potentially chaotic turbulence and transmutation (see Minahen 1992: 157–62).

Writing of the relationship between body and world, Merleau-Ponty (1968: 138) argues that the seer and the visible, the seer and the seen, are flesh to one another. Body and world permeate one another, their limits, their space, more textured, more sensuous, than mathematical. He contends that, 'What we call a visible is . . . a quality pregnant with a texture, the surface of a depth, a cross section upon a massive being, a grain or corpuscle borne by a wave of Being [though] . . . the total visible is always before or after, or between the aspects we see of it' (Merleau-Ponty 1968: 136). The body/world relationships may be vortical or spherical, body and world turning, twisting through one another, folding with one another, smearing and adhering to one another, but whatever they are according to Merleau-Ponty (1968: 138) these relationships are not those of planar, linear topologies. In these phenomenological perceptions, space (and time) are not first and foremost mathematical (Carey 2000: 31).

Bureaucratic logic and the modern state develop historically within and around the same areas of central and northern Europe. Their force is in their synergism, in the emergence of a whole greater than the sum of its parts. Yet this synergism also pulls the state and its infrastructures into vectors of unease, tension, contradiction, rupture. Perhaps the state-form, discussed in Chapter Two, mutates, bifurcating into opposing vectors (apart from its transforming relationship to the rhizomic). One vector pulls towards the mathematical, towards lineal topologies of separating and fitting together parts with exactitude, and governing these territorializations with higher orders of clarity, precision, control. The other pulls towards the modern national, combining the metaphysics of transcendence, of the sublime, with the intense arousing of emotions, their abundance overspilling, uncontainable, rising to crescendos of the national, even as these crests invert into loss through sacrifice and into the absences created in the national. Therefore in one vector, bureaucratic logic and aesthetics do embody the topologies of mathematic-like surfaces, forming angular planes of precision, concision, the exactitude of difference and similarity, organized hierarchically. In this vector the monothetic dominates the forming of infrastructure. The other vector, of the logic and aesthetics of the emotions of holism, swells from within embodiment – of people together in place through time – deeply texturing the sensuous existence of the state. The people sensuously dreaming the national dominates.

The synergic viability of the modern state depend on the torquing together of these two vectors, though their epistemologies consistently clash. This torquing is chiasmic, opening vortices of turbulence, uncertain, unpredictable, in their consequences. In modernity nothing is more machinic in its lineal, angular, controlling and controlled formings of form than is bureaucratic logic. And nothing is more form-less in its swerving, swirling, twirling wildness than is the 'machine' of desire generating emotions of the national, in their manifold textures of sameness and difference, of nationality, race, ethnicity, identity, historicity. The modern state survives through the anxious descent of its transcendental metaphysics, of the utopic imaginary of moral and social order, into the upsurging desire within synchronized bodies territorialized through time. As these downward and upward flows twist and fold into one another, chiasms of the emotional national are generated; and through their energies the peaks of the national flourish, expanding, climbing, surging upwards. The topologies formed through bureaucratic logic aim, hone, direct, and modulate these momenta. Though the folding together of transcendence and desire is deeply textured in its interior complexities, this is less so for the lineal topologies formed through bureaucratic logic. These topologies straighten, fix, and order the emotional national. These lineal surfaces are slick rather than sticky, their capacities to separate, classify, catalogue, attesting to this, as does their monothetic articulation to one another.

The modern state torques together infrastructure and emotion. Mann (1993: 60) argues that, 'the unusual strength of modern states is infrastructural' (see also Torpey 1998). But state infrastructure, formed through bureaucratic logic, must be pervaded by and permeated with metaphysical emotions of the national; otherwise there is little or no identification with and commitment to the state, nor any desire for self-sacrifice. Modern nationalism synergizes bureaucratic logic and emotions of the national. Yet this torquing wavers and wanders, staggering uneasily, variably, radically, between a synergy that shifts the state towards holism shaped as categorical and internally divisive, as the tight, bureaucratic organization and integration of institutions and people, or towards holism shaped as homogeneous by the shared emotionalism of the national. This disjunction between holisms is profound in events of presentation of the modern state, of the Israeli State, even though its overt presence is sewn into the uniform. Perceiving the state through this deep if masked disjunction in its public events, leads me to call Israel a *cyborg state*.

The term, cyborg, short for 'cybernetic organism' (Clynes 1995), indexes the symbiotic joining together of the machinic and the organic (Gray et al. 1995: 2), perhaps inscribing the machinic into the organic (Canguilhem 1992: 54), though the machinic may be understood also as another kind of (perhaps radically different) organic. In Haraway's (1989: 139) terms, 'The cyborg is the figure born of the interface of automaton and autonomy.' The cyborg is not quite a hybrid, since the stress is more on the symbioisis of systems joined through distinctly different premises of existence. Though the cyborg usually refers to this joining through and within the individual body, the term also has been applied to the body politic, to populations organized politically as boundary-defining information systems linked to machineries of organization and control (see, for example, Gray and Mentor 1995: 454–5). The philosophical genealogy of this vision is traceable to Hobbes, among others (Visvanathan 1990: 259–61).

The idea of the cyborg state highlights the power and danger of torquing and intertwining the lineal logic of bureaucratic infrastructure and the dreamings of the national. The bureaucratic, more generally the governmental, is cybernetic in its forming and functioning. The cybernetic is premised on the processing of information that enables the organization of this processing to re-organize itself in response to its processing. The cybernetic depends on self-knowledge, on the system knowing its conditions during its operation, thereby assuming the capacity to predict and control the outcomes of its functioning. Modern bureaucracies, and therefore the state, cannot operate without these teleologies of lineal machinic processes. Yet the energizing fount of these state metaphysics is in the national, with its fiercely erupting, adhesive imaginings of destiny that pierce, rip, and tatter selfness with sacrifice and loss.

The cyborg state is itself the chiasm, the crossover of these forces of presence and absence, the lineal hardness of cybernetic self-knowledge twisting together with the emotionalism of selves melting together through self-sacrifice. The twisting cyborg state veers into cybernetic over-control, needing, arousing, yet fearing the emotions of the national, themselves veering towards the out-of-control. Despite (more accurately, because of) their powers of lineal control, the systems of the cyborg state are poised on the edge of emotional chaos. Relatively slight disruptions of rigid lineal control amplify into massive sliding into the erratic and chaotic out-of-control, and into the violence that does violence to violence – the coercing return to over-control. Though these systems are cybernetic, their degrees of freedom, of interior flexibility, are limited by the hierarchical top-down character of the social taxonomies they operate. In the cyborg state the problem is not one of balancing the arousal of national emotion with lineal machinic control, nor is it one of seeking the right mix of the two. The problem is more that of making one cross over into the other, and so of turning one into the other. Angular planings of the machinic producing sunspots of the national; flaring emotions channeled into controlling gunsights of the machinic. These chiasmic relationships strain the systemics of the cyborg state, continually threatening its capacities to make itself viable.

In its liberal formulations, citizenship – the rational, legal, defining and classifying of individual membership in the state, discussed in Chapter Three – derives from and veers strongly towards the bureaucratic logic of lineality. Small wonder that the Israeli cyborg state maximizes effort into making citizenship national. As is often the case in systems interacting with their own contradictions, what goes around comes around differently. Making citizenship national in the Israeli State is one major crossover of the logic of the lineal into the holism of emotions, holding the state together by homogenizing its Jewish membership on the level of the national. The cyborg state is not a smooth operator of itself. The bifurcation into bureaucratic logic and the national, and their torquing together, generates chiasmic vortices that poise the cyborg state on the edge of the chaotic, as the state collides with and within itself. The lineal and the emotional interact uneasily, their contradictions profound and consequential. The public events discussed throughout this book are in their various ways attempts of the cyborg state to transmute the texturality of national emotion into the mathematic-like topologies of bureaucratic logic, and bureaucratic logic into the emotions of the national, while saving and amplifying both through one another. The emotions of the national are amplified by the purposive goal-directed teleologic vectors of bureaucratic logic; and bureaucratic logic is amplified through the transcendent value, respect, and honor given to emotions of the national.

Chiasm is integral to the cyborg state, since it comes into existence through torquing together radical difference. The cyborg state does not exist without such crossovers and transmutations. Thus bureaucratic logic and national emotion, both basic to the cyborg state, must collide in a variety of venues. They do this in events of presentation. These events shape sentiments of the national through bureaucratic logic, and imbue this logic with the emotions of the national. Yet each of these vectors is still foreign to the other, and so bureaucratic logic and national emotion continue to collide chiasmically in numerous Israeli statist events of presentation, though their collision is not vortical, not turbulent. Why this absence of turbulence in such public events? The very existence of the chiasmic seems to require a high degree of complexity, one that should not be taken for granted. This complexity is that of the human, of free will deliberately driving differences to torque into one another, regardless of collision and turbulence, of potentially chaotic effects. This suggests, then, that the chiasmic can be accomplished also by modulating degrees of human complexity, degrees of free will, while nonetheless remaining human. When free will is dampened and subdued while radical differences are torqued into one another, the collision accomplishes the crossover into cyborgian unity while remaining on the edges of the chaotic, without being sucked into its turbulent vortices. In Israeli public events the presence of the military has this modulating effect, through reducing the complexity of the human without expunging this (the condition of the *muselmann* in the concentration camp).

The recurring presence of the military – its bodies, motifs, metaphors, ethos – in public events of presentation demonstrates how national emotion and bureaucratic logic are torqued into one another without overtly generating turbulence, all the while practicing the stability of the cyborg state. The military is the most prominent and powerful exemplar of clothing bureaucratic logic in the national, demonstratively exhibiting the lineal coolness of this logic while generating national sentiments. Sewn in this way, this logic controls these emotions, all the while maintaining that their amplification is in the best interests of the State. The presence of the military amplifies both bureaucratic logic and the national, while dampening and subduing the free will of those who participate in and partake of their torquing. Though the organization of the modern military is complex in institutional terms, the social constitution of its members while in uniform is reduced in complexity and constrained.

This uni-form is not merely skin deep, but deeply embedded in the psychic and embodied shaping of the individual, his perceptions, practices, judgements. This uni-form embodies both the national and bureaucratic logic, the imaginaries of the former, the monothetic organization, aim, and momentum of the other. In relation to both of these constituents, this uni-form is totalizing, encompassing, hierarchic. The presence of the military in public events reduces human complexity and variation, making these not only more uniform, but similarly responsive to the same stimuli, as free will, individual agency, are dampened. Triggering the military simultaneously activates in tandem the national and bureaucratic logic, but each within the other, each moving through the other, each forming and formed by the other. This torquing via the military obviates much of the danger of the chaotic in the chiasmic. The presence of the military accomplishes the transmutation of the chiasm – here, of the forming power of bureaucratic logic deep within the emotional national, of the dreams of the national deep within the monothetic linealities of bureaucratic logic – without the cyborg state falling into the turbulent vortices opened by its mixing together such unlike, contradictory modes of organizing and interpreting life-worlds.

From this perspective, the military is essential to the well-being of the cyborg state, its presence in public events profoundly stabilizing and energizing relationships between the components of the cyborg, presenting and embodying the project of making citizenship national, but linking this national project inexorably to bureaucratic logic. Each person in uniform, each person standing to attention, each monothetic category separated from all others, each measured movement in sequence through time, makes bureaucratic logic and the national torque into one another over and again, resonating with every cell, as it were, in the structuring of the public event of presentation. More than any other component within these public events –

Versailles, Holocaust Remembrance Day, Remembrance Day, Independence Day, remembrancing in military cemeteries and at war memorials – the presence of the military and military-like formations amplifies torquing without turbulence.

In terms of the rhythms of time, so crucial to the Israeli national, the presence of the military indexes the phase of arisal, the axial reversion from downward to upward movement, the shift from passivity to activity, from victimhood to heroism. This shift depends on opening the vector of self-sacrifice for the sake of the national. Military self-sacrifice is indelibly identified with absence, with the tears in the national fabric, filled with the tears of memory memorializing. These tears must be identified with the doing of violence, with tearing open, with tearing through these openings. Here, in violence and sorrow, bureaucratic logic rejoins the military and the emotionalizing of the national. Monothetic taxonomizing does violence to organic social relationships and communities, dismembering them, slicing through their vital organs, cutting through their essential connectivities, shaping them procrustean-like into parts that fit cleanly (if bloodily) into extant categories of classification. To a significant degree, the Holocaust was predicated on the torquing together of bureaucratic logic and the German national, its emergent chiasmic turbulence displaced by aiming it at the Jews and others. Arising from the ashes of the Holocaust, the Israeli State torques together bureaucratic logic and the Jewish national, seemingly without emergent chiasmic turbulence. Yet . . . is this turbulence displaced . . .?

Zionism is triumphant first and foremost as a cyborg state, as a bureaucratic state whose infrastructures are organized through monothetic classification torqued through with emotions of the national. This is the triumph of the servants and bureaucrats of Zionism, more so than of the ideologues, politicians, theologians. Given the relative absence of turbulence emerging from this torquing, the connection between bureau-cratic logic and the emotionalism of the national is more rather than less synergetic, the whole greater than the sum of its parts. Monothetic order and national emotion are inseparable in the public events of the Israeli State. In Israeli Jewish public spheres, despite all the quarreling, quibbling, qualifying, the only fully legitimate discourse is Zionist or Zionist-related – recycled Zionist, modified Zionist, alternative Zionist, qualified Zionist, variegated Zionist, conflict-ridden Zionist, and on. Citizenship has at best a minimal role in Jewish public events. With few exceptions, all sectors of the Jewish population accept and practice this, even as the face of this struggle over the Jewish national is fingered, mapped, read, dramatized, performed, critiqued. Public events help shape the Jewish national, but they do so on a firm foundation, whatever the doubts of revisionists or Zionist ideologues and theologians. Integral to this firmness are the ways in which governmental infrastructure is shaped so deeply through bureaucratic logic, and the manifold ways in which lives are composed through school, army, bureaucracy, and a myriad of other institutions with which people are so familiar, which are so acceptable and homey, despite the complaints, groans, angers.

Democratic values and ethos are minimally relevant in public events, and this hardly troubles anyone. The tired prayer that Israel is a Jewish and democratic state (always in that order, always suspect for democracy) is intoned relentlessly, a mantra first and foremost for the well-being of the national, with nods, rhetorical and legal, towards the democratic. Democratic citizenship is suspect, since it serves to mask the presence of enemies of Zionism, enabling them to live in relative freedom and comfort within the State. And, too, in the public events discussed and in so many others, Zionism is triumphant in suppressing and excising the presences of rapidly expanding social-class differences, of the poor and oppressed, of ethnicities, of the Israeli–Palestinian conflict. In large measure, this is done through the monothetics of bureaucratic logic. Those who study nationhood and nationalism in modern states should never ever forget just how, and just how penetratingly, the national and national emotions are torqued together with, permeated and shaped by, the linealities and rigidities of bureaucratic logic, itself so often disregarded, treated as a technical adjunct to the evidently more crucial issues of ideology, politics, political philosophy. The Jewish people in place together through time in the Jewish State are held together by the rigidity and exclusivity of bureaucratic logic. Without this, and all it entails, the Jewish people would be shipwrecked on the national shoals of the Promised Land.

> words words
> jump in the air
> like a black cat
> leaping on a white roof
> yet unlike the cat
> lose their balance
> and tumble into space
> landing not on all fours
> but on the question marks
> raised by
> words words

Notes

Chapter 1 The Collapse of Versailles and the Nation-in-Arms

1. I viewed the footage one more time on Swedish television, on the eve of the New Year, 2002, as a segment of a program summarizing the most dramatic, filmed events of the year just concluded.
2. *Yediot Akharonot*, 27 May 2001, p. 8.
3. See, for example, Kapferer 1988, Herzfeld 1992, Hayes 1968, Cassirer 1946.
4. I emphasize that my concerns are not with the logic of logic, studied by philosophers.
5. One exception is Berezin (1994) who argues for the importance of form in the making of meaning in public 'rituals.' She argues that it was the form of Fascist theatre in Italy, not its content, that contained meanings of discipline, order, hierarchy, the value of emotionality, and so forth. She argues for a deep connection between fascism and form, while I think that logics of form are crucial to all public events.
6. Israeli Jews feel the Al-Aqsa Intifada, its tendrils of attack and destruction, as anywhere, anywhen, around them, appearing suddenly, wreaking havoc, disappearing; even more so, at this writing (March 2002). The attacks of the Intifada show borders as artifice, denying the maxim of a recent Israeli prime minister that 'We are here, and they [the Palestinians] are there.' The State's military-administrative response is to impose 'closure' (*seger*) on Palestinian communities in the West Bank and Gaza, an arbitrary demarcation and fortification that suddenly and unequivocally (to the extent possible) stops up, blocks, squeezes, all evident avenues of movement for virtually any purpose among localities. Petrifying space-time, an absolutist response of bureaucratic classification and containment. Such responses raise questions about the state's capacity to comprehend movement beyond its control. It is worth recalling Debord's (1998: 24) comment that, '. . . a perfect democracy constructs its own inconceivable foe, terrorism. Its wish is to be judged by its enemies rather than by its results . . . The spectators must certainly never know everything about terrorism, but they must always know enough to convince them that, compared with terrorism, everything else must be acceptable, or in any case more rational and democratic.'
7. Making way for the military to restore order in times of disaster automatically gives national status to the disaster. Wherever the military appears always signs the presence of national frontiers that interpolate between inside and outside, between the positively valued interior and the potentially hostile exterior. By contrast the

police are expected to deal with small-scale disruptions of civic society, though at times they respond with live fire to put down mass actions by Israeli Palestinians. This occurred in 1976, to shut down protests against the State's expropriation of land. Five people were killed, and the date became known as Land Day, an annual time of commemoration for Israeli Palestinians. In October 2000, police killed thirteen and wounded hundreds, in putting down massive protests by Israeli Palestinians in support of the second Intifada.

8. I discuss intentionality in public events elsewhere (Handelman 1998a). My point there is that the very performance of a particular architectonics of event, whether this configuration is deliberately planned or not, will generate significance because it has particular shapes.

9. I use statist here and elsewhere to refer to public events that, though not officially state-sponsored or sanctioned, support the state. Tellingly, the arm of the police that is military in all but name is called the Border Police, literally, the Border Guard (*Mishmar Hagvul*).

10. Kaddish (literally, 'sanctification') makes no mention of the dead, but praises the unfathomable wisdom of God, of the cosmic order. This prayer has a sense of closure, for in its different variations it is recited at the end of a section in the prayer service, and at its conclusion, as well as by mourners.

11. He was assassinated some months later by a Palestinian from the West Bank.

12. When used within Israel, the phrasing, Am Yisrael, refers to Israeli Jews. *Am Yisrael* refers to the people or nation of Israel.

13. Compare this response to that of the State in 1998, when during the opening event of the Maccabiah Games, often referred to as the Jewish Olympics, a bridge collapsed, dumping Jewish athletes from abroad into a polluted river. Four were killed and dozens injured, some suffering dreadful, crippling injury from the pollutants. The State stonewalled for four years, and only gave in under duress from Jewish communities abroad.

14. Some eight months later the police recommended indictments against thirteen persons, including owners, engineers, and building contractors. But indictment was recommended against only one part-time municipal employee, though suspicions remained of bribe-taking to allow the hall to be used without a valid license (*Jerusalem Post*, 30 January 2002).

15. See Weiss (1997a) on how perceptions of the Israeli body as individualistic shift towards perceptions of the body as more collective in a time of crisis.

16. Brubaker uses the term to refer to perceptions that the state is an 'unrealized' nation-state, the state of and for a particular nation, yet not actualized to a sufficient degree.

17. Though whether the narratives of Zionism are still so dominant is at times strongly contested, though not during the crisis of the Intifada. See the eloquent argument for liberal individualism in Israel by Ezrahi (1997); and also Feige (2001) on how different social movements stake out or deny ideological claims to territory.

18. One can argue in a similar vein about Soviet march-pasts through Red Square, Nazi Nuremberg Rallies, festivals of the French Revolution, and American historical pageants (all are discussed in Handelman 1998a: 41–8).

19. In *Models and Mirrors* (1998a: 22–41, 49–58), I contrasted the event of presentation to the event of modeling. Without going into detail here, the event of modeling makes predictive change – transformation – take place within itself, through its own operations, in contrast to the event of presentation. Numerous rituals of initiation, of healing, of cosmic renewal, and so forth, in traditional social orders can be understood as events of modeling. Modern bureaucracy, on the other hand, does predictive modeling in routine ways, making change through its invention and alteration of taxonomies, that often are organized as systems. There are some events produced through bureaucratic logic that do contain the capacity to question and critique the logic through which they issue (for example, Feige 1999).

Chapter 2 Bureaucratic Logic

1. That bureaucratic logic is used endlessly in social orders that are democratic to organize social life raises questions about the influence of the logic on democratic setups.

2. Bowker and Star (1999: 98) write of how the virus is dealt with through biological classification: '. . . there has been a deliberate effort to create something that looks and feels like other biological classifications, even though the virus itself transgresses basic categories (it jumps across hosts of different kinds, steals from its host, mutates rapidly, and so forth). Even in this most phenomenologically difficult of cases, the world must still be cut up into recognizable temporal and spatial units.' The virus of course is unaffected by scientific classifications.

3. Fuzzier forms of classification are also integral to the routine grounds of everyday living. These include polythetic classification (Sokal 1974; Needham 1975), Wittgenstein's (1953) idea of 'family resemblance,' and Kosko's (1993) notion of multivalence. In these fuzzy classifications, items are brought together through that which psychologists have called 'complexive classes,' or 'chain complexes' (Vygotsky 1962). That is, members of a class of items are connected to one another by attributes not shared by all members of that class. Vygotsky described a child beginning with a small yellow triangle, then adding a red triangle, then a red circle, and so forth. When children used this kind of associative classification in school – classing a chair with a pencil because both are yellow, the pencil with a pointer because both are long and thin, and then regarding all three objects as constituting

a class of objects – they were corrected by the teacher, who insisted on the recognition of a feature common to all members of the class: thus, pencil was classified with pen (as writing instruments), and so forth. In a series of pioneering experiments, Rosch (1975, Rosch et al. 1976) argued that family resemblances, a form of complexive groupings, are integral to how adults compose more abstract levels of classification, so that, for example, the class or level of 'furniture' is arrived at by using complexive groupings of attributes. Note the close association between monothetic classification, racism, and eugenics, in official thinking; and the likely association between fuzzy classification, multiculturalism, and ideas of hybrid and cyborg. In anthropology, attention should be drawn to Strathern's (1988) studies of gender in Melanesia, and to gender's fluid character, such that female is an accentuated version of male, male of female, and which is which may quite depend on context. See also Roy Wagner's recent formulation of a holographic worldview, Handelman and Shulman (1997: 194–7) on the Hindu deity, Siva, as a holographic god, and Handelman (1995b). Yet note Atran's (1996) argument that all biological taxonomies of living kinds seem to have universal properties that accord more or less with monothetic classification.

4. Yet, too, those who put a classification to work also feed their own values into the scheme, and this needs to be taken into account in how classification impacts on that which it classifies. So the bureaucratic innocence in census-taking can be turned easily to horrendous purpose. The Nazis used the Dutch comprehensive population registration system, set up to enable more accurate social-science research, to identify Jews and Gypsies in The Netherlands (Seltzer and Anderson 2001). In 1988 the Iraqi war against the Kurds used the 1987 national census to define the target group of Kurds against whom to practice extermination (Salih 1996).

5. I use Foucault here, despite critiques of his historicism (e.g. Patey 1984: 266–9), given that his formulations offer a useful point of start for tracing this vector of bureaucratic logic.

6. The panopticon is a distant modification of the earlier *Kunstkammer*, the form of museum that in the interests of science brought together greatly disparate objects, natural and artifactual, ahistorical and historical, encouraging the playful forging of metaphoric relationships between unlike objects. Connectivity through metaphor illuminated the ongoing creation and creative potential of the world (Bredekamp 1995: 69ff.). Unlike the Panopticon world, the holism of the Kunstkammer world was predicated on degrees of asymmetry. Utilitarian thought later broke down the playful asymmetries of the Kunstkammer world into units that were combinable through monothetic logic, valuing the resulting symmetries in classification, whether in science or bureaucracy. On symmetries in modern science see Wechsler (1988) and McAllister (1996: 39–44).

7. In Kafka's short story, 'In the penal colony,' the prisoner learns of his guilt and punishment as they are inscribed on (and in) his body by a writing machine,

    thereby forming him into a bureaucratic text – the human being as the embodied, sensuous spectacle of bureaucratic order, not unlike the tattooed arm number invented for prisoners in Auschwitz, one that soon developed its own taxonomic distinctions (numbers for women on the inside of the forearm, for men on the outside).

8. Through the monothetic forming of form, surveillance of the individual comes decisively to the fore through total access to his isolation and display. A century earlier, Leibniz, in his, 'An Odd Thought Concerning a New Sort of Exhibition (or rather, an Academy of Sciences),' written in September, 1675, had proposed a series of 'academies' for the public exhibition of scientific inventions, as well as 'academies' of games and pleasures. Surveillance was important to the covert functioning of the latter, yet here the scopic still was hidden: 'These . . . [academies of pleasure] would be built in such a way that the director of the house could hear and see everything said and done without any one perceiving him, by means of mirrors and openings, something that would be very important for the state . . .' The translation of this passage is in Wiener 1957: 465).

9. Such renditions are the visionary forerunners of the organizational forms we know today as total institutions, service organizations, people-processing organizations, and so forth. Such administrative frameworks use techniques of social, psychologistic, educational, and bureaucratic intervention in the lives of persons defined as their 'clients' (see among others Scott 1969; Dandekar 1990; Rose 1998; Bogard 1996; Handelman 1976, 1978).

10. Weber, however, never used the metaphor of the 'iron cage,' but rather the 'shell as hard as steel,' which has quite different connotations; nor did he metaphorize bureaucracy as this 'shell' (Baehr 2001).

11. Bourdieu (1998: 52) maintains that through its 'molding power' the modern state 'wields a genuinely creative quasi-divine power' (see also Calhoun 1997: 76). Yet the logic of this creativity is that of the bureaucratic, the quasi-divine power emanating from the capacity of this logic to change social worlds by altering their classifications.

12. For example, though the powerful connections during the nineteenth and twentieth centuries among science, statistics, eugenics, and racism are well documented, ideas like that of bureaucratic logic, as the forming of form, are rarely if ever referred to. Thus Evans (1997: 295), writing on the Department of Native Affairs in mid-twentieth-century South Africa, clearly joins together science and racism to that which I am calling bureaucratic logic, but his approach goes no deeper than the study of institutions as such.

13. The forming of bureaucratic logic received impetus from other developments: from European colonialism and colonial administration (Arendt 1958), from the science of statistics, literally, the science of the state (Desrosières 1998; Gigerenzer et al. 1989), from the embracing of numeration (Cohen 1982), and from individualism and its freedoms inherent in ideas of social contract, but also from the

revolutionary reorganization of the military, and from shifts of education towards more universal criteria.

14. Rose (1998: 99–115) argues that in liberal, democratic societies the intention of governmentality is to produce, shape, and regulate the moral order within the psychological individual, rather than to suppress individuality, as is the case under totalitarian regimes.

15. This self-formation may take the shape of the 'individual as enterprise,' the management of personal identity through which one is employed in this enterprise of living throughout one's lifetime (Gordon 1991: 44). This perspective on self-identity dovetails well with the individual internalization of bureaucratic logic, and with the current emphasis on the importance of psychologies of self-actualization, self-autonomy, and the performance of self, raising the issue of how these psychologies contribute to the grounding of bureaucratic logic within the individual. See also Rieff (1966).

16. Here I do not follow developments in Prussia and the shaping of the bureaucratic-military absolutist state, this attempt to construct 'a huge human automaton' (Rosenberg 1958: 38). To no small degree, the model here for bureaucratic absolutism was military (Anderson 1996: 243–6). According to Oestreich (1982: 258–72), in Germany the formation of the absolutist state, of top-down bureaucratic and military order met the more localized, more bottom-up 'science of police' in what became their common goal of shaping and disciplining social and moral order. In Fichte's words (quoted in Hartman 1997: 123), the goal of social order was 'the complete unity and unanimity of all its members.' The developments in the principalities likely have had very long-term effects through German idealism, linking, for example, with the ethnographic insight that German individualism develops best within organic groups (Norman 1991).

17. That group formation not only be imposed top-down but also, quite mysteriously, emerge from within the group has been an ongoing concern of Israeli Jews. In Hebrew this process is often called 'crystallization' (*gibush*), and a group of people brought or thrown together does not have group-ness, this sense of belonging together naturally, until they feel this crystallization of sentiment (see Katriel 1991a). I emphasize 'feel', for there are no conscious, objective social indices of how and when this sense of groupness comes into existence. People just feel when it has. In the Israeli case this crystallization is related to the coming into being of the nation-in-arms and the family-in-arms, and its existence has powerful commonsensical aesthetic qualities for many Israeli Jews.

18. The nation-in-arms is invoked with every declaration that Israel is 'a Jewish and democratic state' – a sequence that privileges and empowers Jewish over democratic (see Kimmerling 2002). So, too, with the declaration that the character of Israeli society, and the future of the state, will be decided on only by Israeli Jews – a pronouncement of inclusion and exclusion, evoking an embattled people who must stand alone, together, otherwise they will lose their knowledge

of who they are. Every such declaration is also a commemoration and a celebration of every other occasion when this was the case, or when it will be so.

19. Walby (1999) argues that the European Union is a new kind of state, a 'regulatory
    state.' A state in which the law, a most powerful generator and applier of linear
    classification, plays a central role. She argues that it is 'the ability to deploy power
    through a regulatory framework, rather than through the monopolization of
    violence or the provision of welfare, which is the key to the distinctive nature of
    the regulatory state' (1999: 123).

20. Laumann and Knoke (1987: 382), in a large-scale study of American government
    bureaucracies, understand the state as 'a complex entity spanning multiple policy
    domains, comprising both government organizations and those core private sector
    participants whose interests must be taken into account.' They found that many
    of the classifications generated by government bureaucracies, that have major
    effects on the worlds beyond these organizations, are intended first and foremost
    for the internal purposes of these bureaucracies, in particular to conserve their
    own existence.

21. So a Californian without a driver's license would not be able to use a credit card
    or cash a check. Such persons are issued with 'non-drivers' driving licenses
    (Herzfeld 1992: 46), thereby capturing them within the taxonomy through whose
    practice they are enabled to live like others.

22. Ironically, bureaucratic logic also reflects aspects of the rhizomic. For all their
    linearity, the trajectories of bureaucratic logic are often tangential, without
    set direction or set sequence of movement in capturing, containing, and de-
    territorializing space and time. Because bureaucratic logic is arbitrary in its
    construction and motion, it moves easily, in any direction, through any vectors,
    in making over space/time as its own.

23. Since 1948, Israeli governments and the IDF have nurtured (in career terms)
    generations of military colonial bureaucrats. Military bureaucrats ruled Palestinian
    citizens of Israel from 1950 until 1966 in areas of concentrated Arab population
    (see Lustick 1980; Shammas 1991); and rule, from 1967 through the present, all
    or part of the occupied territories. Military rule is by administrative order, and
    judicial proceedings are autarchic and and often draconic. Human rights are
    irrelevant to making order through containment and classification. Estimates are
    that since 1967 the military bureaucracy in the West Bank has issued some 1,500
    administrative orders (as of 7 April 2002), each with the binding force of law, and
    together embracing virtually all domains of living and livelihood. The orders set
    in place a complex system of permits, through which permissions are required in
    order to carry out a very long list of activities. The granting and withholding of
    permits function to reward and punish applicants. Military government is the
    extreme shaping of form through bureaucratic logic. On the ambivalence of the
    Israeli Supreme Court towards the military government and its rulings in the
    Territories, see Kretzmer 2002. Kretzmer (2002: 193) argues strongly that the

Court consistently finds in favor of the authorities because, in part, Israel is defined as the State of the Jewish People, and therefore that any action perceived as contrary to the interests of this national collectivity is regarded as a threat to the security of the state.

24. However prevalent, this is but one metaphysics of temporal movement. See, for example, Briggs (1992) on Inuit, and Rosaldo (1980) on Ilongot.

25. Arguments over whether the people who did these tasks were 'bureaucrats,' or whether they were 'functionaries' who behaved as bureaucrats (Carmi and Rosenfeld 1991), seem misplaced. First and foremost they were people who invented and applied a wide range of taxonomies of classification, and who used bureaucratic logic to do so. After 1948 they moved without difficulty into new and renamed offices and positions within the state infrastructures.

26. Thus, an 'Oriental' identity, one that sought common cause between Jews and Palestinians, may have been viable in the pre-state period, at least among some intellectuals (see Eyal 1996; Cordoba 1980). After 1948, governmental taxonomies and their practices made such alliances difficult and costly.

27. Carmi and Rosenfeld (1989) argue that there were limited parallels between the socialist organization of the Yishuv and the state bureaucracy after 1948; so that the state's total bureaucratization of the Arab national and refugee problems constituted a radical transformation in the organization of the social order. Though the scale of things changed drastically with statehood, bureaucratic logic clearly antedates formal statehood.

28. The first Israeli astronaut, who died in the recent disintegration of the space shuttle *Challenger*, took with him into space a small Torah scroll that had survived the Holocaust and a drawing of the earth as seen from the moon, made by a small boy in Theresienstadt (*Ha'aretz*, 2 February 2003, English Edition).

Chapter 3 Making Jews National in their Citizenship

1. Other scholars attend only to aspects of this configuration. Discussions of civil religion ignore how the State has helped to shape and to empower ethnicity as such an active force in Israeli life (see Liebman and Don-Yehiye 1983; Aronoff 1989). Analyses of ethnicity treat the role of the state as a mere bureaucratic setting within which the agendas, agencies, and agents of Jewish 'ethnicities' conflict and contest with one another (see Smooha 1978; Dominguez 1989; Ben-Rafael and Sharot 1991; Weingrod 1985). The Zionist state is an active molder of social and cultural difference; and the patterning of these differences is very much in keeping with bureaucratic logic.

2. Too many of the scholarly arguments define democracy in terms of criteria that this state should have, and then ask whether Israel meets these attributes. These arguments are in themselves exercises in shaping taxonomies, in which more emphasis is put on finalizing what Israel is, essentially, than on following dynamic realities. See, Smooha 1997; Yiftachel 1992; Ghanem 1998; Rouhana 1997; Ghanem et al. 1998; Kimmerling 1999; Gavison 1999; Peled 1992; Peled and Shafir 1996; Shafir and Peled 1998. The conceptual momentum comes from distinctions in classical Western political philosophy between liberalism and individualism on the one hand and republicanism and communitarianism on the other, to which a third type – called ethnic state, ethnic democracy, ethnocracy, and so forth – is added (Smooha 1997; Rouhana 1997). The liberal/republican distinction has limited value in the Israeli case, whose state formation derived less from parliamentary or congressional models. One can argue that the early Zionists in Palestine were influenced also by oriental despotism; and that to a serious degree citizenship became a way to give Jews full and equal rights in the Jewish State, to the detriment of non-Jews. Israeli Palestinians are the subject of administrative, taxonomic exclusion from benefits to which Israeli Jews are entitled. See Rosenhek and Shalev (2000) and Rosenhek (1999). In this regard, Palestinians in the territories are driven into the gutter.

3. In 1985 the Knesset passed an amendment to the election law that made, 'denial of the existence of the State of Israel as the state of the Jewish people,' grounds for disallowing a political party from standing for election (Kretzmer 1987). More recently this law has been amended further. The disjunction between citizenship and Jewishness has vexed scholars of disparate political positions. See, for example, Eisenstadt (1967: 394; 1985: 333), Cohen (1989: 70), Kimmerling (1985), Yuval-Davis (1987: 63).

4. With independence, entry into the country immediately was contested, and decisions depended upon bureaucrats who formed their own classifications. Palestinians were excluded, as were the gentile wives of Jewish husbands (Hacohen 1998: 71). Such issues were dealt with in camera. Today, Palestinians with Israeli citizenship comprise just below 20 percent of the population. Who is a Palestinian is itself problematic: this depends on who does the designating and how this is accepted within particular historical and political contexts. In practice, self-identity may well be situational and multiplex (see Forte 2002).

5. See Provisional State Assembly (*Mo'etzet Hamedina Hazmanit*) Protocol of Discussions: Meetings 22 and 40, Vol. B, 1949, pp. 6–11 and 20–3 (in Hebrew).

6. Recently the Supreme Court ruled that the ORR was intended only to gather statistical information, and that government bureaucrats had no authority to evaluate the truth value of this information (*Ha'aretz*, 7 March 2002, English Edition).

7. The roots of nationality might be in the Ottoman *millet* setup that dealt with the religious, communal organization of non-Muslims in the Ottoman Empire

(*Encyclopedia Judaica* 1971: 1582). However, Braude (1982) questions whether millet was at all institutionalized, and whether it was anything other than a local arrangement. In the 1949 census, 'nationality' was a secular category, distinguished from that of 'religion.' Any significant relationship to millet categorization seems doubtful.

Turn-of-the-century Zionist ideologues questioned whether European Jews existed as anything other than a religion, so that the awareness of peoplehood as a national political entity would have to be inculcated (Pinsker 1966: 32; Almog 1987: 38ff). Ben-Gurion is said to have echoed these intentions, saying that once the Jews had a state, they then had to be formed into a nation.

8. The definition of a Jew according to religious law (*halakha*) is one who is born to a Jewish mother, or one who has been converted to Judaism.

9. See, Judgements of the Supreme Court of Israel, 18–22, Vol. 23, Part II, 1969, pp. 477–82 (in Hebrew).

10. The amendment stated that no one was to be registered as Jewish under nationality unless born of a Jewish mother or a convert to Judaism, with no other religious affiliation (Bin-Nun 1992: 16). See also Jackson (1993) on the case of Brother Daniel, a Jew who had converted to Catholicism and who had asked for Israeli citizenship under the Law of Return. According to religious law, Brother Daniel was still a Jew, and the case challenged the claim of the State to be both Jewish and secular. The Supreme Court denied citizenship to Brother Daniel.

11. See Judgements of the Supreme Court of Israel, 8, Vol. 26, Part I, 1972, pp. 197–224 (in Hebrew).

12. See Judgements of the District Courts in Israel, 8, Part I, 1976–1977, pp. 324–31 (in Hebrew).

13. This attitude towards Israeli Palestinians on the part of Israeli Jewish bureaucrats responsible for their governance holds more or less through the present day. One prominent example of this attitude was the Koenig Report, classified secret but published on 7 September 1976 in the daily newspaper, *Al Hamishmar*. This memorandum, authored by a senior official in the Ministry of the Interior, outlined a series of bureaucratic moves, planned to limit the life chances of Israeli Palestinians.

Israeli Jews expect Israeli Palestinians to prove unceasingly their loyalty to the Jewish State before any substantive discussion of their political and social rights may begin. In practice, there is no way to establish this loyalty, since such 'proof' would destroy the essentialist premise of the discourse, and so would begin to bridge the monothetic divide between Jew and Palestinian. Therefore discussion on civil and political rights is deferred time and again. Note that doing violence is integral to the holding of full citizenship. Since Palestinian citizens rarely serve in the army, they are not full citizens. The doing of violence in the name of the State devolves from citizenship to nationality.

Eyal (1996) argues that Israeli Jews perceive the essence of the Arab as primitive, backward, traditional, an essence that should be modernized, yet that cannot be changed successfully because this would destroy the construction itself. Therefore all Jewish attempts to correct this backward cultural identity fail, because they cannot permit these attempts to succeed. Essences will be different for eternity. Shammas (1988: 9) described this double bind as follows: 'The State of Israel demands that its Arab citizens take their citizenship seriously; but when they try to do so it promptly informs them that their participation in the state is merely social, and that for the political fulfillment of their identity they must look somewhere else [i.e., to the Palestinian nation]. When they do look elsewhere for their national identity, the state at once charges them with subversion; and . . . as subversives they cannot be accepted as Israelis.' See Kimmerling and Migdal 1993.

14. Iconic with this shaping of the ingathering was an official suggestion for celebrating Independence Day in the early years of the state – baking a cake whose ingredients were the 'seven species', the seven fruits for which the Land of Israel is praised in Deuteronomy 8:8, and slicing the cake into four pieces, symbolizing the ingathering of the exiles from the four corners of the earth. See Azaryahu 1995: 99–105.

15. Social scientists and folklorists have contributed to the reification of monothetic ethnicities by classifying 'ethnic' categories of Jews in essentialist fashion, according to place of origin. See Lewis 1985 and Shamgar-Handelman 1996. More generally, the role of scholarship in shaping ethnic categories within state formations is addressed in Wilson 1976, Herzfeld 1982, and Linke 1990.

16. The ethnic paradigm was exemplified during the 1970s and 1980s by the Mimuna festivities organized by middle-class members of the Moroccan 'ethnic group,' then the largest in Israel (Goldberg 1977, 1978). Celebrated in Morocco on the day after the end of the Passover holiday, the Mimuna re-articulated Jewish households to their Muslim neighbors – these relationships were severed during Passover so that Jewish households could maintain ritual purity. In Israel the Mimuna became the great public presentation of the Jewish ethnic map. Representatives of all the Jewish ethnicities gathered in the largest public park in Jerusalem, each 'group' in its allotted space. There they prepared traditional foods, which were shared with other Jewish ethnicities; while various ethnic troupes sang and danced for everyone in the name of their own ethnicity. Israel was presented and displayed as a topology of solidary, egalitarian, Jewish ethnicities, all under the patronage umbrella of the Moroccan community. The event often was addressed by prominent politicians in the name of national solidarity.

17. The Druze in Israel are sometimes referred to by Israeli Jews as an ethnic group. Firro (2001: 45, 49, 51) argues that government policy towards the Druze has been to reclassify Druze nationality from 'Arab' to 'Druze,' so that Druze would see themselves as a separate 'nation' within Israel, one that has no basis for alliance with Israeli Palestinians (see also Oppenheimer 1977).

Part II Prologue

1. The Hebrew term for kindergarten teacher, in the feminine gender, is *gannenet*, literally 'gardener.' The connotations of the term, as in English, are those of one who is an active agent in the processes of growing, cultivating, domesticating. The term likely is a translation of the German ,'kindergärtnerin,' a gardener of children, and is distinguished clearly in Hebrew from 'educator' (fem. *m'khanekhet*) and from 'teacher' (fem. *morah*). The Hebrew term for kindergarten, *gan yeladim*, is again a translation from the German.
2. See Ram 1995, on Zionist narrative and educational policies in post-independence Israel.
3. Though there undoubtedly was the impact of the civic nationalism of the kindergarten movement in nineteenth-century Germany, that emphasized patriotism, citizenship, and political responsibility (Allen 1986: 437); and whose own roots are traced to Fichte, Pestalozzi, and for that matter, to Clausewitz (Paret 1985: 180–3).
4. For the sake of convenience we usually use the masculine gender to refer to the child in general terms.
5. For a brilliant analysis of a culturally different way of counting, among the Iqwaye of New Guinea, one in which the practice of addition turns into cosmic holism, see Mimica 1988.
6. This may be one basis for Western and Israeli preoccupation with the chronological age of young children, and whether the character and accomplishment of youngsters conform to age-related expectations (Hughes 1989: 38). So, too, the obsession with segregating children by age. Children spend an increasing proportion of their lives within frameworks whose structures depend on age-grading (Foner 1975: 151; Suransky 1982: 8, 20, 74), while the modern state takes on extended jurisdiction over enculturation (Tyack 1966), and increasing control over childhood education (Boli-Bennett and Meyer 1978: 802, 810).

Chapter 4 Celebrations of the National

1. Our usage is analogous to that of 'hidden curriculum' (Gearing and Tindall 1973: 103), though we stress the more contested relationship between parents and state, implicit in the maturation of youngsters.
2. For the ambivalent siting of Israeli Palestinian children during such national celebrations – between citizenship (that they have) and nationality (not theirs), see Rabinowitz 1998: 134–5.
3. It is surprising how little analysis has been done on whether and how kindergarten youngsters are exposed to the focused manipulation of symbols and symbolic formations of a supra-familial character, whether in Israel or elsewhere, and how

this use of symbolism is related to nationalism (yet see Gullestad 1997; Furman 1999). Our own argument is closer in spirit to that of Gracey (1972), who contends that the task of teachers in American kindergartens is to prepare children for the rigid routines of bureaucratic, corporate society. Nonetheless, research on ceremonialism in kindergartens is minimal. These comments hold as well for social science in Israel. The major exceptions to date are studies of kindergarten birthday parties (Weil 1986; Doleve-Gandelman 1987).

4. The ethnographers who collected these materials were supervisors employed by the Ministry of Education. They observed kindergartens that they themselves supervised, and with which they were conversant. Their observations and responses, and those of the teachers in these kindergartens, convinced us that the distinction between explicit and implicit agendas was a valid one. The educators consistently understood such events in terms of the obviousness of the celebrations, and the consensus on cooperation between teacher and parent regarding the education of the child. They did not acknowledge that the form and substance of celebratory practices in the kindergarten implicitly conveyed a governmental perspective. However they did agree that the task of the teacher was to educate not only the child but also the parents. All of the kindergartens observed belonged to the secular stream of state education. All their classes consisted of both boys and girls; though for the sake of convenience we usually use the masculine gender to refer to the child in categorical terms.

5. On each of the four sides of the Hanukkah top is inscribed one of the first letters of the Hebrew words, *Ness Gadol Haya Po* ('There was a great miracle here'). Spinning the top is a popular children's game. Regardless of which side remains uppermost when the top topples, its letter signifies the integrity and unity of the whole message, as does the top in its circular spinning.

6. In modern Israel the circle dance (with its invisible, seemingly empty center) became a popular form through which to shape and to express egalitarianism and the dynamism of enduring bonds between persons who, through their cooperative efforts, forged the embracing collectivity of which they were a part. The circle dance was one of the many modes through which Israeli Jews tried to crystallize collectivity. It is especially in this sense that the practice of the circle dance was metonymous with the emerging sense of nation and nationhood.

7. The age to which, legend has it, Moses lived; and a customary greeting of good wishes.

8. See Golden's (n.d.) comments on mothering by the kindergarten teacher, including mothering children as the representative of the national.

9. This is highly contested space. In Muslim cosmology this site is the Haram el-Sherif, from where Mohammed set out on his night journey, one of the holiest places in Islam, the site of the Al-Aqsa mosque and the Dome of the Rock

10. In other children's Jerusalem Day celebrations fathers were invited to reminisce about their soldiering in the battles for Jerusalem. In these instances stress was placed on the obligation to serve the country under any circumstances.

Chapter 5 Celebrations of Bureaucratic Logic

1. Most of these elements have a lengthy provenance, dating to pre-state Palestine (Haskina 1941). The earliest description of a birthday celebration in a Hebrew-speaking kindergarten in Palestine appears to date from 1921.
2. As in Chapter Four, the ethnographers were Ministry of Education supervisors.
3. Ten songs, all with birthday themes, were sung during the party. All emphasized the pleasure of the occasion. In these events, songs are used to shift children in unison from one kind of activity to the next. Most birthday songs rhyme in Hebrew. Kelkin-Fishman (1981) argues that the internalization of musical rhythm (and, one should add, rhyming texts) is used to inculcate control and discipline in Israeli Jewish kindergartens.
4. His mother's signal to Amir is the triangle, and the teacher's, the drum. One should not overlook the contrast in sounds – the delicacy of the triangle and the imperative power of the drum.
5. Here our usage of 'individual' generally follows that of Louis Dumont (1977, 1986), in distinguishing the individual from the social person. In this regard, the person is a negotiated social being, constituted and reconstituted through give-and-take with others. By contrast, the idea of the individual is that of an autonomous, irreducible being, one who constitutes a holistic moral unit in and of himself. This conception of the individual is an important ground for a statistical notion of personhood in the bureaucratic logic of the modern West.
6. Through these activities the child practices the time continuum from opposite perspectives. The order of candle-lighting proceeds from oldest (grandmother) to youngest (grandson); while the chair-lifting begins with the age of 1 and ends in the child's future. The two perspectives are conjoined in the candle lighting. The six candles signify the child's temporal continuum. However, lit in the order of generations, the child's temporal continuum recapitulates the history of his family.
7. This iteration is done also in the first game (VII) following the candle-lighting.
8. Following Plessner (1970), crying may show that the child is capitulating to the agents that are manipulating and redefining his relationships to others and to himself. Crying is the acquiescence of his body to this co-optation, and, simultaneously, the control of selfness by the body. Crying performs the surrender of self to power beyond its control.
9. Kindergarten teachers treat birthday parties as festival celebrations, but ones centered on the little child as 'hero of the day.' It is customary to celebrate all children's birth dates that fall during the school year. Ways often are found to incorporate birth dates that fall outside this period. There is much variation among kindergartens in the scheduling of birthday parties. At one extreme, the birthday is celebrated close to the birth date of the individual child. At the other, a party is held once a month for all those children whose birth dates fall during that period. Perhaps most common is the setting aside of a weekly time slot, within which to

celebrate the birth dates of the past week. In larger classes it is not uncommon for a birthday party to take place almost weekly; and children who spend from two to four years in kindergarten will participate in dozens, and more, of these celebrations.

Part III Prologue

1. From its inception the State embraced the Judaic calendar and its rhythm of holy days, in contrast, for example, to the efforts of certain revolutionary states – France, the Soviet Union – to radicalize the cultural ordering of temporality: see Zerubavel (1985: 27–43). Moreover the period of observance of State Days became that of Jewish holy days: all begin with darkness, as the stars appear, and end with darkness. The few studies on these three Israeli national Days treat each of them as a separate and autonomous occasion. The questions raised in these works highlight the sparse attention given by scholars to state ceremonial in Israel. See Kamen 1977; Don-Yehiye 1984; Dominguez 1989: 42–67; but, too, the historical study by Azaryahu 1995.
2. See Vogt and Abel 1977: 174–6 for a device of national simultaneity that begins Mexico's Independence Day.
3. The stature of Independence Day is brought home by the desire of Ben-Gurion to call this day, the Day of Upright Standing (*Yom Hakomemiyout*), with its meaning of being free to stand erect, but also with the connotations of moral uprightness (see Yarden 1998: 336).
4. I doubt there would be much disagreement among Israeli Jews regarding the basic narrative that the State enacted in promulgating this sequence of the three Days (despite Cohen 1996). With changing historical and situational conditions there is disagreement as to which of these Days has greatest significance in terms of its ethos for the persons in question. In official terms the sequence was understood to move from the least to the most significant of Days, though this aspect of the sequence is more contested today. In recent years, Holocaust Remembrance Day is rising in private and public significance. But these three Days offer people a range of preferences. In this regard, Albanese's (1974: 39) argument regarding the complementarity of Memorial Day parades and picnics in the United States is provocative.

   Based on the celebrations of Israel's fiftieth anniversary in 1998, many of the public events of the three Days were contested over issues that deeply divide Israeli Jews – the rise of Jewish religious fundamentalism, the continued occupation and settlement of the occupied territories, the crippled peace negotiations with the Palestinians. Yet most of the contestation took place in the bureaucratic planning and then in the reaction to the enactment of public events, all outside the performance of the events themselves. In some instances alternative events opposed official ones. In a few instances the performance of events was disrupted by overt expressions of conflict. Nonetheless the value of the three Days and of the existence of the State was not questioned through these contestations.

5. The first proposals to establish a national remembrance authority were made as early as 1945. Zertal (2000: 103) argues that the State repeatedly postponed establishing a national Holocaust memorial until information arrived about memorials planned elsewhere. The opening events of the first Holocaust Remembrance Days were held in the Martyrs' Forest in Jerusalem. In 1958, events were moved to Yad Vashem, the national Holocaust memorial (Ofer 2000: 26, 33, 37). Among the aims of Yad Vashem was the awarding of 'remembrance citizenship' in the State to every one of the Holocaust dead, incorporating them into the Jewish state. This citizenship was bestowed on the Holocaust dead in 1987 by the President of the State during the opening event of Holocaust Remembrance Day.

6. In varieties of Judaism, following the exemplar of biblical creation, the numerical unit of seven is thought to sign completion, closure, unity. The seven days between Holocaust Remembrance Day and Remembrance Day may point to the desire to close the Diaspora chapter of Jewish history, in accordance with Zionist visions of the period.

7. By 1950 Independence Day events were being designed, organized, and supervised by committee, emphasizing bureaucratic logic, and continuing methods used during the Yishuv (Azaryahu 1999: 96; Aronoff 1989: 143–64).

8. Argument over the Hebrew date centered on whether the self-presentation of the new state should focus outwardly, to the world, or inwardly. The issue was prominent in other discussions of national symbolism (Handelman and Shamgar-Handelman 1990).

9. Michael Walzer (1985: 133) argues that the biblical narrative of Exodus became paradigmatic for revolutionary politics in the West.

10. The IDF commissioned a Haggadah, to be read at a festive Independence Day meal, which paraphrased the Passover text, to wit: 'We were slaves of the gentiles in all lands and in all states.' This Independence Day text recounts the return of the exiles, the pioneers, and their triumph over tribulation, culminating in the founding of the State.

11. Correspondence between the legal advisor of the Ministry of Defense and the government secretary, 17 March 1954, 1 April 1954, 13 April 1954.

12. In Israel this rhythm continuously encodes the relating of Holocaust to independence. One example will suffice. In 1981 the first World Gathering of Jewish Holocaust survivors convened in Jerusalem for four days. The program was as follows. The first day, opened at Yad Vashem, was dedicated to the 'remembrance' of the Holocaust. The second, dedicated to 'rebirth and achievement,' was given over to kibbutzim founded by Holocaust survivors. The third was dedicated to

continuity and the next generation, the children of survivors. The fourth, convened in the name of 'lest we forget', was concluded at the Western Wall. The temporal and topological trip from Yad Vashem to the Wall recapitulated the kind of sequence discussed here. So too, the rhetoric of the closing event: the prime minister spoke of the movement 'from the depths of the pit to the peak of independence.' On rhetoric relevant to this sequencing, see Gertz 2000.

13. *Yad Vashem Bulletin*, No. 16, 1965, p. 62.

14. Of the prime ministers, Ben-Gurion and Begin are buried elsewhere, the former in keeping with his ideology of pioneering, and the latter in keeping with his enhancing of the nation over the state.

15. Baumel (1995: 164–5) argues that in individual and communal Holocaust commemoration in Israel, the Holocaust is not linked to national rebirth but is memorialized in and of itself, breaking with Zionist ethos.

16. *Yad Vashem Bulletin,* No. 16, 1965, p. 63. This sequence is practiced to the present day. However since 1969 the eve of Remembrance Day is commemorated at the Western Wall, joining together more powerfully secular Zionism and Judaism.

Chapter 6 Opening Holocaust Remembrance Day

1. In other words, it is done like this because it is done like this – this is how it feels to be done as one does it.

2. This could be called the persuasive self-embodiment of the truth-claims of practice.

3. This sense of an aesthetics of practice, largely unreflective, tries to break decisively with perspectives that, despite their radical turn, continue to emphasize the reflective as integral to the aesthetic (e.g. Welsch 1997).

4. This is so despite claims for the sacralizing qualities of all manners of 'ritual,' including 'secular ritual' (Moore and Myerhoff 1977).

5. This and most other statist rituals are performed at or just after dusk. The darkness also hides the extent of the presence of the military at these events.

6. Systemic military organization projects teleological predictions specifying what happens under variable conditions, and through feedback in communication enables the whole taxonomy to know the ongoing condition and functioning of each of its categories. The military taxonomy is self-correcting and able to alter its condition in response to changing parameters. This quality of systemic organization is absent from public events of presentation.

7. See Rapaport (1994) on the history of the original monument. In the original, one of the figures is that of a bare-breasted mother, one arm raised in defense of her

    infant. In the Yad Vashem copy the bare breast is covered for modesty's sake (see Baumel 1996: 112).

8. See Ofer (1996: 579, 589) on how these terms entered Israeli Jewish discourse.

9. In later years a second state flag has been placed atop the Wall, above the bas-relief, as the sign of the national encompassment and transcendence of the sorrow symbolized by the suffering Jews, beneath.

10. The Hebrew term for Jewish immigration to Israel is *aliyah*, literally, ascent.

11. See Handelman (n.d.) for the analysis of an event in the ancient world that combined modularity, causality, and self-critique.

12. One may argue that the stronger sense of dynamics – archtypal, historicist – is embedded in the poetics of rhetoric, song, and prayer, which I do not discuss here. Nonetheless the speeches usually are stilted and stereotypic set-pieces; the songs, often old favorites; and the psalms and prayers, generic in terms of their insertion into public events.

13. On different sorts of framing – lineal, braided, moebius-like – see Handelman (2001).

14. Righteous Gentiles are non-Jews who are awarded this national recognition because they risked their lives to save Jews during World War II. They are chosen by a committee based in Yad Vashem.

15. In this respect these introductions resembled the Yizkor prayer of remembrance that can be expanded to include a limitless listing of attributes to be remembered.

16. Ascending to light the beacons resonates with the rhythms of time mentioned earlier in this Chapter. This is the segment of the event when lower valence is made higher, when darkness is turned into light, when destruction gives birth to triumph and redemption.

17. In this regard, see the critical comment by Jay (1992b: 103).

18. This is the mirror-image of the Nazi use of bureaucratic logic to detail with precision the war against the Jews.

Chapter 7 Opening Remembrance Day and Independence Day

1. A place of popular veneration, without any formal standing in Jewish religious law, the Wall has become since 1967 the foundation stone of the national religion and identity, though some see its veneration as iconophilia and idolatry. On present day uses of the Wall, see Storper-Perez and Goldberg (1994).

2. The plaza is the venue for the swearing-in of new recruits to many army units. Events held at this Wall inevitably are skewed by religious strictures. The closing event of the Gathering of Jewish Holocaust survivors, held in the plaza (and

mentioned in note 12 of the Prologue to this Part), was to have featured an address by a Knesset Member and heroine of the Warsaw Ghetto uprising. She was prevented from speaking because of her gender.

3. See Handelman and Shamgar-Handelman (1990, 1993) on the choice of Israel's national emblem, Aronoff (1986) on the nationalization of ancient remnants, Y. Zerubavel (1995) on folklore and nationalism, and El-Haj (1998) on archeology and nationalism.

4. Television is the medium of bringing these occasions to the general public. The event was held at the Wall for the first time in 1969. The first telecast of this event, and of that which opens Independence Day, were done a few years later.

5. In the first Remembrance Day opening event at the Wall, the President began his address with, 'In this holy place for all the generations, next to the remnants of the House of Our Delight [i.e. the Temple] ' (from a voice recording in the archives of the Israel Broadcasting Authority).

6. The national imagery of fallen soldiers and the typification of heroic death are discussed in Shamgar-Handelman (1986).

7. The purest sacrifice of ancient Judaism was one wholly consumed by fire, the *korban olah* ('ascending sacrifice'). Sacrifice and purity were intimately related. Though the President says, 'their pure sacrifice' (*korbanam hatahor*), his phrasing partakes of the relationship between total sacrifice and highest value.

8. Fire and light have manifold connotations in Judaism, many associated with junctures of heaven and earth, God and human being, as well-related values. Don-Yehiye (1984: 14) lists the following: good, beauty, belief, hope, freedom, redemption, bravery, growth awakening, revival, unity, eternal rebirth. There are numerous connotations of fire and light in European romanticism and rationalism, including reason, progress, and . . . enlightenment.

9. See also Myerhoff 's (1982: 111) use of re-membering.

10. By the summer of 2003 the religious vote is strong, rightist, and dedicated to the (religious) nation encompassing the state. The allegiance of religious political parties to democracy in Israel is hardly skin-deep.

11. An alternative interpretation would perceive the Wall as the enduring witness to sacrifice; the flag signifying the sacrifice itself; the flame signifying the memory of the sacrifice. Marvin and Ingle (1999: 69) argue that the semiotics of the American flag 'elaborate a drama of male sacrifice and female regeneration.'

12. The lineal series of categories constitutes a monothetic taxonomy of multiple levels of abstraction, one very much the product of bureaucratic logic in the service of the state. Yet in this instance the series also demonstrates how the monothetic joins the monotheistic, how a monothetic taxonomy is itself encompassed within metaphysical categories. In the opposite direction (beginning with the sign of the Wall) the monotheistic metaphysic generates the monothetic. The sign of encompassment distinguishes this event from the Versailles commemoration (discussed in Chapter One), which is formed through lineal rank-ordering.

The extreme condensation of categories into one another demonstrates the affinity between bureaucratic logic and the Durkheimian idea of mechanical solidarity, pointing to Durkheim's underlying concern with issues of solidarity in the modern state. This argument supports Kopytoff's (1988) contention that the organic structuring of modern society produces mechanical structures of solidarity – public events of presentation, in my terms.

13. Thus, Willner's contention (1976: 411) that military 'rituals themselves encode and reiterate a very few basic messages of military life.'

14. Too, the entire event is conducted under an extreme discipline of roles, performers, statuses, movements, texts. In this regard, the over all ethos of the occasion is military (and therefore bureaucratic).

15. The monolithic presentation of the occasion conceals deep divisions in the daily life of the State, some of which are discussed in Chapter Three. An example of how easily such cracks open on the surface is Wright's (1985: 135–59) discussion of British Remembrance Day.

16. The metaphor of family includes in its unity both civilian and military sectors. One complement of this metaphor is the common Hebrew expression that 'the entire people are an army' (*kol ha'am tsava*). The total unity of moral and social order also may be constituted metaphorically through the military. As discussed in Chapter Six the military version of order is the continuation of the civilian. On some modes through which the family supports the army by caring for its own offspring during their military service, see Katriel (1991b). For some points of confrontation, see Weiss (1997b).

    Kinship metaphors in national occasions deserves further attention. See especially Hunt (1992) on metaphors of family destroyed, family rehabilitated, during the French revolution; and Verdery (1999: 41), among others, on the claim that nationalism 'is a kind of ancestor worship.'

17. This flattening of hierarchy holds for the Zionist vision on the summit. It does not obviate the hierarchy of struggle in climbing the mountain, encoded in the ceremonial sequence of Yad Vashem, military cemetery, and Herzl's tomb.

    We note the spatial sense of 'assembly' conveyed by the arrangement of clusters of graves on the summit. To approach these clusters (the Jabotinsky family, the presidents of the World Zionist Organization, the Greats of the Nation) one walks roughly from east to west; while one approaches Herzl's tombstone most frontally by walking roughly from west to east. Although these clusters are not visible from Herzl's tomb, the implicit effect, if one pays attention, is that the clusters 'face' Herzl's tomb, in the arrangement of an assembly over which he presides.

18. The wording of this prayer is modified from its conventional form, that asks God to remember the dead. Hebrew terms for 'memory' (*zekher/zikaron*) have connotations both of identity and of its active retrieval. Thus the term, zekher, is used in the Hebrew Bible as a synonym for 'name' (*shem*). Among the connotations of

'memorial' or 'remembering' are those of the enactment of memory, for example, 'An act deliberately performed with the purpose of preserving something in the heart' (Dinur 1957: 8–9).

19. In the 2003 event the Speaker's address was a paean to ultra-nationalism, in which every movement, every glance, encountered the State flag as the existential horizon. Like the address, the entire occasion was utterly closed in on itself, separated from all else in the world.

20. On the other hand, for example, the theme of 1990, 'One Nation, One Language,' declared the imperative of making citizenship national, excluding Israeli Palestinians, despite Arabic being an official language of the State (Katriel 1990: 321–3).

21. In Yossi Klein, 'A blight unto the nations,' *Ha'aretz Magazine* (English Edition), 25 January 2002, p. 12.

22. The anthem is sung at the end of the event opening Holocaust Remembrance Day, indicating again that this Day is more separated from the other two.

23. In the first years after independence, the official committee charged with planning Independence Day activities advocated top-down organization and coordination of activities. This included opening a time slot intended for mealtime celebration within the family at home. New culinary dishes laden with symbolism were to be created; a text modeled on that read during the Passover meal was commissioned; and the state radio was to broadcast appropriate music for the meal (see Azaryahu 1995: 105–8).

24. Therefore our understanding of histories is aided when we give metaphysical recognition to logics of time (see Handelman 1998b).

25. Deleuze (1991: 31), using Henri Bergson's aphorism of a lump of sugar, shows why space must be opened into process through duration, in order to know its dimensionalities: 'Take a lump of sugar: It has a spatial configuration. But if we approach it from that angle, all we will ever grasp are differences in degree between that sugar and any other thing. But it also has a duration, a rhythm of duration, a way of being in time that is at least partially revealed in the process of its dissolving, that shows how this sugar differs in kind not only from other things, but first and foremost from itself.'

26. Zerubavel (1985: 115) contrasts this unit to 'the astrological model of a seven-day non-pulsating cycle.' It is instructive to contrast lengthy durations of Jewish time to those of classical Indian thought. In the latter, pulsation may be of entropy, the cyclical, the eventual return to points of start and re-start (Nakamura 1981). Complementing these rhythms are modes of belief and action that enable the individual to break free of these toils of time (Pocock 1964). In sharp contrast to Judaic time is that of Javanese gamelan music, in which simultaneous yet separate plots in different times and languages 'coincide' with one another at certain points. Instead of 'a unified causal sequence of actions that reach some climax' (Becker and Becker 1995: 360), the logic of these coinciding times may be more

like a multitude of gyroscopic tops, each swirling separately, yet coinciding with one another's orbits in certain moments of synchronization.

27. Traditional Jewish thought, sensitive to chronicle, is unreflexive about the nature of time itself. Perhaps its unfaltering coherence did not encourage time, 'to be a variable independent of the events it marks' (Fabian 1983: 13), and so, separated reflexively from history.

28. The first four Sabbaths of this sequence are explicitly accorded a special status in traditional Judaism. Their temporal rhythm is accentuated if one adds to this sequence the readings from Prophets of the two subsequent Sabbaths. We are indebted to Shlomo Fischer for bringing this sequence to our attention.

29. The upward impulsion of this sequence continues through the Haftarah from Isaiah, read on the last day of Passover and (as an addition following independence) during the special prayer service of Independence Day (Vainstein 1953: 159). This reading contains the vision of a perfected cosmos, in which wolf and lamb, leopard and kid, will dwell together in harmony (Isaiah 11). Perhaps not the end of time, yet opening to a 'time without limits' (Kochan 1997: 151).

30. Other, still lengthier durations endowed with this rhythm of pulsation could be adduced – thus, the seventh, sabbatical year, and the hypothetical fiftieth year of the Jubilee.

31. The sources used to discuss rhythms of Jewish time are embedded in liturgical texts and schedules. But the penetration of these rhythms into mundane living is necessarily pervasive. Therefore these rhythms are not easily subsumed wholly within the rubric of ritual time, in contrast to that of mundane time: cultural formations likely differ in how they inform living with senses of the rightness of feeling time. There is connectedness in this to aesthetics of practice discussed in Chapter Six. The aesthetics of time are the practice of time – the practice of its rhythms and pulsations – in ways that feel right.

32. The plurality of narratives in today's Israel hardly depart from the forming of this originary narrative structure.

33. The quicker the re-forming of order, the better, even on the small scales of mundane threats of 'terror.' This helps explain the naturalness of immediate armed response, and the sentiment that biting the bullet is unnatural.

34. Not only is peace then perceived as unattainable, but peace itself becomes identified with forms of chaotic disruption. So, the contentions that peace will encourage internal cleavages to explode, wracking social order from within; that peace will lead to cultural subversion by the Arab world from without; that war must continue because the enemy is eternally hostile – the encoding of self-sealing, circular temporal process.

Chapter 8 The Presence of Absence

1. The suffix 'scape,' points to a unifying principle, constructing a part of the land such that this part is practiced as signifying the whole of the land (see Cosgrove 1984: 13). Landscape becomes particular ways of seeing and experiencing (Bender 1993: 2).

2. Baudrillard's (1983: 2) postmodern vision of space is apposite here: 'Simulation is no longer that of a territory, a referential being or a substance, it is the generation by models of a real without origin or reality: a hyperreal. The territory no longer precedes the map, nor survives it. Henceforth, it is the map that precedes the territory . . . It is the map that engenders the territory.' Aware of this artifice of constructedness, can national memorialism still claim to authenticity? Yet death is authentic in its dying, and in the absence it rips opens among the living. No memorialism, however constructed, ever returns the dead to life among the living. Regardless of how space is conceived, the dead map absences among the living. The sacrifice may be demoted, yet is it ever erased from the hyperreal?

3. See Azaryahu (1992: 65–7) for a discussion of private monuments to sacrifice in Israel.

4. Here we address the memorialism of Israeli Jews. However, both Jews and Palestinians use the memorialization of war dead to authenticate claims to territory. During the period immediately after the 1967 War and Israel's capture of East Jerusalem, Jews and Palestinians erected improvised, private memorials for their respective war dead all over that area of the city. The Israeli authorities replaced the individualistic Jewish memorials with uniform memorial plaques inscribed with the names of the dead, and at first did not react to Arab memorials. On the first anniversary of that war, with Jewish and Arab mourners grouped around their respective memorials, tensions ran high. Eventually only one Arab memorial was permitted, and this in the teeth of strong Jewish opposition (M. Benvenisti 1983: 54, 1990: 92).

   This chapter does not discuss a fourth kind of memorialism, that of ancient graves containing the presence of 'ancestors.' Sidra Ezrahi refers to such sites as 'cemeteries without bones.' Examples include the fall of Masada (C.E. 73) (Paine 1994) and the Bar Kokhba revolt (C.E. 132–135) (Aronoff 1986).

5. In contrast to the sacrificial dead, the presence within Israel of Adolph Eichmann, the Nazi officer convicted by an Israeli court of crimes against humanity, was turned into utter absence. He was executed, his body then destroyed by fire. The border authorities took his ashes out in the Mediterranean beyond Israeli territorial waters. At dawn, the movement from darkness into light, his ashes were thrown into the sea to vanish without trace.

6. The voluntarism of sacrifice has deep resonances with the *aqedah*, Abraham's preparedness to sacrifice to God his beloved son, Isaac, and of Isaac's willing acceptance of this (Hayward 1980). The highest form of national death is predicated

not only on sacrifice, but on the still more hermetic and totalistic notion of self-sacrifice, in which the sacrificer is the sacrificed. Conscious sacrifice of oneself connotes also voluntary sacrifice by oneself. One's being transcending the killing ground yet utterly dependent on its earthiness. Self-sacrifice contrasts with suicide, the devolution of being, killing oneself through egotistical sentiments, because one is trapped totally within the mirror imaging of self. In counterpoint, self-sacrifice is always orientated to someone or something beyond oneself. In this regard, it is also self-less sacrifice, the voluntary extinguishing of self for the sake of the other. Complementarily, the other (State, people) is obligated to cherish the memory of the selfless sacrifice within the 'body' of the state, its living national landscapes. The most notable place of this kind is the military cemetery. From this perspective, so-called suicide bombers are self-sacrificers.

Three roles commonly are discussed in relation to sacrifice: the sacrificer, the sacrificed, and the 'sacrifiant' (Herrenschmidt 1978), the latter referring to the agency or person on whose behalf the sacrifice is offered and made. The especially high value attached to self-sacrifice stems from its conjoining sacrificer and sacrificed, the praxis of intent and action within the single self-extinguishing, self-transcending person. Given the synechdocal relationship between the slain soldier (the part) and state and people (the whole), all three sacrificial roles are conjoined within the dead soldier.

In Judaic traditions there is a strong connection amongst earth, creation, and death. In Hebrew, the land of Israel is commonly referred to as 'place of birth' (*moledet*). In Zionist usage this has acquired the meaning of 'motherland,' and it may be contrasted with a place one merely 'comes from' (*houledet*).

7. The State constructs an increasingly greater totality of sacrifice by incorporating into its official pantheon persons who preceded statehood, yet are made to have a direct genealogical connection to the ultimate creation of the state. This includes virtually all Jews who were killed by non-Jews (Ottoman Turks, British, Arabs) in Palestine since 1860, the year Jews first settled outside the walled city of Jerusalem, and the date chosen as of now to signify the modern Jewish battle for Palestine. Most recently, the State is including victims of terror in its expansion of the borders of sacrifice for the national.

8. In the Israeli Jewish cult of the military dead there is no tomb of the Unknown Soldier (see Mosse 1990: 94–8), since the claim is that each and every soldier is known by name, preserving the inviolability of the entire people, living and dead, through time. There are those whose place of burial is unknown. For these soldiers there are name plaques and other memorials. And there are dead soldiers whose religious identity as Jews is in question, and who cannot be buried in the con-secrated ground of a Jewish cemetery. This issue is prominent in the wake of the enormous immigration from the former Soviet Union.

9. Burial and belonging are tightly torqued in Jewish tradition. Eisen (1986: 10) comments that one may sojourn in the land of Israel without possessing it. Yet to

die in the land, a holding (*akhuza*) for a burial plot is needed. Sidra Ezrahi (1992: 482) comments that 'Israel's first real-estate transaction in ancient Canaan was the purchase of the burial cave of the Machpelah [the Tomb of the Patriarchs, in Hebron].' Today the landscape of burial contours Israeli Jewish nationalism in space.

10. Shamir (1989, 1991) compiled descriptions of over nine hundred military memorials, but this listing is incomplete. See also Levinger (1993), and Baumel (1995) on Holocaust memorials.

11. See Casey (1987) and Paine (1990) for discussions of place as the intersection of space and time. Interestingly, Mosse (1991) argued that war memorials in Israel 'are more peace monuments than those [war] monuments [of Western Europe], which are aggressive to the core.'

12. In the past, army regulation of memorialism was stringent, though bypassing regulations was possible (Rubin 1985: 804). In recent years, bereaved parents are putting increasing pressure on the army to loosen its directives regarding the text of the headstone and the artifacts permitted at the grave. In the Mount Herzl cemetery there are numerous examples of this loosening – a photographic engraving on black basalt of the face of a dead soldier, set in front of the official headstone, his details given in Russian; a plaster army boot filled with plants, standing on an inscription covering the body of the grave, stating that the soldier was an outstanding young athlete, felled by friendly fire; a poem to the side of a headstone; a plastic doll of the television Simpsons' youngest, Baby Face, her mouth closed around her teether, resting against the headstone of a young woman soldier who fell in the line of duty. A recent guideline suggested to the army stated that casualties 'belong' first and foremost to their families (*Ha'aretz*, English Edition, 9 August 1999, p. 4).

13. Like all sculpture, these memorials invite touching something of the texture of being there, in different folds, angles, curves.

14. The size of this monument makes difficult its preservation. In 2001 many of the relics were no longer atop their pillars; the site was covered with graffiti, littered with refuse; and the the names of the dead in the inner room were hardly readable. The local administration responsible for the site claimed there were no funds for its upkeep. Too, the size and anonymity of the community of commemoration displaces responsibility.

15. The same sculptor did the bas-relief and sculpture on the site of the Warsaw Ghetto, copies of which are at the Wall of Remembrance at Yad Vashem. See Young (1989a).

16. As noted, the etymology of the English-language term, holocaust, connotes religious sacrifice consumed by fire. The modern Hebrew term for the Jewish genocide is *Shoah*, without religious or sacrificial connotations, meaning simply, destruction, ruin (see Garber and Zuckerman 1989: 199–200). For a more complex exegesis of Shoah, see Tal 1979). In Israel, the name, Shoah, is used

routinely together with the insistence that these dead died for the Sanctification of God's Name, as martyrs.

17. The rhetoric of martyrology hones the problem of claims to the Holocaust. Does it belong to the Jewish people, so that the rest of the world should be made conscious continously of its evil intentions towards Jews? Or is the Holocaust one extreme expression of the universality of evil? Or, of social conditions that have made Jews especial targets and victims (Bauman 1989)?

18. The radical shift in Israeli attitudes towards the Holocaust began with the Eichmannn trial in 1961, crystallizing further with the 1967 War (see the opposing perspectives of Weitz 1996 and Zertal 2000). Prior to that it was especially diaspora Jewry who made the comparison between Israel's isolation and that of Holocaust Jewry. To no small degree, Israeli Jews learned from diaspora Jews that in 1967 Israel had been on the brink of imminent Holocaust; and the power of Israel's self-recognition as the post-Holocaust state of the Jewish people coalesced especially in the wake of the 1967 War. In turn, American Jews learned about the public representation and monumentalism of Holocaust memorialism from Israeli centers like Yad Vashem. Since then Holocaust memorialism flourishes in the United States and elsewhere.

    The rise to power in 1977 of Begin's extreme nationalist Likud Party publicly politicized the Holocaust, making Israel actively diasporic as never before. Begin gloried in the authenticity of prewar Jewish *shtetl* tradition in Eastern Europe, in the growth of religious ways of life, and in the use of Holocaust metaphors and allegories at every opportunity to justify government actions in the spirit of 'the few against the many' (Gertz 1986). At the time of the 1982 Lebanon War, Begin wrote to Reagan: 'May I tell you, dear Mr. President, how I feel these days when I turn to the Creator of my soul in deep gratitude: I feel as a prime minister empowered to instruct a valiant army facing "Berlin" [Beirut] where amongst innocent civilians Hitler [Arafat] and his henchmen hide in a bunker deep beneath the surface' (cited in Cromer 1987: 289). By the 1990s, Israeli teenagers by the thousands were journeying to Poland on trips sponsored by the Ministry of Education in search of authentic relics of the Holocaust and the places of annihilation. One minister of education likened these trips to 'travelling to the Shoah' ('Six after Six,' Israel Radio, 14 September 1992). In Israeli Jewish narratives the Holocaust is increasingly understood as the reason for and the foundation of state formation. Should these trends continue to develop apace, the Holocaust will become a radical critique of the Zionist state.

    Military and Holocaust memorialism have quite distinct circulations. Military memorialism circulates *as* the borders, historical and eternal, of the State. The consumption and contestation of military memorialism are local, as are its pilgrims and tourists. Holocaust memorialism is exported, circulating widely. Its electronic technologies of showing and telling are competitive with one another, as are its master narratives and meanings in different countries. Publics whose centers of power are outside Israel contest the shaping of Holocaust memorialism in Israel. In 1995, gays held a memorial occasion at Yad Vashem, disrupted by Orthodox Jews for whom homosexuality is anathema. And Ultra-orthodox Jews threatened to boycott Yad Vashem if photographs of Jewish women, naked and herded by Nazi guards, were not removed from the historical museum.

19. In a similar vein the Yad Vashem World Council passed a resolution in 1957 stating that, 'The Council considers it desirable that Memorial Day [for the Holocaust dead] be observed in a similar manner in all parts of the country and that this manner be determined in cooperation with the government' (*Yad Vashem Bulletin*, No. 2, December 1957, p. 25). So, too, the head of the Yad Vashem Executive declared in 1962 that, 'We have made a close study of how to make memory of the Catastrophe strike root [in Israel] '(*Yad Vashem Bulletin*, No. 11, April-May 1962, p. 99). From its beginnings, Yad Vashem struggled with the tensions between sponsoring basic research on and national commemoration of the Holocaust, in which the latter was integral to the pedagogy of making citizenship national (Stauber 2000).

20. The Avenue was inaugurated on Holocaust Martyrs' and Heroes' Remembrance Day, 1962. Among the first Righteous to plant a tree was Oskar Schindler (*Yad Vashem Bulletin*, No. 12, December 1962, p. 99).

21. The ashes are a signal reminder of the significance of embodiment (however ephemeral) and burial in Judaism, and of the implications of these for Israeli nationalism and its relationship to religion. In 1947 a former Polish partisan 'illegally' brought into Palestine ashes from the death camp of Treblinka (*Yad Vashem Bulletin*, No. 22, May 1968, p. 64).The term 'illegal' in this text evoked the 'illegal immigration' (*Aliyah Bet*) of Holocaust survivors through the British sea blockade against all Jewish immigration before the founding of the state. Thus ashes of the martyred dead also suffered the depredations that living survivors underwent in order to make their place in the pre-state landscape.

    At the initiative of a senior official of the Ministry of Religious Affairs, ashes from the death camp of Flossenburg were buried on Mount Zion in Jerusalem, in what became another memorial, The Cellar of the Holocaust (*Martef HaShoah*), under the aegis of the Ministry. These ashes were one of the first foci of memorial services for the Holocaust dead in Israel. Mount Zion is the traditional burial place of King David. The Messiah is expected to come from the lineage of David – linking ashes of the Holocaust dead to Mount Zion invokes the rhythm of time discussed in Chapter Seven.

22. A comment on the Hall of Remembrance: 'My own thought is that . . . this Jerusalem hillside . . . marks one absolutely sacred patch of earth. You may retort: and if that is the case, why was it necessary to erect a building, construct walls, a roof, a gate? The patch of earth could just as well have been marked by a simple palisade. The eternal flame would burn under an open sky; ceremonies and prayers would be conducted directly beneath the heavens . . . in fact, that is often

what happens' (Lishinsky 1983: 16–17). The 'simple palisade' describes military memorialism. Toponyms as forms of commemoration were extremely popular in the early years of the state, and among these was the memorial forest (Azaryahu 1992: 63; Y. Zerubavel 1996). Such a forest was planted by Yad Vashem, but as it grew it disapeared within other forests planted for other purposes, losing its distinctive contours in the broader Israeli landscape. Were the Holocaust to be commemorated as the comment suggested, it would dissipate into the Israeli landscape.

23. The Children's Memorial is built as a developing architectonic sequence that moves from its exterior layer done in the style of socialist realism, to its interior core, designed in the indeterminate style of a postmodern vision, opening simultaneously in all directions. One enters the memorial from the outside by passing the bas-relief of a young boy's face, the donor's son who perished in the Holocaust. This figure was a condition of the donor's subsidizing the memorial. One comes into a lit ante-chamber, facing a wall of black-and-white photographs of children who died in the Holocaust, passing then into the blacked out sight-scape of momentary blindness and flickering reflections. Here the Children's Memorial comes closest to Baudrillard's postmodern dilation of reality as simulation. The sudden loss of direction, the blurring of vertical and horizontal axes and borders, the onset of tiny surges of vertigo, the need to feel rather than see one's way through, all imbalance and fragment the totality of reality that is itself a fragmented totality – the infinity of separate lights that are not connected to one another, except by the nullity of darkness. This memorial is the most seductive to the senses (Baudrillard 1990) at Yad Vashem, in its mastery of artifice to evoke the lost innocence of childhood (the infinity of tiny lights) and its loss (the recognition of the artifice behind them). As eyes adjust to blackness, the body once again sees more than feels, and we lose the reality of fragmentation that this memorial evokes. One exits from this cave into the near-blinding daylight, high above a vista of valley and mountains, an authentic and integrated vision (or is it?) which once more eye and body must adjust to. The exit from this memorial is no less brilliant than the entry. The memorial is open to a wide range of interpretations. On a recent visit in 2003 I overheard a teacher explaining to her class that the memorial is symbolic of a death-camp gas chamber.

24. In general the photographs conform to Brink's (2000: 149) argument that, 'Photographs showing the Nazi crimes have to be unequivocal . . . It is deeply confusing if these photographs, these "photographic icons," become readable, if their meaning shifts according to the context in which they are shown and looked at.'

25. The Historical Museum is being rebuilt. The preliminary designs call for it to be located largely beneath the surface, a burial site echoing our comments on closed memorial sites at Yad Vashem.

26. During the 1980s there was a significant increase in artifacts given to Yad Vashem by Holocaust survivors, conscious of their age and seeking a home for these

authentic, personal mementos (Mais 1988: 18). By contrast the Museum of the Jewish Diaspora in Tel-Aviv deliberately uses only models and copies of artifacts to describe the history of Jewish life around the world. Golden (1996) argues that this policy stresses the 'inauthenticity of the [diasporic] life that is on display.' See also Shenhav-Keller (2000).

27. In their study of Remembrance Day and Holocaust Remembrance Day events in Israeli schools, Ben-Amos and Bet-El (1999: 275) found that in contrast to those of Remembrance Day, Holocaust Remembrance Day events 'concentrate on recreating the victims' world in an attempt to bring home to the pupils the tragedy of the event' – in other words, these events build Europe in Israel.

28. To some degree this is offset by the fact that areas of Yad Vashem are 'living memorials' (Barber 1949: 66), with immediate instrumental purposes – archives, library, pedagogy. Numerous organizations are constructing the generational paradigm of survivorship – the children of survivors become the inheritors of Holocaust, the Second Generation, while the offspring of second-generation survivors become the Third Generation of survivors. The intention is to continue the obligation of the living to remember through metaphors of family.

29. Thomas Laqueur (personal communication) maintains that this relationship is not shared with the commemoration of military dead in the West (see Laqueur 1994). Yet we are not arguing for the universality of this inverse relationship in the memorializing of national death. Of greater significance to the human condition is the problem of presence and absence, and the creation of the presence of absence. (See Schieffelin 1976 for a striking example of practicing absence into presence.) This is no less a problem for postmodernist thinking, given the emphasis on loosening of structures, social fragmentation, hybridization, and social simulation.

30. See Handelman (1992) on self-negating paradox.

Chapter 9 Absence Rising

1. All names of persons are changed. The transcripts of stories and descriptions of interaction are based on videotapes of the workshop.

2. I use the phrasing, 'Holocaust self,' to refer to the sense of being of the person who has lived through the Holocaust. This sense of being is neither singular nor monolithic, nor is this the person's entirety of selfness. But the Holocaust self often is self-guarding – its traffic with the outside world may be one-way, absorbing outside influences but responding apprehensively, cautiously.

3. Persons who lived through the Holocaust usually are called 'saved.' However, unless the Holocaust self asserts agency on the social surface, I regard this sense of being as still victimized, and prefer to call these persons, 'victims.'

4. My use of 'embodiment' refers, as in dictionary usage, to the coalescence, incorporation, and forming of a whole. In the human being, self pervades body and body pervades self – each existentially embodies the other, and together they are the bodied. How this is accomplished culturally (and the consequences of this) are then the issue. Therefore Cartesian mind/body dualism is no less an accurate depiction of being than is, say, a premise of the indefinite boundaries of mind/body and their high degree of integration.

5. My concern here is with how the absence of the Holocaust self is turned into presence through stories, bringing with it the absences that are the Holocaust. I do not discuss how the stories themselves are put together, nor how, in the main, their organization and effectiveness are critiqued.

6. My use of 'un-story' differs from Blanchot's (1986: 128). Blanchot's usage of un-story emphasizes the activity of passivity: '. . . forgetfulness as thought. That which . . . cannot be forgotten because it has already fallen outside memory,' so, 'keep watch over absent meaning,' he admonishes (1986: 42). I stress the absence of narrative in the narrative that destroys narrative. So, too, in using the term, 'un-meaning,' I refer to that absence of meaning that corrodes meaning.

7. See Agamben's (1999: 41–83) meditation on the muselmann.

8. The forty years may allude also to the biblical wanderings of the Israelites in the wilderness after leaving Egypt, as against her own Holocaust self, parched and deserted for decades by others in the wilderness of Israel.

9. The reference likely is to reparation payments made by the German government to Holocaust survivors from Germany, yet often seen popularly as monies received by all Holocaust survivors.

10. Why does the performing body have to tell the bulk of the story in words? The status of language, of the 'word' in witnessing, of historiographic detail ('This happened . . . there . . . then . . . to . . .') and emotional tones ('I felt. . . ') in words must be considered. In this culture the Holocaust is hardly performed through song, dance, music, mime. But the words are so bountiful. So, too, the occasions of remembrance are primarily composed of words and texts. How do other cultures enact catastrophe?

11. Including absence to itself, perhaps the not-me that did the experiencing. See Delbo 1995.

12. 'Vus-vus' is a derogatory term, based on the Yiddish interrogative, *vus,* meaning 'what,' but generally used to deride Ashkenazim categorically as know-it-alls. The 'Northern North' refers stereotypically to Ashkenazi-dominated, middle-class North Tel-Aviv.

13. The European qualities of the Holocaust and its social consequences for children of Easterner parentage is shown subtly but emphatically in the documentary film, *Slaves of Memory* (1989), directed by Eyal Sivan. In one scene, Easterner high school students rehearse a Holocaust Remembrance Day event. Mispronouncing the names of concentration and death camps, they must repeat them – apparently because these names do not appear in their routine talk.

14. In 1996 the Chief Ashkenazi Rabbi (himself a survivor and an extremely active witness and publicist) struck from the official liturgy for Holocaust Remembrance Day the phrase, 'like sheep to the slaughter,' commonly used to describe the passivity of the victims.
15. Telling these stories in the workshop and beyond may be a form of therapy for the victims. (This is the aim of one of the organizations involved in the workshop.) Philip Rieff (1966) argues that therapy has replaced religion in modernity. Terry Evens (personal communication, February 1998) comments that many of these stories have an irrepressible religious character. This religious character of the stories may be enabling therapy to impact on the political ordering of the social.

Bibliography

Abramov, Zalman. 1976. *Perpetual Dilemma*. Rutherford, NJ: Farleigh Dickinson University Press.

Agamben, Giorgio. 1999. *Remnants of Auschwitz: The Witness and the Archive*. New York: Zone Books.

Albanese, Catherine. 1974. 'Requiem for Memorial Day: dissent in the redeemer nation,' *American Quarterly*, 26: 386–98.

Allen, A.T. 1986. 'Gardens of children, gardens of God: kindergartens and day-care centers in nineteenth-century Germany,' *Journal of Social History*, 19: 433–50.

Allen, Nicholas J. 2000. *Categories and Classifications: Maussian Reflections on the Social*. New York: Berghahn.

Almog, Shmuel. 1987. *Zionism and History: The Rise of a New Jewish Consciousness*. New York: St Martin's Press.

Amichai, Yehuda. 1971. *Selected Poems*. Trans. Assia Guttmann and Harold Schimmel with the collaboration of Ted Hughes. Harmondsworth: Penguin.

—— 1986. *The Selected Poetry of Yehuda Amichai*. [Edited and translated by Chana and Stephen Bloch.] New York: Harper and Row.

—— 1995. *Yehuda Amichai: A Life of Poetry 1948–1994*. Selected and trans. Benjamin and Barbara Harshav. New York: Harper Perennial.

Anderson, Benedict. 1991. *Imagined Communities: Reflections on the Origin and Spread of Nationalism*. rev. ed. London: Verso.

Anderson, Perry. 1996. *Lineages of the Absolutist State*. London: Verso.

Arendt, Hannah. 1958. *The Origins of Totalitarianism*. New York: Meridian.

Aronoff, Myron J. 1986. 'Establishing authority: the memorialization of Jabotinsky and the Burial of the Bar Kochba Bones in Israel under the Likud,' In *The Frailty of Authority*, M.J. Aronoff, ed., pp. 105–30. New Brunswick, NJ: Transaction.

—— 1989. *Israeli Visions and Divisions: Cultural Change and Political Conflict*. New Brunswick, NJ: Transaction.

Atran, Scott. 1996. 'Modes of thinking about living kinds: science, symbolism, and Common Sense,' In *Modes of Thought: Explorations in Culture and Cognition*, D.R. Olson and N. Torrance, eds., pp. 216–60. Cambridge: Cambridge University Press.

Azaryahu, Maoz. 1992. 'War memorials and the commemoration of the Israeli War of Independence, 1948–1956,' *Studies in Zionism*, 13: 57–77.

—— 1993. 'From remains to relics: authentic monuments in the Israeli landscape,' *History and Memory*, 5: 82–103.

—— 1995. *State Cults: Celebrating Independence and Commemorating the Fallen in Israel, 1948–1956*. Beersheva: Ben-Gurion University of the Negev Press (in Hebrew).

—— 1999. 'The Independence Day military parade: a political history of a patriotic ritual.' In *The Military and Militarism in Israeli Society*, E. Lomsky-Feder and E. Ben-Ari, eds., pp. 89–116. Albany: State University of New York Press.

Baehr, Peter. 2001. 'The "iron cage" and the "shell as hard as steel": Parsons, Weber, and the *Stahlhartes Gehause* metaphor in *The Protestant Ethic and the Spirit of Capitalism*,' *History and Theory*, 40: 153–69.

Barber, Bernard. 1949. 'Place, symbol and utilitarian function in war memorials,' *Social Forces*, 28: 64–8.

Baudrillard, Jean. 1983. *Simulations*. New York: Semiotext(e).

—— 1990. *Seduction*. New York: St Martin's.

Bauman, Zygmunt. 1989. *Modernity and the Holocaust*. Ithaca: Cornell University Press.

—— 1998. 'The Holocaust's life as a ghost,' *Tikkun*, 13, no. 3: 33–8.

Baumel, Judith Tydor. 1995. '"In everlasting memory": individual and communal Holocaust commemoration in Israel,' *Israel Affairs*, 1, no. 3: 146–70.

—— 1996. '"Rachel laments her children" – representation of women in Israeli Holocaust memorials,' *Israel Studies*, 1: 100–26.

Becker, Alton and Judith Becker. 1995. 'A musical icon: power and meaning in Javanese Gamelan music.' In *Beyond Translation: Essays Toward a Modern Philology*, by Alton Becker, pp. 349–64. Ann Arbor: University of Michigan Press.

Ben-Amos, Avner. 1989. 'State funerals of the French Third Republic,' *History and Memory*, 1: 85–108.

—— and Ilana Bet-El. 1999. 'Holocaust Day and Memorial Day in Israeli schools: ceremonies, education and history.' *Israel Studies*, 4, no. 1: 258–84.

Ben-Ari, Eyal. 1987. 'Disputing about day-care: care-taking roles in a Japanese day nursery.' In, *Alternative Patterns of Family Life in Modern Societies*, Lea Shamgar-Handelman and R. Palomba, eds., pp. 483–502. Rome: Istituto Di Ricerche Sulla Popolazione.

—— 1998. *Mastering Soldiers: Conflict, Emotions, and the Enemy in an Israeli Military Unit*. New York: Berghahn.

Bender, Barbara. 1993. 'Introduction: Landscape – meaning and action.' In *Landscape: Politics and Perspectives*, B. Bender, ed., pp. 1–17. Oxford: Berg.

Ben-Eliezer, Uri. 1995. 'A nation-in-arms: state, nation, and militarism in Israel's first years,' *Comparative Studies in Society and History*, 37: 264–85.

—— 1998a. *The Making of Israeli Militarism*. Bloomington: University of Indiana Press.

—— 1998b. 'State versus civil society? A non-binary model of domination through the example of Israel,' *Journal of Historical Sociology*, 11: 370–96.

—— 2001. 'From military role-expansion to difficulties in peace-making: The Israeli Defense Forces 50 years on.' In *Military, State, and Society in Israel*, Daniel

Maman, Eyal Ben-Ari, and Zeev Rosenhek, eds., pp. 137–72. New Brunswick, NJ: Transaction.

Benjamin, Walter. 1969. 'The work of art in the age of mechanical reproduction.' In his *Illuminations*, Hannah Arendt, ed., pp. 217–51. New York: Schocken.

Ben-Rafael, Eliezer and Stephen Sharot. 1991. *Ethnicity, Religion and Class in Israeli Society*. Cambridge: Cambridge University Press.

Bentham, Jeremy. 1995. *The Panopticon Writings*, ed. M. Bozovic. London: Verso.

Benvenisti, Eyal. 1990. *Legal Dualism: The Absorption of the Occupied Territories into Israel*. Boulder, CO: Westview.

Benvenisti, Meron. 1983. *Jerusalem: Study of a Polarized Community*. Jerusalem: West Bank Data-base project.

—— 1990. *Jerusalem's City of the Dead*. Jerusalem: Keter (in Hebrew).

Berdoulay, Vincent. 1987. 'Place, meaning and discourse in French language geography.' In *The Power of Place*, J.A. Agnew and J.S. Duncan, eds., pp. 124–39. Boston: Unwin Hyman.

Berezin, Mabel. 1994. 'Cultural form and political meaning: state-subsidized theater, ideology, and the language of style in Fascist Italy,' *American Journal of Sociology*, 99: 1237–86.

Bernstein, Michael A. 1998. 'A homage to the extreme: the Shoah and the rhetoric of catastrophe,' *Times Literary Supplement*, 6 March, pp. 6–8.

Bilu, Yoram and Eliezer Wiztum. 2000. 'War-related loss and suffering in Israeli society: an historical perspective,' *Israel Studies*, 5, no. 3: 1–31.

Bin-Nun, Ariel. 1992. *The Law of the State of Israel*. Jerusalem: Rubin Mass.

Blanchot, Maurice. 1986. *The Writing of the Disaster*. Lincoln: University of Nebraska Press.

Blau, Herbert. 1990. 'Universals of performance: or, amortizing play.' In *By Means of Performance*. Richard Schechner and Willa Appel, eds., pp. 250–72. Cambridge: Cambridge University Press.

Bloch, Maurice and Jonathan Parry, eds. 1982. *Death and the Regeneration of Life*. Cambridge: Cambridge University Press.

Bogard, William. 1996. *The Simulation of Surveillance: Hypercontrol in Telematic Societies*. Cambridge: Cambridge University Press.

—— 2000. 'Smoothing machines and the constitution of society,' *Cultural Studies*, 14: 269–94.

Boli-Bennett, J. and J.W. Meyer. 1978. 'The ideology of childhood and the state: rules distinguishing children in national constitutions, 1870–1970,' *American Sociological Review*, 43: 797–812.

Borges, Jorge Luis. 1970. 'A new refutation of time.' In his *Labyrinths*, pp. 252–69. London: Penguin.

Bourdieu, Pierre. 1977. *Outline of a Theory of Practice*. Cambridge: Cambridge University Press.

—— 1998. 'Rethinking the state: genesis and structure of the bureaucratic field.' In his *Practical Reason*. Cambridge: Polity, pp. 35–63.

Bowker, Geoffrey C. and Susan Leigh Star. 1999. *Sorting Things Out: Classification and its Consequences*. Cambridge, MA: MIT Press.

Bozovic, Miran. 1995. 'Introduction: "an utterly dark spot".' In J. Bentham, *The Panopticon Writings*, M. Bozovic, ed., pp. 1–27, London: Verso.

Braude, Benjamin. 1982. 'Foundation myths of the *millet* system.' In *Christians and Jews in the Ottoman Empire*, Vol. 1, B. Braude and B. Lewis, eds., pp. 69–88. New York: Holmes and Meier.

Bredekamp, Horst. 1995. *The Lure of Antiquity and the Cult of the Machine: The Kunstkammer and the Evolution of Nature, Art and Technology*. Princeton: Markus Wiener.

Briggs, Jean. 1992. 'Lines, cycles, and transformations: temporal perspectives on Inuit action.' In *Contemporary Futures*, S. Wallman, ed., pp. 83–108. London: Routledge.

Brink, Cornelia. 2000. 'Secular icons: looking at photographs from Nazi concentration camps,' *History and Memory*, 12, no. 1: 135–50.

Brubaker, Rogers. 1995. 'National minorities, nationalizing states, and externalizing national homelands in the new Europe,' *Daedalus*, 124, no. 2: 107–32.

Bruner, Edward M. and Phyllis Gorfain. 1984. 'Dialogic narration and the paradoxes of Masada.' In *Text, Play, and Story: The Construction and Reconstruction of Self and Society*, E.M. Bruner, ed., pp. 56–79. Washington, DC: American Ethnological Society.

Bunn, James H. 1981. *The Dimensionality of Signs, Tools, and Models*. Bloomington: Indiana University Press.

Calhoun, Craig. 1997. 'Nationalism and the public sphere.' In *Public and Private Thought and Practice*, J. Weintraub and K. Krishan, eds., pp. 75–102. Chicago: University of Chicago Press.

Canguilhem, Georges. 1992. 'Machine and organism.' In *Incorporations*, J. Crary and S. Kwinter, eds., pp. 44–69. New York: Zone Books.

Carey, Seamus. 2000. 'Cultivating ethos through the body,' *Human Studies*, 23: 23–42.

Carmi, Shulamit and Henry Rosenfeld. 1989. 'The emergence of militaristic nationalism in Israel,' *International Journal of Politics, Culture and Society*, 3: 5–49.

—— and —— 1991. 'The radical change: from a socialist perspective to militarism (rejoinder to Ben-Eliezer and Shamir),' *International Journal of Politics, Culture and Society*, 4: 577–87.

Casey, Edward S. 1987. *Remembering: A Phenomenological Study*. Bloomington: Indiana University Press.

Cassirer, Ernst. 1946. *The Myth of the State*. New Haven: Yale University Press.

Clynes, Manfred E. 1995. 'Cyborg II: Sentic space travel.' In *The Cyborg Handbook*, Chris Hables Gray, ed., pp. 35–42. New York: Routledge.

Cohen, Anthony P. 1996. 'Personal nationalism: a Scottish view of some rites, rights, and wrongs,' *American Ethnologist*, 23: 802–15.

Cohen, Erik. 1989. 'Citizenship, nationality and religion in Israel and Thailand.' In *The Israeli State and Society: Boundaries and Frontiers*, B. Kimmerling, ed., pp. 66–92. Albany: State University New York Press.

Cohen, Patricia Cline. 1982. *A Calculating People: The Spread of Numeracy in Early America*. Chicago: University of Chicago Press.

Connell, R.W. 1990. 'The state, gender, and sexual politics,' *Theory and Society*, 19: 507–44.

Cordoba, Avraham. 1980. 'The institutionalization of a cultural center in Palestine: the case of the Writers' Association,' *Jewish Social Studies*, 42: 37–62.

Corsaro, William. 1988. 'Routines in the peer culture of American and Italian nursery school children,' *Sociology of Education*, 61: 1–14.

Cosgrove, Denis E. 1984. *Social Formation and Symbolic Landscape*. London: Croom Helm.

Cromer, Gerald. 1987. 'Negotiating the Meaning of the Holocaust,' *Holocaust and Genocide Studies*, 2: 289–302.

Csordas, Thomas J. 1994. 'Introduction: the body as representation and being-in-the-world.' In *Embodiment and Experience*. T.J. Csordas, ed., pp. 1–24. Cambridge: Cambridge University Press.

Dandekar, Christopher. 1990. *Surveillance, Power and Modernity: Bureaucracy and Discipline From 1700 to the Present Day*. Cambridge: Polity.

Debord, Guy. 1998. *Comments on the Society of the Spectacle*. London: Verso.

Delbo, Charlotte. 1995. *Auschwitz and After*. New Haven: Yale University Press.

Deleuze, Gilles. 1991. *Bergsonism*. New York: Zone Books.

—— and Felix Guattari. 1986. *Nomadology: The War Machine*. New York: Semiotext(e).

—— and —— 1988. *A Thousand Plateaus: Capitalism and Schizophrenia*. London: Athlone.

Desrosières, Alain. 1998. *The Politics of large Numbers: A History of Statistical Reasoning*. Cambridge, MA: Harvard University Press.

Dinur, Benzion. 1957. 'Problems confronting "Yad Vashem" in its work of research,' *Yad Vashem Studies*, 1: 7–30.

Doleve-Gandelman, Tzili. 1987. 'The symbolic inscription of Zionist ideology in the space of Eretz Yisrael: why the native Israeli is called tsabar.' In *Judaism From Within and From Without: Anthropological Studies*, H. Goldberg, ed., pp. 257–84. Albany: State University of New York Press.

Dominguez, Virginia R. 1989. *People as Subject, People as Object: Selfhood and Peoplehood in Contemporary Israel*. Madison: University of Wisconsin Press.

Don-Yehiye, Eliezer. 1984. 'Festival and political culture: the celebration of Independence Day in the early years of statehood,' *State, Government and International Relations*, 23: 5–28 (in Hebrew).

—— 1992. 'Hannukah and the myth of the Maccabees in Zionist ideology and in Israeli society,' *Jewish Journal of Sociology*, 34: 5–24.

Douglas, Mary. 1966. *Purity and Pollution*. London: Routledge & Kegan Paul.

—— 1987. *How Institutions Think*. London: Routledge & Kegan Paul.

—— 1999. *Leviticus as Literature*. Oxford: Oxford University Press.

Drury, Richard Toshiyuki and Robert C. Winn. 1992. *Plowshares and Swords: The Economics of Occupation in the West Bank*. Boston: Beacon.

Dufrenne, Mikel. 1973. *The Phenomenology of Aesthetic Experience*. Evanston, IL: Northwestern University Press.

Dumont, Louis. 1970. *Homo Hierarchicus: The Caste System and its Implications*. London: Paladin.

—— 1977. *From Mandeville to Marx: The Genesis and Triumph of Economic Ideology*. Chicago: University of Chicago Press.

—— 1979. 'The anthropological community and ideology,' *Social Science Information*, 18: 785–817.

—— 1986. *Essays on Individualism: Modern Ideology in Anthropological Perspective*. Chicago: University of Chicago Press.

Durkheim, Emile. 1956. *Sociology and Education*. Glencoe: Free Press.

—— and Marcel Mauss. 1963. *Primitive Classification*. London: Cohen and West.

Eco, Umberto. 1985. 'At the roots of the modern concept of symbol,' *Social Research*, 52: 385–402.

Eisen, Arnold. 1986. *Galut: Modern Jewish Reflections of Homelessness and Homecoming*. Bloomington: Indiana University Press.

Eisenstadt, Shmuel Noah. 1967. *Israeli Society*. London: Weidenfeld & Nicolson.

—— 1985. *The Transformation of Israeli Society*. London: Weidenfeld & Nicolson.

El-Haj, Nadia Abu. 1998. 'Translating Truths: nationalism, the practice of archeology, and the remaking of past and present in contemporary Jerusalem,' *American Ethnologist*, 25: 166–88.

Elias, Norbert, 1988. 'Violence and civilization: the state monopoly of physical violence and its infringement.' In *Civil Society and the State: New European Perspectives,* J. Keane, ed., pp. 177–98. London: Verso.

Eliav-Feldon, Miriam. 1982. *Realistic Utopias: The Ideal Imaginary Societies of the Renaissance, 1516–1630*. Oxford: Oxford University Press.

Ellen, Roy. 1979. 'Introductory essay.' In *Classifications in Their Social Context*, R.F. Ellen and D. Reason, eds., pp. 1–32. London: Academic Press.

Evans, Ivan. 1997. *Bureaucracy and Race: Native Administration in South Africa*. Berkeley: University of California Press.

Evron, Boas. 1995. *Jewish State or Israeli Nation?* Bloomington: Indiana University Press.

Eyal, Gil. 1996. 'The discursive origins of Israeli separatism: the case of the Arab village,' *Theory and Society*, 25: 389–429.

Ezrahi, Sidra. 1985–86. 'The Holocaust in Hebrew literature,' *Salmagundi*, 68–9: 245–70.

—— 1992. 'Our homeland, the text . . . our text, the homeland: exile and homecoming in the modern Jewish imagination,' *Michigan Quarterly Review*, 31: 463–97.

Ezrahi, Yaron. 1990. *The Descent of Icarus: Science and the Transformation of Contemporary Democracy*. Cambridge, MA: Harvard University Press.

—— 1997. *Rubber Bullets: Power and Conscience in Modern Israel*. New York: Farrar, Straus & Giroux.

Fabian, Johannes. 1983. *Time and the Other: How Anthropology Makes its Object*. New York: Columbia University Press.

Fayence-Glick, S. 1957. 'Kindergartens in Eretz Yisrael.' In *The Book of the Fiftieth Anniversary of the Teachers' Union*, pp. 132–44. Tel-Aviv: Histadrut Hamorim B'Eretz Yisrael (in Hebrew).

Feige, Michael. 1998. 'Peace Now and the legitimation crisis of "civil militarism",' *Israel Studies*, 3, no. 1: 85–111.

—— 1999. 'Rescuing the person from the symbol: "Peace Now" and the ironies of modern myth,' *History and Memory*, 11, no. 1: 141–68.

—— 2001. 'Where is "here"?: Scientific practices and appropriating space in the discourse of Israeli social movements.' In *Israel as Center Stage*, A.P. Hare and G. Kressel, eds, pp. 43–71. Westport, Conn: Bergin and Garvey.

Feldman, Jackie. 2000. *'It is My Brothers Whom I am Seeking': Israeli Youth Voyages to Holocaust Poland*. Ph.D. Thesis, Department of Sociology and Anthropology, Hebrew University of Jerusalem.

Ferrari, Giovanna. 1987. 'Public anatomy lessons and the carnival: the anatomy theatre of Bologna,' *Past and Present*, 117: 50–106.

Firer, Ruth. 1985. *The Agents of Zionist Education*. Tel-Aviv: Oranim School of Education of the Kibbutz Movement (in Hebrew).

Firro, Kais M. 2001. 'Reshaping Druze particularism in Israel,' *Journal of Palestine Studies*, 30: 40–53.

Foner, A. 1975. 'Age in society: structure and change,' *American Behavioral Scientist*, 19: 144–65.

Forte, Tania. 2002. 'Shopping in Jenin: women, homes and political persons in the Galilee,' *City and Society*, 13: 211–44.

Forty, Adrian. 1999. 'Introduction'. In *The Art of Forgetting*, A. Forty and S. Kuchler, eds., pp. 1–18. Oxford: Berg.

Foucault, Michel. 1973. *The Order of Things: An Archeology of the Human Sciences*. New York: Vintage.

—— 1979. *Discipline and Punish: The Birth of the Prison*. New York: Vintage.

—— 1980. *Power/Knowledge*. New York: Pantheon.

—— 1982. 'The subject and power,' *Critical Inquiry*, 8: 777–95.

—— 1991. 'Governmentality.' In *The Foucault Effect: Studies in Governmentality*, G. Burchell, C. Gordon, and P. Miller, eds., pp. 87–104. Hemel Hempstead: Harvester Wheatsheaf.

Frangsmyr, Tore, ed. 1994. *Linnaeus: The Man and His Work*. Canton, MA: Science History Publications/USA.

Fredman, Ruth Gruber. 1981. *The Passover Seder: Afikoman in Exile*. Philadelphia: University of Pennsylvania Press.

Frenkel, Michal, Yehouda Shenhav, and Hanna Herzog. 1997. 'The political embeddedness of managerial ideologies in pre-state Israel: the case of PPL 1920–1948,' *Journal of Management History*, 3: 120–44.

Friedlander, Saul and Adam Seligman. 1994. 'The Israeli memory of the Shoah: on symbols, rituals, and ideological polarization.' In *HereNow: Space, Time and Modernity*, R. Friedland and D. Boden, eds., pp. 356–71. Berkeley: University of California Press.

Furman, Mirta. 1999. 'Army and war: collective narratives of early childhood in contemporary Israel.' In *The Military and Militarism in Israeli Society*, E. Lomsky-Feder and E. Ben-Ari, eds., pp. 141–68. Albany: State University of New York Press.

Garber, Zev and Bruce Zuckerman. 1989. 'Why do we call the Holocaust "the Holocaust"? An inquiry into the psychology of labels,' *Modern Judaism*, 9: 197–211.

Garfinkel, Harold. 1967. *Studies in Ethnomethodology*. Englewood Cliffs, NJ: Prentice-Hall.

Gavison, Ruth. 1999. 'Jewish and democratic?: a rejoinder to the "ethnic democracy" debate,' *Israel Studies*, 4, no. 1: 44–72.

Gearing, Fred and Bruce Allan Tindall. 1973. 'Anthropological studies of the educational process,' *Annual Review of Anthropology*, 2: 95–105.

Gell, Alfred. 1992. *The Anthropology of Time: Cultural Constructions of Temporal Maps and Images*. Oxford: Berg.

Gerth, Hans and C. Wright Mills. 1958. *From Max Weber*. New York: Oxford University Press.

Gertz, Nurit. 1984. 'The few against the many,' *Jerusalem Quarterly*, 30: 94–104.

—— 1986. 'Social myths in literary and political texts,' *Poetics Today*, 7: 621–39.

—— 2000. *Myths in Israeli Culture: Captives of a Dream*. London: Valentine Mitchell.

Ghanem, As'ad. 1998. 'State and minority in Israel: the case of the ethnic state and the predicament of its minority,' *Ethnic and Racial Studies*, 21: 428–48.

——, Nadim Rouhana, and Oren Yiftachel. 1998. 'Questioning "ethnic democracy": a response to Sammy Smooha,' *Israel Studies*, 3, no. 2: 253–67.

Gigerenzer, Gerd, Zeno Swijtink, Theodore Porter, Lorraine Daston, John Beatty, Lorenze Kruger. 1989. *The Empire of Chance: How Probability Changed Science and Everyday Life*. Cambridge: Cambridge University Press.

Gilbert, Martin. 1985. *The Holocaust: A History of the Jews of Europe During the Second World War*. New York: Holt Rinehart & Winston.

Goldberg, Harvey. 1977. 'Introduction: culture and ethnicity in the study of Israeli society,' *Ethnic Groups*, 1: 163–86.

—— 1978. 'The Mimuna and the minority status of Moroccan Jews,' *Ethnology*, 17: 75–87.

Golden, Deborah. 1990. 'Memory in and out of the body: an enquiry into the links between memory, place and Jewish identity.' Manuscript.

—— 1996. 'The Museum of the Jewish Diaspora tells a story.' In *The Tourist Image: Myth and Myth Making in Tourism*. Tom Selwyn, ed., pp. 223–50. New York: John Wiley.

—— 2001. '"Now like real Israelis, let's stand up and sing": Teaching the national language to Russian newcomers in Israel,' *Anthropology and Education Quarterly*, 32: 52–79.

—— n.d. 'Hugging the teacher: reading bodily practice in an Israeli kindergarten,' *Teachers and Teaching*, forthcoming.

Goldman, Alan. 2001. 'The aesthetic.' In *The Routledge Companion to Aesthetics*, B. Gant and D.M. Lopes, eds., pp. 181–92. London: Routledge.

Gordon, Colin. 1991. 'Governmental rationality: an introduction.' In *The Foucault Effect: Studies in Governmentality*, G. Burchell, C. Gordon, and P. Miller, eds., pp. 1–51. London: Harvester Wheatsheaf.

Gould, Stephen Jay. 1987. *Time's Arrow, Time's Cycle: Myth and Metaphor in the Discovery of Geological Time*. Cambridge, MA: Harvard University Press.

Gracey, Harry L. 1972. 'Learning the student role: kindergarten as an academic boot camp.' In *Readings in Introductory Sociology*, D. Wrong and H.L. Gracey, eds., pp. 243–73. New York: Macmillan.

Gray, Bennison. 1978. 'The semiotics of taxonomy,' *Semiotica*, 22: 127–50.

Gray, Chris Hables and Steven Mentor. 1995. 'The cyborg body politic.' In *The Cyborg Handbook*, Chris Hables Gray, ed., pp. 453–67. New York: Routledge.

——, —— and Heidi J. Figueroa-Sarrieria. 1995. 'Cyborgology: constructing the knowledge of cybernetic organisms.' In Chris Hables Gray, *The Cyborg Handbook*, pp. 1–14. New York: Routledge.

Greenhouse, Carol J. 1989. 'Fighting for peace.' In *Peace and War: Cross-Cultural Perspectives*, M. LeCron Foster and R.A. Rubinstein, eds., pp. 49–60. New Brunswick, NJ: Transaction.

Greenspan, Henry. 1992. 'Lives as texts: symptoms as modes of recounting in the life histories of Holocaust survivors.' In *Storied Lives: The Cultural Politics of Self-Understanding*, G.C. Rosenwald and R.L. Ochberg, eds., pp. 145–64. New Haven: Yale University Press.

Gross, David. 1985. 'Temporality and the modern state,' *Theory and Society*, 14: 53–82.

Grossman, David. 1990. *See Under: Love*. New York: Washington Square Press.

Gullestad, Marianne. 1997. 'A passion for boundaries: Reflections on connections between the everyday lives of children and discourses on the nation in contemporary Norway,' *Childhood*, 4: 19–42.

Hacohen, Dvora. 1998. 'The Law of Return as an embodiment of the link between Israel and the Jews of the Diaspora,' *Journal of Israeli History*, 19: 61–89.

Haines, David W. 1990. 'Conformity in the face of ambiguity: a bureaucratic dilemma,' *Semiotica*, 78, 3/4: 249–69.

Halbwachs, Maurice. 1992. *On Collective Memory*. Lewis A. Coser, ed. Chicago: University of Chicago Press.

Handelman, Don. 1976. 'Bureaucratic transactions: the development of official-client relationships in Israel.' In *Transaction and Meaning*, Bruce Kapferer, ed., pp. 223–75. Philadelphia: ISHI.

——— 1978. 'Bureaucratic interpretation: the perception of child abuse in urban Newfoundland.' In Don Handelman and Elliott Leyton, *Bureaucracy and World View: Studies in the Logic of Official Interpretation*, pp. 15–69. St. John's: Institute of Social and Economic Research, Memorial University of Newfoundland.

——— 1985. 'Rites of the living, transformations of the dead,' *Reviews in Anthropology*, 12: 220–31.

——— 1992. 'Passages to play: paradox and process,' *Play and Culture*, 5: 1–19.

——— 1995a. 'Cultural taxonomy and bureaucracy in ancient China: The Book of Lord Shang,' *International Journal of Politics, Culture and Society*, 9: 263–93.

——— 1995b. 'The guises of the goddess and the transformation of the male: Gangamma's visit to Tirupati and the continuum of gender.' In *Syllables of Sky: Studies in South Indian Civilization in Honor of Velcheru Narayana Rao*, D. Shulman, ed., pp. 281–335. Delhi: Oxford University Press.

——— 1998a. *Models and Mirrors: Towards an Anthropology of Public Events*. 2nd edn. New York: Berghahn.

——— 1998b. 'The transformation of symbolic structures through history and the rhythms of time,' *Semiotica*, 119, no. 3/4: 403–25.

——— 2000. 'Telling a good Holocaust story: the narrator as a doubled subject in witnessing.' In *Telling, Remembering, Interpreting, Guessing: A Festschrift for Anniki Kaivola-Bregenhoj*, M. Vesenkari, P. Enges, and A-L Siikala, eds., pp. 39–45. Joensuu: Suomen Kansantietouden Tutkijain Seura.

——— 2001. 'Postlude: framing, braiding, and killing play,' *Focaal: European Journal of Anthropology*, 37: 145–56.

——— n.d. 'Designs of ritual: the City Dionysia of fifth-century Athens.' In *Celebrations: Sanctuaries and the Vestiges of Cult Activity*. Athens: Norwegian Institute at Athens, in press.

——— and Lea Shamgar-Handelman. 1990. 'Shaping time: the choice of the national emblem of Israel.' In *Culture Through Time: Anthropological Approaches*, Emiko Ohnuki-Tierney, ed., pp. 193–226. Stanford: Stanford University Press.

——— and ——— 1993. 'Aesthetics versus ideology in national symbolism: the creation of the emblem of Israel,' *Public Culture*, 5: 431–49.

——— and David Shulman. 1997. *God Inside Out: Siva's Game of Dice*. New York: Oxford University Press.

Haraway, Donna. 1989. *Primate Visions: Gender, Race and Nature in the World of Modern Science*. New York: Routledge.

Hardin, Kris L. 1993. *The Aesthetics of Action: Continuity and Change in a West African Town*. Washington, DC: Smithsonian Institution Press.

Hartman, Geoffrey H. 1997. *The Fateful Question of Culture*. New York: Columbia University Press.

Haskina, T. 1941. 'Birthday party in the kindergarten,' *Hed Hagan*, 5: 34–7 (in Hebrew).

Hayes, Carleton J.H. 1968. *The Historical Evolution of Modern Nationalism*. New York: Russell and Russell.

Hayward, Robert. 1980. 'The Aqedah.' In *Sacrifice*, M.F.C. Bourdillon and Meyer Fortes, eds., pp. 84–7. New York: Academic Press.

Hendry, Joy. 1986. 'Kindergarten and the transition from home to school education,' *Comparative Education*, 22: 53–8.

Henry, Jules. 1965. *Culture Against Man*. New York: Vintage.

Herrenschmidt, O. 1978. 'A qui profite le crime? Cherchez le sacrifiant: un désir fatalement meurtrier,' *l'Homme*, 18: 7–18.

Hertz, J. 1938. *The Pentateuch and Haftorahs*. London: Soncino.

Herzfeld, Michael. 1982. *Ours Once More: Folklore, Ideology, and the Making of Modern Greece*. Austin: University of Texas Press.

—— 1992. *The Social Production of Indifference: Exploring the Symbolic Roots of Western Bureaucracy*. Oxford: Berg.

Heschel, Abraham Joshua. 1951. *The Sabbath: Its Meaning for Modern Man*. New York: Farrar, Straus, and Young.

Hirsch, Samson Rafael. 1985. *The Collected Writings*, Vol. II. New York: Feldhein.

Hobsbawm, Eric. 1983. 'Introduction: Inventing traditions.' In *The Invention of Tradition*, E. Hobsbawm and T. Ranger, eds. Cambridge: Cambridge University Press.

Horgan, John. 1998. *The End of Science*. London: Abacus.

Hoskin, Keith. 1996. 'The "awful idea of accountability": inscribing people into the measurement of objects.' In *Accountability: Power, Ethos and the Technologies of Managing*, R. Munro and J. Mouritsen, eds., pp. 265–82. London: International Thomson Business Press.

—— and Richard H. Macve. 1995. 'Accounting and the examination: a genealogy of disciplinary power.' In *Michel Foucault (2): Critical Assessments*, B. Smart, ed., pp. 99–138. London: Routledge.

Hubert, Henri and Marcel Mauss. 1964. *Sacrifice*. London: Routledge & Kegan Paul.

Hughes, J. 1989. 'Thinking about children.' In *Thinking About Children: Children, Parents and Politics*, G. Scarre, ed., pp. 36–51. Cambridge: Cambridge University Press.

Hunt, Lynn. 1992. *The Family Romance of the French Revolution*. London: Routledge.

Huntington, Richard and Peter Metcalf. 1979. *Celebrations of Death: The Anthropology of Mortuary Ritual*.Cambridge: Cambridge University Press.

Illich, Ivan. 1995. 'Guarding the eye in the age of show,' *Res*, 28: 47–61.

Ingersoll, Daniel W. and James N. Nickel. 1987. 'The most important monument: the Tomb of the Unknown Soldier.' In *Mirror and Metaphor: Material and Social Constructions of Reality*, D.W. Ingersoll and G. Bronitsky, eds., pp. 199–225. Lanham, MD: University Press of America.

Inglis, David and John Hughson. 2000. 'The beautiful game and the proto-aesthetics of the everyday,' *Cultural Values*, 4: 279–97.

Jackson, Bernard S. 1993. 'Brother Daniel: the construction of Jewish identity in the Israel Supreme Court,' *International Journal for the Semiotics of Law*, 6, no. 17: 115–46.

Jay, Martin. 1992a. 'Scopic regimes of modernity.' In *Modernity and Identity*, S. Lash and J. Friedman, eds., pp. 178–95. Oxford: Blackwell.

—— 1992b. 'Of plots, witnesses, and judgements.' In *Probing the Limits of Representation*, Saul Friedlander, ed., pp. 97–107. Cambridge: Harvard University Press.

Johnstone, J.C. 1970. 'Age-grade consciousness,' *Sociology of Education*, 43: 56–68.

Kafka, Franz. 1999. *Metamorphosis and Other Stories*. London: Vintage.

Kahane, Reuven. 1997. *The Origins of Postmodern Youth: Informal Youth Movements in a Comparative perspective*. Berlin: Walter de Gruyter.

Kamen, Charles S. 1977. 'Affirmation or enjoyment? The commemoration of independence in Israel,' *Jewish Journal of Sociology*, 19: 5–20.

Kanter, Rosabeth Moss. 1972. 'The organization child: experience management in a nursery school,' *Sociology of Education*, 43: 56–68.

Kapferer, Bruce. 1988. *Legends of People, Myths of State: Violence, Intolerance, and Political Culture in Sri Lanka and Australia*. Washington, DC: Smithsonian Institution Press.

Katerbursky, Z. 1962. *The Ways of the Garden*. Tel-Aviv: Otsar Hamoreh (in Hebrew).

Katriel, Tamar. 1990. 'Celebrating language: the "Hebrew language year" as cultural performance,' *Text and Performance Quarterly*, 10: 321–3.

—— 1991a. '*Gibush*: the crystallization metaphor in Israeli cultural semantics.' In her *Communal Webs: Communication and Culture in Contemporary Israel*. Albany: State University of New York Press, pp. 11–34.

——1991b. 'Picnics in a military zone: rituals of parenting and the politics of consensus'. In her *Communal Webs: Communication and Culture in Contemporary Israel*. Albany: State University of New York Press, pp. 71–91.

—— 1997. *Performing the Past: A Study of Israeli Settlement Museums*. Mahiah, NJ: Lawrence Erlbaum.

—— and Aliza Shenhar. 1990. '"Tower and stockade": dialogic narration in Israeli settlement ethos,' *Quarterly Journal of Speech*, 76: 359–80.

Katz, Jack. 1999. *How Emotions Work*. Chicago: University of Chicago Press.

Kauffmann, Yehezkel. 1972. *The Religion of Israel*. New York: Schocken.

Kelkin-Fishman, D. 1981. 'Tune and control: the acquisition of the concept of music in the kindergarten,' *Notebooks for Research and Criticism*, 6: 5–25 (in Hebrew).

Kharkhordin, Oleg. 2001. 'What is the state? The Russian concept of *Gosudarstvo* in the European context,' *History and Theory*, 40: 206–40.

Kidron, Carol. 2000. *Amcha's Second Generation Holocaust Survivors: A Recursive Journey into the Past to Construct Wounded Carriers of Memory*. M.A. Thesis, Department of Sociology and Anthropology, Hebrew University of Jerusalem.

Kimmerling, Baruch. 1999. 'Religion, nationalism and democracy in Israel,' *Constellations*, 6: 339–63.

—— 2001. *The Invention and Decline of Israeliness: State, Society, and the Military*. Berkeley: University of California Press.

—— 2002. 'Jurisdiction in an immigrant settler society: the "Jewish and democratic state",' *Comparative Political Studies*, 35: 1119–44.

Kimmerling, Baruch, in collaboration with Irit Backer. 1985. *The Interrupted System: Israeli Civilians in War and Routine Times*. New Brunswick, NJ: Transaction.

—— and Joel S. Migdal. 1993. *Palestinians: The Making of a People*. New York: Free Press.

King, Michael. 1993. 'The "truth" about autopoeisis,' *Journal of Law and Society*, 20: 218–36.

Kirmayer, Laurence J. 1996. 'Landscapes of memory: trauma, narrative, and dissociation.' In *Tense Past: Cultural Essays in Trauma and Memory*. Paul Antze and Michael Lambek, eds., pp. 173–98. New York: Routledge.

Kochaa, Lionel. 1997. *Beyond the Graven Image*. London: Macmillan.

Kopytoff, Igor. 1988. 'Public culture: a Durkheimian perspective,' *Public Culture Bulletin*, 1, no. 1: 11–16.

Kosko, Bart. 1993. *Fuzzy Thinking: The New Science of Fuzzy Logic*. New York: Hyperion.

Krakowski, Shmuel. 1984. *The War of the Doomed: Jewish Armed Resistance in Poland, 1942–1944*. New York: Holmes and Meier.

Kretzmer, David, assisted by Osama Halabi. 1987. *The legal Status of the Arabs in Israel*. Tel-Aviv: International Center For Peace in the Middle East.

—— 2002. *The Occupation of Justice: The Supreme Court of Israel and the Occupied Territories*. Albany: State University New York Press.

Kuchler, Susanne. 1993. 'Landscape as memory: the mapping of process and its representation in a Melanesian society.' In *Landscape: Politics and Perspective*, B. Bender, ed., pp. 85–106. Oxford: Berg.

Kundera, Milan. 1990. *The Art of the Novel*. London: Faber & Faber.

Kunz, P. R. and J. Summers. 1979–1980. 'A time to die: a study of the relationship of birthday and time of death,' *Omega*, 10: 281–9.

Lahav, Pnina. 1993. 'Rights and democracy: the Court's performance.' In *Israeli Democracy Under Stress*, E. Sprinzak and L. Diamond, eds., pp. 125–52. Boulder: Lynne Rienner Publishers.

La Mettrie, Julien Offray de. 1993 [1748]. *Man A Machine*. La Salle, IL: Open Court.

Lang, Berel. 1990. *Act and Idea in the Nazi Genocide*. Chicago: University of Chicago Press.

Langer, Lawrence L. 1991. *Holocaust Testimonies: The Ruins of Memory*. New Haven: Yale University Press.

—— 1995. 'Memory's time: chronology and duration in Holocaust testimonies.' In his *Admitting the Holocaust*, pp. 13–23. New York: Oxford University Press.

Langer, Suzanne. 1953. *Feeling and Form*. London: Routledge & Kegan Paul.

Laqueur, Thomas W. 1994. 'Memory and naming in the Great War.' In *Commemorations: The Politics of National Identity*, J.R. Gillis, ed., pp. 150–67. Princeton: Princeton University Press.

Laumann, Edward O. and David Knoke. 1987. *The Organizational State: Social Choice in National Policy Domains*. Madison: University of Wisconsin Press.

Lee, Dorothy. 1959. *Freedom and Culture*. Englewood Cliffs, NJ: Prentice-Hall.

Lefebvre, Henri. 1991. *The Production of Space*. Translated by Donald Nicholson-Smith. Oxford: Blackwell.

Lefort, Claude. 1986. *The Political Forms of Modern Society: Bureaucracy, Democracy, Totalitarianism*. Cambridge, MA: MIT Press.

Lemke, Thomas. 2001. '"The birth of bio-politics": Michel Foucault's lecture at the College de France on neo-liberal governmentality,' *Economy and Society*, 30: 190–207.

Lévi-Strauss, Claude. 1966. *The Savage Mind*. London: Weidenfeld and Nicolson.

Levinger, Esther. 1993. 'Socialist-Zionist ideology in Israeli war memorials of the 1950s,' *Journal of Contemporary History*, 28: 715–46.

Levinsky, Yom-Tov. 1957. *The Book of Times*. Tel-Aviv: Dvir (in Hebrew).

Lewis, Arnold. 1979. *Power, Poverty and Education: An Ethnography of Schooling in an Israeli Town*. Ramat Gan, Israel: Turtledove Publishing.

—— 1985. 'Phantom ethnicity: "Oriental Jews" in Israeli society.' In *Israeli Ethnicity: After the Ingathering*, A. Weingrod, ed., pp. 133–57. New York: Gordon & Breach.

Lieblich, Amia. 1989. *Transition to Adulthood During Military Service: The Israeli Case*. Albany: State University of New York Press.

Liebman, Charles S. and Eliezer Don-Yehiye. 1983. *Civil Religion in Israel: Traditional Religion and Political Culture in the Jewish State*. Berkeley: University of California Press.

Linde, Charlotte. 2001. 'The acquisition of a speaker by a story,' *Ethos*, 28: 608–32.

Linke, Uli. 1990. 'Folklore, anthropology, and the government of social life,' *Comparative Studies in Society and History*, 32: 117–48.

Lishinsky, Yosef. 1983. 'Yad Vashem as art,' *Ariel*, 55: 14–25.

Luhmann, Niklas. 1999. 'The paradox of form.' In *Problems of Form*, D. Baecker, ed., pp. 15–26. Stanford: Stanford University Press.

Lustick, Ian. 1980. *Arabs in the Jewish State: Israel's Control of a National Minority*. Austin: University of Texas Press.

Maimonides, Moses. 1956. *The Guide for the Perplexed*. New York: Dover.

Mais, Yitzchak. 1988. 'Institutionalizing the Holocaust,' *Midstream*, December, pp. 16–20.

Mann, Michael. 1988. *War, States and Capitalism*. Oxford: Blackwell.

—— 1993. *The Sources of Social Power, Vol. 2: The Rise of Classes and Nation-States, 1760–1914*. New York: Cambridge University Press.

Marvin, Carolyn and David W. Ingle. 1999. *Blood Sacrifice and the Nation: Totem Rituals and the American Flag*. Cambridge: Cambridge University Press.

McAllister, James W. 1996. *Beauty and Revolution in Science*. Ithaca: Cornell University Press.

McNeil, David. 1992. *Hand and Mind: What Gestures Reveal about Thought*. Chicago: University of Chicago Press.

McNeil, William H. 1986. *Mythistory and Other Essays*. Chicago: University of Chicago Press.

Merleau-Ponty, Maurice. 1968. *The Visible and the Invisible*. Evanston: Northwestern University Press.

Mills, C. Wright. 1959. *The Sociological Imagination*. New York: Oxford University Press.

Mimica, Jadran. 1988. *Intimations of Infinity*. Oxford: Berg.

Minahen, Charles D. 1992. *Vortex/t: The Poetics of Turbulence*. University Park: Pennsylvania State University Press.

Ministry of Education and Culture. 1967. *Hannukah, Festival of Lights*. Jerusalem: Ministry of Education and Culture [Israel] (in Hebrew).

Moore, Sally Falk and Barbara Myerhoff, eds. 1977. *Secular Ritual*. Assen: Van Gorcum.

Mosse, George L. 1979. 'National cemeteries and national revival: the cult of the fallen soldiers in Germany,' *Journal of Contemporary History*, 14: 1–20.

—— 1990. *Fallen Soldiers: Reshaping the Memory of the World Wars*. New York: Oxford University Press.

—— 1991. 'The Holocaust, death, and scenes of war.' Lecture at Confederation House, Jerusalem, June 6.

Musgrove, F. and R. Middleton. 1981. 'Rites of passage and the meaning of age in three contrasted social groups: professional footballers, teachers, and Methodist ministers,' *British Journal of Sociology*, 32: 39–55.

Myerhoff, Barbara G. 1982. 'Life history among the elderly: performance, visibility, and re-membering.' In *A Crack in the Mirror: Reflexive Perspectives in Anthropology*, Jay Ruby, ed., pp. 99–117. Philadelphia: University of Pennsylvania Press.

—— 1984. 'A death in due time: construction of self and culture in ritual drama.' In *Rite, Drama, Festival, Spectacle: Rehearsals Toward a Theory of Cultural Performance*, J.J. MacAloon, ed., pp. 149–78. Philadephia: ISHI.

Naftali and Nir-Yaniv. 1974. *Subjects of Instruction: Day-Care Centers*. Jerusalem: Ministry of Education and Culture [Israel] (in Hebrew).

Nakamura, Hajime. 1981. 'Time in Indian and Japanese thought.' In *The Voices of Time* (2nd ed.), J.T. Fraser, ed., pp. 77–91. Amherst: University of Massachusetts Press.

Needham, Rodney. 1975. 'Polythetic classification: convergence and consequences,' *Man* (N.S.), 10: 349–69.

Newton-Smith, W.H. 1980. *The Structure of Time*. London: Routledge & Kegan Paul.

Nora, Pierre. 1989. 'Between memory and history: *Les Lieux de Mémoire*,' *Representations*, 26: 7–25.

Norman, Karin. 1991. *A Sound Family Makes a Sound State: Ideology and Upbringing in a German Village* (Stockholm Studies in Social Anthropology, No. 24). Stockholm: Almqvist and Wiksell.

Oestreich, Gerhard. 1982. *Neostoicism and the Early Modern State*. Cambridge: Cambridge University Press.

Ofer, Dalia. 1996. 'Linguistic conceptualization of the Holocaust in Palestine and Israel, 1942–53,' *Journal of Contemporary History*, 31: 567–95.

—— 2000. 'The strength of remembrance: commemorating the Holocaust during the first decade of Israel,' *Jewish Social Studies*, 6: 24–55.

Ohnuki-Tierney, Emiko. 1994. 'The power of absence: zero signifiers and their transgressions,' *l'Homme*, 130: 59–76.

Ong, Aihwa. 1996. 'Cultural citizenship as subject-making: immigrants negotiate racial and cultural boundaries in the United States,' *Current Anthropology*, 37: 737–51.

Oppenheimer, Jonathan. 1977. 'Culture and politics in Druze ethnicity,' *Ethnic Groups*, 1: 221–40.

Paine, Robert. 1983. 'Israel and totemic time?' *RAIN*, 59: 19–22.

—— 1990. 'Jewish ontologies of time and political legitimation in Israel.' In *The Politics of Time*, Henry Rutz, ed., pp. 150–70. Washington, D.C.: American Ethnological Society.

—— 1994. Masada: a history of memory,' *History and Anthropology*, 6: 371–409.

Paret, Peter. 1985. *Clausewitz and the State*. Princeton: Princeton University Press.

Pasquino, Pasqualle. 1991. 'Theatrum politicum: the genealogy of capital – police and the state of prosperity.' In *The Foucault Effect: Studies in Governmentality*, G. Burchell, C. Gordon, and P. Miller, eds., pp. 105–18. Hemel Hempstead: Harvester Wheatsheaf.

Patai, Raphael. 1970. *Israel Between East and West: A Study in Human Relations* (2nd ed.) Westport, CN: Greenwood.

Patey, Douglas Lane. 1984. *Probability and Literary Form*. Cambridge: Cambridge University Press.

Patton, Paul. 2000. *Deleuze and the Political*. London: Routledge.

Pavic, Milorad. 1989. *Dictionary of the Khazars: A Lexicon Novel*. New York: Vintage.

Peled, Yoav. 1992. 'Ethnic democracy and the legal construction of citizenship: Arab citizens of the Jewish state,' *American Political Science Review*, 86: 432–43.

—— and Gershon Shafir. 1996. 'The roots of peacemaking: the dynamics of citizenship in Israel, 1948–93,' *International Journal of Middle East Studies*, 28: 391–413.

Perec, Georges. 1999. *Species of Spaces and Other Pieces*. London: Penguin.

Peretz, Don. 1991. 'Early state policy towards the Arab population, 1948–1955.' In *New Perspectives on Israeli History*, L.J. Silberstein, ed., pp. 82–102. New York: New York University Press.

Piaget, Jean. 1969. *The Child's Conception of Time*. London: Routledge & Kegan Paul.

Pinsker, J.L. 1966. 'The renewal of national bonds.' In *Israel Among the Nations*, Zvi Zohar, ed., pp. 32–36. Jerusalem: World Zionist Organization.

Pintner, Walter M. and Don K. Rowney. 1980. 'Officialdom and bureaucratization: an introduction.' In *Russian Officialdom*, W.M. Pintner and D.K. Rowney, eds., pp. 3–18. Chapel Hill, NC: University of North Carolina Press.

Plessner, Helmuth. 1970. *Laughing and Crying: A Study of the Limits of Human Behavior*. Evanston: Northwestern University Press.

Pocock, David F. 1964. 'The anthropology of time-reckoning,' *Contributions to Indian Sociology* (N.S.), 7: 18–29.

Polanyi, Michael. 1962. *Personal Knowledge: Towards a Post-Critical Philosophy*. New York: Harper Torchbooks.

—— 1966. *The Tacit Dimension*. London: Routledge & Kegan Paul.

Poster, Mark. 1990. *The Mode of Information: Poststructuralism and Social Context*. Chicago: University of Chicago Press.

Rabin, Yitzhak. 1989. 'Introduction.' In *Gal-ed: Memorials for the Fallen in the Wars of Israel*, Ilana Shamir, ed., pp. 6–7. Ministry of Defense, State of Israel (in Hebrew).

Rabinowitz, Dan. 1998. 'National identity on the frontier: Palestinians in the Israeli education system.' In *Border identities: Nation and State at International Frontiers*, T.M. Wilson and H. Donnan, eds., pp. 142–61. Cambridge: Cambridge University Press.

Rabinowitz, Esther, ed. 1958. *Holidays and Times in Education*. Tel-Aviv: Urim (in Hebrew).

Raeff, Marc. 1983. *The Well-Ordered Police State: Social and Institutional Change Through Law in the Germanies and Russia, 1600–1800*. New Haven: Yale University Press.

Ram, Uri. 1995. 'Zionist historiography and the invention of modern Jewish nationhood: the case of Ben Zion Dinur,' *History and Memory*, 7, no. 1: 91–124.

Rapaport, Nathan. 1994. 'Memoir of the Warsaw Ghetto Monument.' In *The Art of Memory: Holocaust Memorials in History*, James E. Young, ed., pp.103–7. New York: Prestal Verlag.

Rearick, Charles. 1977. 'Festivals in modern France: the experience of the Third Republic,' *Journal of Contemporary History*, 12: 435–60.

Ricoeur, Paul. 1984. *Time and Narrative*, Vol. 1. Chicago: University of Chicago Press.

Rieff, Philip. 1966. *The Triumph of the Therapeutic: Uses of Faith After Freud*. New York: Harper and Row.

Rimmon-Kenan, Shlomith. 1984. *Narrative Fiction: Contemporary Poetics*. London: Methuen.

Rizzi, Bruno. 1985. *The Bureaucratization of the World: The USSR: Bureaucratic Collectivism*. London: Tavistock.

Roche, Maurice. 1987. 'Citizenship, social theory, and social change,' *Theory and Society*, 16: 363–99.

Rosaldo, Renato. 1980. *Ilongot Headhunting*. Stanford: Stanford University Press.

Rosch, Eleanor. 1975. 'Cognitive representations of semantic categories,' *Journal of Experimental Psychology*, 104, no. 3: 192–233.

——, Carolyn B. Mervis, Wayne D. Gray, David M. Johnson, Penny Boyes-Bream. 1976. 'Basic objects in natural categories,' *Cognitive Psychology*, 8: 382–439.

Rose, Nikolas. 1989. *Governing the Soul: The Shaping of the Private Self*. London: Routledge.

—— 1996a. 'The death of the social? Re-figuring the territory of government,' *Economy and Society*, 25: 327–56.

—— 1996b. 'Governing "advanced" liberal democracies.' In *Foucault and Political Reason: Liberalism, Neo-Liberalism and Rationalities of Government*, A. Barry, T. Osborne, and N. Rose, eds., pp. 37–64. Chicago: University of Chicago Press.

—— 1998. *Inventing Our Selves: Psychology, Power, Personhood*. Cambridge: Cambridge University Press.

Rosenberg, Hans. 1958. *Bureaucracy, Aristocracy and Autocracy: The Prussian Experience, 1660–1815*. Boston: Beacon.

Rosenhek, Zeev. 1999. 'The exclusionary logic of the welfare state: Palestinian citizens in the Israeli welfare state,' *International Sociology*, 14: 195–215.

—— and Michael Shalev. 2000. 'The contradictions of Palestinian citizenship in Israel.' In *Citizenship and State in the Middle East*, N. Butenschor, U. Davis, and M. Kassassian, eds., pp. 288–315. Syracuse: Syracuse University Press.

Roskies, David G. 1988. *The Literature of Destruction: Jewish Responses to Catastrophe*. Philadelphia: Jewish Publication Society.

Rouhana, Nadim N. 1997. *Palestinian Citizens in an Ethnic Jewish State: Identities in Conflict*. New Haven: Yale University Press.

Rubin, Nissan. 1985. 'Unofficial memorial rites in an Army unit,' *Social Forces*, 63: 795–809.

Salih, Khaled. 1996. 'Demonizing a minority: the case of the Kurds in Iraq.' In *National Minorities and Diasporas: Identities and Rights in the Middle East*, K.E. Schulze, M. Stokes, and C. Campbell, eds., pp. 81–94. London: I.B. Tauris.

Scarry, Elaine. 1985. *The Body in Pain*. New York: Oxford University Press.

Schieffelin, Edward. 1976. *The Sorrow of the Lonely and the Burning of the Dancers*. New York: St Martin's Press.

Scholem, Gershom. 1971. 'The Star of David: history of a symbol.' In his *The Messianic Idea in Judaism*, pp. 257–81. New York: Schocken.

Schwartz, Barry. 1981. *Vertical Classification: A Study in Structuralism and the Sociology of Knowledge*. Chicago: University of Chicago Press.

——, Yael Zerubavel, and Bernice M. Barnett. 1986. 'The recovery of Masada: a study of collective memory,' *Sociological Quarterly*, 27: 147–64.

Scott, James C. 1998. *Seeing Like a State*. New Haven: Yale University Press.

Scott, Robert. 1969. *The Making of Blind Men*. New York: Russell Sage Foundation.

Segal, Daniel. 1988. 'Nationalism, comparatively speaking,' *Journal of Historical Sociology*, 1: 301–21.

Segev, Tom. 1993. *The Seventh Million: The Israelis and the Holocaust*. New York: Hill and Wang.

Seligman, Adam. 1992. *The Idea of Civil Society*. New York: Free Press.

Seltzer, William and Margo Anderson. 2001. 'The dark side of numbers: the role of population data systems in human rights abuses,' *Social Research*, 68: 481–513.

Shafir, Gerson. 1998. 'Introduction: the evolving tradition of citizenship.' In *The Citizenship Debates*, G. Shafir, ed., pp. 1–28. Minneapolis: University of Minnesota Press.

—— and Yoav Peled. 1998. 'Citizenship and stratification in an ethnic democracy,' *Ethnic and racial Studies*, 21: 408–27.

Shalev, Michael. 1992. *Labour and the Political Economy in Israel*. Oxford: Oxford University Press.

Shamgar-Handelman, Lea. 1986. *Israeli War Widows: Beyond the Glory of Heroism*. South Hadley, MA: Bergin and Garvey.

—— 1990. *Childhood as a Social Phenomenon. National Report: Israel*. Vienna: Eurosocial Report, European Centre for Social Welfare Policy and Research.

—— 1996. 'Family sociology in a small academic community: family research and theory in Israel,' *Marriage and Family Review*, 23, no. 3/4: 377–416.

Shamir, Ilana, ed. 1989. *Gal-ed: Memorials for the Fallen in the Wars of Israel*. Ministry of Defense, State of Israel (in Hebrew).

—— 1991. *Gal-ed: Memorials for the Fallen in the Wars of Israel – Additions and Corrections*. Ministry of Defense, State of Israel (in Hebrew).

Shammas, Anton. 1988. 'A stone's throw,' *New York Review of Books*, March 31, pp. 9–10.

—— 1991. 'At half-mast – myths, symbols, and rituals of the emerging state: a personal testimony of an "Israeli Arab".' In *New Perspectives on Israeli History*, L.J. Silberstein, ed., pp. 216–24. New York: New York University Press.

Shapiro, Jonathan. 1976. *The Formative Years of the Israeli Labour Party: The Organization of Power, 1919–1930*. London: Sage.

—— 1993. 'The historical origins of Israeli democracy.' In *Israeli Democracy Under Stress*, E. Sprinzak and L. Diamond, eds., pp. 65–80. Boulder: Lynne Rienner Publishers.

Sharron, Avery. 1982. 'Dimensions of time,' *Studies in Symbolic Interaction*, 4: 63–89.

Sheets-Johnstone, M. 2000. 'Kinetic tactile-kinesthetic bodies: ontogenetical foundations of apprenticeship learning,' *Human Studies*, 23: 343–70.

Shemer, A. ed. 1966. *Ways of Work in Kindergartens*. Tel-Aviv: Tarbut V'Khinukh (in Hebrew).

Shenhav-Keller, Shelly. 2000. *'Looking Back to the Future': Representation, Memory and Identity at the Museum of the Jewish Diaspora (Beth Hatfutsoth)*. Ph.D. Thesis, Department of Sociology and Anthropology, The Hebrew University of Jerusalem (in Hebrew).

Shields, Rob. 1991. *Places on the Margin: Alternative Geographies of Modernity*. London: Routledge.

Simmel, Georg. 1968 [1896]. 'Sociological aesthetics.' In his *The Conflict in Modern Culture and Other Essays*, pp. 68–80. New York: Teachers College Press.

Smith, Anthony D. 1991. *National Identity*. London: Penguin.

Smith, Brian K. and Wendy Doniger. 1989. 'Sacrifice and substitution,' *Numen*, 36: 189–224.

Smooha, Sammy. 1978. *Israel: Pluralism and Conflict*. London: Routledge & Kegan Paul.

—— 1997. 'Ethnic democracy: Israel as an archtype,' *Israel Studies*, 2, no. 2: 198–241.

Sokal, Robert R. 1974. 'Classification: purposes, principles, progress, prospects,' *Science*, 185, no. 4157: 1115–23.

State of Israel Yearbook. 1954. Jerusalem: Government Printing Press.

Stauber, Roni. 2000. 'Confronting the Jewish response during the Holocaust: Yad Vashem – a commemorative and a research institute in the 1950s,' *Modern Judaism*, 20: 277–98.

Stevens, Wallace. 2001. *Harmonium*. London: Faber & Faber.

Stites, Richard. 1989. *Revolutionary Dreams: Utopian Vision and Experimental Life in the Russian Revolution*. New York: Oxford University Press.

Stone, Deborah. 1988. *Policy Paradox and Political Reason*. Glenview, IL: Scott, Foresman & Co.

Storper-Perez, Danielle and Harvey E. Goldberg. 1994. 'The Kotel: toward an ethnographic portrait,' *Religion*, 24: 309–32.

Strathern, Marilyn. 1988. *The Gender of the Gift*. Berkeley: University of California Press.

Straus, Erwin W. 1966. *Phenomenological Psychology*. London: Tavistock.

Sturken, Marita. 2001. 'Absent images of memory: remembering and reenacting the Japanese internment.' In *Perilous Memories: The Asia-Pacific War(s)*, T. Fujitani, G.M. White, and L. Yoneyama, eds., pp. 33–49. Durham, NC: Duke University Press.

Suransky, Valerie P. 1982. *The Erosion of Childhood*. Chicago: University of Chicago Press.

Swirsky, Shlomo. 1976. 'Community and the meaning of the modern state: the case of Israel,' *Jewish Journal of Sociology*, 18, no. 2: 123–40.

—— 1981. *Orientals and Ashkenazim in Israel: The Ethnic Division of Labor*. Haifa: Makhberot Lemekhkar Ulebikoret (in Hebrew).

Tal, Uriel. 1979. 'Excursus on the term: Shoah,' *Shoah*, 1, no. 1: 4–11.

Tamarin, Georges R. 1973. *The Israeli Dilemma: Essays on a Warfare State*. Rotterdam: Rotterdam University Press.

Tarn, Nathaniel. 1976. 'The heraldic vision: a cognitive model for comparative aesthetics,' *Alcheringa: Ethnopoetics* (N.S.), 2, no. 2: 23–41.

Taylor, Charles. 1990. 'Modes of civil society,' *Public Culture*, 3: 95–118.

Taylor, Simon. 1985. *Prelude to Genocide*. London: Duckworth.

Tillyard, Eustace M.W. n.d. *The Elizabethan World Picture*. New York: Vintage.

Torpey, John. 1998. 'Coming and going: on the state monopolization of legitimate "means of movement",' *Sociological Theory*, 16: 239–59.

Trouillet, Michel-Rolph. 2001. 'The anthropology of the state in the age of globalization: close encounters of the deceptive kind,' *Current Anthropology*, 42: 125–33.

Tumarkin, Nina. 1983. *Lenin Lives! The Lenin Cult in Soviet Russia*. Cambridge, MA: Harvard University Press.

Tyack, D. 1966. 'Forming the national character,' *Harvard Educational Review*, 36: 29–41.

Tzetnik, K. 1988. 'Quintessence,' *Tel-Aviv Review*, 1: 325–31.

Vainstein, Yaacov. 1953. *The Cycle of the Jewish Year*. Jerusalem: World Zionist Organization.

Verdery, Katherine. 1996. *What was Socialism and What Comes Next?* Princeton: Princeton University Press.

—— 1999. *The Political Lives of Dead Bodies: Reburial and Postsocialism*. New York: Columbia University Press.

Visvanathan, Shiv. 1990. 'On the annals of the laboratory state.' In *Science, Hegemony and Violence*, A. Nandy, ed., pp. 257–88. Delhi: Oxford University Press.

Vogt, Evon Z. and Suzanne Abel. 1977. 'On political rituals in contemporary Mexico.' In *Secular Ritual*, S.F. Moore and B. Myerhoff, eds., pp. 173–88. Assen: Van Gorcum.

Vygotsky, Lev S. 1962. *Thought and Language*. Cambridge, MA: MIT Press.

Walby, Sylvia. 1999. 'The new regulatory state: the social powers of the European Union,' *British Journal of Sociology*, 50: 118–40.

Waltzer, Michael. 1985. *Exodus and Revolution*. New York: Basic.

Weber, Max. 1964. *Theory of Social and Economic Organization*. Glencoe: Free Press.

Wechsler, Judith, ed. 1988. *On Aesthetics in Science*. Boston: Birkhauser.

Weil, Shalva. 1986. 'The language and ritual of socialization: birthday parties in a kindergarten context.' *Man* (N.S.), 21: 329–41.

Weingrod, Alex, ed. 1985. *Studies in Israeli Ethnicity: After the Ingathering*. New York: Gordon & Breach.

Weinstock, John, ed. 1985. *Contemporary Perspectives on Linnaeus*. Lanham, MD: University Press of America.

Weiss, Meira. 1997a. 'War bodies, hedonist bodies: dialectics of the collective and the individual in Israeli society,' *American Ethnologist*, 24: 813–32.

—— 1997b. 'Bereavement, commemoration, and collective identity in contemporary Israeli society,' *Anthropological Quarterly*, 70: 91–101.

Weitz, Yechiam. 1996. 'The Holocaust on trial: the impact of the Kasztner and Eichmann trials on Israeli society,' *Israel Studies*, 1, no. 2: 1–26.

Welsch, Wolfgang. 1997. *Undoing Aesthetics*. London: Sage.

Westoby, Adam. 1985. 'Introduction.' In *The Bureaucratization of the World*, by Bruno Rizzi. London: Tavistock, pp. 1–33.

Weyl, Hermann. 1952. *Symmetry*. Princeton: Princeton University Press.

Wiener, Philip P. 1957. 'Leibniz's project of a public exhibition of scientific inventions.' In *Roots of Scientific Thought: A Cultural Perspective*, P.P. Wiener and A. Noland, eds., pp. 460–8. New York: Basic.

Williams, Colin and Anthony D. Smith. 1983. 'The national construction of social space,' *Progress in Human Geography*, 7: 503–18.

Williams, Raymond. 1977. *Marxism and Literature*. New York: Oxford University Press.

Willke, Helmut. 1999. 'The contingency and necessity of the state.' In *Problems of Form*, D. Baecker, ed., pp. 142–54. Stanford: Stanford University Press.

Willner, Dorothy. 1976. 'Ritual, myth, and the murdered president.' In *The Realm of the Extra-Human: Agents and Audiences*, A. Bharati, ed., pp. 401–20. The Hague: Mouton.

Wilson, William. 1976. *Folklore and Nationalism in Modern Finland*. Bloomington: Indiana University Press.

Wittgenstein, Ludwig. 1953. *Philosophical Investigations*. Oxford: Blackwell.

Wright, Patrick. 1985. *On Living in an Old Country: The National Past in Contemporary Britain*. London: Verso.

Wyschogrod, Edith. 1985. *Spirit from Ashes: Hegel, Heidegger, and Man-Made Mass Death*. New Haven: Yale University Press.

Yanai, Nathan. 1996. 'The citizen as pioneer: Ben-Gurion's concept of citizenship,' *Israel Studies,* 1: 127–43.

Yarden, Ophir. 1998. 'The sanctity of Mount Herzl and Independence Day in Israel's civil religion.' In *Sanctity of Time and Space in Tradition and Modernity*, A. Houtman, M.J.H.M. Poorthuis, and J. Schwartz, eds., pp. 317–48. Leiden: Brill.

Yerushalmi, Yosef Hayim. 1982. *Zakhor: Jewish History and Jewish Memory*. Seattle: University of Washington Press.

Yiftachel, Oren. 1992. 'The concept of "ethnic democracy" and its applicability to the case of Israel,' *Ethnic and Racial Studies*, 15: 125–36.

Young, James E. 1989a. 'The biography of a memorial icon: Nathan Rapaport's Warsaw Ghetto monument,' *Representations*, 26: 69–106.

—— 1989b. 'The texture of memory: Holocaust Memorials and Meaning,' *Holocaust and Genocide Studies*, 4: 63–76.

—— 1990. 'When a day remembers: a performative history of Yom Ha-Shoah,' *History & Memory*, 2, no. 2: 54–75.

—— 1993. *The Texture of Memory: Holocaust Memorials and Meanings*. New Haven: Yale University Press.

Young, Katherine. 2000. 'Gestures and the phenomenology of emotions in narrative,' *Semiotica*, 131, no. 1/2: 79–112.

Yuval-Davis, Nira. 1987. 'The Jewish collectivity and national reproduction in Israel.' In *Women in the Middle East,* M. Salman, H. Kazi, N. Yuval-Davis, L. al-Hamdani, S. Botman, and D. Lerman, eds., pp. 61–93. London: Zed.

—— 2000. 'Multi-layered citizenship and the boundaries of the "nation-state",' *HAGAR,* 1: 112–27.

Zanbank-Wilf, A. 1958. 'The kindergarten as a component in creating a holiday atmosphere at home.' In *Holidays and Times in Education,* Esther Rabinowitz, ed., pp. 57–9. Tel-Aviv: Urim (in Hebrew).

Zempleni, Andras. 1999. 'Sepulchral land and the territory of the nation: reburial rituals in contemporary Hungary.' Paper read to the conference on The Land of the Dead, Johns Hopkins University, November 19.

Zertal, Idith. 2000. 'From the People's Hall to the Wailing Wall: a study in memory, fear, and war,' *Representations,* 69: 96–126.

Zerubavel, Eviatar. 1981. *Hidden Rhythms: Schedules and Calendars in Social Life.* Chicago: University of Chicago Press.

—— 1985. *The Seven Day Circle: The History and Meaning of the Week.* New York: Free Press.

Zerubavel, Yael. 1986. 'The holiday cycle and the commemoration of the past: history, folklore, and education'. Mimeo.

—— 1995. *Recovered Roots: Collective Memory and the Making of Israeli National Tradition.* Chicago: University of Chicago Press.

—— 1996. 'The forest as a national icon: literature, politics, and the archeology of memory,' *Israel Studies,* 1: 60–99.

Index

Breinigsville, PA USA
17 March 2010
234370BV00002B/14/P